MW00805723

Jewish Babylonia between Persia and Roman Palestine

Jewish Babylonia between Persia and Roman Palestine

RICHARD KALMIN

OXFORD
UNIVERSITY PRESS
2006

OXFORD
UNIVERSITY PRESS

Oxford University Press, Inc., publishes works that further
Oxford University's objective of excellence
in research, scholarship, and education.

Oxford New York
Auckland Cape Town Dar es Salaam Hong Kong Karachi
Kuala Lumpur Madrid Melbourne Mexico City Nairobi
New Delhi Shanghai Taipei Toronto

With offices in
Argentina Austria Brazil Chile Czech Republic France Greece
Guatemala Hungary Italy Japan Poland Portugal Singapore
South Korea Switzerland Thailand Turkey Ukraine Vietnam

Copyright © 2006 by Oxford University Press, Inc.

Published by Oxford University Press, Inc.
198 Madison Avenue, New York, New York 10016

www.oup.com

Oxford is a registered trademark of Oxford University Press

All rights reserved. No part of this publication may be reproduced,
stored in a retrieval system, or transmitted, in any form or by any means,
electronic, mechanical, photocopying, recording, or otherwise,
without the prior permission of Oxford University Press.

Library of Congress Cataloging-in-Publication Data
Kalmin, Richard Lee.
Jewish Babylonia between Persia and Roman Palestine / Richard Kalmin.
p. cm.
Includes bibliographical references and index.
Contents: Roman persecutions of Jews—Kings, priests, and sages—
Jewish sources of the second Temple Period in rabbinic compilations of late
antiquity—Anxious rabbis and mocking nonrabbis—Idolatry in late antique
Babylonia—Persian persecutions of Jews—Josephus in Sasanian Babylonia.
ISBN-13 978-0-19-530619-4
1. Judaism—History—Talmudic period, 10-425. 2. Jews—Iraq
—Babylonia—Intellectual life. 3. Jews—Iraq—Babylonia—Social conditions.
4. Rabbis—Iraq—Babylonia—Office. 5. Tannaim. 6. Amoraim. 7. Talmud—
Criticism, interpretation, etc. 8. Jews—Persecutions. 9. Rabbinical literature—
History and criticism. 10. Babylonia—History. I. Title.
BM177.K34 2006
296.1'206—dc22 2006042518

9 8 7 6 5 4 3 2

Printed in the United States of America
on acid-free paper

For Sam and Adele Kleinburd,
with love and appreciation

Preface

The Babylonian Talmud, or Bavli, was composed by rabbis who flourished from the third to the sixth or seventh centuries CE. Babylonian rabbis lived under Sasanian Persian domination between the Tigris and Euphrates rivers, in what corresponds to part of modern-day Iraq. The Bavli consists primarily of Tannaitic, Amoraic, and unattributed statements, although many post-Talmudic comments were added to the text during the lengthy course of its transmission from late antiquity to the present.

Tannaitic statements, or Baraitot, comprise the Bavli's earliest layer, dating from the first century CE until the early third century CE. Virtually all Tannaitic statements derive from Palestine, although a small number of Tannaim lived in Babylonia.[1] Amoraic statements derive from rabbis who lived between the early third and the early sixth centuries CE in Babylonia, and between the early third and the late fourth centuries CE in Palestine. Unattributed materials in the Bavli tend to be later, to postdate the Amoraic layer, although a significant amount of this material may derive from the Amoraic period;[2] particularly from the mid–fourth century CE and later. Identification of the unattributed materials is facilitated by their unique stylistic characteristics, most notably their character as lengthy, Aramaic argumentation. Tannaitic and Amoraic materials, in contrast, are often in Hebrew and tend to be prescriptive and interpretive. In addition, Tannaitic and Amoraic argumentation tends to be relatively brief.[3]

Some Talmudic material predates the destruction of the second Temple in 70 CE, but this material derives from groups or individuals other than rabbis, since the earliest rabbis appeared after the destruction of the Temple. Study of second Temple literature, for example, reveals that the Talmud contains a significant amount of pre–70 CE literature, but the Talmud does not explicitly distinguish this material from Tannaitic statements per se. In addition, much of this material has been rabbinized, that is, made to conform to rabbinic standards, such that it often tells more about the rabbis who transmitted it than the prerabbinic figures who are its purported authors and protagonists.[4]

Much of the Bavli is a commentary on the Mishnah, a Tannaitic work of Palestinian origin consisting primarily of legal statements by rabbis who lived between the first and early third centuries CE. It would be a gross oversimplification, however, to characterize the Talmud as a mere commentary on the Mishnah, since frequently the Bavli's discussions are based on Baraitot or Amoraic statements, or consist entirely of sources whose connection to the Mishnah is fragile or artificial.[5]

The Bavli contains legal pronouncements on civil, criminal, and ritual matters. It also contains sententious sayings, advice, dream interpretations, magical incantations, medical cures, polemics, folk tales, fables, legends, scriptural interpretations (midrash), legal case reports, and numerous other literary genres. Much more so than Palestinian rabbinic compilations, the Bavli is encyclopedic in character, meaning that it contains more varieties of rabbinic literature than roughly contemporary Palestinian compilations.[6] The Bavli, for example, is much richer in nonlegal scriptural commentary (aggadic midrash) than is the Yerushalmi, which is more narrowly focused on law and Mishnah commentary. Apparently, the relatively narrow focus of the Yerushalmi is due in part to the fact that compilations of aggadic midrash circulated in Palestine, in contrast to the situation in Babylonia. In Babylonia, aggadic midrash survived in the context of a compilation only if it was incorporated into the Bavli. In Palestine, in contrast, there was more specialization, with midrashic compilations the primary repositories of aggadic scriptural commentary, and the Yerushalmi the primary repository of law and Mishnah commentary.[7]

As noted above, much of the Babylonian Talmud is composed of anonymous discussions. Their unattributed character makes them difficult to analyze, and many basic questions about them have yet to be answered. It is not known, for example, when the unattributed materials were by and large complete, with scholarly guesses ranging from the mid–sixth century CE until the Muslim conquest of Persia in 657 CE.

Throughout this book I observe the convention of using the honorific "Rav" to refer to Babylonian Amoraim, and the honorific "R.," short for "Rabbi," to refer to Tannaim and Palestinian Amoraim. "Rav Yehudah," therefore, is a Babylonian Amora, while "R. Yehudah" is a Tanna, and "R. Yoḥanan" is a Palestinian Amora.[8]

This book is based primarily on examination of the Bavli and the following Palestinian compilations: (1) the Mishnah; (2) the Tosefta; (3) Mekhilta de-R. Yishmael; (4) Sifrei Deuteronomy; (5) the Yerushalmi; (6) Genesis Rabba; (7) Leviticus Rabbah; and (8) Pesikta de-Rav Kahana. At times, the enormity of the relevant material precluded examination of the entire Bavli or Yerushalmi.

At other times, it was necessary or feasible to examine only one or the other Talmud, and occasionally it was necessary or possible to examine additional Palestinian compilations. I will specify in the notes each time I base my conclusions on compilations other than those listed here.

Throughout this book, quotations from the Mishnah are introduced by a lower-case "m.," from the Tosefta by a lower-case "t.," from the Yerushalmi by a lower-case "y.," and from the Bavli by a lower-case "b."

I am delighted to thank Isaiah Gafni and Seth Schwartz, who read and critiqued the entire manuscript. I also wish to thank Carol Bakhos, Daniel Boyarin, Yaakov Elman, Alyssa Gray, Judith Hauptman, Geoffrey Herman, Catherine Hezser, Chaim Milikowsky, Hillel Newman, and Michael Satlow, who read earlier versions of parts of the book and made several thoughtful suggestions. Any remaining errors of fact or judgment, of course, are my responsibility alone.

It is also my pleasure to thank Ismar Schorsch and Jack Wertheimer of the Jewish Theological Seminary, who encouraged this project every step of the way. A fellowship at the Institute for Advanced Studies at Hebrew University enormously facilitated the final stages of research and writing. I am particularly grateful to Joshua Levinson, from whose wisdom and friendship I benefited greatly. I would also like to thank Ronit Meroz, head of our research project, and Benjamin Kedar, director of the Institute, for inviting me to join the group and for their help in creating an atmosphere conducive to collegiality and contemplation.

I presented an earlier version of (1) chapter 3 at the conference "The Talmud Yerushalmi and Graeco-Roman Culture" (Princeton University, November 12–14, 2000); (2) chapter 2 at the conference "The Contemporary Study of Halakhah: Methods and Meaning" (Hebrew Union College, New York, March 18–20, 2001); (3) chapter 4 at the conference "Creation and Composition: The Contribution of the Bavli Redactors (Stammaim) to the Aggada" (New York University, February 9–10, 2003); (4) chapter 5 at the conference "The Sculptural Environment of the Roman Near East: Reflections on Culture, Ideology, and Power" (University of Michigan, Ann Arbor, November 7–10, 2004); (5) chapter 6 at the conference "History and Literature: The Ancient Period" (Hebrew University, December 22, 2004); (6) chapter 7 at a lecture delivered at Bar-Ilan University (Janauary 3, 2005); and (7) the introductory and concluding chapters at a conference honoring David Weiss-Halivni, sponsored by Columbia University (May 29–30, 2005).

Much of the material in this book, having taken preliminary form as articles, has been revised substantially for publication in this book. These articles are as follows. A few sections of the introduction: "The Formation and Character of the Babylonian Talmud," in *The Cambridge History of Judaism*, vol. 4, *The Late Roman-Rabbinic Period* (Cambridge: Cambridge University Press, 2006); chapter 1: "Rabbinic Traditions about Roman Persecutions of the Jews: A Reconsideration," *Journal of Jewish Studies* 54, no. 1 (2003); chapter 2: "Kings, Priests, and Sages in Jewish Literature of Late Antiquity," in *Netiot LeDavid: Jubilee Volume for David Weiss Halivni*, ed. Ephraim Halivni et al.

(Jerusalem: Orhot Press, 2004); chapter 3: "Jewish Literature of the Second Temple Period in Rabbinic Compilations of Late Antiquity," in *The Talmud Yerushalmi and Graeco-Roman Culture*, vol. 3, ed. Peter Schäfer (Tübingen: Mohr/Siebeck, 2003); chapter 5: "Babylonian Rabbinic Literature on Idolatry in its Persian Context," in *The Sculptural Environment of the Roman Near East: Reflections on Culture, Ideology, and Power*, ed. Yaron Eliav et al. (Leuven: Peeters Publishing, forthcoming); chapter 6: "Persian Persecutions of the Jews: A Reconsideration of the Talmudic Evidence," in *Irano-Judaica*, vol. 6, *Studies Relating to Jewish Contacts with Persian Culture Throughout the Ages*, ed. Shaul Shaked and Amnon Netzer (Jerusalem: Ben-Zvi Institute, forthcoming); chapter 7: "Between Rome and Mesopotamia: Josephus in Sasanian Persia," in *Judaism in Its Hellenistic Context*, ed. Carol Bakhos (Leiden: Brill, 2004). I thank the editors for permission to publish revised versions of these articles.

I would also like to thank Adam Parker for compiling the index, and Theo Calderara, Julia TerMaat, and Christine Dahlin of Oxford University Press for making the process of publication a pleasurable one. Finally, *aḥaron, aḥaron ḥaviv*, I thank my wife, Freda. Busy with her own work, she was not involved in the writing of this book, but without her sense of humor and love of learning, I never would have been able to complete the project.

Contents

Manuscripts and Early Editions

Unless otherwise indicated, citations of the Mishnah follow Albeck's edition; citations of Tosefta follow Lieberman's or Zuckermandel's edition; citations of the Yerushalmi follow the Venice edition; and citations of the Bavli follow the standard Romm printed edition. Significant variants based on medieval testimonia, the early printed editions, manuscripts, and Genizah fragments are provided in the notes. The most significant source of variants is the computerized Sol and Evelyn Henkind Talmud Text Data Bank of Talmudic manuscripts provided by the Saul Lieberman Institute for Talmudic Research at the Jewish Theological Seminary of America in New York.

MISHNAH

Albeck, Ḥanokh, ed. *Shishah Sidrei Mishnah.* 6 vols. Tel Aviv: Devir, 1957–59.

TOSEFTA

Lieberman, Saul, ed. *The Tosefta.* 5 vols. Jerusalem: Jewish Theological Seminary, 1955–88.
Zuckermandel, M. S., ed. *Tosefta, Based on the Venice and Vienna Codices.* Reprint, Jerusalem: Wahrmann Books, 1970.

YERUSHALMI (PALESTINIAN TALMUD)

Ms. Leiden, Scaliger no. 3. Facsimile edition with introduction by Saul Lieberman: Jerusalem: Kedem, 1971.

First printed edition, based upon the Leiden ms. *Talmud Yerushalmi*. Venice: Bomberg, 1523–24. Facsimile edition: Berlin: Sefarim, 1925.

BABYLONIAN TALMUD (BAVLI)

Standard printed edition: *The Babylonian Talmud*. Vilna: Romm, 1880–86.

Jewish Babylonia between Persia and Roman Palestine

Introduction

Fourth-Century Judaism and Christianity between Persia and the Eastern Roman Provinces

This book advances our understanding of late antique Babylonia as partly eastern (i.e., Persian) and partly western (i.e., Palestinian and provincial Roman) in character.[1] The book supports my claim in earlier work that Babylonian rabbis tended to avoid contact with other Jews, particularly those they perceived as their inferiors, and therefore as unable to benefit them socially or economically. Babylonian rabbis avoided (1) informal interactions with nonrabbinic Jews; (2) marriage into their families; and (3) the acceptance of such Jews into the rabbinic movement on the basis of acquired merit.[2] In this respect, Jewish society in Babylonia had more in common with Persian than with Roman models, since Persian society discouraged movement and interaction between classes,[3] in contrast to Rome, where upward (and downward) movement from one class to another was a relatively common phenomenon.[4] Richard Frye and Nina Garsoïan documented an obsession with genealogical purity on the part of Georgians and Armenians, minority cultures within the Sasanian Persian Empire, comparable to that of Babylonian rabbis as documented in the Babylonian Talmud.[5] In addition, Talmudic portrayals of rabbis conform to the behavior demanded of Christians training at the school of Nisibis, in Persia, close to the rabbinic centers of Babylonia. For example, according to the statutes of this Christian school, compiled in the late sixth century but containing much material deriving from earlier centuries, students were to avoid unnecessary contact with the inhabitants of the city. Isaiah Gafni points out many structural and terminological similarities between Babylonian rabbinic and Nestorian Christian schools of approximately the same time and place,[6] and observes that the Christian school's statutes reveal its "inner-directed character," resembling that of a monastery.[7]

This book utilizes a method of reading rabbinic literature that has found widespread acceptance,[8] but is still considered inefficacious by several leading scholars.[9] I refer to the fact that throughout this book, I pay close attention to the Talmud's markers of geography and chronology, which sometimes enables me to trace the development of institutions and ideas. This, in turn, makes possible documentation of what appears to be a significant change in rabbinic literature and society during the mid–fourth century CE, a time when traditions and modes of behavior amply documented in pre-fourth-century Palestine are attributed to Babylonian rabbis, often for the first time. One striking illustration of this conclusion is my demonstration, in chapter 7 and in the conclusion,[10] that some culturally significant traditions from Josephus, or from a source drawn upon independently by Josephus and the rabbis, are known to Babylonian rabbis who flourished in the mid–fourth century, resulting in a dramatic shift in Babylonian rabbinic portrayals of important figures from the distant past.[11]

It would certainly be premature to conclude from these few examples that the Bavli's familiarity with Josephus or Josephus's sources, as well as with other compilations composed in Palestine or elsewhere in the Roman Empire,[12] date largely from the fourth century. Combined with other data, however, surveyed in detail in the conclusion, the Josephan or Josephus-like material in the Bavli forms part of a larger picture pointing to the mid–fourth century as a time when later rabbinic Babylonia is portrayed as (and, I will argue, becomes) receptive to Palestinian literature and modes of behavior. This book, therefore, builds on the work of Ẓvi Dor, who documented approximately fifty years ago many of the important ways in which the learning of later Babylonian Amoraim was based on and shaped by traditions deriving from the land of Israel.[13] The fact that Palestinian literary motifs and modes of behavior manifest themselves in mid-fourth-century (and later) Babylonia may constitute the literary record of a process set in motion, or, to be more precise, accelerated, in the mid–third century, when King Shapur I of Persia transplanted thousands of inhabitants of the eastern Roman Empire and settled them in Mesopotamia, eastern Syria, and western Persia (see below).

Armenia, which bordered Babylonia to the north and west, converted to Christianity in the early fourth century CE,[14] and thus may have manifested the effects of the same process, as did the Babylonian rabbis vis-à-vis the west (i.e., the eastern Roman provinces) at approximately the same time.[15] This process began earlier and was more powerful in Armenia than in Babylonia, because Armenia was a border province, subject to fierce and protracted competition between the rival empires.[16] Babylonia, also a border province,[17] was Armenia's neighbor to the south and east, and was thus closer to the administrative heart of the Sasanian Empire.[18]

I am not claiming, it bears emphasizing, that prior to the fourth century the border regions between Rome and Persia were free of influence from the west. The acceptance by Babylonian rabbis of the Mishnah, a Palestinian compilation, obviously belies such a claim, as does the activity of the *naḥotei*, scholars who traveled back and forth between Palestine and Babylonia, carrying with them Palestinian rabbinic traditions to Babylonia. Nor is it my claim that influences never flowed in the opposite direction as well, namely from Persia and Mesopotamia to Rome. Third-century Babylonian rabbinic statements are found frequently in the Palestinian Talmud, and Manichaeism's expansion throughout the Roman Empire beginning in the late third century is well attested.[19] Rather, it is my contention that the Jewish and Christian developments in the region during the fourth century, continuing until the advent of Islam in the seventh century, may be closely related, and that processes accelerated by Shapur's dramatic conquests of the third century may have had pronounced literary and practical consequences in Babylonia and surrounding territories.

This book, therefore, may contribute to the question of the extent to which the various cultures comprising Syria and Mesopotamia developed or reinforced their Syrian and Mesopotamian identities throughout the period under study. The book provides a modicum of support for those scholars who characterize the territory between the two Empires as culturally linked,[20] although it would be a mistake to minimize the very significant differences that remained within this vast expanse of territory until the end of antiquity and on into the Middle Ages.

Other developments may similarly mark the fourth century as a significant turning point in the history of Christianity east of Byzantium. For example, Georgia, to the north of Armenia and also a border province between Rome and Persia, also converted to Christianity in the early fourth century CE. In the words of Gillman and Klimkeit, "while the seeming rapid acceptance of Christianity [in Georgia] in the fourth century would support some long standing foundations, hard evidence is scarce."[21] In addition, David Bundy notes the paucity of documentation of Syriac Christianity prior to the fourth century, and observes that no Christian documents written in the Syriac language have survived between the writing of Bardaisan (ca. 212 CE) and the early decades of the fourth century.[22]

The fourth and early fifth centuries were also a time of rapid development and consolidation for Persian Christianity. The major pioneering figure in Persian monasticism, Mar Awgin, may have introduced Egyptian monastic models into Persia during the mid–fourth century.[23] The first Christian synod in the Sasanian Empire met in 410 CE,[24] and in a synod convened in 424 CE, the Persian Church placed itself outside the authority of Rome, Constantinople, Alexandria, Antioch, and Jerusalem, thereby declaring its independence from all Church authority in the Roman Empire.[25] Along the same lines, Sebastian Brock writes, "although later tradition traces back the origins of the Christianity in Persia to apostolic times, it is not until the fourth century that we have reliable sources in any quantity."[26] The fourth century witnesses a period of intense literary production and Christian activity in eastern Syria and in the Persian Empire. Most notable, but by no means unique, are Aphrahat (d. ca. 350) and Ephrem (d. 373). Bundy, for example, claims that "Ephrem's influence in the Syriac-speaking churches was perhaps the most important factor in their intellectual and spiritual development. His work largely determined the relationships between theological investigation, spirituality, and liturgy."[27] Brock similarly characterizes the development of early Christianity in Edessa, the major city of the province of Osrhoene in western Mesopotamia.[28]

This is not to suggest that the Christianity of the fourth-century Syriac authors is the same as those who worked in the Christian Roman Empire. The Christological debates provoked by the Arian controversy are absent from the work of Aphrahat, for example, whose primary concern in this area is to demonstrate that the Christian concepts of God and the Son are compatible with monotheism.[29] Brock, however, overemphasizes the distinctions between (1) Syrian and north Mesopotamian Christianity in the fifth and sixth centuries and (2) the Christianity that existed in this area prior to the fifth century.[30] Distinctions there certainly were, but the flowering of Syriac Christian literature in the fourth century is at least as significant as its later development. Van Rompay, for example, remarks judiciously that "despite its genuine Semitic character, Syriac literature was never isolated from the Graeco-Roman world. . . . In Syria and Mesopotamia [between the fourth and sixth centuries], the conjunction of traditions of Semitic origin and Graeco-Roman culture has given Syriac Christianity its own distinctive characteristics."[31] Similarly, Murray observes, "as regards the cultural milieu of Aphrahat and Ephrem, it was probably F. C. Burkitt (with a touch, perhaps, of protestant romanticism) who exaggerated its nonhellenistic character. . . . It must be recognized to what extent the whole Near and Middle East was a culturally hybrid world."[32]

Van Rompay observes that "Aphrahat must have been quite isolated from Christianity as it developed in the Roman Empire. The Council of Nicaea (325 [CE]) did not touch [Aphrahat's] theology and he probably knew no Greek."[33] It is not at all surprising that Nicaea left no mark on Aphrahat's work, however, since his *Demonstrations* were written between 337 and 345 CE, at most two decades after the famous church council. Van Rompay himself, furthermore, writes that "the artistic style of [Aphrahat's] work attests to his full participation in the literary culture of his day, which was highly complex, and moulded by both Semitic and Hellenistic traditions."[34] In short, Van Rompay means that Aphrahat was strongly influenced by Greco-Roman culture, but he had no direct access to it *via the Greek language*, and he was probably unfamiliar with the most recent fourth-century developments of that culture. This is to be expected, however, if I am correct that the Christianity that manifested itself during the fourth century in Mesopotamia is evidence of indigenous Mesopotamian developments accelerated by events of the previous century, that is, prior to the advent of Nicaea.

As noted, a critically important question addressed by this book is why the hypothesized changes in Mesopotamian Jewish and Christian society took place at precisely this time and in precisely these places. While certainty on this question is unfortunately beyond our grasp at present, we are at least able to begin to hazard a guess. As noted, it is well documented that King Shapur I of Persia deported large numbers of people from their homes in the eastern provinces of the Roman Empire, and resettled them in the western border provinces of the Persian Empire in the wake of his conquests of the middle decades of the third century CE, between 242 and 260.[35] Christian centers such as Antioch were profoundly affected by Shapur's resettlement policy.[36] In the words of Josef Wiesehöfer,

> Christian communities had already started spreading in Mesopotamia and Iran in the second century.... However, the crucial role in the establishment of Christianity in the Sasanian Empire was not played by this "first evangelization," but by the deportation of... inhabitants of Roman Syria, Cilicia and Cappadocia by Shapur I.[37] Both Shapur's great *res gestae* and the Christian-Arabic Chronicle of Se'ert[38] confirm that those deported were settled in Mesopotamia, Persis and Parthia.[39]

Similarly, according to Richard Frye,

> The campaign of Shapur had delivered many captives into his hands and he settled them in Khuzistan and Fars provinces where traces of their activities exist to the present, such as the Band-e Kaisar or "Caesar's Dam" on the Karun River at Shustan, attributed to the war prisoners of Shapur by Tabari (I, 827),[40] while mosaics found in a palace at Bishapur also have been attributed to Roman prisoners. The origins of Christianity in the southern part of Iran have been traced primarily to these war prisoners brought and settled by Shapur in his last two campaigns, and the town of Weh Antiok Shapur, "the better Antioch of Shapur," later Gundeshapur, was settled almost exclusively by war prisoners.[41]

It is probably no coincidence that Gundeshapur, or, as it was known in Syriac sources, Beth Lapat,[42] later became a great Christian center,[43] the site of a major synod in 484 at which Persian Christians officially rejected the Nicene doctrine[44] and accepted the Nestorian creed.

In addition to the Persian sources, several late antique Roman historians describe the Persians conquering Roman cities throughout Syria, all the way to and including Antioch,[45] and from there venturing deep into Asia Minor. We know from other sources that Shapur's armies were not repulsed until they reached Emesa (modern-day Homs, Syria), approximately 150 miles northeast of Palestine.[46] The Sasanian practice of settling Roman captives in Persian territory is confirmed as well by several late antique Roman historians,[47] and is taken for granted by the tenth-century author Magdasi.[48]

This movement of whole populations perhaps contributed to important changes in the cultural life of Babylonian Jews as well as Christians, since western Syria was also an important center of Jewish life.[49] It is not unreasonable to suggest that different communities and literatures within eastern Syria, Mesopotamia, and western Persia showed the effects of Shapur's policy at differing times during this century, and that these effects developed and deepened throughout the region, until the Muslim conquests of the seventh century drastically altered the political and cultural landscape.

Babylonian Rabbis between Persia and Roman Palestine

Many scholars read Palestinian rabbinic literature in the context of the Greco-Roman world, but it is extremely rare to find scholars who read Babylonian rabbinic literature in its larger cultural context.[50] As Yaakov Elman observes, furthermore, scholars who comment on the place of Jewish Babylonia within the Persian Empire tend to confine the discussion to the realm of popular religion and folk practice, despite the fact that the boundary separating elite and popular culture is extremely difficult, if not impossible, to define when speaking about the ancient world.[51] This book attempts in part to refine our understanding of Babylonian rabbis, bearers of elite Jewish culture, in the context of Persian culture and society.

As noted, chapters 1–4 of this book support my claim in earlier research that Babylonian and Palestinian rabbis relate to nonrabbinic Jews in strikingly dissimilar ways, and that these differences are linked to the larger Persian and Roman contexts within which these rabbis flourished. These chapters support my characterization of Babylonian rabbis as internally focused, their reality to a significant extent bounded by the four walls of the study house, in contrast to Palestinian rabbis, who were more fully integrated into the mainstream of nonrabbinic Jewish life. Chapter 6 further supports this claim, by challenging the conventional portrayal of early Babylonian rabbis as important players in the late antique Jewish political realm. This chapter argues that nonrabbinic Jews did not wait eagerly for Babylonian rabbis to express themselves on the important "foreign policy" issues of their day, such as (1) the relative merits of Persia and Rome, and (2) how the Jewish community should relate to its imperial masters. Rather, Babylonian rabbis delivered their pronouncements on these subjects in the privacy of their own study houses, before an audience of fellow rabbis and their disciples, in keeping with their strongly internal focus. Chapter 7 further supports this thesis, arguing that the Babylonian Talmud's hostility to Sadducees is motivated not by the presence of Sadducee-like groups within the Babylonian rabbis' midst, but more likely by the introduction within Babylonia of literary traditions that portrayed the Sadducees as an ancient group that espoused views that made them anathema to the rabbis. Chapter 5 provides evidence that Sasanian Persian policy with respect to idols and cultic worship affected late antique Babylonia, further supporting my claims regarding Babylonia's partially Persian character.

It is important to emphasize once again, however, that my claim is not that Babylonian rabbis were totally cut off from the outside world, and that all Babylonian rabbis, over a period of several centuries, never left the confines of their study houses. Yaakov Elman, for example, has shown convincingly that Rav Naḥman, a Babylonian rabbi of the late third century, was criticized by his contemporaries for "putting on Persian airs," which he appears to have cultivated in his capacity as an official in the exilarch's bureaucracy, a position that required regular interaction with the Persian government.[52] In addition, I argued in earlier research that Babylonian rabbis tended to depart from their usual aloofness vis-à-vis the exilarch, aristocratic Jews, and officials of the Persian government, since such powerful individuals were in a position to assist the rabbis socially and economically.[53] Any distinctions between two cultures in the ancient or modern world, furthermore, cannot be drawn too starkly, but of necessity must be described as varying degrees of gray rather than as black versus white. If we found no exceptions to our generalizations concerning the behavior of Babylonian rabbis, in other words, we would have to hypothesize their existence, since no culture can realistically be thought of as totally static for centuries over a vast geographic expanse, and no elite group can survive without some significant contact with members outside the group. In this respect, as in others, therefore, Babylonian rabbis resembled late antique monks and holy men, both Christian and pagan, who managed to be both dissociated from and part of the world, detached from society in certain contexts and capable of exercising a leadership role in others.[54]

In addition, substantial portions of this book serve as a necessary corrective to a conclusion one might be inclined to draw from my claim that Babylonian rabbis tended to view the rabbinic study house as the sum total of their experience. Chapters 2, 3, and 7, for example, demonstrate that the rabbis' monklike quality did not serve to seal them off from all contact with the outside world, since, as noted, we will find abundant evidence that nonrabbinic *literature* reached Babylonian rabbis and found a receptive audience there. We will see that they attempted to rabbinize this literature, for example, by transforming the protagonists of stories from kings and priests to sages; but often the nonrabbinic traditions remain visible despite the rabbinic tampering, and often the rabbis only partly succeeded in domesticating their nonrabbinic sources. It is revealing that a significant amount of rabbinic exposure to the nonrabbinic world took the form of the incorporation of *literary texts* into the developing Talmud. For example, chapter 7's analysis of the Bavli's attempt to grapple with the issue of belief in the inefficacy of sages and the authority of the written Torah alone is most likely due to Babylonian rabbinic confrontation with *texts* that express this opinion rather than with *real people* in Babylonian Jewish society who held such a view.[55]

My intent in this book is not to "flatten" the rabbis, to portray them as one-dimensional and unchanging. I have no doubt that another book could be written that would focus on the ways Babylonian rabbis impinged on nonrabbinic society. That other book, however, would have to contend with this book, which examines afresh evidence that earlier scholars maintained depicts the rabbis as politicians or as contending with actual groups in society, and discovers in key instances that the same evidence attests instead to their internally focused character.

The conclusion surveys the evidence that mid-fourth-century and later Babylonian rabbis behaved, or were portrayed as behaving, like Palestinian rabbis, most notably in the form of traditions depicting later Babylonian rabbis as open to and encouraging of informal contacts with nonrabbinic Jews. As noted, these findings are particularly significant, since we appear to find Babylonian rabbis behaving like Palestinians even in situations where the exilarch, the wealthy, or Persian officials were not involved, and thus the contact did not advance the rabbis' social or economic interests. These portrayals of later Babylonians appear to show that they participated in the region's fourth-century reorientation vis-à-vis the west without abandoning their Persian character. In this respect as well, the history of rabbinic Babylonia conforms to that of Armenia, which retained its Persian character long after its conversion to Christianity in the early fourth century.[56]

While the concentration of evidence of the process of Palestinianization in the mid–fourth century, I believe, is difficult to deny, the precise extent to which this period in Babylonian Jewish history represents a departure from the past must await careful study of third- and early fourth-century Babylonian Jewish history. In addition, I have made the case that Mesopotamia's fourth-century "Syrianization" and rabbinic Babylonia's fourth-century "Palestinianization" may be closely related, stimulated, perhaps, by the same mid-third-century events. The parallels are striking, but less than fully exact, since the rabbinic evidence derives almost exclusively from Palestine and the Christian evidence concerns western Syria. It is hoped, however, that this book will stimulate further studies that will decide whether the fourth-century developments in rabbinic Babylonia and Christian Mesopotamia amount to more than an interesting coincidence.

Dating and Interpreting Rabbinic Traditions

The historical conclusions described above depend on methods of interpreting the Talmud that are neither self-evident nor agreed upon by all. Most historians of late antique Judaism, for example, have yet to incorporate the most recent methodological advances of modern Talmudic text criticism, and therefore fail to distinguish adequately between the anonymous, editorial layer of the Talmud and earlier, attributed materials.[57] As noted, concentration on the layered nature of Talmudic discourse enables me to distinguish between (1) Palestinian and Babylonian and (2) early and later Babylonian traditions, and to discover significant ways in which Babylonia, without losing its Persian character, behaves like Roman Palestine in the fourth century. Absolutely crucial to my work is the ability to identify (1) authentically Palestinian traditions in the Babylonian Talmud and (2) the overlay of later Babylonian commentary on earlier traditions.

In addition, some influential scholars of rabbinic literature today tend to concentrate on the work of the Talmud's later editors,[58] and thus fail to appreciate the extent to which statements attributed to Palestinian and early

Babylonian rabbis in the Bavli are not sixth-century pseudepigraphs, but rather derive, at least approximately, from the period or place they purport to derive from. While Jeffrey Rubenstein, for example, acknowledges that some, even many, statements in the Bavli attributed to Palestinian or early Babylonian rabbis are what they purport to be,[59] in practice he builds his theories around exaggerated claims that purported Baraitot and Palestinain Amoraic statements are of sixth-century Babylonian provenance.[60] This book is not a systematic refutation of his arguments. In fact, it is theoretically possible that he is correct about the chronology and geography of the traditions he analyzes, since he bases his conclusions on traditions not analyzed in this book. Nevertheless, the frequency with which this book supports the claims of earlier scholars that the Bavli's markers of chronology and geography are at least partially and approximately accurate[61] (often, but by no means always) casts serious doubt on Rubenstein's tendency to disregard the sources' chronological and geographical markers, and his persistent claims that the Bavli routinely presents us with the pseudepigraphical inventions of later editors.[62]

Correct dating of rabbinic traditions is not simply a matter of antiquarian concern, since inevitably we will fail to understand the Jewish experience of late antiquity if we improperly date rabbinic materials, the most abundant historical source for the period. The relationship between ancient Judaism and Christianity will serve as a case in point. Daniel Boyarin, for example, rejects the traditional conception of Christianity as Judaism's "daughter religion," and a significant part of his argument depends on demonstrating that phenomena that scholars claim manifest themselves in Jewish sources already in the first or second centuries CE actually date from the fifth or sixth centuries, contemporaneous with or postdating the Christian evidence.[63] If Boyarin's dating is incorrect, then the persuasiveness of his theory is seriously undermined. Along the same lines, we learn much about the relationship between the Jewish and Christian communities in Mesopotamia if both experienced similar transformations in the fourth century, partly in response to the same third-century events. If the Jewish sources turn out to derive from the sixth or seventh centuries, then obviously our understanding of this relationship needs to be revised.

Often, the arguments of this book depend on detailed comparison between parallel versions of a tradition preserved in the Bavli on the one hand and a Palestinian compilation such as the Yerushalmi on the other. While this method of analysis is extremely important and useful, it is insufficient when not accompanied by examination of the full gamut of Babylonian and Palestinian literature to see if the absence of motifs, attitudes, emotions, institutions, or modes of interaction from the Palestinian or Babylonian version of a tradition is part of a consistent pattern, or is simply an idiosyncratic feature of a single text. In addition, analyzing literature preserved in a variety of different Palestinian compilations (which, as noted in the preface, tend to be specialized compared to the more encyclopedic Bavli) decreases the likelihood that the absence of a particular feature of a text from its Palestinian parallel is simply a function of the genres which the Palestinian compilation tends to exclude or include, or is the result of the less than perfect transmission of a single text over a period of well over a thousand years, including centuries of oral transmission. Due to its vastness, it is often feasible to examine only part of the rabbinic corpus, but this book is characterized, I believe uniquely, by exhaustive scrutiny of large amounts of material beyond the comparison of parallel texts, which makes possible accurate assessments of what is Babylonian about the Bavli and what is Palestinian, as well as what is early in the Bavli and what is late.

Fundamentally, therefore, this book is a series of textual analyses intended to serve as models for analyzing rabbinic discussions and identifying their component parts. The textual analyses in the present book distinguish systematically between (1) material attributed to Babylonian rabbis in the Bavli; (2) material attributed to Palestinian rabbis in the Bavli; and (3) material attributed to Palestinian rabbis in Palestinian compilations. These analyses often result in surprising revisions of our understanding of the two rabbinic communities that produced the texts. Other scholars have approached rabbinic sources with the same goals, but they have tended to focus on distinctions between parallel texts rather than viewing individual texts against the background of as much as half or even the entire rabbinic corpus. In addition, scholars have tended to approach the rabbinic material with interpretive goals (what does this specific text mean?) rather than with significant historical questions in mind (what does this text, when read against the backdrop of rabbinic literature as a whole, say about rabbinic culture?).

Competing Theories of the Character of the Bavli and Its Proper Use as Historical Evidence

To utilize the Talmud as a historical source, however, it is not enough to divide a story or a discussion into its component parts. For, as I will have occasion to observe elsewhere in this book, a tradition can be early but still a fiction, or Palestinian but still worthless as evidence regarding Palestinian Jewish history. To use a tradition as historical evidence, it is also necessary to know who composed and transmitted it, what its intended message and intended audience were, and, occasionally, what it looked like before it reached the rabbis' hands.

A theory that radically contests the historicity of the Bavli's portrayals of interactions between rabbis and nonrabbis, for example, conceives of the Talmud as "internal rabbinic discourse."[64] According to this theory, ostensible dialogues and interactions between rabbis and nonrabbis are actually Babylonian rabbinic monologues, occasions for rabbis to work out their anxieties, aggressions, or fantasies, or to imagine how such interactions might take place in a perfect world. According to this theory, the Bavli's obsession with genealogical purity, for example, is no proof that Babylonian rabbis were any less involved in nonrabbinic society than their Palestinian counterparts.

People routinely say or think one thing and do another; why assume that Babylonian rabbis were any different?

This theory is problematic, however, first because it does not explain why a single compilation, the Bavli, portrays Babylonian and Palestinian rabbis so differently. If the Bavli presents us with little or nothing but internal Babylonian rabbinic discourse, why does it distinguish between rabbis from different localities? Why do we find geographical patterns rather than randomness and inconsistency? Why does the Bavli not attribute to Palestinian rabbis as well as to Babylonian rabbis a powerful concern for genealogical purity? If the Bavli is simply a forum for Babylonian rabbis to exorcise their demons and give expression to their anxieties, why does it depict rabbis differently depending on their geographical provenance?

In addition, it bears mentioning that if we concede (which I do not) that the Bavli is "internal rabbinic discourse," then we may have another argument in favor of my characterization of Babylonian rabbis as relatively removed from the rest of Jewish society. If the Bavli is little or nothing more than a collection of rabbinic monologues, then my point regarding the detachment of Babylonian rabbis receives significant support. It is important for my argument to reject this characterization of the Bavli, however, since if Babylonian rabbis talked to no one but themselves, then it is more difficult to argue that we can (1) discern within the pages of the Talmud evidence that Babylonia was both a Persian and a provincial Roman (i.e., Palestinian) province; and (2) that a significant body of nonrabbinic literature found its way into the rabbinic study house and from there into the pages of the Babylonian Talmud.

Other considerations further support the claim that the Talmud contains rabbinic responses to stimuli from the nonrabbinic world. First, the Talmud is a historical artifact, and it is the nature of historical artifacts to be embedded in a historical context, to serve the purposes of individuals and groups within a society situated within a larger culture. To view the Talmuds as *primarily* a record of rabbinic discourse, by rabbis for rabbis, seems to me eminently reasonable, a point to which I will return later. To say that the boundary separating rabbinic literature from the community at large is all but totally impermeable is counterintuitive, not to mention counter to the explicit claims of the literature itself. In addition, it is one thing to claim that it is extremely difficult to derive reliable information about nonrabbinic society based on rabbinic texts, which refract everything through the spectacles of the rabbis. It is another thing to claim that we can say nothing whatsoever about nonrabbis, that it is impossible to correct for the distortions caused by the rabbinic lenses we look through when we read rabbinic texts. I find extremely improbable the notion that rabbinic encounters with nonrabbis are not occasionally documented, in however distorted a manner, in rabbinic texts, and that we can never draw reliable conclusions about these encounters.

It is at times indisputable, in fact, that rabbinic corpora preserve nonrabbinic traditions. Several stories in rabbinic compilations, for example, have parallels in Josephus, a pre- and nonrabbinic author.[65] As noted, rabbinic storytellers and editors tend to rabbinize such stories, for example, by transforming the protagonist from a king or a priest into a rabbi. Often, however, the process of rabbinization is incomplete; the priest or king is dominant and the rabbi only secondary or absent altogether, a claim I will substantiate in detail in chapters 2 and 3. Sometimes, in other words, nonrabbinic voices find a place, albeit muted, within rabbinic documents, and a source's nonrabbinic features survive the process of editorial homogenization. And if nonrabbinic voices deriving from Josephus find their way into the Bavli, then why should the same not occur, at least occasionally, with nonrabbinic voices deriving from late antique Babylonia itself?

Further proof that rabbinic corpora contain accurate information about relationships between rabbis and nonrabbis is provided by stories that portray Jews not explicitly identified as rabbis appearing before rabbis for judgment. Modern scholarship has shown that sometimes these stories yield a picture not of disciples appearing before their masters but of nonrabbis appearing before rabbis. A significant number of these stories do not portray rabbis adjudicating every aspect of life; instead, there are important emphases and omissions that we would not expect were the Talmud simply comprised of rabbinic monologues. Contrasts between these portrayals and portrayals of conversations between individuals explicitly labeled "rabbi" lead Jacob Neusner to conclude that the Bavli routinely depicts Babylonian rabbis litigating cases "involving exchanges of property, torts and damages" and "court-enforced documents" but only rarely cases involving "points of religious observance."[66] If the Talmud depicts rabbis judging cases involving nonrabbis, one can understand this lacuna in the sources: nonrabbis did not need or want rabbis to determine their religious observances. They apparently preferred to decide such questions on their own or to consult nonrabbinic authorities. According to the claim that the Talmud contains little besides internal rabbinic discourse, in contrast, this lacuna is incomprehensible.

It has also been argued (in my opinion, incorrectly), that the evidence surveyed above is attributable to the differing audiences to which Palestinian and Babylonian rabbinic literature is directed.[67] What was characterized above as the insular nature of Babylonian rabbis, in other words, is perhaps a function of the inner-directed character of the Babylonian Talmud. What was characterized above as the greater openness of Palestinian rabbis to nonrabbinic Jewish society is perhaps a function of the more outer-directed nature of Palestinian rabbinic compilations. In the ensuing discussion I refer to this theory as the "theory of audience."

The Bavli, according to this theory, is intended for a rabbinic audience, which explains the inner-directed character of the rabbis it depicts. This theory also explains another phenomenon heretofore unmentioned: the fact that statements by and stories involving Babylonian rabbis tend to emphasize Torah study to the exclusion of all else, that is, to emphasize the importance of values and preoccupations unique to the rabbinic elite.[68] More of Palestinian literature, according to this theory, is intended for a nonrabbinic audience, which explains why this literature depicts a more outer-directed Palestinian rabbinate, and why statements by and stories involving Palestinian rabbis emphasize values and preoccupations shared by rabbis and nonrabbis alike: the importance of charity to the poor, hospitality to the wayfarer, observance of the Sabbath, and the like.

The theory of audience, however, fails to explain why statements attributed to Palestinian rabbis in the Bavli tend to exhibit the same outer-directed character as do statements attributed to Palestinian rabbis in Palestinian compilations. Were the inner-directed portrayals of Babylonian rabbis attributable solely to the inner-directed nature of the Bavli, we would expect Palestinian and Babylonian rabbis to be depicted by this Talmud in basically the same fashion. Why is this not the case? Why are Palestinian rabbis often depicted as outer-directed in the Bavli as well as the Yerushalmi? Why does the Bavli routinely contain accounts of Palestinian rabbinic encounters with nonrabbis, or quote statements by Palestinian rabbis expressing values they shared with nonrabbis, but tend to exclude such encounters and such statements when they involve Babylonian rabbis, apparently (according to the theory of audience) on the grounds that they would not be of interest to the Bavli's audience? Why is such material of interest to the Bavli's audience when it depicts interaction between Palestinian rabbis and nonrabbis, but not when it depicts interaction between Babylonian rabbis and nonrabbis? It is likely, therefore, that the differing portrayals are evidence of distinct rabbinic roles in society and not merely of distinctions between Palestinian and Babylonian rabbinic literature.

In addition, the theory of audience needs to explain why Babylonian Jewish society is structured differently from other societies within the Persian Empire.[69] Why is Babylonian Jewish society less hierarchical, why are boundaries between classes less rigid, in Babylonian Jewish society than in Persian society in general, including the societies of non-Jewish minorities within that empire? The structure of Persian society, in contrast, conforms well to the theory that Talmudic sources in this one instance accurately reflect historical reality. The Persian intellectual and judicial elites had relatively little to do with other groups in Persian society, corresponding to the rabbis' character as an intellectual and judicial elite in Babylonian Jewish society.

The inner-directed nature of Babylonian rabbinic literature, in contrast, versus the more outer-directed nature of Palestinian rabbinic literature is easily explicable according to the theory that the literary portrayals in the Talmud in this one instance reflect historical reality. If I am correct that Babylonian rabbis tend to be more aloof from nonrabbis than are their Palestinian counterparts, it is easy to understand (1) why Babylonian rabbis produced a literature intended almost exclusively for rabbinic consumption, and (2) why Palestinian rabbis authored and transmitted for posterity some traditions intended more for a nonrabbinic Jewish audience.

One final argument that has been raised against the attempt to derive history from Talmudic sources bases itself on the fact that rabbinic compilations of late antiquity have been subjected to centuries of imperfect transmission, such that it is extremely difficult, if not impossible, to make far-reaching generalizations about the history, culture, or society of the Jews of this time period.[70] We are so often uncertain, for example, that a statement attributed to the Babylonian Amora Abaye was actually said by Abaye that it is impossible to draw historical conclusions based on statements he ostensibly made.

It should be noted, however, that my claim is not that it is possible to write biographies of rabbinic figures such as Abaye.[71] My claim, rather, is that it is possible to draw some general distinctions between Palestinian and Babylonian rabbis, and early and later periods of Jewish history of late antiquity. For this purpose, it is necessary only to have confidence that significant numbers of traditions that purport to be Palestinian or Babylonian are what they claim to be, and that markers of Tannaitic, Amoraic, or anonymous editorial provenance are often (but by no means always) reliable. For my purposes it is enough to be reasonably confident that significant numbers of statements preserved in independently edited rabbinic compilations (for example, the Yerushalmi and Bavli) yield substantially the same picture of Palestinian rabbinic attitudes, social roles, or institutions. Our tools, in other words, are often blunt, but they are effective tools nonetheless.

It is also important to emphasize that my claim is not that all sources attributed to Palestinian rabbis in the Talmud (1) were authored by the rabbis to whom they are attributed, or (2) necessarily reflect a Palestinian point of view.[72] Some statements attributed to Palestinian rabbis in the Bavli are more Babylonian than Palestinian, and other sources attributed in the Bavli to early rabbis were invented or tampered with by later editors.[73] It is advisable to look for general patterns characterizing Palestinian and Babylonian, and early and later rabbis, all the while remaining alert to the possibility that the transmitters and editors of these traditions altered them in subtle or not-so-subtle ways. Information about Palestinian rabbis preserved only in the Bavli is of course suspect and can be used as historical evidence only with due caution. Prima facie, it can neither be rejected nor accepted as evidence about conditions in Palestine; each individual case must be examined on its own terms. The same is true, *mutatis mutandis,* of early rabbis whose statements and actions are recorded only in compilations edited centuries after the fact.

As noted, often we can use other rabbinic compilations of late antiquity as controls for the picture supplied by the Bavli. Granted, the textual problems impeding our use of Palestinian midrashic compilations are even more serious than those of the Bavli, since manuscript versions of the former often preserve a veritable chaos of variants, particularly where names of rabbis are concerned. In many cases it is at present impossible to decide which manuscript version is correct. Nevertheless, Palestinian midrashic compilations almost exclusively contain statements attributed to Palestinian rabbis. Often we cannot be sure who authored a particular statement, but generally we can be sure that it reflects a Palestinian point of view.[74] And we can compare that Palestinian view to the view attributed to Palestinian rabbis in the Bavli. If these views correspond, the various compilations independently confirm one another. If they differ, we must attempt to explain why. Has the Bavli fabricated an attitude and falsely attributed it to Palestinian rabbis? If so, why? Is the difference a function of differences in genre, since Palestinian midrashic compilations consist almost exclusively of rabbinic Bible commentary and the Bavli contains numerous other genres as well? That is, a rabbi interpreting scripture might behave or speak very differently from the same rabbi speaking without scriptural support, and the "contradiction" might be no contradiction at all. Does the Bavli preserve an authentically Palestinian attitude, deriving from circles other than those that predominate in extant Palestinian compilations? Markers of geographical and chronological provenance supplied by rabbinic compilations, therefore, raise significant questions and yield potentially significant conclusions, questions we would not have posed and conclusions we would not have reached had we assumed without further inquiry that these markers are historically useless.

Throughout this study, except where explicitly indicated otherwise, the term "Palestinian rabbinic traditions" denotes statements attributed to and stories involving Palestinian rabbis in Palestinian rabbinic compilations of late antiquity. The term "Babylonian rabbinic traditions" denotes statements attributed to and stories involving Babylonian rabbis in the Babylonian Talmud (or Bavli). Statements attributed to and stories involving Palestinian rabbis in the Bavli present a particularly thorny methodological problem.[75] On the one hand, they may be Babylonian creations, fully reflective of Babylonian attitudes and/or reality; on the other hand, they may accurately reflect the opinions or actions of the Palestinian rabbis to whom they are attributed. Such traditions also may have originated in Palestine and been subjected to greater or lesser tampering by Babylonian authors or editors during the course of their journey to and/or transmission in Babylonia. In short, such sources may belong to one of several different categories, and it would be a mistake to prejudge this material or to ignore it entirely. I will decide on a case-by-case basis whether or not a particular statement is best classified as Palestinian, Babylonian, or some combination of the two, or whether we lack a sufficient basis on which to decide the question. In so doing, we attempt to steer a middle course between (1) scholars who a priori tend to view all traditions in the Bavli, even those designated as Tannaitic or Palestinian Amoraic, as having been subjected to the heavy hand of Babylonian editor and (2) scholars who consider all material designated in the Bavli as Tannaitic or Palestinian Amoraic—as precisely what it purports to be.

In the next chapter, the data will require the use of different terminology in referring to Palestinian and Babylonian traditions, since all of the material under investigation in this chapter is attributed to Tannaim (nearly all of whom derive from Palestine), and I will be examining a distinction between purportedly Tannaitic statements in the Bavli and purportedly Tannaitic statements in Palestinian compilations. The precise nature of the investigation and the data in each chapter, therefore, will require a certain amount of terminological flexibility, but as a rule, the foregoing generalization applies for the entire book, except where explicitly noted otherwise.

I

Roman Persecutions of the Jews

This chapter surveys ancient rabbinic accounts of Roman interference with the practice of Judaism during the first few decades of the second century CE. What Jewish practices do the rabbis describe as having been affected by the second Palestinian Jewish revolt? Do Babylonian portrayals differ from Palestinian portrayals? Since virtually all of the relevant sources are attributed to Tannaim (pre-third-century CE rabbis who are almost exclusively Palestinian), I will approach this question by comparing sources attributed to Tannaim in the Bavli to those attributed to Tannaim in Palestinian compilations. If there is a difference, was the difference due in part to distinctive Babylonian rabbinic values that left their mark on Palestinian rabbinic traditions? I will attempt to show that Babylonian portrayals tend to emphasize Roman prohibition of Torah study, while Palestinian portrayals do so only rarely, if at all. This will be the first of many respects in which Babylonian rabbis place greater stress on Torah study than do Palestinian rabbis, which is easily explicable according to my claim that the universe of experience of Babylonian rabbis, more so than of Palestinians, tended not to extend beyond the four walls of the study house.

As noted in the introduction, furthermore, important scholars in the field today treat material attributed to Palestinians in the Bavli as Babylonian. Acknowledging in theory that the Bavli contains Palestine traditions, they tend in practice to ignore the attributions of statements and stories to Palestinian rabbis. It is my contention that the approach to this problem must be more nuanced, and the conclusions drawn in this chapter and the methods used to derive these conclusions will guide me throughout this book. Often, I will attempt to show, Palestinian traditions have been partially Babylonianized during the process of transfer from Palestine to Babylonia, but many of their Palestinian features have survived intact.

For the purposes of this chapter, the terms "Babylonian portrayals" or "Babylonian traditions" refer to statements and stories preserved in the Babylonian Talmud, while the terms "Palestinian portrayals" or "Palestinian traditions" refer to statements and stories preserved in Palestinian compilations.[1]

Babylonian rabbis preserved for posterity much Palestinian material, for example traditions deriving from Palestine that purport to describe (1) the impact of the Romans' bloody suppression of the Bar Kokhba revolt upon the observance of Judaism; and/or (2) Roman decrees prohibiting specific Jewish practices. The question of the historical truth or falsity of these traditions has been discussed in detail by Peter Schäfer and others, and I am persuaded by Schäfer's fundamental thesis: that the rabbinic materials tell us extremely little about the actual conduct of the Romans against the Jews.[2]

Rabbinic materials do tell us, however, about the concerns of rabbis.[3] What the rabbis describe as having been prohibited by the Romans, and/or as having been difficult or impossible to fulfill during "the time of danger," is for the most part what these rabbis viewed as most precious about Judaism.[4] Perhaps some traditions focus on those Jewish observances that were most likely to have been adversely affected by or fall victim to a period of chaos, bloodshed, and violence, but I doubt that a desire for verisimilitude was uppermost in the minds of rabbinic storytellers. These traditions were intended to inspire pathos in their audience, to dramatize the deeds of great Jewish martyrs, and to instruct people about the importance of the observances for which these martyrs gave their lives.

In most respects, Babylonian and Palestinian traditions describe the Romans interfering with the same set of Jewish practices. This is no argument in favor of the historicity of these traditions, but it does show that much was absorbed into the Bavli from Palestine without substantive change. The prominence given to the issue of Torah study in the Bavli, however, is evidence that occasionally the Babylonians did make important changes, the significance of which I will explore below.

One of the important results of Peter Schäfer's analysis was the discovery that it is extremely difficult to determine the precise chronology of many of the traditions that earlier scholars assigned with confidence to the period immediately prior to, during, or immediately after the Bar Kokhba war.[5] In addition, several traditions considered by earlier scholars to have been causes of the war are just as easily explicable as consequences, and several traditions considered to have been general descriptions of the Jewish experience during the Bar Kokhba period (e.g., imperial decrees affecting all of Palestinian Jewry), were more likely (if they were historical at all) responses by provincial Roman authorities to local disturbances. They were more likely Roman responses of limited duration and geographical compass.

For someone interested in writing the history of second-century Palestine, Schäfer's observations were revolutionary. For the purposes of this chapter, many of his conclusions matter little, since I am interested in attitudes reflected by the rabbinic sources, which with rare exceptions do not distinguish between localities within Palestine, and which make no effort to indicate their relative chronology. I am interested in distinctions between Palestinian and Babylonian rabbinic attitudes, and for this purpose it makes no difference whether or not a tradition accurately describes the event or period it purports to describe. To make this chapter of manageable proportions, I confine the discussion to traditions that purport to describe the events of the Bar Kokhba period, a term I use to refer to events leading up to, consequent upon, or taking place during the Bar Kokhba war.[6]

I also confine the discussion to stories, that is, to reports of events or actions, and also to actions or statements found within a narrative framework that begins with a description of the physical setting in which the action took place or the statement was made. I exclude from the discussion abstract legal statements, or prescriptive statements that are not embedded in a narrative framework.[7] My interest is in what the rabbis thought took place and not with what they thought the law was or should have been. I want to avoid lumping diverse categories in a single analysis, although my conclusion would not be altered significantly even if I included this material.

Palestinian Traditions in the Bavli: Torah Study

Examination of a fascinating narrative in b. Rosh Hashanah 19a will help illustrate my claim regarding the difference between Palestinian and Babylonian rabbinic traditions:[8]

> (A) On the twenty-eighth of [Adar] came good tidings to the Jews, that they should not cease from the Torah.
>
> (B) For one time a decree was decreed[9] against Israel that they should not occupy themselves in Torah [study], nor circumcise their sons, and that they should profane the Sabbath. What did Yehudah ben Shamua and his colleagues do? They went and took counsel with a matron who was frequently visited by all the greats of Rome.[10]
>
> She said to [Yehudah ben Shamua and his colleagues], "Stand and cry out at night."
>
> They went and cried out at night.
>
> They said, "By heaven! Are we not brothers? Are we not children of one father? Are we not children of one mother? How are we different from every nation and language, such that you decree against us evil decrees?" And [the Romans] annulled [the decrees] and [the Jews] made that day a holiday [*yom tov*].

It will be revealing to compare the Bavli's version of the story with that preserved in the Parma manuscript of the scholion to Megillat Ta'anit. Vered Noam persuasively characterizes this manuscript as relatively early and reliable, compared to other manuscript versions of the scholion, in part because it tends to be free of "corrections" and emendations based on the text of the Bavli.[11] This manuscript version reads as follows.

> (A) On the twenty-eighth of [Adar] came good tidings to the Jews, that they should not cease from the Torah and that they should not eulogize.
>
> (B) For the wicked kingdom decreed a persecution against Israel that they should not circumcise their sons, nor observe the Sabbath, and that they should worship idols. Until Yehudah ben Shamua and his colleagues went to a certain matron who gave them advice.
>
> They went and cried out at night and said, "By heaven! Are we not brothers? Are we not the sons of one father? Are we not the sons of one mother? How are we different from all of the nations, such that you decree against us these decrees?"
>
> They did not depart from there until they permitted these three commandments to Israel, that they should circumcise their sons, observe the Sabbath, and not worship idols. The day on which [these commandments] were permitted to them, they made it a holiday [*yom tov*].

As numerous scholars have noted, Megillat Ta'anit is a list, composed in Aramaic and for the most part deriving from the period of the second Temple, of dates on which great things happened to the Jewish people. In the selection quoted here, this early list is designated (A). A commentary, composed in Hebrew and designated here (B), expands upon the brief, often cryptic references found in the earlier list. It is the consensus of modern scholars that the Hebrew commentary, or scholion, is a later commentary on the Aramaic scroll, and that this Hebrew commentary does not necessarily understand or accurately interpret the Aramaic text upon which it is based.[12]

The Hebrew commentary, according to the Bavli and the Parma manuscript of the scholion, attempts to explain the phrase "that they should not cease from the Torah" found in the Aramaic substratum. The two versions of the commentary agree that in decreeing that Israel should "cease from the Torah" (*Oraita*), the Romans forbade circumcision and Sabbath observance. The Bavli, however, identifies the third decree as a prohibition of Torah study, while the Parma manuscript of the scholion identifies it as forced idolatry.[13] This story is the first of several Babylonian Talmudic traditions examined in this chapter that emphasize the importance of Torah study.

When did this story purportedly take place? Most versions of the Bavli, as well as the Parma manuscript of the scholion, employ the terminology "the wicked kingdom decreed a persecution" (*shemad*), and Lieberman and Herr convincingly argue that the word *shemad* is a technical term denoting a persecution that took place during the Bar Kokhba period.[14] Some versions of the Bavli, however, read simply "decreed a decree," without the word *shemad*.[15]

The chronology of the story's protagonist, Yehudah ben Shamua, provides another clue to the story's purported date. On the basis of a tradition that depicts Yehudah ben Shamua quoting R. Meir,[16] the Bavli concludes here that he was R. Meir's student, and according to numerous rabbinic sources, R. Meir flourished during the generation following the suppression of the Bar Kokhba revolt. In addition, Yehudah ben Shamua may have been the brother of R. Elazar ben Shamua, apparently a contemporary of R. Meir.[17] This evidence is likewise less than fully probative, however, since a single tradition is a fragile basis upon which to determine a rabbi's chronology.[18]

Perhaps, therefore, although not necessarily, this story illustrates the point that Babylonian traditions about the Bar Kokhba period tend to emphasize the importance of Torah study, but that Palestinian traditions (e.g., the scholion to Megillat Ta'anit as preserved in the Parma manuscript) do not.

A lengthy narrative, or rather series of narratives, in b. Avodah Zarah 17b–18a further supports this claim:[19]

> (A, in Hebrew) Our rabbis taught [in a Baraita]: When R. Elazar ben Perata and R. Ḥanina ben Teradion were arrested, R. Elazar ben Perata said to R. Ḥanina ben Teradion, "Happy are you, who was arrested because of one matter; woe to me, who was arrested because of five matters."
>
> R. Ḥanina [ben Teradion] said to him, "Happy are you, who was arrested because of five matters and you will be saved; woe to me, who was arrested because of one matter and I will not be saved, for you occupied yourself with Torah [study] and with deeds of lovingkindness, but I only occupied myself with Torah [study]." ...
>
> (B, in Aramaic) The [Romans] brought R. Elazar ben Perata [in for questioning].
>
> They said to him, "Why did you study and why did you steal? ...
>
> The [Romans] said to him, "Why did they call you 'Rabbi?' " ...
>
> The [Romans] said to him, "Why did you not go to the House of Avidan [the local pagan temple]?[20] ...
>
> [The Romans said to him], "Why did you free your slave?" ...
>
> The [Romans] brought R. Ḥanina ben Teradion [in for questioning]. They said to him, "Why have you occupied yourself with Torah [study]?"
>
> He said to them, "I have done as the Lord my God commanded me."
>
> (C, in Hebrew) Immediately the [Romans] decreed that [R. Ḥanina ben Teradion] should die by burning, that his wife should die by the sword, and that his daughter should sit in a brothel." ...
>
> (D, in Hebrew) Our rabbis taught [in a Baraita]: When R. Yosi ben Kisma became sick, R. Ḥanina ben Teradion went to visit him.
>
> [R. Yosi ben Kisma] said to [R. Ḥanina ben Teradion], "Ḥanina, my brother, don't you know that this nation [Rome] was made to rule by heaven, that [it] destroyed [God's] house, burned His palace, killed His pious ones, and destroyed His worthy ones, and still it endures? Yet I have heard that you sit and occupy yourself with

> Torah [study], [and gather crowds in public][21] with a Torah scroll resting in your bosom."
>
> [R. Ḥanina] said to [R. Yosi], "Heaven will have mercy."
>
> [R. Yosi] said to [R. Ḥanina], "I say reasonable things to you and you say, 'Heaven will have mercy?' I will be astonished if they don't burn you and your Torah scroll in fire." . . .
>
> It was said: "It was not long before R. Yosi ben Kisma died, and all of the Roman aristocrats went to bury him, and they eulogized him with a great eulogy. And when they returned, they found R. Ḥanina ben Teradion sitting and busying himself with Torah [study], and gathering crowds in public with a Torah scroll resting in his bosom. They wrapped him in his Torah scroll, surrounded him with bundles of wood, and set them on fire."

I have divided this lengthy narrative into four parts, and have translated only the sections relevant to this discussion. The Bavli identifies part A as a Tannaitic statement, and it is entirely in Hebrew; part B is in Aramaic and is apparently later commentary on part A; part C reverts back to Hebrew; and part D is in Hebrew and is introduced by a technical term that serves (1) to distinguish it from parts A–C as a separate source,[22] and (2) to indicate its Tannaitic provenance.

A partial parallel to this narrative is preserved in Sifrei Deuteronomy, a largely Tannaitic work of Palestinian provenance.[23] It will be illuminating to compare the accounts of the Sifrei and the Bavli. The Sifrei reads as follows:

> Another matter: "The rock, His deeds are perfect" (Deut. 32:4).
>
> When they arrested R. Ḥanina ben Teradion, he was condemned to be burned with his [Torah] scroll.
>
> They said to him, "You have been condemned to be burned with your Torah scroll."
>
> He recited this verse: "The rock, His deeds are perfect" (Deut. 32:4).
>
> They said to his wife, "Your husband has been condemned to be burned, and you to die by the sword."
>
> She recited this verse: "God is faithful and does no evil" (Deut. 32:4).
>
> They said to his daughter, "Your father has been condemned to be burned, your mother to die by the sword, and you [are sentenced] to forced labor."
>
> She recited this verse: "Wondrous in purpose and mighty in deed, Your eyes observe [all the ways of man]" (Jer. 32:19).
>
> Said Rabbi [Yehudah Hanasi], "How great are these righteous people, for in the time of their sorrow they summoned three verses declaring the righteousness of God's judgment."

The version of the story in the Sifrei, a Palestinian compilation, does not explain why the Romans arrested Ḥanina ben Teradion. The Sifrei is concerned with *ẓidduk ha-din*, with dramatizing Ḥanina's as well as his wife's and daughter's acceptance of their cruel fate without the slightest murmur of complaint against God. In contrast, at first glance the reason for Ḥanina's and Elazar's arrest appears to occupy the center of the Bavli's concern. Closer examination, however, reveals that this concern is front and center at some points in the Bavli's narrative but absent at others.

As noted, part B of the Bavli's version is in Aramaic and part A is in Hebrew, suggesting that they derive from different sources. Part A purports to be a Baraita, a Tannaitic source deriving from Palestine, while part B is apparently Babylonian commentary on the Palestinian source. Viewing part A in isolation from part B, we find that the central concern of part A is the inadequacy of Torah study alone, and the need for study to be accompanied by deeds of lovingkindness.

This point bears restating. Part A mentions that Ḥanina ben Teradion occupied himself with Torah study alone, while Elazar ben Perata occupied himself with Torah study and good deeds. Part B, which appears to be commentary on part A, induces us to view differently the role of Torah study and good deeds in part A. Part B suggests that we view Torah study (in the case of Ḥanina ben Teradion) and Torah study and good deeds (in the case of Elazar ben Perata) as the offenses for which these rabbis were arrested by the Romans. Viewing part A in isolation from part B, however, shows the likelihood of another interpretation. Part A's reference to Ḥanina occupying himself with one matter, Torah study, explains why he lacks sufficient merit and therefore will not be saved from the Romans; part A's reference to Elazar occupying himself with deeds of lovingkindness and Torah study explains why he has sufficient merit and therefore will be saved. According to part A, Torah study and deeds of lovingkindness are not the reasons for the rabbis' arrest; that point is not made until part B. Part A emphasizes that one acquires greater merit from occupying oneself with both Torah and good deeds than from occupying oneself with Torah alone, and this greater merit serves to protect one from this-worldly harm.[24]

To sum up the discussion thus far, the first Palestinian tradition in the Bavli (part A), like the Palestinian tradition in Sifrei Deuteronomy, is not concerned with the question of why the Romans arrested Ḥanina ben Teradion and Elazar ben Perata. My point is not that part A and the text of the Sifrei should be interpreted in light of one another. They are very different: the Sifrei is concerned with the issue of *ẓidduk ha-din*, and part A is concerned with the inadequacy of Torah study unaccompanied by good deeds. Rather, my point is that both Palestinian traditions contain no mention of Torah study as a factor motivating Roman persecution of the Jews. Significantly, one of the Palestinian traditions that is preserved in the Bavli *deemphasizes* the importance of Torah study, teaching that by itself this religious duty is not sufficient to protect one from arrest by the Romans.

Turning now to parts B and C, we find that the Bavli's anonymous editors have subjected part A to a radical new interpretation. Throughout the Talmud, the anonymous editors often radically interpret the Tannaitic and Amoraic sources at their disposal, and it is no surprise to see them doing so here.[25] The anonymous editors understand "Torah study" to be the "offense" for which the Romans arrested Ḥanina ben Teradion. The editors demonstrate this most clearly when they juxtapose the Roman cross-examination of Ḥanina ("Why have you busied yourself with Torah [study?]") with (1) Ḥanina's bold confession ("He said to them, 'I have done as the Lord my God commanded me'") and (2) part C's report that "immediately the [Romans] decreed that he should die by burning, that his wife should die by the sword, and that his daughter should sit in a brothel." Part C is apparently Tannaitic, since it is in Hebrew and constitutes the Bavli's closest parallel to the text from Sifrei Deuteronomy. By placing it immediately after the Roman cross-examination of Ḥanina and Ḥanina's confession, therefore, the anonymous editors of the Bavli enlist Tannaitic material in support of their claim that Torah study was the "crime" for which the Romans arrested Ḥanina ben Teradion.

It is likely that the anonymous editors explain in part B the nature of the "five matters" on account of which the Romans arrested Elazar ben Perata. First, their "bringing" Elazar to be cross-examined is described in the same terms used to describe their cross-examination of Ḥanina, and second, they bring a total of five charges against Elazar in part B, one of which is Torah study.[26]

According to the Babylonian section of the discussion (part B), therefore, the Romans considered Torah study to be a capital offense; according to the Palestinian sections (parts A and C), we do not know why the Romans arrested the rabbis. Part D of the discussion, however, is identified as a Baraita ("Our rabbis taught") and is entirely in Hebrew, yet it twice specifies Torah study as the "crime" for which Ḥanina ben Teradion was executed.

This fact, however, does not negate the conclusions reached above. As we saw above, and as we shall see repeatedly throughout this book, other purportedly Palestinian traditions were Babylonianized during the course of their transmission from Palestine to Babylonia, and while Palestinian traditions in Palestinian compilations do not identify Torah study as a capital offense, Palestinian traditions in the Bavli sometimes do. It should not surprise us that (1) some Palestinian traditions in the Bavli were not Babylonianized at all, while (2) other traditions were partially Babylonianized but retained several or most of their Palestinian features. In addition, it is possible that part D's Babylonianization was attempted by post-Talmudic scribes, and even then only with partial success, a possibility strengthened by the multiplicity of manuscript variants,[27] which Shamma Friedman argues persuasively is often a sign of textual emendation or corruption.[28]

Many other rabbinic texts describe the impact of the conflict with Rome upon Jewish observance. Do we find further support for our claim that some Palestinian traditions underwent partial Babylonianization during the course of their journey from Palestine to Babylonia? The answer is yes, since a purportedly Tannaitic tradition[29] in b. Berakhot 61a dramatizes Roman prohibition of Torah study, but texts in Palestinian compilations do not.[30] The text is as follows:

> Our rabbis taught [in a Baraita]: One time the wicked government decreed that Israel should not busy themselves with Torah [study].
>
> Papos ben Yehudah came and found R. Akiba gathering crowds in public and busying himself with Torah [study].[31]
>
> [Papos] said to him, "Akiba, are you not afraid on account of the kingdom?"
>
> [R. Akiba] said to him, "I will tell you a parable: To what can this matter be compared? To a fox that walked along the side of a river and saw fish gathering from one place to another. [The fox] said to them, 'Why are you fleeing?' [The fish] said to him, 'Because of the nets which people bring upon us.' [The fox] said to them, 'Do you want to come up to dry land so that you and I will live together just like my ancestors lived with your ancestors?' [The fish] said to him, 'You are the one they call the cleverest of beasts? You are not clever, but stupid! If we are afraid in the place where we live, in a place where we die how much the more so [will we be afraid]?' [Akiba continued]: So too with us: Now we are sitting and occupying ourselves with Torah study, about which it is written, 'For it is your life and the length of your days' (Deut. 30:20) [and we are afraid], if we stop [studying Torah], how much the more so [will we be afraid]?"
>
> They said, "It was not long before they arrested R. Akiba and put him in prison, and they arrested Papos ben Yehudah and imprisoned him next to [R. Akiba]."
>
> [R. Akiba] said to him, "Papos, what brought you here?"
>
> [Papos] said to him, "Happy are you, R. Akiba, for you were arrested for words of Torah. Woe to Papos, who was arrested for worthless matters."

The fact that the story describes the arrest and execution of R. Akiba is unequivocal proof that the storyteller has in mind Roman persecutions during the Bar Kokhba war.

There are obvious similarities between this story and the story analyzed above involving Ḥanina ben Teradion and Elazar ben Perata. In both cases, the two protagonists are arrested by the Romans and put together in prison. Both stories employ the formula, "Happy are you . . . Woe to . . ." and both stories depict rabbinic figures arrested for Torah study.[32] Finally, both stories describe the protagonist "gathering crowds in public," and some versions of both stories describe him with "a Torah scroll in his lap." The stories show traces of (mutual?) influence or a common ancestry, although the precise nature of this influence and/or ancestry is not clear.

What does this text view as the crimes for which R. Akiba was arrested? Certainly Torah study is one, but several modern scholars claim that Akiba was also arrested for the crime of "gathering crowds in public."[33] This issue is significant, for my concern in this survey is to describe rabbinic portrayals of Roman behavior during the period of Bar Kokhba, with special emphasis on the difference between Palestinian and Babylonian rabbinic portrayals. The story is most likely useless as evidence regarding early second-century Palestine, but it tells us much about later rabbinic attitudes.

It is likely that this story does not view "gathering crowds in public" as one of the crimes for which Akiba was arrested. The story opens by informing us that the Romans prohibited Torah study, and later on informs us that Akiba was arrested for Torah study. "Gathering crowds in public" is mentioned only when the story relates what Akiba is doing when he is arrested. "Gathering crowds in public," in other words, is not described as illegal, nor is it cited as one of the reasons for Akiba's arrest. Rather, it is evidence of the lengths to which Akiba went in defying the Roman decree. He gathered crowds in public even though this increased the visibility of his "crime," and he held on to a Torah scroll even though this signaled to the Romans that he was the one most responsible for violating Roman law.

Why have scholars concluded incorrectly that the story depicts R. Akiba breaking the law by gathering crowds in public? Perhaps because they approached the text with historical questions uppermost in their minds, which left them insufficiently attuned to the story's didactic purposes. That Akiba gathered crowds in public tells us about his devotion to teaching Torah to the Jewish people, but tells us nothing at all about what Palestinian or Babylonian storytellers thought that the Romans (or Persians) outlawed. It is significant that in Avodah Zarah 17a, R. Ḥanina ben Teradion is said to be guilty of only one crime, that is, Torah study, even though he also "gathered crowds" (see part D, above). If "gathering crowds" were a crime, why is R. Ḥanina not said to have transgressed two prohibitions?

Other purportedly Palestinian Tannaitic texts in the Bavli further indicate that Babylonian tradents and storytellers, in accordance with Babylonian preoccupations, depict the Romans prohibiting Torah study during the Bar Kokhba period. A tradition in b. Pesaḥim 112a–b reads as follows:[34]

> R. Akiba recommended five things to R. Shimon bar Yoḥai when [R. Akiba] was in jail.
>
> [R. Shimon] said to him, "Rabbi, teach me Torah."
>
> [R. Akiba] said, "I will not teach you."
>
> [R. Shimon] said to him, "If you don't teach me, I will tell father Yoḥai and he will hand you over to the government."
>
> [R. Akiba] said to him, "My son, more than the calf wants to nurse the cow wants to suckle."
>
> [R. Shimon] said to him, "But which one is in danger? Isn't the calf in danger?"
>
> [R. Akiba] said, "If you want to be choked, hang yourself from a large tree. And when you teach your son, teach him from a scroll that has been corrected."

Apparently, R. Shimon asks R. Akiba to teach him, in defiance of the Roman ban.[35] Akiba refuses for reasons that are at first unclear: is Akiba afraid for his own life or for that of his student, R. Shimon? Shimon threatens to tell his father to denounce Akiba to the government if he withholds Torah from him, an outrageous expression of his desperate need for Torah.[36] Akiba responds that he is full to bursting with Torah and would like nothing more than to teach, but something, apparently concern for his student's safety, holds him back.

Shimon's response puts an ironic twist on the dialogue. The real "danger" is not the Roman threat to execute students and teachers of Torah. The "danger" is not that Akiba or Shimon might be arrested by the Romans, but that R. Shimon, the student, will weaken and eventually die if R. Akiba denies him Torah, which is as necessary for life as mother's milk.[37]

A statement in b. Yevamot 108b,[38] finally, says that unnamed rabbis took the extraordinary step of hiring someone to take their halakhic question to R. Akiba in jail. This story perhaps presupposes a Roman prohibition of Torah study, according to which the money compensates the messenger for exposing himself to danger.[39] Alternatively, however, this story imagines Akiba in solitary confinement, with all contact between him and the outside world forbidden by his Roman captors. Accordingly, the messenger exposes himself to danger simply by making contact with Akiba, and the story perhaps says nothing about Roman prohibition of Torah study.

Other Palestinian Traditions in the Bavli

We have established, therefore, that an ostensible Roman ban of Torah study is featured in several of the Bavli's traditions about the Hadrianic persecutions. It is by no means the only preoccupation, however, and the ensuing discussion examines other relevant traditions. Modern scholars have cited b. Me'ilah 17a–b as evidence that the Romans prohibited circumcision and the observance of the Sabbath, and either forbade ritual immersion[40] or compelled Jewish men to have sex with menstruants.[41]

The Bavli's account, which purports to be Tannaitic,[42] is as follows:

> For one time the kingdom decreed a decree that [the Jews] shall not observe the Sabbath nor circumcise their sons, and that they shall have intercourse with their wives [when they are] menstruants. R. Reuven son of Istroboli cut his hair in the style of a pagan and sat with them.
>
> He said to them, "He who has an enemy, should [the enemy] become poor or rich?"
>
> They said to him, "[The enemy] should become poor."
>
> He said to them, "If so, they should not do work on the Sabbath so that they will become poor."
>
> They said, "You [speak] well."
>
> He said, "Annul [the decree]."
>
> And they annulled it.

> He then said to them, "One who has an enemy, should [the enemy] grow weak or strong?"
> They said to him, "He should grow weak."
> He said to them, "If so, let them circumcise their sons on the eighth day [so that] they grow weak."
> They said, "You [speak] well."
> He said, "[Annul it]," and they annulled it.
> He then said to them, "One who has an enemy, should [the enemy] increase or decrease in number?"
> They said to him, "He should decrease."
> [He said to them], "If so, they should not have intercourse with menstruants."
> They said, "You [speak] well."
> He said, "[Annul it]," and they annulled it.

The prohibition against Sabbath observance and circumcision is documented in other traditions, and the only "new" information supplied by this tradition is the supposed Roman decree that Jewish men should have intercourse with menstruants.[43]

To Peter Schäfer's cogent arguments against the historicity of the story's claim that the Romans coerced Jewish men to have intercourse with menstruants, I would add that the issue of forced intercourse is mentioned here only because it makes for a better story. Like Sabbath observance and circumcision, refraining from intercourse during menstruation is a *mizvah* that, using purely human logic, weakens the Jewish people. It decreases, think the storytellers, the ability of Jews to reproduce, and granting the Jews permission to observe this *mizvah* would seem to be sound political strategy on the part of the Romans. The "joke," of course, which the story's authors and Jewish audience share at the Romans' expense, is that it is precisely by observing these *mizvot* that the Jewish people keep their covenant with God and therefore guarantee their survival.

In all, my study yielded the following results. According to the Bavli, Roman persecutions of the Bar Kokhba period interfered with the performance of the following *mizvot*: (1) Torah study: three to five traditions;[44] (2) circumcision: four traditions;[45] (3) Sabbath observance: two traditions;[46] (4) tefillin: one or two traditions;[47] (5) public reading of the Torah: one tradition;[48] (6) "the week of the child:" one tradition;[49] (7) sukkah building: one tradition;[50] (8) marriage on Wednesday: one tradition;[51] (9) the prohibition of idolatry: one tradition;[52] (10) lighting Ḥanukkah lamps: one tradition;[53] (11) ordination of rabbis: one tradition;[54] (12) deeds of lovingkindness: one tradition;[55] (13) the prohibition of sex with menstruants: one tradition;[56] and possibly (14) properly issued divorce bills: one tradition.[57]

In all, we find mention of 20–23 *mizvot* in 13–16 traditions. Torah study and circumcision are mentioned most frequently; besides these two *mizvot*, only Sabbath observance and possibly tefillin are mentioned more than once. The prominence of circumcision is easily explicable: it is the one *mizvah* that non-Jewish sources claim aroused Roman opposition,[58] and there is widespread modern scholarly agreement (but not unanimity) that Roman prohibition of circumcision was either a cause or a result of the Bar Kokhba revolt.[59] The prominence of Torah study, however, is more difficult to explain, since as noted, Torah study is not featured in relevant sources preserved in Palestinian compilations, a point to which I will return.[60]

Palestinian Compilations

Thus far we have examined statements attributed to and stories involving Palestinian rabbis preserved in the Bavli. Turning to traditions preserved in Palestinian compilations, we find some interesting differences. T. Berakhot 2:13, for example, attributes to R. Meir the view that Rome prohibited the *mizvah* of chanting the *shema*, a liturgical act, but *permitted* the study of Torah.[61] The text is as follows:

> "A *ba'al keri* [a man who is ritually impure by reason of a seminal emission] who has no water in which to immerse himself [in order to become ritually pure], chants the *shema* but does not do so loudly enough for his ears to hear," [these are] the words of R. Meir.
>
> The sages say, "He chants the *shema* loudly enough for his ears to hear and he blesses before and after."
>
> Said R. Meir, "One time we were sitting in the study house before R. Akiba, and we were chanting the *shema*, but not loudly enough for our ears to hear, on account of a *quaestor* who stood at the door."
>
> They said to him, "A time of danger is no proof."

The story, which involves R. Akiba and R. Meir, clearly purports to take place during the period of Bar Kokhba.[62] The Vienna manuscript and the printed edition have the phrase "in the study house," but the Erfurt manuscript does not. Even without these words, however, the phrase "we were sitting before R. Akiba" probably implies a study context.[63] The rabbis are not afraid to study Torah in the presence of the *quaestor*, apparently because this narrative assumes that the Romans did not prohibit Torah study.

Peter Schäfer claims that the story does not imply Roman prohibition of recitation of the *shema*. According to Schäfer, R. Meir equates the unclean *ba'al keri* and the unclean *quaestor*; he interprets R. Meir to be saying that just as the rabbis said the *shema* quietly in the presence of the unclean *quaestor*, so too the ritually unclean *ba'al keri* recites the *shema* quietly.

Schäfer reaches this conclusion because there is a problem with interpreting the story in what seems to be a more straightforward fashion. At first glance, the issue seems to be quite simple: can the ritually unclean *ba'al keri* recite the *shema* out loud or not? The sages say yes, and R. Meir says no. As "proof," however, R. Meir quotes a story about ritually clean individuals who chant the *shema* quietly in the presence, but not within earshot, of a Roman *quaestor*. This story does not seem to prove Meir's point, since the individuals who chant the *shema* quietly in Meir's story are not ritually impure. R. Meir's proof does not match the case he is apparently trying to prove.

Schäfer's interpretation, however, does not solve the problem. Schäfer's interpretation renders the proof brought by R. Meir totally inadequate, because the Roman *quaestor* is not and cannot be ritually unclean, since the categories of ritual purity and impurity apply in Jewish law only to Jews. In addition, for the two cases (the *ba'al keri* and the *quaestor*) to be truly equivalent, according to Schäfer, there should be a prohibition against someone who is ritually clean chanting the *shema* loudly enough for the unclean *ba'al keri* to hear, just as the ritually clean rabbis chanted the *shema* softly so the unclean *quaestor* could not hear. Neither R. Meir nor any other rabbi holds that position, however, and the two cases are therefore not equivalent.

More likely, we are to understand R. Meir's proof as one of similarity rather than complete identity. R. Meir, who asserts that "a man who is ritually impure by reason of a seminal emission . . . chants the *shema* but does not do so loudly enough for his ears to hear," wishes to show his opponents that there is another case in which special circumstances make it necessary to say the *shema* quietly. The action of R. Akiba and his students proves that there is religious value in saying the *shema* quietly when it is not possible or feasible to say it out loud.

It is likely, furthermore, that R. Meir's report of the halakhic action of R. Akiba did not originate in the present context. Rather, R. Meir originally told a story about his teacher, R. Akiba, and the editors of the Tosefta placed it in its present argumentational context, adding a rejection of the proof by R. Meir's interlocutors. Such redactional activity in rabbinic texts is routine,[64] and it is preferable to posit this development than to resort to a forced interpretation.

In traditions preserved in other Palestinian compilations, a Roman prohibition of Torah study is likewise notably absent. According to a statement attributed to R. Natan in the Mekhilta, for example, Jews were lashed because they waved the lulav on Sukkot, and were executed because they (1) observed the *mizvah* of circumcision; (2) publicly read the Torah; and (3) ate matzah on Passover.[65] The fact that the statement is attributed to R. Natan, who flourished during the generation following the Bar Kokhba war, makes it likely that the statement's author intends it as a characterization of Jewish suffering during and/or shortly after the second rebellion.

Public reading of the Torah, one of the three prohibited *mizvot* according to the Mekhilta, is clearly distinguishable from Torah study. Public reading of the Torah requires a quorum of 10 men and a fixed text (the weekly Torah portion) and is performed only on fixed days and at fixed times. Torah study requires none of these things. Most important for my purposes, the liturgical act of reading from the Torah was limited to biblical texts and was performed by and for nonrabbis as well as rabbis. The act of Torah study, on the other hand, primarily involved rabbinic texts and was the distinguishing mark of a rabbi.[66]

Two additional texts, placed back-to-back in y. Yevamot 12:6 (12d), are also relevant to the issue of purported Roman prohibition of Torah study. A Baraita[67] reports that R. Akiba judged a case that came before him in jail. The Yerushalmi continues in Aramaic:

> R. Yoḥanan Hasandlar pretended to be a peddler. One day he passed before the jail cell of R. Akiba and announced, "Who wants pins? Who wants hooks? If she performed *ḥaliẓah*[68] with only the levir present, what is the law? [Is the *ḥaliẓah* valid or not]?"
>
> R. Akiba peered at him from the window.
>
> He said to him, "Do you have spindles [*kashin*]? Do you have *kasher* [valid]?"

The Aramaic story is apparently a post-Tannaitic attempt to explain the extraordinary conditions under which the case came before R. Akiba in jail. R. Yohanan Hasandlar came in disguise to the street outside his teacher's cell and communicated the question while pretending to be a peddler announcing his wares. Akiba recognized his student and gave Yoḥanan the answer while pretending to be an interested buyer.

The Baraita on which this Aramaic story is based, therefore, perhaps implies that the Romans *permitted* Torah study, at least in the form of answers to practical questions. It will be recalled that the Baraita states simply that a halakhic case came before R. Akiba in jail and he delivered judgment. The post-Tannaitic story, however, commenting on the Baraita, perhaps implies that the Romans prohibited Torah study.[69] The student, R. Yoḥanan Hasandlar, and the teacher, R. Akiba, must communicate in secret, perhaps out of fear that they will be arrested for violating Roman law.

Neither the Baraita, however, nor the post-Tannaitic story compel these interpretations. With regard to the Baraita, perhaps R. Akiba was able to judge the case because the Romans permitted Torah study, but just as plausibly someone brought the case to Akiba in secret. This is in essence the Aramaic story's interpretation of the Baraita, and it is not at all far-fetched.

As for the story itself, perhaps it indicates only that the Romans forbade contact between Akiba and his students while he was in jail. Why the Romans did so is another matter. Perhaps the story claims that they did so out of fear that such contact might serve military purposes and might contribute to the Jewish war effort. Or perhaps the Romans forbade such contact as part of R. Akiba's punishment, to deny him precious contact with his students. These traditions do not serve as clear proof that Rome was thought either to have permitted or to have forbidden Torah study, although neither possibility can be dismissed.

T. Sotah 15:10 also bears very much on this question, although this text is difficult to evaluate because it survives in two very different versions. The Erfurt manuscript of the Tosefta reads as follows:

> Said Rabban Shimon ben Gamliel, "Since they decree that we cannot study Torah, let us decree that Israel cannot marry, and Israel will become desolate and the seed of Abraham will cease. But leave Israel alone; it is better that they sin unwittingly than that they sin intentionally."

This version states explicitly that the Romans prohibited Torah study. The attribution of the statement to Rabban Shimon ben Gamliel, furthermore, indicates that the story's background is the period of Bar Kokhba.[70]

A very different version, however, is preserved in the Vienna manuscript and in the printed edition of the Tosefta:

> Said R. Yishmael . . . "Since they uproot the Torah from among us, we should decree that the world should be desolate, that a man should not marry, that he should not father children, and that he should not establish 'the week of the son,' until the seed of Abraham will cease by itself."[71]
>
> They said, "It is better for the community to sin unintentionally than to sin intentionally."

This version makes no mention of a Roman decree against Torah study, speaking in vague generalities and providing no clues of the precise manner in which the Romans "uproot the Torah." Peter Schäfer correctly notes that at present we have no basis upon which to prefer one version over the other.[72]

In all, we have found that Palestinian texts preserved in Palestinian compilations portray Roman prohibition of the following *mizvot*: (1) circumcision: four traditions;[73] (2) public reading of the Torah: three traditions;[74] (3) Sabbath observance: three traditions;[75] (4) marriage on Wednesday: two traditions;[76] (5) eating matzah on Passover: two traditions;[77] (6) building a sukkah: two traditions;[78] (7) returning lost articles: two traditions;[79] (8) waving the lulav: two traditions;[80] (9) wearing tefillin: one tradition;[81] (10) chanting the *shema*: one tradition;[82] (11) use of specially dyed wool in *tsitsit*: one tradition;[83] (12) public reading of the scroll of Esther: one tradition;[84] (13) tithing: one tradition;[85] (14) Hebrew documents: one tradition;[86] (15) sex with a virgin: one tradition;[87] and study of Torah: zero to two traditions.[88]

In all, we found a total of 17–19 traditions that mention 26–28 *mizvot*. If we confine the discussion to post-Tannaitic compilations, the figure is 9–10 traditions that mention 15–16 *mizvot*; and if we limit ourselves to Tannaitic compilations, the figure is 13–14 traditions that mention 16–17 *mizvot*. Circumcision was mentioned most frequently (four times); followed by public reading of the Torah and observance of the Sabbath (three times each); followed next by marriage on Wednesday, eating matzah on Passover, building a sukkah, wearing tefillin, and returning lost articles (two times each). I found only two doubtful references to a prohibition of Torah study, and one or two cases that suggested that the Romans permitted Torah study.[89]

As noted, the prominence of circumcision is most likely due in part to its central importance within rabbinic Judaism, but also in part to the likelihood that the Romans did, in fact, attempt to interfere with the observance of this *miẓvah*. The other *miẓvot* are also of primary importance to the rabbis, and their presence on this list is not at all surprising.[90]

Two important facts emerged during the course of this chapter: (1) on the whole, there is very little difference between the portrayal of Roman persecutions (a) in the Bavli, and (b) in Palestinian compilations, and (2) the most significant difference is Torah study, mentioned more frequently in the Bavli than any other *miẓvah*, with the possible exception of circumcision, while in Palestinian compilations it is mentioned perhaps not at all, and may even be referred to occasionally as having been permitted by the Romans.

The substantial uniformity between compilations from the two rabbinic centers indicates that, on the whole, Babylonian storytellers and editors did not invent out of whole cloth their picture of Roman behavior during the period of Bar Kokhba. This is to claim not that the Bavli's traditions are historical (although some of them may be) but simply that in this case, with regard to basic content, the Bavli exercised restraint in tampering with the legends, fabrications, and traditions it received from Palestine.

As noted in the introduction, the Bavli's greater emphasis on Torah study may be evidence of a significant cultural difference between rabbis in the two localities. For Babylonian rabbis, Torah study was the *summum bonum* of human existence. For Palestinian rabbis, Torah study was only one among many important religious observances and practices; significant, yes, but not to the extent that it overshadowed other religious activities as it did for their Babylonian counterparts. This distinction, combined with all of the evidence gathered in earlier studies and briefly summarized in the introduction, supports my contention that Babylonian rabbis tended to draw a tight circle around themselves and to venture outside the rabbinic study house as little as possible. For Babylonian rabbis, whose lives revolved around Torah study, it is unimaginable that the Romans would not make it a significant focus of their efforts to damage or destroy the Jewish people. More closely involved with nonrabbinic Jews, Palestinian rabbis tended more than Babylonian rabbis to emphasize the importance of religious observances other than Torah study, observances precious to rabbis and nonrabbis alike. These differing preoccupations influenced their differing portrayals of the Jewish past, a tendency we will observe in subsequent chapters as well.

One qualitative difference between the Bavli on the one hand and Palestinian corpora on the other is the tendency of traditions in the Bavli to be more elaborate. This difference, however, characterizes traditions in the Bavli in general as compared to traditions in Palestinian corpora. In other words, this distinction between the Bavli and Palestinian compilations is one of genre and genre alone, and/or of differing storytelling capabilities or conventions.[91]

Other differences between portrayals found in the Mishnah and Tosefta on the one hand and the Bavli on the other are likewise due to considerations of genre. It is no surprise, for example, that the Mishnah and Tosefta contain relatively few relevant traditions, since these texts are primarily compilations of law that set forth rabbinic standards of proper behavior.[92] The Mishnah and Tosefta concentrate on the rabbinic norm rather than on extraordinary circumstances and extraordinary individuals. To a far greater extent, on the other hand, the Bavli tells stories and reports traditions that deliver a didactic message or a moral lesson rather than simply prescribe the norm. The Bavli's more abundant corpus of traditions that describe Roman interference with Jewish observances during the Bar Kokhba period is very likely a function of literary genre rather than explicable in terms of the differing chronology and geography of the Babylonian and Palestinian compilations. Other than the Bavli's emphasis on Torah study, the picture presented in the two Talmuds is in most ways the same, differing quantitatively, both in terms of the number of traditions and the degree of their complexity, but not qualitatively. In terms of quantity, the Yerushalmi occupies a middle ground between the extremes represented by the Mishnah and Tosefta on the one hand and the Bavli on the other. But this quantitative difference is likewise attributable to genre, since, as noted in the preface, the Yerushalmi is more tightly focused on law and Mishnah commentary than the Bavli. The Bavli finds space for a multiplicity of genres and styles, focusing more than the Yerushalmi on the hagiographical and homiletical in addition to the exegetical and legal.

2

Kings, Priests, and Sages

This chapter attempts to describe differences between Palestinian and Babylonian rabbinic narratives that purport to portray events of the second Temple period, and thus continues our examination of rabbinic depictions of the past and the light they shed on the rabbinic present. I attempt to show that Babylonian portrayals emphasize the importance of rabbis, especially at the expense of kings, in particular depicting sages rather than kings in control of the priests and the Temple cult. Palestinian rabbinic portrayals, on the other hand, tend to assign to rabbis a less prominent role and allow for a greater role for kings.[1]

Babylonian rabbis visualized Jewish society of the distant past as dominated by rabbis, perhaps in part because the study house was, to a significant degree, the sum total of their experience. Palestinian rabbis were more integrated into society; perhaps in conformity with their experience, they sometimes visualized Jewish society in the past as being dominated by groups and individuals other than rabbis, notably priests and kings. In addition, it is possible that Babylonian rabbis told these stories to strengthen their belief and the belief of their disciples that rabbis were entitled to be the leaders of Babylonian Jewish society.

Once again, I will conclude, the Bavli partially emends the Palestinian traditions at its disposal in accordance with Babylonian concerns, while transmitting much of the Palestinian traditions without significant change. Only rarely are we able to determine when these emendations were made, and it is likely that they were made throughout the entire period of the Bavli's formation.[2] This chapter contains additional examples of the methods by which traditions in the Bavli can be divided into their component parts, with some editorial additions responding to hermeneutical instead of or in addition to cultural concerns.

We know from numerous sources that priests and, during the Hasmonean and Herodian periods, kings wielded temporal authority in second Temple Palestinian Jewish society.[3] My conclusion that Babylonian Talmudic sources tended to emphasize the contribution of sages at the expense of kings and priests, therefore, is one of several indications that Babylonian aggadot are less reliable than Palestinian aggadot on the issue of the role of rabbis in second Temple Jewish society.[4] These findings demonstrate the necessity of carefully distinguishing between Palestinian and Babylonian, earlier and later, and briefer and lengthier aggadot with regard to their historicity, since not all types of aggadah distort reality in the same way and to the same extent.

This chapter also examines the relationship between the Talmuds and the Tosefta and in one case supports Shamma Friedman's claim that early versions of the Bavli's Baraitot closely resemble those of the Tosefta.[5] Current versions of Baraitot in the Bavli are often very different from those of the Tosefta, while Baraitot in the Yerushalmi more closely resemble those of the Tosefta. According to Friedman, the Yerushalmi's editors and tradents apparently did not emend their sources as freely as did the editors of the Bavli, and the final editing of the Bavli took place roughly two centuries after that of the Yerushalmi. The Bavli's texts passed through many more hands before they reached their final form, and these hands shaped, molded, and sometimes transformed these texts in accordance with contemporary realities, needs, desires, and assumptions.

I find it very unlikely that the aforementioned differences between Palestinian and Babylonian sources are due simply to the greater freedom with which Babylonian editors emended their sources, or the longer duration of the Bavli's redaction. In other words, I find it unlikely that the Bavli substitutes sages for kings, for example, while parallel stories in the Yerushalmi do not, simply because Babylonian editors tended to tinker with their sources but Palestinian editors did not. I reject this explanation because the phenomenon under consideration—the tendency of Babylonian Talmudic sources to downplay the role of kings and to emphasize the role of sages in controlling priests and the priestly cult during the second Temple period—is too persistent to be dismissed as a mere byproduct of the editing process, with no larger significance. Were the differences between Babylonia and Palestine simply a function of more versus less editing, we would expect a more random distribution of evidence, with the Bavli less systematically privileging sages at the expense of kings.

The difference between the Palestinian and Babylonian versions of these traditions is not a function of the different audiences to which the various versions were addressed. The theory of audience, in other words, outlined in the introduction does not satisfactorily account for the evidence. Both the Palestinian and Babylonian versions transform a tradition that in an earlier form was a diverting anecdote into a legal precedent, which supports a particular halakhic viewpoint. In no case do we find that one of the rabbinic versions, Palestinian or Babylonian, is more appealing or accessible to a nonrabbinic audience than any of the others.

Finally, this chapter documents several instances in which nonrabbinic traditions have found their way into the Bavli. This finding supports my claim in the introduction that Babylonian rabbis, despite their internal focus, were not totally cut off from the nonrabbinic world, although this world is often mediated to them through the prism of literary texts. The findings of this chapter indicate that Palestinian rabbis did not need to emend nonrabbinic traditions as radically as did Babylonian rabbis to transform them into what they considered to be appropriate objects of Torah study.

A Baraita found in b. Yoma 12b and paralleled in Palestinian compilations (see below) will exemplify these claims:[6]

> Our rabbis taught [in a Baraita]: "If [the high priest] became [ritually] unfit [to serve as high priest] and they appointed another in his place, the first resumes his duties [when he is no longer ritually unfit] and the second, all the commandments of the high priesthood apply to him." [These are] the words of R. Meir.
>
> R. Yosi says, "[When he is no longer ritually unfit], the first [high priest] resumes his duties and the second is not fit [to serve] as a high priest or as a common priest."
>
> Said R. Yosi, "It once happened to Yosef ben Elem from Sepphoris[7] that the high priest became unfit and they appointed [Yosef ben Elem] in his place.
>
> The sages said, '[When he is no longer ritually unfit] the first [high priest] resumes his duties and the second is not fit [to serve] as a high priest or as a common priest.' "

A parallel but lengthier version of the Baraita is found in t. Yoma 1:4:

> R. Ḥananya the adjutant high priest said, "For this [reason] an alternate [high priest] is appointed: [When] a [high] priest is found to be [ritually] unfit, an alternate serves in his place."
>
> "[When he is no longer ritually unfit], the high priest resumes his duties, and the one who served in his place, all the commandments of the [high] priesthood apply to him." [These are] the words of R. Meir.
>
> R. Yosah[8] says, "Even though they said, 'All the commandments of the [high] priesthood apply to him,' he is not fit [to serve] as a high priest or as a common priest."
>
> Said R. Yosah, "It happened that Yosef ben Ilim from Sepphoris served for a brief period [as high priest] in place of the [regular] high priest, and [after the latter resumed his duties, Yosef ben Ilim] was not fit [to serve] as a high priest or as a common priest. When he came out [of the holy of holies, Yosef ben Ilim] said to the king, 'The bull and goat that were offered today, who incurs the expense? Me

> or the high priest?' The king knew what [Yosef ben Ilim] meant. [The king] said to him, 'What is this, ben Ilim? Is it not enough that you served briefly in place of the high priest before He who spoke and the world came into being, but that you also want to take for yourself the high priesthood?' At that moment ben Ilim knew that he had been removed from the [high] priesthood."

Still another version of this Baraita is preserved in y. Yoma 1:1 (38d):[9]

> It happened to ben Ilem from Sepphoris that the [regular] high priest had a seminal emission on Yom Kippur, [rendering him ritually unfit], and ben Ilem entered and served in his place as high priest.
>
> And when [ben Ilem] exited [the holy of holies] he said to the king, "My lord, the king, the bull and the goat of Yom Kippur, are they offered at my expense or at [the expense] of the high priest?"
>
> And the king knew what [ben Ilem] was asking him.
>
> [The king] said to him, "Ben Ilem, is it not enough for you that you served briefly before He who spoke and the world came into being?"
>
> And ben Ilem knew that he had been removed from the high priesthood.

Before I attempt to draw historical conclusions based on these texts, it is necessary to determine the literary relationship between them. The case before us would appear to contradict Friedman's claim regarding the relationship between the Tosefta and the two Talmuds (see above), since the Yerushalmi's version of the Baraita much more closely resembles that of the Tosefta than does that of the Bavli. A closer reading of the evidence, however, supports Friedman's theory, and I will argue that the Bavli originally had before it the Tosefta's version of the particular Baraita under consideration. This earlier version was emended in accordance with third- to seventh-century Babylonian preoccupations, and the resulting source is a hybrid of early Tannaitic or pre-Tannaitic Palestinian elements and Amoraic or post-Amoraic Babylonian components.

What is the evidence for these claims? According to versions of the Baraita in Palestinian compilations (the Tosefta and Yerushalmi), the king decides who will serve as high priest. According to the Baraita in the Bavli, sages decide that the original high priest returns to his duties when he is no longer ritually unfit, replacing the priest who served as his substitute (but see below). While mathematical certainty on this issue is not possible, it is entirely in character for Babylonian rabbis to have found it unacceptable that a king made a halakhic decision. It is very likely that Babylonian rabbis emended the Palestinian story and made sages[10] rather than the king in control of the high priesthood and responsible for the functioning of the Temple cult.

My conclusion that the Bavli emended an earlier text that depicted the king deciding Yosef ben Elem's[11] fate sheds interesting light on still another version of the Baraita preserved in the Munich manuscript of Horayot 12b. This version does not end with a ruling by "the sages" but instead concludes:

"and [Yosef ben Elem's] brothers the priests did not permit him to be a high priest or a common priest." According to this version, the priests themselves decided that Yosef must step down. The differing versions in the Bavli agree that the king did not decide, but they disagree about whom to put in his place. While this issue falls outside the purview of this book, it would be interesting to examine the degree to which tractate Horayot, and perhaps other tractates of the Bavli, assign prominent roles to priests, as opposed to sages, in their depiction of the past or the present. The Paris manuscript of Horayot reads "the sages" rather than "the priests," although it is likely that the reading of the Paris manuscript is the work of scribes who "corrected" Horayot in conformity with the version of the Baraita in b. Yoma 12b.

Josephus also preserves a version of this story.[12] Comparison between the versions of Josephus and the rabbis will support my claim that an earlier version of the Bavli's Baraita closely resembled that of the Tosefta, and that the presence of sages in the narrative is a Babylonian rabbinic invention. Josephus's version of the story dates from the first century CE at the latest; in all likelihood it predates the rabbinic versions of the story, which are found in compilations redacted centuries after Josephus wrote. Josephus's version is as follows:

> Because of [Herod's] savage state and out of fear that in his fury he might avenge himself upon them, those present said that these things had been done without their consent, and it seemed to them that the perpetrators should not be exempted from punishment. Herod therefore dealt rather mildly with these others but removed the high priest Matthias from his priestly office as being partly to blame for what had happened, and in his stead appointed his wife's brother Joazar as high priest. Now it happened during this Matthias's term as high priest that another high priest was appointed for a single day—that which the Jews observe as a fast—for the following reason. While serving as priest during the night preceding the day on which the fast occurred, Matthias seemed in a dream to have intercourse with a woman, and since he was unable to serve as priest because of that experience, a relative of his, Joseph, the son of Ellemus, served as priest in his place. Herod then deposed Matthias from the high priesthood. As for the other Matthias, who had stirred up the sedition, he burnt him alive along with some of his companions. And on that same night there was an eclipse of the moon.

There is no mention of a king in Josephus's version of the Joseph ben Ellemus story, but neither is there mention of sages, priests, or anyone else deciding Joseph ben Ellemus's fate. The surrounding context in Josephus, however, maintains clearly that the king determined who would be high priest, and Josephus is consistent on this point throughout his works.[13]

The version of the story in Josephus is obviously related only tangentially to its larger context. Josephus reports the story simply because it is an unusual event that he thinks will interest his readers.

According to the version of t. Yoma 1:4, in contrast (see above), R. Yosah quotes the story as proof for his position that, after the regular high priest resumes his duties, the substitute high priest can serve neither as high priest nor as common priest. Only one line in the Tosefta's version of the story, however, explicitly indicates that this law can be derived from the story, and it is a line missing from the version in the Yerushalmi, which quotes the story to prove a different halakhic point.[14] Without this line: "And [after the regular high priest resumed his duties, Yosef ben Ilim] was not fit [to serve] as a high priest and as a common priest," the story does not explicitly support R. Yosah's position in the slightest. Most likely the line was added to the Tosefta, perhaps at a very late date, to make explicit precisely how the story could be understood as conforming to its present halakhic context. According to the Yerushalmi's version, and according to the Tosefta's version minus the one suspicious line, nothing explicit in the story itself indicates that the king's decision that ben Ilim should step down is a general rule applicable to all substitute high priests. Palestinian rabbinic storytellers or editors enlist an early story, which originally served no halakhic purpose, in support of diverse halakhic views. Josephus's use of the story as nothing more than a diverting anecdote supports our claim that the story originally served no legal purpose. In the versions of the story in the Palestinian rabbinic compilations, the king's decision is not a legal precedent but a decision by a particular individual applicable to one specific case.

According to the version in the Bavli, in contrast, the story fits the halakhic context very well. So well, in fact, that we have reason to suspect that the Bavli's version is the result of emendation, to avoid the impression that the case involving ben Elem was never intended to serve as a binding precedent. That is, in Babylonia the Baraita was emended to remove all ambiguity, so that it would no longer be possible to read the story as a description of an individual's opinion applicable only to a particular case rather than as a binding precedent. According to the Bavli's emended text, the story describes an event exactly like the situation contemplated by R. Yosi, and it concludes with a decision that is clearly intended as a general rule applicable to all cases involving substitute priests. Babylonians emended the story more radically than did Palestinians, eliminating all parts of the story that are irrelevant to or distracting from its halakhic point.

Despite the obvious differences between the Bavli's version of the Baraita and that of the Tosefta, therefore, the Bavli's version is the product of emendation in accordance with Babylonian Amoraic or post-Amoraic preoccupations. It is very likely, despite appearances to the contrary, that this case supports Friedman's contention that earlier versions of many of the Bavli's Baraitot looked very much like those of the Tosefta. Interestingly, in this instance the Tosefta itself was emended, albeit not as radically as the Bavli, to clarify how the story about Yosef ben Ilim serves as a halakhic precedent. The Bavli's unemended text, I am claiming, closely resembled the Tosefta's unemended text, which in turn closely resembled the version preserved in the Yerushalmi.

It should also be noted that the Tosefta's version as currently formulated is probably later than the Yerushalmi's version. That is, the Yerushalmi's version is probably the earliest rabbinic version (it is closest to Josephus's version, and the story does not fit its context particularly well), and the Tosefta's and the Bavli's versions contain later emendations.

Other rabbinic sources describing events of the second Temple period confront us with the same contrast between Palestinian and Babylonian attitudes toward the role of the king in the distant past.[15] We read in m. Yevamot 6:4:

> If [a priest] betrothed a widow and was then appointed high priest, he can marry [the widow].
> It once happened that Yehoshua ben Gamla betrothed Marta bat Baitos and the king appointed him high priest and he married her.

B. Yevamot 61a, based on this mishnah, reads as follows:

> "[The king] appointed him," yes, but if he was appointed [by others], no.[16]
> Said Rav Yosef, "I see a conspiracy here, for Rav Asi said, 'Marta bat Baitos bribed Yannai the king with two *kav* of dinars so that he appointed Yehoshua ben Gamla as high priest.'"

The mishnah unabashedly asserts that the king appointed a high priest, and Sifra Emor Perek 2:6 and Lamentations Rabbah 1:46,[17] also of Palestinian provenance, record the same story. As we saw above, the notion that the king appointed a high priest provokes no discomfort in Palestinian literature.

It clearly bothers Rav Yosef, however, a Babylonian Amora who flourished early in the fourth century CE. He cites a statement by Rav Asi to the effect that characters in the brief mishnaic story perform actions that violate halakhic norms. The king appoints Yehoshua ben Gamla as high priest, not because he acted appropriately and had halakhic authority to do so but because he was bribed and, presumably, arrogated to himself the authority to appoint a high priest. Once again we see a distinction between Palestine and Babylonia on the question of the king's prerogative to appoint high priests.[18]

Another story found in Palestinian and Babylonian rabbinic compilations further supports my claim that Babylonian sources, to a greater degree than Palestinian sources, depict rabbis dominating Jewish society and institutions of the distant past. The ensuing discussion argues that a story in b. Gittin 55b–56a, like the stories examined above, has been Babylonianized, that is, subtly altered in conformity with Babylonian concerns and preoccupations. Once again, the date of this editorial tampering cannot be determined. It is likely, although not certain, that this story derives from a nonrabbinic source (see below):

> Said R. Yoḥanan, "What is the meaning of the verse, 'Happy is the man who is always afraid, but one who hardens his heart encoun-

ters evil?' (Prov. 28:14)? On account of Kamẓa and Bar Kamẓa Jerusalem was destroyed. . . ."

For there was a certain man whose friend was Kamẓa and whose enemy was Bar Kamẓa. [The man] made a feast.

He said to his attendant, "Go and bring me Kamẓa."

[The servant] brought him Bar Kamẓa. [The host] found [Bar Kamẓa] sitting.

[The host] said to him, "Wait a minute. You're my enemy.[19] What are you doing here? Get up and leave."

[Bar Kamẓa] said to [the host], "Since I have come, let me stay and I will pay for what I eat and drink."

[The host] said to him, "No."

[Bar Kamẓa] said to him, "I will pay for half of the feast."

[The host] said to him, "No."

[Bar Kamẓa] said to him, "I will pay for the entire feast."

[The host] said to him, "No."

[The host] grabbed hold of him, stood him up, and threw him out.

[Bar Kamẓa] said, "Since the rabbis sat there and did not protest, I will inform on them to the government."[20]

He said to the emperor, "The Jews have rebelled against you."

[The emperor] said, "Says who?"

[Bar Kamẓa] said to [the emperor], "Send a sacrifice to them and see if they offer it."

[The emperor] sent a three-year-old calf[21] in the hand of [Bar Kamẓa]. On his way, [Bar Kamẓa] put a blemish in its lip, and some say in its eye, a place where to us [Jews] it is a blemish [and therefore unfit as a sacrifice] and to them [the Romans] it is not a blemish.

The rabbis wanted to offer it [despite the blemish] to avoid offending the government.

R. Zekhariah ben Avkulas said to [the rabbis], "People will say that it is permissible to offer blemished animals on the altar."

[The rabbis] wanted to kill [Bar Kamẓa] so he would not tell [the emperor].

R. Zekhariah [ben Avkulas] said to them, "People will say that one who intentionally blemishes a sacrificial animal should be executed."

Said R. Yoḥanan, "The humility [modesty? patience?][22] of R. Zekhariah ben Avkulas caused our holy sanctuary to be destroyed, our Temple to be burnt, and caused us to be exiled from our land."

This rich, enigmatic story has given rise to an extensive scholarly literature.[23] Perhaps the most serious interpretive crux is R. Yoḥanan's concluding statement. What is the meaning of the word *anvetanuto*, translated above as "humility," "modesty," or "patience," its usual meaning in rabbinic literature? These translations are ill suited to the context, since they poorly describe R. Zekhariah's behavior.[24] A bewildering variety of alternative explanations have been suggested by scholars, none of which suit the context and conform to the meaning of *anvetanuto* elsewhere in rabbinic literature.[25]

Among the more likely suggestions are "tending to compromise" and "pleasing to other people," first because these translations conform to the meaning of R. Zekhariah's name (ben Avkulas, probably related to the Greek word *eukolos*),[26] and second because it is at least possible to interpret R. Zekhariah's actions as exhibiting these characteristics. Another suggested possibility, "lacking self-confidence," might also conform to R. Zekhariah's behavior, although it does not conform to the meaning of the Greek word.[27] As noted, these and other translations do not correspond to the meaning of *anvetanut* as used elsewhere in rabbinic literature and are therefore problematic.[28]

In addition, R. Yoḥanan's exclusive focus on Zekhariah as the cause of the destruction is peculiar.[29] Why does R. Yoḥanan make no mention of the host who offended Bar Kamẓa or of the rabbis who did nothing to stop the host? Finally, Yoḥanan's first statement as well as the entire story are in Aramaic, while his concluding remark as well as the statement of Zekhariah are in Hebrew. What accounts for the change of language?[30]

The concluding statement by R. Yoḥanan is found in two other contexts. Perhaps they will yield answers to these questions. We read in t. Shabbat 17:6:

> Beit Hillel says, "It is permissible to lift bones and shells from the table [on Shabbat]."
>
> Beit Shammai says, "One [must] remove the entire tablet [the surface on which people eat] and shake it [to remove bones and shells]."
>
> Zekhariah ben Avkulas acted in accordance with neither Beit Shammai nor Beit Hillel. Rather, he threw [bones and shells] behind the bed.
>
> Said R. Yosah, "The humility [modesty? patience?] of R. Zekhariah ben Avkulas caused the burning of the Temple."

Most likely, R. Yosah's statement did not originate as a comment based on this Tosefta.[31] Zekhariah's action in the Tosefta, which is either an attempt to avoid controversy or a third opinion in contrast to that of Beit Hillel and Beit Shammai, is entirely unremarkable. Actions like it are found throughout Tannaitic literature, and it is not at all clear why Zekhariah is singled out for special opprobrium. Most likely, R. Yosah's statement originated in a different context; perhaps it is quoted here because a later editor thought Zekhariah's actions exemplified a consistent mode of behavior that led to the destruction of the Temple. Alternatively, it may be quoted here simply because of the Tosefta's mention of Zekhariah ben Avkulas, an extremely obscure figure quoted elsewhere only in the context of the Kamẓa and Bar Kamẓa story.

Here, again, the word *anvetanuto* is problematic. Once again "humility" and related meanings do not fit the context, and "lacking self-confidence,"[32] which better fits the context, and "pleasing to other people," which better fits the meaning of the Greek word *eukolos*, are problematic as translations of *anvetanuto*. And Zekhariah's actions in the Tosefta are ambiguous. Do his actions betray a failure of nerve, an unwillingness to cause offense by taking a halakhic stand, or do they boldly reflect his own independent view, contrary to the views of both Beit Hillel and Beit Shammai?[33] R. Yosah's statement about Zekhariah is too ambiguous to use as the basis for a didactic lesson.

Lamentations Rabbah, a Palestinian compilation the dating of which relative to the Bavli is unclear,[34] preserves another version of the Kamẓa and Bar Kamẓa story. The standard printed edition of the midrash is unfortunately full of errors. Solomon Buber published a manuscript version, liberally tampered with by scribes who incorporated numerous additions based on the Bavli. Fortunately, a version of the particular story of concern to us here, largely free of textual corruptions, was found in the Cairo Genizah and published by Ẓvi Rabinovitz in 1977.[35] Pinḥas Mandel published an improved rendering,[36] upon which the following translation is based.

> It once happened that one of the great men of Jerusalem made a feast, and he invited everyone.
> [He said] to his [servant] boy, "Go bring me Bar Kamẓa my friend."
> But he brought him Bar Kamẓora [his] enemy. [The host] entered and found [Bar Kamẓora] sitting among [the guests].
> [The host] said to him, "Get up and get out of here."
> [Bar Kamẓora] said to him, "I will pay [for my meal. Just don't] humiliate me by throwing me out."
> [The host] said to [Bar Kamẓora], "You must get out of here."
> [Bar Kamẓora] said to him, "[I will pay] for the entire meal. Just don't humiliate me by throwing me out."
> [The host] said to [Bar Kamẓora], "You must [get out of here]."
> [Bar Kamẓora] said to him, "I will pay twice what the meal costs. Just don't humiliate me by throwing me out."
> [The host] said to [Bar Kamẓora], "You must [get out] of here."
> R. Zekhariah bar Avkalis was there. He could have protested [but he did not protest].
> When [Bar Kamẓora] left he said, "I went out in shame and left them sitting there in peace?"
> He went [to] the king.
> [Bar Kamẓora] went and said to the king, "The Jews eat the sacrifices that you send [instead of offering them on the altar]."
> [The king] rebuked him and said to him, "You're lying because [you] want to slander them."
> [Bar Kamẓora] said to [the king], "Send sacrifices with me and send [with me a trusted man]. You will discover the truth."
> [The king] sent with him a trusted man and he sent [with him sacrifices].

> At night he put blemishes on [the animals] in secret. When the pr[iest saw them, he did not offer them.
>
> (The priest) said to the (king's agent)], "I will not offer them. Tomorrow I will offer them."
>
> Came day and he did not off[er them. Came d]ay and he did not offer them.
>
> Immediately he sent to the king, "What the J[ew] told you is true."
>
> Immediately [the king] destroyed the Temple. Therefore peop[le] say, "On account of Kamẓa and Kamẓora the Temple was destroyed."
>
> Said R. Yosi bar R. Abun,[37] "The humility [modesty? patience?] of R. Zekhariah bar Avkalis burned the Temple."

How do these traditions contribute to my larger thesis? Three rabbinic compilations, the Tosefta, Lamentations Rabbah, and the Bavli assign a critical role to a rabbi, R. Zekhariah ben Avkulas, in the destruction of the Temple.[38] Only the Bavli, however, claims that he controlled the priests and the Temple cult, ruling that the priests should not offer the king's sacrifice. Only in the Bavli's version of the story do we find rabbis at the two most critical junctures of the story: at the banquet and in the Temple.

Both the Bavli and Palestinian compilations rabbinize their sources, but as noted throughout this book, the Bavli does so to a much greater extent.[39] The present case, in which the Bavli portrays sages performing an action performed in a Palestinian tradition by someone other than sages, is another example of a much wider phenomenon. Earlier scholars, however, have not explained why villains as well as heroes are rabbinized in rabbinic sources of late antiquity, and in Babylonian compilations far more than in Palestinian ones.

In my opinion, the answer lies in the fact, noted in the introduction, that Babylonian rabbis, in conformity with their own experience, tended to visualize rabbis virtually everywhere, controlling most of what truly mattered in the world. Both for good and ill, in the imaginations of Babylonian rabbis, it was the sages who determined the fate of the Jewish people. If embarrassment to an individual led to the destruction of the Temple, it was because rabbis were there and failed to stop it. If the failure to offer the king's sacrifice caused the destruction of the Temple, it was because a rabbi was there and would not allow the sacrifice to be offered.

Due to their insularity and their relatively secure social position, Babylonian rabbis were unconcerned about nonrabbinic Jewish opinion. They therefore felt free to portray rabbis in an unfavorable light.[40] Palestinian rabbis, more integrated into society, more dependent upon nonrabbinic Jews for financial support and social advancement and therefore more sensitive to criticism, were less willing to create and transmit portrayals of sinful sages. This conclusion does not require that we view Palestinian stories as having been read by and/or performed before a nonrabbinic audience. For my purposes, it is enough that rabbis anticipated such an audience and felt the need to head off criticism because of their sensitivity to nonrabbinic opinion. Palestinian rabbis interacted with nonrabbis and were therefore sensitive to what they might say or think. Some of their statements are formulated at least in part with nonrabbis as the anticipated (if not actual) audience for their remarks.

The Lamentations Rabbah text, however, cautions us to emphasize again that the difference between Palestinian and Babylonian sources is one of degree rather than total opposition,[41] since Lamentations Rabbah depicts a sinful sage in one context (R. Zekhariah ben Avkulas at the banquet). Significantly, however, it is a single sage who failed to protest in the Lamentations Rabbah version rather than "the rabbis" in general as in the Bavli. In addition, as noted by Pinḥas Mandel, the story in Lamentations Rabbah moves from the interpersonal to the international, revealing "a deep understanding of a complicated set of relationships between nations, and a realistic portrayal of the process by which the conqueror and the conquered can be dragged into a war" without provocation at all commensurate with the gravity of the consequences.[42] The story in the Bavli, in contrast, is primarily (although not exclusively) a story about rabbis, who depict themselves as inadequate leaders of the people and as therefore responsible for the destruction of the Temple. The story in the Palestinian compilation depicts the actions of the Jewish protagonists on an international stage. The story in the Bavli focuses much less on the international dimension, mentioning Rome only briefly in the story's middle section.[43] The Bavli's version turns its attention inward to a much greater degree, using the story as an occasion for self-criticism and internal reflection.

What is the relationship between the Palestinian and Babylonian versions of the story? Do these strikingly similar yet far from identical versions help us answer our question about the original context of the concluding statement, attributed in the Bavli to R. Yoḥanan, in Lamentations Rabbah to R. Yosi bar R. Abun, and in the Tosefta to R. Yosah?

A. A. Halevi claims that the Lamentations Rabbah version is the original. According to Halevi, the word *anvetanuto* fits the context in Lamentations Rabbah but not in the Bavli.[44] David Rokeaḥ argues for the priority of the Bavli's version, and claims that Lamentations Rabbah changed the story to conform it to the concluding pronouncement about Zekhariah. The editors of Lamentations Rabbah, claims Rokeaḥ, had difficulty understanding Zekhariah's behavior in the Bavli as *anvetanut*. They therefore emended the story so that R. Yosi bar R. Abun no longer responds to Zekhariah's refusal to allow halakhic compromise in the Temple, but instead condemns Zekhariah's failure to stop Bar Kamẓora's humiliation at the banquet. The editors of Lamentations Rabbah, claims Rokeaḥ, interpreted *anvetanut* as "lack of self-confidence."

Daniel Schwartz rejects Rokeaḥ's argument, arguing that it is not at all clear that the Bavli's text was before the editors of the midrash. Schwartz bases his claim on the fact that one of the central motifs of the Lamentations Rabbah version, the possibility of substituting the sacrifice of the king with another sacrifice, is missing from the Bavli.[45] Rokeaḥ is unable to explain, claims Schwartz, why the editors of the Bavli omitted this and other motifs from the Lamentations Rabbah text.[46]

I find both Rokeaḥ's and Halevi's arguments unconvincing. In addition to the objections raised above, neither scholar explains why the story is in Aramaic and the Amora's concluding comment is in Hebrew. Furthermore, only one other line in the Lamentations Rabbah version,[47] the comment "R. Zekhariah bar Avkalis was there. He could have protested..." is in Hebrew. How do we account for the change of language?

Finally, I fail to understand why the Bavli's editors, confronted with the text of Lamentations Rabbah (according to Halevi), removed Zekhariah from the banquet and placed him only at the conclusion of the story. If Zekhariah is responsible for the destruction of the Temple, why did the Bavli's editors deny that he committed a clearly sinful act? Why did they claim, instead, that he committed only an act of uncertain moral character? Why was it necessary for Zekhariah to appear in the story only once?

The two versions of the story are clearly too closely related to have originated independently. As we have seen, however, attempts to identify the original context and to explain how the later version developed out of the earlier have been unsatisfactory. In my view, the problem lies in the assumption of scholars that one version of the story is based on the other. If we posit that an early version of the story made no mention of Zekhariah, then our problem is solved. The statement, either by R. Yoḥanan, R. Yosi bar R. Bun, or R. Yosah,[48] blaming Zekhariah's "humility, modesty, or patience" for the destruction of the Temple originated in a context we no longer have. Accounts in Josephus about an individual with a strikingly similar name (Zacharias son of Amphicalleus), whose actions contributed to the Romans' decision to attack Jerusalem, sack the city, and destroy the Temple, perhaps support the claim that the statement about R. Zekhariah ben Avkulas in rabbinic literature derives from an ancient tradition, independent of its present contexts.[49] In addition, Joseph Derenbourg notes the similarity between the names Kamẓa and Bar Kamẓa and Campsos son of Campsos, also mentioned by Josephus in connection with the events leading up to the rebellion against Rome.[50] Two independent sources, the Kamẓa-Bar Kamẓa (Kamẓora) story and the statement about Zekhariah ben Avkulas, were combined during the Amoraic or post-Amoraic period by editors who (1) sought a context for the striking statement by R. Yoḥanan (or R. Yosi, or R. Yosi bar Abun), and (2) wished to identify an anonymous character in the Kamẓa-Bar Kamẓa (Kamẓora) story, in keeping with the tendency of aggadah to avoid anonymity.[51] The two versions of the story, the Bavli's and Lamentations Rabbah's, are the result of diverse decisions about how the two traditions should best be combined. According to Lamentations Rabbah, Zekhariah caused the destruction of the Temple when he sinfully failed to intervene at the banquet, while according to the Bavli he caused the destruction at the climax of the story when he decided not to offer the king's sacrifice. The two versions may be the result of the originally oral nature of the traditions, constituting a record of two discrete oral performances of the material.

This explanation, incidentally, also accounts for the change of language. The description of Zekhariah's behavior together with the concluding comment are in Hebrew, while the story is in Aramaic, because they derive from diverse sources.

Our conclusion, once again, is that an independent statement by a Palestinian rabbi ("The *anvetanuto* of R. Zekhariah ben Avkulas . . .") was incorporated into a story that originally made no reference to Zekhariah, and that these traditions appear to have roots in nonrabbinic sources. It is unclear whether this combination of sources took place also in Babylonia, or took place only in Palestine and in this form was transmitted to Babylonia.

A story in b. Baba Batra 3b-4a further supports my claim that Babylonian aggadot routinely depict rabbis besting groups and individuals known to have dominated Jewish society during the second Temple period, most notably kings and priests.[52]

The story is as follows:

> Herod was the slave of the house of the Hasmoneans. He lusted after[53] a [Hasmonean] girl.
>
> One day he heard a voice[54] say, "Every slave that rebels now will succeed."
>
> [Herod] killed all of his masters but left [alive; *shiarah*] the girl.[55]
>
> When this girl saw that [Herod] wanted to marry her [*leminsevah*, literally, "to take her"],[56] she went up to the roof and cried out.
>
> She said, "Whoever says, 'I am descended from the Hasmonean house' is a slave, for I am the only Hasmonean left[57] and I[58] am about to fall from the roof to the ground."[59]
>
> [Herod] hid her for seven years in honey.[60] Some say he had sex with her, others say he didn't have sex with her. Those who say he had sex with her [think] he hid her to satisfy himself sexually. Those who say he didn't have sex with her [think] he hid her so that [people] would say he married [*nasav*, literally, he "took"] a princess.
>
> [Herod] said, "Who interprets, 'Be sure to set [as king] over yourself one of your people' (Deut. 17:15) [thereby excluding me]? The rabbis."
>
> [Herod] killed all of the rabbis. He left [alive; *shiarei*][61] Baba ben Buta to take [*lemisav*][62] counsel from him. He crowned him with a garland of lizards[63] and put out his eyes. One day [Herod] came and sat before [Baba].
>
> [Herod] said, "Did the master [i.e., Baba] see what that evil slave [Herod] did?
>
> [Baba] said to [Herod], "What shall I do to him?"
>
> [Herod] said to him, "Let the master curse him."
>
> [Baba] said to him, "[It is written], 'Even in your thoughts don't curse a king' " (Eccles. 10:20).
>
> [Herod] said to him, "He is not a king."

> [Baba] said to him, "Even if he is only a rich man, it is written, 'and do not curse the rich man in private' " (Eccles. 10:20).
>
> [Herod said to him], "And if he is a prince it is written, 'Do not curse a prince of your people' (Exod. 22:27), this refers to [a prince] who behaves like one of your people, and this one does not behave like one of your people."[64]
>
> [Baba] said to [Herod], "I am afraid of him."
>
> [Herod] said to him, "No one will tell him, for you and I sit here alone."
>
> [Baba] said to him, "It is written, 'For a bird of the air may carry the utterance, and a winged creature may repeat the word' " (Eccles. 10:20).
>
> [Herod] said to him, "I am he. Had I known that the rabbis were so discreet,[65] I would not have killed them. What is my[66] solution?"
>
> [Baba] said to him, "You[67] extinguished the light of the world, [the rabbis],[68] as it is written, 'For commandment is a lamp and the Torah is light' (Prov. 6:23), go and busy yourself with the light of the world, [the Temple],[69] as it is written, 'And all the nations shall be illuminated by [the Temple]'[70] (Isa. 2:2). . . ."[71]
>
> [Herod] said to [Baba], "I am afraid of the government."
>
> [Baba] said to him, "Send a messenger [to the government]. [The messenger] will travel for a year, tarry for a year, and return for a year. In the meantime you can tear down [the Temple] and build it up again."
>
> [Herod] did this.
>
> [The Romans] sent to him, "If you haven't torn it down already, don't tear it down. And if you have [already] torn it down, don't rebuild it. And if you have [already] torn it down and rebuilt it, those who do evil, after they do they seek counsel. If your weapons are upon you, your [genealogical] book is here: 'Neither a king nor the son of a king.'[72] Herod, [slave], your [free] country becomes a colony."[73]

This narrative is of interest here primarily because of two vivid scenes, the first dealing with Herod and the Hasmoneans and the second with Herod and the rabbis. These two scenes in several respects repeat one another, and I will attempt to show that this twin narrative structure is an important key to the story's message. The first scene has some striking features in common with Josephus's account of the death of Mariamme, suggesting that at least portions of the scene are early (at least first century CE), nonrabbinic, and Palestinian (or "western" vis-à-vis Babylonia, i.e., deriving from somewhere in the Roman Empire).[74] Supporting this claim is the fact that an undefined but apparently well-known sexual perversion referred to as "the act of Herod" is attested in diverse contexts in Tannaitic literature.[75]

The second scene recapitulates the first in several ways. Herod's actions against the Hasmoneans parallel those he takes against the rabbis, a connection strengthened by linguistic parallels.[76] In both instances, Herod "arises and kills" all those who stand in his way. In the first scene "he leaves [*shiarah*]" one survivor (the girl), and in the second scene "he leaves [*shiarei*]" one survivor, Baba ben Buta. In both instances, Herod needs to establish a close, personal relationship with the lone survivor to strengthen his claim to the throne. In the first scene, Herod wants to "take her in marriage [*leminsevah*]," and in the second scene Herod wants to "take counsel [*lemisav ezah*]" with the sage. The narrative parallels the plight of a woman facing an unwanted marriage to a tyrant, a nauseatingly close relationship with a man who murdered her entire family but who needs her to support his claim to the throne or to satisfy his sexual needs, with the predicament of a rabbi asked to serve as personal counselor to the same tyrant, to consort with a miscreant who murdered his colleagues, and who keeps him alive to exploit his wisdom and support his claim to the throne.

Further strengthening the connection between rabbi and girl, Baba is blind and therefore physically vulnerable, and according to most versions of the story, Baba and the rabbis are described as discreet, *ẓanitu*,[77] a word typically used to describe the rabbinic ideal of behavior in a woman.[78]

Given these striking commonalities, the differences between the two scenes stand out all the more sharply. The girl publicly declares Herod's slave status from the rooftops; Baba refuses to curse Herod even in his thoughts. Baba allows Herod to take counsel with him, and the result is the building of the Temple and the Romans' public proclamation of Herod's slave status. In contrast, the Hasmonean girl refuses to have anything to do with Herod, and instead climbs up to the roof and announces to the world that Herod is an illegitimate pretender to the throne. She throws herself to the ground, committing suicide rather than be taken in marriage by the despicable slave.

If the story ended with the girl's suicide, we would have a standard tale of a hero who kills himself or herself in order to escape sexual violation at the hands of a terrible villain. These tales arouse our sympathy for the unfortunate victim and our admiration for his or her courageous choice of a noble death in preference to a degraded life.[79] Our story does not end with the girl's heroic death, however. Her suicide does not lead to her canonization as hero, but to Herod's realization that he must take further action to prop up his flimsy claim to the throne. He does so by dishonoring the Hasmonean maiden in death and murdering the rabbis. The audience's expectations are reversed. The trope of the courageous suicide does not yield the expected results, since the noble suicide ends in disaster.

For the Hasmonean girl and the rabbi, the natural response is to run away in disgust, which is in essence what the girl hopes to do by committing suicide. In the end she cannot run away, and the story teaches that a distastefully close relationship with a horrible but powerful ruler is preferable to a dignified death.

How does this narrative contribute to my thesis about the portrayal of rabbis, priests, and kings in Babylonian rabbinic narratives about the second

Temple period? The story claims that a rabbi (Baba ben Buta) bests the murderous, sexually perverted King Herod, convincing him to repair the Temple and manipulating events so that Herod's non-Jewish sponsors reduce Judaea to the status of a colony, effectively stripping Herod of his status as a king.[80] The story also relates that the Hasmoneans, kings and priests, spectacularly fail on both counts. On the one hand, the Hasmoneans are Herod's innocent victims; on the other, they lack the wherewithal to foil the wicked usurper, Herod, and to trick him into doing their will, which only the rabbis accomplish. The Hasmonean dynasty comes to an end, leaving Herod stronger and more murderous than ever.

Nothing in the story explicitly connects its events or characters to the Babylonian rabbinic present or to the contemporary priesthood. The story's image of a brilliant sage in the distant past besting a murderous pretender to the throne, in contrast to the legitimate kings' failure to do so, would very likely have been of intense interest to Babylonian Amoraim without the need to view ancient figures as stand-ins for specific groups or individuals in the rabbinic present.[81]

In addition, for reasons discussed in the introduction, this story was most likely not propaganda addressed by rabbis to nonrabbis. Rather, the story was (1) designed to strengthen the conviction of the rabbis and their students that rabbis were best suited to lead the Jewish people; and/or (2) an expression of Babylonian rabbis' extreme myopia, their penchant for visualizing the past through the prism of their own experience.

The ensuing discussion compares strikingly similar versions of a story found in Josephus and in the Bavli and further supports my claim that the Bavli (1) is receptive to nonrabbinic Jewish traditions, which it attempts to rabbinize; (2) depicts sages more positively than an earlier Palestinian[82] story depicts Pharisees; and (3) belittles a Hasmonean king.[83] In addition, the Bavli's version of the narrative struggles to problematize the king's claim to the high priesthood by casting doubt on his Aaronide lineage. This narrative, we argue, has been tampered with by Babylonian tradents and editors and made to conform to its larger context (the Bavli and Babylonian rabbinic culture), but at least one feature of the story—its treatment of King Yannai as something other than a total villain—has been preserved, despite the fact that it runs counter to Babylonian rabbinic thinking. Most likely, this one feature characterized the story before it reached Babylonia, and it survived the process of Babylonian editorial homogenization. As we saw in the previous chapter, and as we will see throughout this book, it is often inadequate to characterize traditions in the Bavli as unproblematically early and Palestinian, or late and Babylonian. Often such traditions, as in this case, are a hybrid: partly early and partly later, partly Palestinian and partly Babylonian. Any historical or literary treatment of these traditions will need to take all of these possibilities into account.

The Bavli's version of the story, in b. Kiddushin 66a, is as follows:

> Yannai the king went to Koḥlit in the desert and conquered 60 cities.
>
> When he returned, he rejoiced greatly and called to all of the sages of Israel.

> [He] said to [them], "Our ancestors ate mallows when they built the Temple, so too we shall eat mallows in memory of our ancestors."
>
> They placed mallows on golden tables and ate. And there was an elder there, a scoffing, evil, worthless man named Elazar ben Po'erah.
>
> And Elazar ben Po'erah said to Yannai the king, "Yannai the king, the hearts of the Pharisees are against you."
>
> [Yannai] said to him, "What shall I do?"
>
> [Elazar] said to him, "Make them swear an oath[84] by the frontlet between your eyes [which symbolizes your status as high priest]."
>
> [Yannai] made them swear an oath by the frontlet between his eyes. There was an elder there and Yehudah ben Gedidi'ah was his name.
>
> And Yehudah ben Gedidi'ah said to Yannai the king, "Yannai the king, the crown of kingship is enough for you; leave the crown of priesthood to the seed of Aaron."
>
> For people had said, "His mother had been taken captive in Modi'im."
>
> The matter was investigated but not confirmed, and the sages departed in anger.
>
> And Elazar ben Po'erah said to Yannai the king, "Yannai the king, such is the law for a commoner in Israel. For you who are king and high priest should such be the law?"
>
> [Yannai said to him], "What shall I do?" [Elazar said to Yannai], "If you listen to my advice, trample them."
>
> [Yannai said to Elazar], "And what will become of the Torah?"
>
> [Elazar said to Yannai], "It is bound up and lying in a corner. Whoever wants to learn it, let him come and learn."
>
> Said Rav Naḥman bar Yiẓḥak, "Immediately heresy was cast into him,"[85] for [Yannai] should have said, "It is well [with regard to] the written Torah. What about the oral Torah?"[86]
>
> Immediately the evil sprouted forth as a result of Elazar ben Po'erah [and as a result of Yehudah ben Gedidi'ah],[87] and all of the sages were killed, and the world was desolate until Shimon ben Shetach came and restored the Torah as of old.

The strikingly similar account in Josephus[88] is as follows:

> As for Hyrcanus, the envy of the Jews was aroused against him by his own successes and those of his sons; particularly hostile to him were the Pharisees, who are one of the Jewish schools, as we have related above. And so great is their influence with the masses that even when they speak against a king or high priest, they immediately gain credence. Hyrcanus too was a disciple of theirs, and was greatly loved by them. And once he invited them to a feast and en-

tertained them hospitably, and when he saw that they were having a very good time, he began by saying that they knew he wished to be righteous and in everything he did tried to please God and them—for the Pharisees profess such beliefs; at the same time he begged them, if they observed him doing anything wrong or straying from the right path, to lead him back to it and correct him. But they testified to his being altogether virtuous, and he was delighted with their praise. However, one of the guests, named Eleazar, who had an evil nature and took pleasure in dissension, said, "Since you have asked to be told the truth, if you wish to be righteous, give up the high-priesthood and be content with governing the people."

And when Hyrcanus asked him for what reason he should give up the high-priesthood, he replied, "Because we have heard from our elders that your mother was a captive in the reign of Antiochus Epiphanes." But the story was false, and Hyrcanus was furious with the man, while all the Pharisees were very indignant.

Then a certain Jonathan, one of Hyrcanus's close friends, belonging to the school of the Sadducees, who hold opinions opposed to those of the Pharisees, said that it had been with the general approval of all the Pharisees that Eleazar had made his slanderous statement; and this, he added, would be clear to Hyrcanus if he inquired of them what punishment he deserved—for, he said, he would be convinced that the slanderous statement had not been made with their approval if they fixed a penalty commensurate with the crime—, and they replied that Eleazar deserved stripes and chains; for they did not think it right to sentence a man to death for calumny, and anyway the Pharisees are naturally lenient in the matter of punishments. At this Hyrcanus became very angry and began to believe that the fellow had slandered him with their approval. And Jonathan in particular inflamed his anger, and so worked upon him that he brought him to join the Sadducean party and desert the Pharisees, and to abrogate the regulations which they had established for the people, and punish those who observed them. Out of this, of course, grew the hatred of the masses for him and his sons, but of this we shall speak hereafter. For the present I wish merely to explain that the Pharisees had passed on to the people certain regulations handed down by former generations and not recorded in the Laws of Moses, for which reason they are rejected by the Sadducean group, who hold that only those regulations should be considered valid which were written down, and those which had been handed down by former generations need not be observed. And concerning these matters the two parties came to have controversies and serious differences, the Sadducees having the confidence of the wealthy alone but no following among the populace, while the

> Pharisees have the support of the masses. But of these two schools and of the Essenes a detailed account has been given in the second book of my *Judaica*.
>
> And so Hyrcanus quieted the outbreak, and lived happily thereafter; and when he died after administering the government excellently for thirty-one years, he left five sons. Now he was accounted by God worthy of three of the greatest privileges, the rule of the nation, the office of high priest, and the gift of prophecy; for the Deity was with him and enabled him to foresee and foretell the future; so, for example, he foretold of his two elder sons that they would not remain masters of the state. And the story of their downfall is worth relating, to show how far they were from having their father's good fortune.

As earlier scholars have noted, in precisely those instances where narratives in Josephus and in rabbinic compilations most closely parallel one another, the narratives are most easily detachable from their contexts within Josephus's larger discussion. In addition, such narratives are typically found only in *Antiquities* but not in the parallel in Josephus's earlier work, *The Jewish War*.[89]

The case before us is no exception. Numerous factors indicate that Josephus's account of the Pharisees' rift with Hyrcanus derives from a source independent of his main narrative.[90] To cite just a few of the most obvious proofs: (1) Josephus first says that the Pharisees are particularly envious of Hyrcanus's successes,[91] while almost immediately thereafter he writes that Hyrcanus is a disciple of the Pharisees and is greatly loved by them; (2) Josephus first writes that the Jewish people dislike Hyrcanus out of envy; later he writes that they hate him because he abrogated Pharisaic regulations and punished those who followed them; still later Josephus writes that Hyrcanus died after administering the government excellently for 31 years; and (3) Josephus interrupts his lengthy account of (a) the Pharisees' rift with Hyrcanus, and (b) the differences between the Pharisees and Sadducees to inform us that Hyrcanus "quieted the outbreak," an outbreak Josephus made no mention of previously.[92]

It bears noting that the sources most closely paralleled in Josephus and in rabbinic compilations are also easily detachable from their contexts in rabbinic literature. In this instance, the narrative serves a halakhic purpose that is clearly remote from the narrative's main concern. The implication is very likely that between his composition of *The Jewish War* and *Antiquities*, Josephus gained access to sources that were subsequently incorporated into rabbinic literature. It is not out of the question that Josephus himself was the rabbis' source.[93]

The story is also significant in that it runs counter to Josephus's tendency to glorify John Hyrcanus,[94] which we see, for example, in Josephus's remark that Hyrcanus "was accounted by God worthy of three of the greatest privileges, the rule of the nation, the office of high priest, and the gift of prophecy." The narrative also runs counter to the Babylonian rabbinic tendency to treat Hasmonean kings, especially Yannai, as unqualified villains, and to the Palestinian rabbinic tendency to portray Hasmonean kings in a positive or neutral light.[95] The narrative, it will be recalled, purports to be a Palestinian source (a Baraita) quoted in the Bavli; its depiction of King Yannai is atypical of both Palestinian and Babylonian rabbinic sources.

These points bear restating in greater detail. As noted, Josephus is very favorably disposed toward Hyrcanus, an attitude that continues up to and including Josephus's assertion that tension between Hyrcanus and the Jews, particularly the Pharisees, was the result of envy toward the king for his great successes.[96] The Pharisees, therefore, are portrayed as petty[97] and Hyrcanus as totally blameless.

In the continuation, however, Josephus, or rather Josephus's source, depicts the Pharisees in more positive terms, and Hyrcanus diminishes in stature. One of the guests, Elazar, who may or may not have been a Pharisee,[98] is at fault, falsely claiming that Hyrcanus is genealogically unfit, while all of the (other?) Pharisees are outraged by Eleazar's public slander of the king. No longer is it envy that rouses the Jews, especially the Pharisees, against Hyrcanus, but instead it is the king's decision to abolish Pharisaic regulations and to punish those who follow them. A Sadducee named Jonathan, one of Hyrcanus's closest friends, dupes the king into believing that the Pharisees approved of Eleazar's calumny. In contrast to his previous portrayal, Josephus thus depicts a less than perfect king and an unjustly persecuted sect.

In the rabbinic version of the story, the sages come off even better than do the Pharisees in Josephus's version. The king, in contrast, comes off worse, even though the story holds Elazar ben Po'erah rather than Yannai the king directly responsible for the atrocities committed against the rabbis and the Torah. The king in the rabbinic story is totally incapable of independent action, with the exception of the first scene, about which more will be said below. With the exception of the first scene, the king does nothing but ask questions and carry out the wishes of his wicked adviser, Elazar ben Po'erah. The story casts doubt on the king's Aaronide descent (see below), and Babylonian rabbinic commentary on the story declares that he was a heretic. And the sages, with one possible exception, are totally blameless in the rabbinic story. The possible exception is Yehudah ben Gedidi'ah, who takes the place of Josephus's Elazar in urging the king to give up the high priesthood. Yehudah ben Gedidi'ah is not referred to as a sage but as an elder, although it is possible that Yehudah is a sage, for the term "elder" frequently, although not always, designates a sage in rabbinic literature.

Even if Yehudah is a sage, however, he is not described as wicked, in contrast to Josephus's wicked Eleazar.[99] As noted, the main villain in the rabbinic story is Elazar ben Po'erah, the king's adviser, who takes the place of Josephus's Sadducee, Jonathan. And whereas Josephus says explicitly that the charge against Hyrcanus (i.e., that he was unfit for the high priesthood) was false, the Bavli simply says that the charge was not confirmed. Josephus's Sadducee, furthermore, is a schemer who convinces the king to join the Sadducean party, but he is not the "scoffing, evil, worthless" villain of the rabbinic story, who convinces the king to murder the sages and nearly succeeds in stamping out the Torah. For Josephus, the enemy of the Pharisees (Jonathan the Sadducee) need not be a total miscreant; for the rabbis, the enemy of the sages (Elazar ben Po'erah) must be a "scoffing, evil, worthless man."

This narrative is another example of the Bavli's tendency to deprecate kings, in this case portraying a hapless, heretical monarch and weakening his connection to the high priesthood. According to the Bavli, Yannai the king wants to pass himself off as high priest. "The crown of kingship is enough for you," says Yehudah ben Gedidi'ah. "Leave the crown of priesthood to the seed of Aaron," after which the story's unnamed narrator adds: "For they said that his mother was captured in Modi'im." Only the latter charge is mentioned in Josephus; nothing at all is said about the king not being of the seed of Aaron.

In the rabbinic story, the narrator's charge of captivity is apparently the basis for Yehudah's claim that Yannai is not of the seed of Aaron, but Yehudah's claim is blunt and brutally direct; that of the narrator is roundabout, requiring several logical steps before we appreciate its significance. In addition, the phraseology of the story in this crucial context is strangely ambiguous; one can form the impression that the charge of captivity is separate from Yehudah's challenge; that two charges are leveled against the king, only one of which is investigated and the first of which (the lack of Aaronide descent) is uncontested.

And, as noted, the rabbinic narrative does not say that the charge about the king's mother is false, but only that it is not confirmed. In addition, the sages depart in anger, but it is not clear who they are angry with or why. There is no reason to assume that they are (only?) angry with Yehudah for calling upon the king to renounce the high priesthood. Just as plausibly, they are (also?) angry with the king for usurping the role of high priest.

Why did Babylonian storytellers or editors, in contrast to Josephus, omit discussion of the punishment appropriate for one who slanders the king? The most likely answer to this question depends on my conclusion above that the Bavli's version of the story takes seriously the charge that Yannai is not an Aaronide, even after "the matter was investigated but not confirmed." In this story, as in the stories analyzed earlier, Babylonian rabbis struggle to weaken the king's connection to the high priesthood. In their eyes, Yehudah ben Gedidi'ah might not be guilty of slander. In addition, Babylonian rabbis find it unacceptable that sages would recommend harsh punishment for one who spoke publicly against the foolish king, who after all consented to the slaughter of rabbis and allowed Elazar ben Po'erah to put the Torah itself in jeopardy. At the very least, the rabbinic story wants it to be unclear whether or not the king has a legitimate claim to the high priesthood and is in fact a legitimate priest at all. It will not do, therefore, for the sages to claim that Yehudah, the man who spoke against the king, deserves to be whipped for his bravery.

The foregoing discussion assumes that b. Kiddushin 66a is based on a very early source that Babylonian rabbis altered on the basis of their own preoccupations. The close parallel in Josephus, of course, is the strongest proof of the story's antiquity, but other facts support my claim that the story is ancient and not simply archaizing.

As several scholars have noted, the rabbinic version of the story uses a biblical style of Hebrew, with a series of verbs that indicate past tense by means of the *vav*-consecutive and the imperfect.[100] Only the opening scene lacks traces of biblical Hebrew, and only the opening scene is without parallel in Josephus. This scene's portrayal of Yannai as a decisive military commander is at odds with his portrayal in the rest of the story, and the issue of concern in the opening scene—the connection between Yannai's conquests and the building of the Temple—is abruptly dropped. Only the opening scene lacks evidence of antiquity, therefore, and this scene clearly derives from a source different from that of the rest of the story.[101]

We have repeatedly seen that only (or in one case, primarily) the Bavli claims that the rabbis played critical roles in second Temple Jewish society, and only the Bavli claims that rabbis controlled kings (at least Hasmonean kings) and the priests and the priestly cult prior to the destruction of the second Temple.

I suggested that these portrayals of the wisdom, discretion, courage, and resourcefulness of sages in the distant past (1) bolstered the confidence of Babylonian rabbis in the legitimacy of their claim to lead contemporary Jewish society; and (2) reflected the Babylonians' conviction that the values of the rabbinic study house were the only values that truly mattered, and perhaps supported my claim that Babylonian rabbis seldom ventured beyond the walls of the study house.

In addition, I argued that subtle distinctions need to be drawn between early and later, Palestinian and Babylonian, and briefer and lengthier narratives, to determine whether some aggadot tend to be more accurate than others or to distort reality in particular ways but not in others. Editors and/or storytellers in Babylonia were particularly willing to emend earlier sources to reflect realities and/or attitudes in third- to seventh-century Babylonia. Our ability to make more refined distinctions will improve our ability to predict which kinds of distortions are likely to be present in a particular source found in a particular compilation, and better equip us to make use of rabbinic sources as historical evidence.

Without question, rabbis were uninterested in history and in general did not hesitate to portray sages as the leaders of Israel's central institutions of the distant past. Some early storytellers, however, some of them rabbis, some of them nonrabbis, portrayed the distant past, if not with total accuracy, then at least without the gross anachronisms and self-aggrandizing distortions that so often characterize ancient storytelling. Some later, for the most part Babylonian rabbis, in contrast, portrayed their ancient counterparts as communal leaders, as supervising nonsages in their own domain. The ancients distorted history to differing degrees and in varying ways, and any description of ancient conceptions of the past must take these nuanced distinctions into account.[102] Scholars have noted differences in the degree of historical reliability of halakhic and aggadic texts.[103] I am advocating that distinctions be drawn within the realm of aggadah itself.[104]

Of course we should not credit early Palestinian rabbinic storytellers with a concern for the disinterested reporting of historical facts simply because they distort reality less, and/or in different ways, than do later Babylonian storytellers. As noted, the distinctions between Palestinian and Babylonian rabbis surveyed throughout this book are linked to tendencies in the contemporary non-Jewish world, with Babylonian rabbinic detachment corresponding to strict hierarchical divisions within Persian society, and Palestinian rabbinic integration corresponding to the somewhat more permeable boundaries between classes in the Roman Empire. Differences between Palestinian and Babylonian rabbinic storytelling, therefore, have much to do with the larger cultural context within which these two literatures were produced and nothing to do with a greater or lesser desire to avoid anachronisms or distortions in the narration of past events.

Finally, I examined the relationship between the Tosefta and the Talmuds and supported Shamma Friedman's claim that earlier versions of the Bavli's Baraitot closely resembled those of the Tosefta. I examined one instance in which the substantial differences between them are due to (1) the relatively great freedom with which Babylonian tradents and editors emended their sources in accordance with Babylonian rabbinic preoccupations and presuppositions, and (2) the likelihood that the editing of the Bavli continued for roughly two centuries after the final redaction of the Yerushalmi.

3

Jewish Sources of the Second Temple Period in Rabbinic Compilations of Late Antiquity

This chapter further exemplifies my claim regarding the Bavli's tendency to depict the most powerful groups and the major institutions of the distant past as controlled by rabbis, as opposed to the tendency of Palestinian rabbis to acknowledge the prominent role played by nonrabbis. In addition, this chapter further supports my claim that the nonrabbinic Jewish world penetrated the walls of the Babylonian rabbinic study house in the form of literary traditions deriving from Roman Palestine, and perhaps from elsewhere in the Roman provincial world. Once again, the rabbis domesticated these traditions by supplying them with a rabbinic veneer that transformed them into fit objects of Torah study. We will find that several pre- and nonrabbinic traditions have been incorporated into the Tosefta, the Yerushalmi, and the Bavli, and all have been subjected to varying degrees of editorial revision and distortion. Once again, we will see that Palestinian rabbis emended these stories less radically than Babylonian rabbis, for reasons discussed in the previous chapter. This finding is significant, since it means that if we are able to correct for the distortions, rabbinic literature is a fruitful repository of nonrabbinic thought, belief, behavior, and gossip.[1] Often the Bavli only partially "Babylonianizes" the traditions, however, while leaving much or most of them intact.

The phrase "When the sages heard about the matter..." and rabbinic statements and actions introduced by this phrase will be this chapter's mode of entry into these issues. The phrase has important historical implications, in part because it is almost always based on narratives that purport to describe the distant past. It is thus distinguishable from similar phrases, such as "When the matter came before the sages ..." which usually introduce narratives but which do not purport to derive from the distant past.

Analysis of traditions found at the end of tractate Sukkah will illustrate these points. These traditions are found in the context of m. Sukkah 5:8, which reads:

> The entering [priests] divide [the showbread] in the north and the exiting [priests] divide in the south. [The priestly division] Bilga always divides in the south. And [Bilga's] ring is fixed and [Bilga's] window is shut [making it impossible for this priestly division to perform any sacrificial labors].[2]

Baraitot in b. Sukkah 56b provide additional details:

> (1) Our rabbis taught [in a Baraita]: The [priests] who enter divide in the north so that it will be apparent that they are entering. And the [priests] who exit divide in the south so it will be apparent that they are exiting.
>
> "[The priestly division] Bilga always divides in the south" (m. Sukkah 5:8).
>
> (2) Our rabbis taught [in a Baraita]: It once happened that Miriam the daughter of Bilga apostatized.[3] She went and married an officer[4] of the Greek government. When the Greeks entered the Temple, she struck the altar with her sandal.
>
> She said, "Wolf, wolf, how long will you consume the property of Israel and not stand up for them in their hour of need?"
>
> *And when the sages heard about the matter, they fixed [Bilga's] ring and sealed [Bilga's] window.*
>
> And some say [Bilga's][5] priestly watch delayed coming, and Yeshebav [Bilga's] brother entered[6] and served in [Bilga's] stead. Even though the neighbors of the wicked do not profit, the neighbors of Bilga profited, for Bilga always divides in the south and Yeshebav [Bilga's] brother in the north.

A parallel to the second Baraita is found in t. Sukkah 4:28. We read there:

> "Bilga always divides in the south, and [Bilga's] ring is fixed and [Bilga's] window is shut" (m. Sukkah 5:8).
>
> Because of Miriam the daughter of Bilga who apostatized.[7] She went and married an officer of the Greek government. And when non-Jews entered the temple, she went and hit the roof of the altar.
>
> She said to it, "Wolf, wolf, you destroy the property of Israel but do not stand up for them in their time of distress."
>
> And some say because of the delay of priestly watches, Yeshebav entered and served instead of [Bilga]. Therefore Bilga always appears to be exiting and Yeshebav always appears to be entering. All of the

> neighbors of the wicked did not receive a reward except for Yeshebav, who was the neighbor of Bilga and did receive a reward.

Still another parallel is found in y. Sukkah 5:8 (55d):

> "Bilga always divides in the south" (m. Sukkah 5:8).
>
> Because of Miriam the daughter of Bilga who apostatized[8] and went and married an officer of the Greek kingdom. And she went and hit the roof of the altar.
>
> She said to it,[9] "Wolf, wolf, you destroyed the property of Israel and did not stand up for them in the hour of their need."
>
> And others say [Bilga's] time came to ascend [to the altar] and [Bilga] did not ascend. Yeshebav entered and served in Bilga's stead as high priest. Therefore Bilga is always like one who is leaving and Yeshebav is like one who enters.

It will be noted that the phrase "When the sages heard about the matter," italicized here, is found only in the Bavli's version of the Baraita. I will consistently find this to be the case, with one exception, the significance of which I will discuss below.

Turning now to the three versions of the Bilga story, we find them to exhibit several features in common with the other sources that contain the aforementioned phrase in at least one version. First, in all three versions of the story, the source is purportedly Tannaitic. Second, all three versions are quoted in the context of the same mishnah. Third, all three versions are strikingly similar (but not identical) in terms of content, structure, and language. Fourth, according to all three versions, the story involves nonrabbis (priests). Fifth, the story purports to derive from the distant past. The story describes an event that ostensibly took place during the time of the Greeks, that is, the Macedonian dynasties who divided Alexander the Great's empire upon his death in 323 BCE and who ruled Judaea until the Maccabean victory in the second century BCE.[10]

I will argue below that these facts indicate that the source's claim to be early is true, although we have no way to precisely determine its date. The fixity of the source's text and context in multiple locations, I will argue, are marks of its antiquity, of the standardization at a relatively early date of both its text and context. This conclusion will be strengthened by the fact that (1) several of the traditions examined in this chapter have parallels, or at least distant echoes, in early nonrabbinic works; (2) several of these traditions are divisible into earlier and later components; and (3) most of the earlier parts of the traditions involve only nonrabbis (especially priests), who we know were among the dominant figures in prerabbinic Jewish society.

As noted, in this chapter I am primarily interested in the historical implications of the phrase "When the sages heard about the matter" and statements and actions introduced by this term. In the case under discussion, in the Bavli's version, the statement "When the sages heard about the matter, they fixed her ring and sealed her window" implies that the actions of Miriam the daughter of Bilga were brought to the attention of rabbis. These rabbis punished the priestly division, Bilga, by "fixing her ring and sealing her window."

This statement has important historical implications. If we accept the source's historicity, it attests to the existence, already during the time of the Seleucid Greeks, of sages who had the power to impose their will on an important priestly clan and to determine how the priestly service in the Temple was conducted. If we reject the source's historicity, it shows that the rabbis believed and wanted their audience to believe that sages controlled the cult and priesthood while the Temple still stood.

Both alternatives assume, in my opinion correctly, that the source believes and wants its audience to believe that the sages who "heard about the matter" are contemporaries of Bilga, Yeshebav, and the other priests mentioned in the story. Modern scholars share this understanding of the term under consideration. David Halivni, for example, writing about a narrative in b. Rosh Hashanah 18b (see below), states that it is unlikely that a substantial time period separates the sages who "heard" about an action and the Hasmoneans who performed the action.[11] Similarly, Avraham Aderet, writing about another usage of the term, assumes that the sages who "heard about the matter" are contemporaries of the person who performed the action.[12]

Compelling evidence, however, reveals that the sages are not contemporaries of the ancient priests in the Bilga story. The story's claim that the sages comment contemporaneously on the priestly actions is most likely false. The statement about the sages, in other words, is worthless as historical evidence for the period it purports to describe.

What is the proof for this claim? The Bavli's version of the Baraita, the only version to mention sages, is problematic as it stands. According to the Bavli's Baraita, it will be recalled,

> when the sages heard about the matter, they fixed [Bilga's] ring and sealed [Bilga's] window. And some say [Bilga's] priestly watch delayed coming, and Yeshebav [Bilga's] brother entered and served in [Bilga's] stead. . . . Bilga always divides in the south and Yeshebav [Bilga's] brother in the north.

The problem with this Baraita is that it is unclear why the Baraita sets up the following either-or situation: either (1) the priestly clan Bilga was punished for the behavior of Miriam by having its ring fixed and its window sealed; or (2) the priestly clan was punished for failure to perform the Temple service at the proper time by always dividing the showbread in the south. Why is it necessarily the case that only one of the two misdeeds led to one of the two punishments? Given the usual implication of the term "some say" throughout the Talmud, namely, to introduce an irreconcilable difference between two versions of the same event, one would expect the Baraita to record disagreement either about the priestly crime alone or the punishment alone, but not about both the crime and the punishment. Why does the Baraita introduce its description of the second crime and punishment with the phrase "some say" when there is no necessary contradiction between the first and second halves of the Baraita? Why does the Baraita not simply state that two separate priestly crimes led to two separate punishments? One crime was that of Miriam the daughter of Bilga, and Bilga the priestly division was punished by having its ring fixed and its window sealed. The second crime was that of Bilga the priestly division, which was slow to ascend the altar to perform its priestly duties. It was punished by perpetually having to divide the showbread in the south.

If we say, however, that the statement "When the sages heard about the matter, they fixed her ring and sealed her window" is a later addition to the Baraita, then our problem is solved. Without that phrase, the Baraita contains accounts of two priestly crimes, the first that of Miriam daughter of Bilga and the second that of Bilga the priestly division. One of the two crimes led to the punishment described in the conclusion of the Baraita, namely, that henceforth Bilga would divide the showbread in the south. The phrase "some say" is necessary, since the two versions disagree about which crime led to the punishment but agree about the punishment itself. Without mention of the sages and the second punishment, that is without the statement, "When the sages heard about the matter, they fixed her ring and sealed her window," the Bavli closely resembles the Tosefta and the Yerushalmi, neither of which mention the sages reporting the punishment of "fixing her ring and sealing her window." The Tosefta and the Yerushalmi, as noted, make no mention of sages at all.

Whoever added the second punishment to the Bavli's Baraita evidently wished to bring the Baraita in line with the mishnah. The mishnah, it will be recalled, lists two punishments, while the Baraita originally listed only one. Whoever added the second punishment wished to resolve this contradiction, unmindful or unconcerned about the difficulty described above.

According to this reconstruction of the evidence, the original version of the Baraita (or the closest to the original that we can reconstruct) attested neither to the rabbis' credulity nor to their vast powers of anachronism. The original version of the Baraita did not claim that sages controlled a powerful priestly clan and the Temple cult during the period of the Greeks. The author of the statement "When the sages heard about the matter they fixed her ring and sealed her window" very likely assumed rabbinic control of the priests, but his primary purpose was to reconcile the Baraita with the mishnah.

We must distinguish, therefore, between the earlier Palestinian authors of the "original" version of the Baraita and the later Babylonian rabbis who added the statement and very likely understood the sages to have had the final word in a narrative that purports to derive from the distant past.

There is some evidence, furthermore, that the "original version" of the source was not authored by a rabbi, but rather was a nonrabbinic story, a piece of gossip, or perhaps a priestly source taken over by the rabbis. While no exact nonrabbinic parallel to the story survives, echoes of it may be preserved in 2 Maccabees 4:23–5:27 and 3:4. According to Old Latin and Armenian manuscripts of 2 Maccabees,[13] Menelaus, a member of the priestly clan Bilga, is a depraved sinner: brutal, greedy, and responsible for the desecration of the

Temple by Antiochus and the Seleucid Greeks. Menelaus had the audacity to seize the high priesthood from the family of Ẓadok after centuries of hereditary succession.[14] According to 2 Maccabees 5:15–16,

> The king had the audacity to enter the holiest temple on earth, guided by Menelaus, who turned traitor both to his religion and his country. [Antiochus] laid impious hands on the sacred vessels; his desecrating hands swept together the votive offerings which other kings had set up to enhance the splendor and fame of the shrine.

As earlier scholars have suggested, the rabbinic traditions about Bilga in tractate Sukkah may be connected to 2 Maccabees' traditions about the wicked Menelaus, priest of the clan of Bilga. Martin Hengel goes too far when he suggests[15] that 2 Maccabees

> is supplemented by the old Mishnah that the priestly clan of Bilga was excluded from offering sacrifices for all time . . . because of its conduct in the religious distress under Antiochus IV: "Its ring of slaughter is closed and its niche is shut up" (Sukkah 5:8c). A Baraita explains this punishment in two ways: according to one view, Miriam had become an apostate from the priestly order of Bilga, had married a Greek officer, desecrated the altar and blasphemed God. According to the other, the order of Bilga allowed itself to be deterred from exercising priestly office. Both reasons probably conceal a more severe charge which alone could match the uniqueness and magnitude of the punishment, namely, the chief responsibility for the desecration of the temple in 167 BC.[16]

I am not persuaded by Hengel's claim that the rabbis knew the truth as recorded in 2 Maccabees but "concealed" it. More likely, the rabbis believed the explanations recorded in the mishnah to be the actual reasons why Bilga was punished. Hengel's treatment of the mishnah seems to me an example of the scholarly tendency to project modern concerns onto the ancients. The issue is not what would prompt modern westerners to punish a priestly clan but what would prompt ancient rabbis to do so, and Hengel assumes what he needs to prove. In addition, 2 Maccabees does not purport to explain the punishment of Bilga; the book does not even express awareness of such a punishment.

Nevertheless, the negative portrayals of (an individual member of?) the priestly clan Bilga in 2 Maccabees (according to some manuscripts) and in rabbinic sources may be distantly related. The rabbinic and nonrabbinic accounts may share in common the notion that (individual members of?) the priestly clan Bilga misbehaved during the time of the Maccabees. And if 2 Maccabees and the rabbinic sources are related, I have further support for my conclusion that the core of the rabbinic narrative is early.

As noted in previous chapters, this conclusion says nothing about the story's reliability. Stories may be chronologically close to the events they describe and historically worthless, or later and more reliable. My claim concerns the story's relative chronology and says nothing at all about its historical accuracy.

It also bears emphasizing that the discussion above, which concluded that a crucial difference between the Bavli's Baraita and the parallels in the Yerushalmi and Tosefta was due to emendation by Babylonian editors, further supports Friedman's theory regarding the relationship between Baraitot in the Tosefta, the Yerushalmi, and the Bavli.[17]

Examination of a Baraita in b. Rosh Hashanah 18b leads to several of the same conclusions. Rav Aḥa bar Huna, a fourth-century Babylonian Amora, raises an objection by citing the following source from Megillat Ta'anit, the Fasting Scroll. According to the Talmud, the source is Tannaitic:

> On the third of Tishrei the mention [of God's name] in documents was abolished. For the kingdom of Greece[18] decreed a persecution[19] that the name of heaven should not be uttered. And when the Hasmonean kingdom grew strong and defeated [the Greeks], they ordained that the name of heaven should be mentioned even in documents. And thus they would write: "In such and such a year of Yoḥanan the High Priest of the Most High God."[20]
>
> *And when the sages heard about the matter they said: "Tomorrow this one will pay his debt and the document will end up in the trash."*
>
> And they abolished them. And that very day they made a holiday.

Megillat Ta'anit and its scholion, discussed preliminarily in chapter 1, contain a parallel to the foregoing Baraita.[21] It will be helpful to translate the Parma and Oxford manuscript versions of the story, since, as noted in chapter 1, these manuscripts are the most reliable. They often contain traditions that derive from Palestine and that, particularly in the case of the Oxford manuscript, were not subjected to Babylonianization.

The Parma manuscript reads as follows:

> (A) On the third of Tishrei, the mention [of God's name] was removed from documents.
>
> (B) Because the wicked Greek kingdom decreed a persecution against Israel and said to them, "Deny the kingdom of heaven and say, 'We have no portion in our God in heaven.'"
>
> And when the hand of the Hasmonean house grew strong they removed [the persecution] from them, and they wrote the name of heaven in documents. And thus they wrote: "In such and such a year of Yoḥanan the High Priest of the Most High God."
>
> Said the sages of blessed memory, "Is it possible that the name of heaven will be written in documents?"
>
> They took a vote about them and hid [the documents. That is, they put them away for safekeeping so that they would not be treated with disrespect.]
>
> The day they hid them, they made it a holiday.

The Oxford manuscript reads:

> (A) On the third of Tishrei the mention [of God's name] was annulled from documents.
>
> (B) In the days of the Greek kingdom they wrote God's name in documents, that there would be no portion for Israel[22] in the world to come. And when the kingdom of the Hasmonean house grew strong, they wrote, "In such and such a year of the High Priest,[23] and he was a priest of the Most High God."
>
> When the court saw that a person would take his document when it was paid and throw it into the fire or into the garbage, they decreed that the Name not be written in documents.

Neither version wants for textual problems. However, for present purposes it is important to note that (1) for Megillat Ta'anit, as for the Bavli, the reason for the holiday is the annulment of the Hasmonean practice of writing God's name in documents; (2) neither version of Megillat Ta'anit reads "When the sages heard about the matter," which is true of most Palestinian versions of traditions examined in this chapter; and (3) the Oxford manuscript, which Vered Noam characterizes as less Babylonian than the Parma manuscript,[24] makes no explicit mention of sages.

This narrative resembles the narrative about Bilga in several ways. First, it purports to be Tannaitic. Second, it involves nonsages (Greeks, Hasmoneans, and Yoḥanan the High Priest). Third, it purports to derive from the distant past, that is, the Hasmonean period and the "time of the Greeks" (see above). Fourth, the sages' statement is most likely a later addition to the narrative;[25] and fifth, Babylonian editors very likely added rabbis to a Palestinian narrative that made no mention of them.

An important proof that the sages' statement is a later addition is the story's anomalous nature, particularly viewed within the context of Megillat Ta'anit as a whole. Throughout (1) the scholion to Megillat Ta'anit[26] and (2) traditions from the scholion recorded in the Talmuds,[27] we frequently encounter the following pattern: (1) a crisis befalls or threatens the Jewish community; (2) the Jews "gain in strength"[28] or meet the challenge in some way that defuses the crisis, for example by issuing a counter-decree which shows publicly that the enemy has been defeated, God has prevailed, and a new era has begun; and (3) the day or days of victory are proclaimed a *yom tov*, a holiday, on which fasting and/or funeral orations are prohibited.

It will be helpful to describe in detail one of the many cases that follow this pattern. B. Shabbat 21b, for example, reports:

> On the twenty-fifth of Kislev, the days of Hanukah are eight, that one should not deliver funeral orations on them nor fast on them. For when the Greeks entered the Temple, they defiled all of the oils in the Temple. And when the kingship of the Hasmonean house grew strong and defeated them, they checked and found only one container of oil with the seal of the high priest intact, and it

> contained only enough [oil] to light for one day. A miracle happened with [the container of oil] and they used it for lighting for eight days. The following year, they established these [days] and made them a holiday.[29]

The narrative in b. Rosh Hashanah 18b (and parallel), however, does not follow this pattern. This narrative adds a surprising twist at the end, alone among (1) all of the stories recorded in the scholion to Megillat Ta'anit and (2) all of the Talmudic stories that purport to derive from the scholion. According to b. Rosh Hashanah 18b (and parallel), after the victory of the Jewish heroes (the Hasmoneans) and the public demonstration that the crisis is past (the Hasmonean ordinance overturning the decree of the Greeks), the public demonstration of the Jewish victory is itself overturned, an anomaly without parallel elsewhere in the scholion and related sources.

Phrased differently, this anomalous source opens with an account of the Greek decree forbidding mention of the name of God. The Hasmoneans grow in strength until they defy the decree by ordaining that the name of God should be included even in documents. The source concludes with the sages pointing out a problem with the Hasmonean ordinance and abolishing it as a result. Strangely, it is the annulment of the Hasmonean ordinance rather than the end of the Greek decree that is the occasion for jubilation. In other words, the only explicitly mentioned Jewish act of defiance of the Greek decree, the placing of God's name in documents, is annulled, and it is this annulment rather than the abolition of the evil Greek decree that the source deems worthy of commemoration. It is the only instance in the scholion to Megillat Ta'anit and related sources (see above) where the heroes of the story author injurious legislation, and it is the undoing of the act of the story's heroes rather than of its villains that the story celebrates.

Further indication that the sages' comment is a later addition is the fact that in b. Rosh Hashanah 18b a holiday is declared, even though there is no divine intervention. In other quotations from the scholion to Megillat Ta'anit, holidays are declared or commemorative measures taken in response to some event that is explicitly labeled a miracle, or is so surprising and significant it is easy to understand why it resulted in the declaration of a holiday. To cite only one of many possible examples, in b. Shabbat 21b (see above), the "miracle" of the oil lasting for eight days is the explicitly stated reason for the holiday of Hanukkah.

In b. Rosh Hashanah 18b (and parallel), however, where the holiday is declared in response to the repealing of the ordinance of the Hasmoneans, it is not at all clear why the event was considered extraordinary enough to warrant the institution of a holiday. Rashi is sensitive to this anomaly, and comments: "They annulled mention of the name of heaven from documents. And they annulled it with difficulty, for the people already acted [in accordance with the Hasmonean decree]. And when the sages heard and annulled [this practice] it was good [in the people's] eyes and it was considered by [the sages] to be a miracle, and they made it a holiday.[30] Rashi, in other words, struggles to explain the annulment of the Hasmonean ordinance as a miracle, but his explanation is forced, since there is no hint of any popular opposition in the narrative itself.

It is once again likely, therefore, that the statement introduced by the phrase "When the sages heard about this matter,"[31] together with the phrase itself, is a later addition to the story. Without this addition, the source is not exceptional or anomalous, since the holiday is declared as a result of the annulment of the evil decree of the Greeks. The addition of the sages' statement was made, most likely, for reasons stated explicitly within the source itself, by rabbis bothered by the halakhic consequences of writing God's name in documents and the resulting possibility that His name would be treated with disrespect.

If the above analysis is correct, we gain insight into the composition of Megillat Ta'anit and the scholion. The Aramaic scroll states the holiday's date and briefly describes the "historical event" that led to its establishment. The scholion is Hebrew commentary, usually a narrative, that elaborates upon the brief Aramaic description. As noted in chapter 1, modern scholars agree that the Aramaic scroll derives largely from the second Temple period, and the Hebrew scholion is of later provenance. The discussion above supports this consensus, since I concluded that the scholion is a later attempt to interpret the Aramaic scroll. We are dealing with three stages in the development of the source: (1) the early Aramaic substratum;[32] (2) the "original" Hebrew story (i.e., part B above minus the comment of "the sages"); and (3) a later Hebrew addition to the "original" Hebrew story ("When the sages heard about the matter"). The "original" Hebrew story plus the comment of the sages became attached to the Aramaic substratum as its authoritative commentary.

More important for my purposes, if the source is taken at face value, we have what appears to depict halakhic innovation by sages who were contemporaries of the Hasmoneans. The source appears at first glance to attest to communal leadership and halakhic activity by sages who lived in the second or first centuries BCE. According to the conclusions above, however, an earlier source advances no historical claims regarding the leadership role of sages in the distant past, while a later, very likely Babylonian addition[33] shows the anachronistic nature of some later sources that assume that the Hasmonean period was dominated by sages. Once again, whoever added the statement did so primarily for halakhic reasons, to make the point that documents should not contain the name of God.

Some support for my conclusion regarding the composite nature of the narrative can be found in the interpretation presupposed by the objection of the Babylonian Amora Rav Aḥa bar Huna in b. Rosh Hashanah 18b. Rav Aḥa bar Huna quotes the Baraita as an objection against the view that the holidays listed in Megillat Ta'anit were annulled when the second Temple was destroyed. Rav Aḥa quotes the source and adds: "And if you think that Megillat Ta'anit was annulled, would they annul the first days when the Temple was destroyed and then add holidays after the destruction?" According to Rav Aḥa, in other words, the second part of the source ("When the sages heard about the matter") postdates the destruction of the Temple, long after the period of the Greeks and Hasmoneans. Rav Aḥa finds it unlikely that the holidays mentioned in Megillat Ta'anit would be annulled due to the destruction of the Temple, given the fact that sages after the destruction added a day on which it is forbidden to fast. Therefore, he thinks, Megillat Ta'anit was not annulled, and it is no longer problematic that sages added a day after the destruction. Rav Aḥa, in other words, reads the source as I claim it should be read: it consists of an early layer that describes the Greek decree and the Hasmonean annulment of that decree, followed by a later layer that relates the sages' annulment of the Hasmonean ordinance. Within late antiquity itself, therefore, the sages who "heard about the matter" were understood not as participants in the action but as later commentators upon an early source. The difference between Rav Aḥa's approach and my own is that (1) Rav Aḥa does not view the later addition as an attempt to read sages back into Israel's ancient history as the leaders of Jewish society; and (2) he does not doubt the source's claim that the third of Tishrei was declared a holiday because of the annulment of the Hasmonean ordinance.[34]

Rav Aḥa bar Huna, incidentally, is a mid-fourth-century Babylonian rabbi,[35] suggesting strongly that this tradition reached Babylonia from Palestine during or shortly before the mid–fourth century. I provisionally discussed the importance of this dating in the introduction, and will return to this point in the conclusion.

It also bears mentioning that one of two alternative versions of m. Yadayim 4:8 reports the following dispute between the Pharisees and a Galilean heretic:[36]

> Said a Galilean heretic, "I complain about you Pharisees, for you write in documents the [name of the] ruler with the [divine] name."[37]
>
> Said the Pharisees, "We complain about you, Galilean heretic, for you write [the name of] the ruler on a page [of the Torah] with the [divine] name."

According to this version of the mishnah, the Pharisees write God's name in documents.[38] This practice accords with the Hasmonean practice described in b. Rosh Hashanah 18b and in the scholion to the Fasting Scroll, and is contrary to (or, more likely, ignorant of) the ruling of the sages. According to this version, therefore, this mishnah supports my claim that the "original" version of the scholion in this instance is nonrabbinic (i.e., it is Pharisaic rather than rabbinic) and that the ruling of the sages in the scholion is relatively late, since it is unknown, apparently, to the authors of the mishnah in Yadayim.

Finally, it should be noted that the portion of the source that I claim is its early Hebrew core refers to "Yoḥanan the High Priest of the Most High God." This unusual designation, found nowhere else in rabbinic literature, seems to be an authentic historical reminiscence deriving from Hasmonean times. Yoḥanan the High Priest in rabbinic sources corresponds to John Hyrcanus in the books of the Maccabees and Josephus, and he is referred to as "Hyrcanus, high priest of the Most High God" in a decree of Augustus quoted by Josephus.[39] We have further proof, therefore, that in this instance the Hebrew scholion is very early and nonrabbinic in origin.[40]

Examination of a narrative in b. Shabbat 121a leads to similar conclusions. Once again I will conclude that the phrase "When the sages heard about the matter," together with the statement it introduces, is a later addition to the narrative. Once again I will distinguish between the authors of the "original" story, who make no claims regarding the leadership role of sages in the distant past, and the authors of the later addition.

The story in b. Shabbat 121a is quoted in the context of the following mishnah: "A non-Jew who comes to extinguish [a fire on the Sabbath], we don't say to him, 'Extinguish' or 'Don't extinguish,' because his Sabbath observance is not your responsibility." The story is as follows:

> Our rabbis taught: "It once happened that a fire broke out in the courtyard of Yosef ben Simai[41] in Shiḥin.[42] The Roman garrison[43] of Sepphoris came to extinguish it because [Yosef] was the guardian of the king, but he didn't allow them to because of the honor of the Sabbath. A miracle took place for him and rain fell and extinguished [the fire]. That evening [after the Sabbath was over] he sent to each one [of the soldiers] two *sela'im* and to their leader [he sent] 50 [*sela'im*]."
>
> *When the sages heard about the matter, they said, "He didn't need to do this, for we have learned, 'A non-Jew who comes to extinguish [a fire on the Sabbath], we don't say to him, "Extinguish" or "Don't extinguish"'"* (m. Shabbat 16:6).

T. Shabbat 13:9 and y. Shabbat 16:7 (15d) preserve parallel versions of the same story in the context of the same mishnah. It will be helpful to quote them in full to see the extent of their similarity. The Tosefta's version is as follows:

> A non-Jew who comes to extinguish, we don't say to him, "Extinguish" or "Don't extinguish" (m. Shabbat 16:6).
>
> It once happened that a fire broke out in the courtyard of Yosef ben Simai of Shiḥin. The Roman garrison of Sepphoris came to extinguish it, but [Yosef] did not allow them to. A cloud descended and extinguished it.
>
> The sages said, "He didn't have to [stop them]."
>
> Even so, after the Sabbath was over he sent each one of them a *selah* and to their leader he sent 50 *denarim*.

The Yerushalmi's version is as follows:[44]

> It happened that a fire broke out in the courtyard of Yosi ben Simai in Shiḥin. The Roman garrison of Sepphoris descended to extinguish it, but [Yosi] did not allow them to.

He said to them, "Allow the Collector to collect his debt."

Immediately a cloud gathered and extinguished [the fire]. After the Sabbath he sent each one of them a *selah* and to their leader [he sent] 50 [*sela'im*].

The sages said, "He didn't need to do this."

This narrative is similar in several respects to the other narratives examined in this chapter. First, the story is virtually identical in three different compilations: the Tosefta, the Yerushalmi, and the Bavli. Second, the source purports to be Tannaitic. Third, all three versions are quoted in the same context based on the same mishnah. Fourth, the story involves nonrabbis (the Roman soldiers), although it is unclear from the narrative whether or not Yosef (=Yosi) ben Simai[45] is to be considered a rabbi.[46] Yosef's observance of the Sabbath does not decide the issue, since there is nothing improbable about a nonrabbi observing the Sabbath. Fifth, the Bavli's version of the source may purport to be ancient, ostensibly taking place during a period when a Jewish king ruled Palestine (see below). In all likelihood, the Bavli's reference to a "king" is to a Jewish king of the Herodian dynasty, which flourished from 40 BCE to approximately 100 CE,[47] ending with the death of Agrippa II.[48] As noted, the fixity of the Baraita's text and context, among other factors, support the narrative's claim to derive from the relatively distant past.

Who are the sages who "heard" what happened to Yosef ben Simai? Are they contemporaries of Yosef whose reaction to the event was almost immediate? The ensuing discussion argues that the story is most likely composite, with the statement by the sages a later addition to a preexisting narrative that made no mention of sages. What supports this contention?

As the text now stands, Yosef ben Simai performs a halakhic action, and the sages inform us that Yosef's practice, while not forbidden, is not the halakhic norm. The story is weighted toward the view of the sages, who have the final word and are the majority passing judgment on the action of an individual who may not even be a rabbi.

The story is strange, however, given the fact that Yosef's practice is supported by an act of God, by the miracle of the rain or the cloud extinguishing the fire at precisely the right moment. Even according to the Tosefta and Yerushalmi, which do not explicitly label the event a miracle, divine intervention is no doubt intended. If a cloud descends at just the right time to put out the fire on Shabbat, it follows that God approves of Yosef's action. It is surprising when the sages assert that his opinion is not the authoritative norm.

Perhaps the story's point is that it is improper to decide law in accordance with miracles. Even though heaven approved of Yosef's action, it does not follow that his opinion is law. Were the story a unity and this extraordinary claim its point, however, we would expect it to be made more clearly, as it is, for example, in the story of the excommunication of R. Eliezer ben Hyrcanus, when R. Yehoshua announces, "[Torah] is not in heaven."[49] It stretches credulity to believe that the story before us expects its audience to fill such a large gap in the narrative, to infer (1) that the story's purpose is to make the remarkable claim that human decision making takes precedence over the divine will in determining halakhah; and (2) that the sages as well as the story's authors appropriately defy God's will as expressed through the miracle.

Other attempts to interpret the story as a unity also fail. For example, it is unlikely that the story depicts the sages' disapproval of Yosef ben Simai's hubris in going beyond the letter of the law, for there is no clear-cut evidence of any disapproval in their statement. Neither is there any hint that the story depicts the sages' disapproval of Yosef's brush with the miraculous, that they react to him, for example, the way Shimon ben Shetach reacts to Ḥoni Hame'agel in m. Ta'anit 3:8. Ḥoni is a miracle worker, whereas the miracle simply happens to Yosef ben Simai. There is no reason to equate the sages' matter-of-fact reaction to Yosef ben Simai with Shimon ben Shetach's angry response to Ḥoni.

Perhaps it will be argued that the story is a unified composition that teaches that while the halakhah follows the sages, Yosi's practice is highly praiseworthy. Yosi goes beyond the letter of the law, and heaven rewards him for it. The structure of the story, however, belies this interpretation, since if the account of the miracle is intended to convince us of the righteousness of Yosef bar Simai's action, then the sages respond to it with surprising indifference. If the text means to praise Yosef for going beyond the letter of the law, it does so in an extremely anticlimactic and self-defeating manner, allowing the sages to dismiss his action as unnecessary and ending the story on a peculiarly sour note.

What we have before us, therefore, is most likely a composite. The "original" source is the miracle story that confirms as normative, or at least expresses approval, of Yosef's practice. At some later date the opinion of the sages was added, an opinion that rejects the halakhic point of the preexisting miracle story because it conflicts with the mishnah. Once again, the primary purpose of the addition is halakhic, to express the halakhic point that Jews are not responsible for the Sabbath observance of non-Jews.[50]

Despite the tension within the narrative created by this addition, the original version of the story[51] was preserved intact. We observed a similar phenomenon in the cases examined above, where the original narratives were preserved intact, despite later additions that rendered them problematic. It would be a simple matter to provide additional examples of this phenomenon.

Once again, we are confronted by (1) an earlier narrative that makes no claims regarding the sages' jurisdiction in the past over the ritual observances of nonsages (if Yosef ben Simai is, in fact, not a rabbi), and (2) a later source (the comment by the sages) that very likely assumes this jurisdiction.

Further supporting my conclusions regarding the composite nature of the narrative is the fact that in the Tosefta, the sages' statement precedes the account of Yosef ben Simai's gift to the Roman soldiers, while in the two Talmuds, the statement follows this account. Shamma Friedman has observed that later additions to a text frequently enter different versions of the text in different places.[52] The varying context of the sages' statement supports my claim that the statement is a later addition to the story.

Analysis of a Baraita in b. Menaḥot 109b leads to similar conclusions.[53] The Baraita reads as follows:

> As it is taught [in a Baraita]: The year that Shimon the Righteous died, he said to them, "This year I[54] will die."
>
> They said to him, "How do you know?"
>
> He said to them, "Every Day of Atonement an elder meets me, wearing white and wrapped in white. He enters with me and leaves with me. This year an elder met me dressed in black and wrapped in black. He entered with me but did not leave with me."
>
> After the holiday, [Shimon the Righteous] was sick for seven days and died, and his brothers the priests refrained from blessing with God's name.[55]
>
> At the time of his death, he said to [the other priests], "Ḥonio my son will serve in my place."
>
> Shimi, [Ḥonio's] brother, was jealous of him, for [Shimi] was two and half years his senior.
>
> [Shimi] said to [Ḥonio], "Come and I will teach you the proper way to serve."
>
> [Shimi] dressed [Ḥonio] in a dress[56] and girded him with a girdle[57] and stood him next to the altar.
>
> [Shimi] said to his brothers the priests, "See what vow [Ḥonio] fulfilled for his lover: 'The day on which I serve as high priest I will wear your dress and gird myself with your girdle.' "
>
> His brothers the priests wanted to kill [Ḥonio]. He ran from them and they ran after him. He went to Alexandria of Egypt and built an altar there, and raised up idolatrous [offerings].
>
> *And when the sages heard about the matter, they said, "If this one [Ḥonio], who did not take office, [acts] in this fashion, one who takes office, all the more so [will he act in this fashion]."*
>
> [These are] the words of R. Meir.
>
> R. Yehudah said to [R. Meir], "That wasn't how it happened. Rather, Ḥonio did not accept [the high priesthood] upon himself, for Shimi his brother was two and half years his senior. And even so, Ḥonio became jealous of his brother Shimi.
>
> [Ḥonio] said to [Shimi], "Come and I will teach you the proper way to serve."
>
> And [Ḥonio] dressed [Shimi] in a dress and girded him with a girdle and stood him next to the altar.
>
> [Ḥonio] said to his brothers the priests, "See what vow he fulfilled for his lover: 'The day on which I serve[58] as high priest, I will wear your dress and gird myself with your girdle."

[Shimi's] brothers the priests wanted to kill him. [Shimi] told them the whole story. They wanted to kill Ḥonio. He ran from them and they ran after him. All who saw [Ḥonio] said, "This is the one! This is the one!" He went to Alexandria of Egypt and built an altar there, and he offered up [offerings] for the sake of heaven, as it is said, "On that day there will be an altar to God in the land of Egypt and a monument near its border to God" (Isa. 19:19).

And when the sages heard about the matter, they said, "If this one [Ḥonio], who fled from [office, acts] in this fashion, one who seeks [office], how much the more so [will he act in this fashion]?"

The Palestinian Talmudic version of the story, found in y. Yoma 6:3 (43c–d), is as follows:

For 40 years Shimon the Righteous served Israel in the high priesthood, and in the last year he said, "This year I will die."

They said to him, "Who shall we appoint after you?"

[Shimon] said to them, "Behold, Neḥunion my son is before you."

They went and appointed Neḥunion, and Shimon his brother was jealous. [Shimon] went and dressed [Neḥunion] in a dress and girded him with a girdle.

[Shimon] said to them, "Look what [Neḥunion] vowed to his lover. He said to her, 'When I serve in the high priesthood I will wear your dress and gird myself with your girdle.' "

They investigated but didn't find [Neḥunion; or: the report to be true].

They said, "[Neḥunion] fled from the altar to the King's Mountain. From there he fled to Alexandria and built there an altar and applied to it this verse: 'On that day there will be an altar to God in the land of Egypt' " (Isa. 19:19).

And behold it is an a fortiori argument. If this one [Neḥunion], who fled from office, see how he went looking for it in the end, one who entered office and left, how much the more so [will he go looking for it].

It is taught: These are the words of R. Meir.

R. Yehudah says, "No, rather they appointed Shimon, and Neḥunion his brother was jealous. [Neḥunion] went and dressed him in a dress and girded him with a girdle.

[Neḥunion] said to them, 'Look what he vowed to his lover,' " and so on, as above.[59]

And behold it is an a fortiori argument. If one who did not enter office [Neḥunion], see how he compelled Israel to worship idols, one who entered and left, how much the more so [will he compel Israel to worship idols]."

In several respects the two versions of this narrative conform to narratives examined throughout this chapter. First, the narrative is preserved in two parallel versions, one in the Bavli and the other in the Yerushalmi. Second, the source purports to be Tannaitic. Third, the narrative features nonrabbis, and the nonrabbis involved are priests. Fourth, the story purports to be ancient, to describe the circumstances of the construction of the Leontopolis temple, which modern scholars date to the second century BCE.[60] And fifth, the Palestinian version of the story makes no claim that sages witnessed and pronounced judgment on events of the distant past, while the Babylonian version does make this claim.

This narrative may be composed in part of traditions dating back as far as the second century BCE. The rabbis obviously know about the temple of Onias, they know the names of the principal protagonists, and they know as well that this temple was associated with descendants of the authentic high priestly dynasty of Jerusalem. These facts derive from the first century CE at the latest, since the temple closed in 73 or 74 CE, and from the second century BCE at the earliest, when the temple was built. Resemblances between the rabbinic stories and accounts in Josephus may indicate the rabbis' familiarity with centuries-old priestly gossip, to which they added a rich blend of fantasy, polemics, and moralizing.

In addition to the accounts in Josephus[61] and rabbinic sources, our knowledge of Onias and the Leontopolis temple is provided (1) by epigraphic evidence referring, for example, to the major area of Jewish settlement in ancient Egypt as "the land of Onias," the Greek equivalent of Ḥonio,[62] and (2) by a letter found near Leontopolis written by a high-ranking Egyptian official to a certain "Oni..." (most likely to be reconstructed as Onias). The "Onias" addressed in this letter is clearly an important personage, a high-ranking member of the Egyptian Jewish community, confirming in part the status attributed to him by Josephus and the rabbis.[63]

Once again, the rabbinic accounts are of very limited historical significance regarding the period they purport to describe, but they provide significant information about the attitudes and polemical preoccupations of the rabbis themselves. While certainty on these questions is not possible, it is likely that according to R. Meir's version as preserved in the Bavli, the story is a polemic against (1) cultic centers outside of Jerusalem; (2) dynastic succession as the criteria for determining communal and priestly status; (3) a father's right to choose his own successor; and possibly (4) the priests in general.[64]

These points bear restating in greater detail. It is necessary first, however, to remove from consideration a section that is most likely a later addition to the Bavli's version of the Baraita:

> They said to [Shimon the Righteous], "How do you know [that this year you will die]?"
>
> [Shimon the Righteous] said to them, "Every Day of Atonement an elder meets me, wearing white and wrapped in white. He enters with me and leaves with me. This year an elder met me dressed in black and wrapped in black. He entered with me but did not leave with me."

> After the holiday, [Shimon the Righteous] was sick for seven days and died, and his brothers the priests refrained from blessing with God's name.

This section of the Baraita is part of an independent source in b. Yoma 39b, and a very similar source is found in t. Sotah 13:8, y. Yoma 5:2 (42c), and Leviticus Rabbah.[65] In addition, the remainder of the Baraita, that is, everything other than the brief section just quoted above, is paralleled in y. Yoma 6:3 (43c–d) (see above).

What we have before us in Bavli Menaḥot, therefore, is most likely a combination of two Baraitot. R. Meir's contribution, basing ourselves on y. Yoma 6:3 (43c–d), became combined with another Baraita (that of b. Yoma 39b) because both describe what took place at the time of Shimon the Righteous's death.

This conclusion is important, because the latter Baraita treats Shimon as a hero who foretells his own death, a death that devastated the priests to the point that they refrained from blessing in God's name. R. Meir's version, in contrast, is sharply critical of Shimon or, more precisely, depicts his conduct negatively to teach the lessons described above.

According to R. Meir in Bavli Menaḥot, it will be recalled, the priests ask Shimon who will succeed him. "Ḥonio, my son," he answers, despite the fact that his son Shimi is older and more knowledgeable about the priestly craft. Dynastic succession and a father's right to pick his own successor as high priest, to my knowledge attested nowhere else in rabbinic sources,[66] set in motion the tragic events of the story. The story also emphasizes the negative consequences of lineage as a factor determining power and priestly status by repeatedly mentioning the father-son relationship between Shimon the Righteous and his sons, as well as the "brotherly" relationship of the priests.[67] The irony of this designation is particularly evident when Ḥonio's "brothers, the priests," wish to kill him on the basis of Shimi's trumped-up charge, without bothering to investigate the possibility of extenuating circumstances.

The story also problematizes inherited authority as such, since even if Shimon the Righteous had picked as his successor Shimi, the older and more knowledgeable son, Shimi's wickedness would have made him a very poor high priest. Very likely (but by no means certainly) the story according to R. Meir emphasizes the problematic nature of inherited priestly status, a theme we encounter frequently in rabbinic literature.[68]

R. Yehudah's version in the Bavli, however, reveals the rabbis as exegetes, and demands a different understanding of the significance of this story for second-century-CE (or later) rabbis. To be specific, R. Yehudah's version arose in response to R. Meir's version, as an attempt to bring R. Meir's attitude toward Ḥonio's temple in line with that of the mishnah. The cause of the trouble from start to finish is Ḥonio, as well as the human proclivity to seek power revealed by his example.

Support for the claim that R. Yehudah's version is a reworking of R. Meir's is the fact that its conclusion is incongruous, given R. Yehudah's negative depiction of Ḥonio's behavior. According to R. Yehudah, it will be recalled, Ḥonio is jealous of his brother, Shimi, who he dresses in ridiculous garb to perform the sacrifices. Ḥonio arranges for Shimi to be observed by other priests, who he knows will be enraged by Shimi's apparent disregard for the sanctity of the altar and the Temple service. When Ḥonio is chased out of Jerusalem and flees to Alexandria, however, he builds an altar and offers sacrifices "for the sake of heaven." Given the portrayal of Ḥonio prior to this point, the favorable evaluation of Ḥonio's Egyptian altar is surprising.

According to R. Meir's version, which portrays Ḥonio more positively, Ḥonio's Egyptian altar is idolatrous, which serves to heighten the tragic nature of the entire affair. In R. Meir's version, the unfortunate denouement powerfully drives home the point about the ill-advised nature of (1) the priestly insistence on inherited succession, and (2) Shimon the Righteous's insistence on dynastic succession. In R. Yehudah's version, however, this denouement was changed to conform to the mishnah, which partially acknowledges the legitimacy of Ḥonio's Egyptian altar, and falls short of the condemnation of the altar in R. Meir's version. R. Yehudah's version reflects the hand of tradents and/or later editors, who "corrected" R. Meir's version, unmindful or unconcerned about the resulting incongruities.

Interestingly, the rabbinic accounts are reminiscent of Josephus's story of Manasses the high priest and the foundation of the Samaritan temple on Mount Gerizim, in addition to their obvious affinities with Josephus's account of the founding of the Leontopolis temple. The Samaritan temple was built, apparently, in the fourth century BCE (or later) and destroyed in 128 BCE (or later).[69]

Josephus's story of Manasses is as follows:

> Now the elders of Jerusalem, resenting the fact that the brother of the high priest Jaddus was sharing the high priesthood while married to a foreigner, rose up against him. . . . They therefore told Manasses either to divorce his wife or not to approach the altar. And, as the high priest shared the indignation of the people and kept his brother from the altar, Manasses went to his father-in-law Sanaballetes and said that while he loved his daughter Nokaso, nevertheless the priestly office was the highest in the nation and had always belonged to his family, and that therefore he did not wish to be deprived of it on her account. But Sanaballetes promised not only to preserve the priesthood for him but also to procure for him the power and office of high priest and to appoint him governor of all the places over which he ruled, if he were willing to live with his daughter; and he said that he would build a temple similar to that in Jerusalem on Mount Garizein–this is the highest of the mountains near Samaria. . . . When, therefore, Alexander gave his consent, Sanaballetes brought all his energy to bear and built the temple and appointed Manasses high priest.[70]

Josephus's story of Manasses and the two rabbinic stories examined above deal with (1) conflict between two brothers competing for the office of high priest; (2) a woman who (allegedly) plays a prominent role in the brotherly conflict; (3) a father (-in-law) who handpicks his son (-in-law) for the office of high priest; (4) a familial conflict that has consequences for the entire nation when it leads to the construction of a rival cultic center outside of Jerusalem. Perhaps the most striking of these parallels is the third, the father (-in-law) who picks his son (-in-law) as his successor, since, as noted, to my knowledge this motif is found nowhere else in rabbinic literature. This anomaly is apparently an indication that the motif entered rabbinic literature from a nonrabbinic source.

The rabbinic narrative, therefore, is in part a conflation of ancient, nonrabbinic traditions about the founding of the Mount Gerizim and Leontopolis temples. Once again the sages' comment in the rabbinic narrative is based in part on early traditions, possibly gossip, possibly formal sources, that originated outside of rabbinic circles.

A narrative in b. Sanhedrin 44b adds to our understanding of the phrase under discussion, "When the sages heard about the matter." First, this narrative supports my claim that rabbinic storytellers use the phrase to introduce comments by sages who they believe participated in the action as leaders. Second, here, as elsewhere in this chapter, (1) the story on which the sages' comment is based involves a nonrabbi; (2) the Bavli's version is closely paralleled by versions in the Tosefta and Yerushalmi;[71] (3) in all three compilations the source purports to be Tannaitic; (4) all three versions of the story are preserved in the same context based on the same mishnah; and (5) the story purports to derive from the relatively distant past, during a period when the Jews had the power to put people to death.[72]

The narrative reads as follows:

> Our rabbis taught [in a Baraita]: There is a story of a man who went out to be executed.
>
> He said, "If I am guilty of this sin, let my death not be atonement for all of my sins. But if I am not guilty of this sin, let my death be atonement for all of my sins. And the court and all of Israel are innocent. But the witnesses should never be forgiven."
>
> *And when the sages heard about the matter, they said, "To bring him back is impossible, for the verdict has already been decided. Rather, let him be executed and let the burden [of guilt] hang on the necks of the witnesses."*

As noted, the authors of this story believe that the sages who "heard about the matter" are participants in the action and are in charge of the judicial proceedings. The proof is the sages' declaration: "To bring him back is impossible, for the verdict has already been decided. Rather, let him be executed." This understanding is even clearer in the versions of the Tosefta and Yerushalmi, where the sages burst into tears before ruling that the execution must proceed. Were the sages merely commenting on a source, then their personal involvement, as indicated by the shedding of tears, would make little sense.

Examination of a Baraita in b. Yoma 38a and paralleled in t. Yoma 2:5–6; y. Yoma 3:9 (41a); y. Shekalim 5:2 (48d–49a); and Song of Songs Rabbah 3:5

also yields important information about our term. The Baraita in the Bavli reads as follows:

> Our rabbis taught [in a Baraita]: Beit Garmu were expert in making showbread but they didn't want to teach [others how to make it]. The sages sent and brought artisans from Alexandria of Egypt. They knew how to bake like [Beit Garmu], but they didn't know how to remove [the bread from the oven] like them, for they [light the fire] from the outside and bake from the outside, while the others [light the fire] from inside and bake from inside. Their bread spoiled, and the others' bread did not spoil.
>
> *And when the sages heard about the matter, they said, "Everything that the Holy One, blessed be He created, He created for His honor, as it is said, 'All that was called [into being by God's speech], by My name and in My honor I created it'" (Isa. 43:7).*
>
> Beit Garmu returned to their places. The sages sent for them, but they didn't come. They doubled their salary, and they came. Every day they took 12 *maneh*, but that day they took 24.
>
> R. Yehudah says, "Every day they took 24, and that day 48."

What does this story about Beit Garmu reveal about our phrase?[73] In several respects, it is typical of the narratives examined throughout this chapter. First, versions of the story preserved in the Tosefta, Yerushalmi, and Bavli closely parallel one another.[74] Second, the parallels in the three compilations are all taught in the same context based on the same mishnah. Third, the story on which their comments are based purports to describe the actions of nonrabbis, and once again the nonrabbis are priests. Fourth, the story purports to derive from the relatively distant past, describing events that took place while the Temple still stood.[75] Fifth, the sources purport to be Tannaitic.

In one important respect, however, the present case is atypical. In this case and only in this case, the phrase itself, "When the sages heard about the matter," is found in Palestinian compilations.[76] That is, the phrase and not simply the content of the statements is paralleled in the Tosefta and in the Yerushalmi. The term, therefore, is attested in Palestine, although it is in the Babylonian Talmud, or, more precisely, in purportedly Tannaitic sources found in the Bavli, that it achieves an appreciable degree of currency. It may be significant that the one case in which the term is found in Palestinian compilations depicts sages who are powerless in the face of intransigent priests, and who are forced to assent to the priests' demands for more money (see below).[77]

What conclusions can we draw from this diverse body of evidence? It will be recalled that in several cases we were able to show that the term and statements introduced by the term were later additions to earlier narratives. In several other cases, only the Bavli's version of a story mentioned sages; parallel versions in Palestinian compilations did not.[78] It is likely that the Palestinian versions preserve the earlier reading in these cases and the mention of sages is a later addition by Babylonian editors, although at present we have no way to determine when the editors did their work. Any time during the development of the Talmud in Babylonia is a possibility.

Several preliminary observations are possible. First, (1) the absence of the term from statements by Amoraim[79] and (2) its presence in Baraitot found in the Babylonian Talmud (as well as one source preserved in the Tosefta, the Yerushalmi, and Song of Songs Rabbah) is unexpected. If, as seems likely, the term is of Palestinian, Tannaitic provenance, as indicated by its presence in the Tosefta and by the fact that the Talmuds cite it almost exclusively as part of Baraitot, why is it so scarce in Palestinian compilations and found with relative frequency in the Bavli?

Perhaps the answer is to be found in the fact, noted above, that most of the narratives examined above involve priests, and all but two or three involve individuals who are not sages.[80] To be specific, of the 9 or 10 cases in which the term is found in the Bavli, five or six explicitly involve priests,[81] three make no mention of the protagonists being either priests or nonpriests, and only one involves a figure, R. Akiba, who we can be reasonably certain was not a priest.[82] It has yet to be shown, however, that rabbinic attitudes toward nonrabbinic priests were different in Babylonia from in Palestine, and the question warrants further study.

One contributing factor may have been the Bavli's greater tendency to tamper with and add to earlier sources. As noted, the Bavli underwent a relatively protracted editorial process, which continued roughly two centuries after the final editing of the Yerushalmi; for this reason, we find editorial additions more frequently in the Bavli than in Palestinian compilations. The specific type of editorial addition under consideration here, namely, the addition of rabbis into narratives that originally made no mention of them, however, is easily explicable in terms of my theory regarding the tendency of Babylonian rabbis to depict the past in terms of their experience of the present, dominated by rabbis and rabbinic concerns.

What other conclusions can we draw from the evidence collected above? We found that several earlier narratives derived from or had more or less strong affinities with pre- and nonrabbinic sources. In a few cases, even though a parallel nonrabbinic source was not extant, the earlier rabbinic narrative showed signs of influence by or derivation from nonrabbinic roots.[83] Once again, we see that rabbinic compilations incorporate much nonrabbinic material, which they subject to varying degrees of editorial manipulation.

It remains for me to discuss additional factors supporting the claim of the narratives, at least the core narratives, to be relatively ancient. One factor was the frequency with which our phrase is featured in sources that (1) have close parallels in the Tosefta, the Yerushalmi, and the Bavli; and (2) are transmitted in the same context based on the same mishnah in all three compilations. The fact that their form, content, and context is so stable suggests that they assumed their present shape in their present contexts at a relatively early date.

In addition, we found that the narratives' earlier core depicts the deeds of nonsages and makes no mention of sages as the leaders of ancient Jewish society. This finding further supports their claim to derive from the distant past, since Jewish society, particularly prior to the destruction of the Temple, was dominated by figures other than sages. It is unlikely that these core narratives were invented relatively late in the Tannaitic or post-Tannaitic period and that they involve nonsages because their authors wanted to create believable fiction. It is unlikely that for the sake of verisimilitude, rabbinic authors made nonsages (especially priests) who flourished in earlier eras the protagonists of their tales.

I reject this possibility because it fails to explain why nearly all of the narratives are preserved in the same context in two or three compilations. I can understand a later storyteller inventing a narrative that attempts to describe convincingly an early period. I cannot understand how basically the same source repeatedly made its way into the same context in two or three different compilations. Unless we posit that the three compilations—the Tosefta, the Yerushalmi, and the Bavli—underwent a process of coordinated editing beyond anything we have reason to suspect,[84] the presence of the core sources in the same context in multiple compilations is difficult to explain if we posit a late date of composition.

This is not to say, of course, that these narratives originated precisely at the time they purport to describe or that they portray events as they actually took place. True, the sources are relatively early, but as noted, early sources are as capable of distorting historical reality as are later sources. And, as noted in the previous chapter, we should not credit the early, Palestinian storytellers responsible for the core narratives with a concern for the disinterested reporting of historical facts simply because they distort reality less, and/or in different ways, than do later Babylonian storytellers. As also noted in the previous chapter, the differences between Palestinian and Babylonian rabbinic storytelling described herein have much to do with the larger cultural context within which these two literatures were produced, and nothing to do with a greater or lesser desire to avoid anachronisms or distortions in the narration of past events.

Appendix

Stories in b. Gittin 35a, b. Bekhorot 51b, b. Eruvin 21b, and possibly b. Baba Kamma 50a also contain statements introduced by our phrase. Since these cases add little to our understanding of the term, I discuss them briefly in this appendix.

B. Bekhorot 51b reads as follows:

> We taught [in m. Bekhorot 8:8] that which our rabbis taught [in the following Baraita]: If he gave [the money required to redeem one's firstborn son] to 10 priests at one time, he has fulfilled his obligation. [If he gave the money to] one after the other, he has fulfilled his obligation. If [the priest] took [the money] and returned it to him, he

> has fulfilled his obligation. And thus was the practice of R. Tarfon, that he would take and return.
>
> *And when the sages heard about the matter, they said, "This one fulfilled this law."*

This narrative has several points in common with the narratives examined above. First, it is closely paralleled by a story in the Tosefta.[85] There is no parallel in the Yerushalmi, but this is not surprising, since no Palestinian Talmud on tractate Bekhorot has survived. Second, the parallels in the Tosefta and Bavli are preserved in identical contexts. Third, the source deals with nonrabbis, once again with priests. Fourth, the source purports to be a Baraita. Fifth, the parallel in the Tosefta makes no mention of sages.

The usage of the term here differs from other usages in that (1) the story on which the sages' comment is based involves a rabbi, R. Tarfon (although the story clearly identifies R. Tarfon as a priest),[86] and (2) the story does not purport to be ancient.

A story found in the printed edition of b. Baba Kamma 50a also contains the phrase "When the sages heard about the matter." The reading of the printed edition is corroborated by Halakhot Gedolot,[87] but the Munich, Hamburg, Florence, Rome,[88] Escorial, and Vatican 116 manuscripts read: "When the matter came to the sages" (as does t. Baba Kamma 6:5), and R. Alfasi reads: "When the matter came before the sages."

Perhaps the reading of the printed edition of b. Baba Kamma arose on account of the narrative's similarity to b. Bekhorot 51b (see above), the only other place in the Bavli where sages say "This one fulfilled this law." According to all versions of the latter story, the sages' statement is introduced by the phrase "When the sages heard about the matter," and the usage there perhaps influenced the scribes in Baba Kamma. This conclusion is tentative, however, because of the support for the reading of the printed edition provided by Halakhot Gedolot.

In any event, the usage in b. Baba Kamma exhibits most of the features of the other narratives examined throughout this study: (1) the source purports to be a Baraita; (2) it involves a nonrabbi, Neḥunia the digger of cisterns, ditches, and caves, who, according to m. Shekalim 5:1, was a priest; (3) the story purports to derive from the distant past (according to this mishnah, Neḥunia lived during the time of the Temple); and (4) the narrative is closely paralleled by a source found in the same context in t. Baba Kamma 6:5.

The text of b. Gittin 35a, which also contains our phrase, is as follows:

> For Rav Kahana said (others say Rav Yehudah said)[89] Rav said, "It once happened in a time of famine that a certain man left a gold denar in the charge of a widow. She placed it in a jar of flour and baked it into bread and gave it to a poor man. Eventually the owner of the denar came to her and said, 'Give me my denar.'
>
> She said to him, 'May poison kill one of my children[90] if I have benefited at all from your denar.'

> They said, 'It wasn't long before one of her children died.'
> *And when the sages heard about the matter they said, 'If this happens to one who swears honestly, how much the more so will it happen to one who swears falsely.'"*

In contrast to all of the other cases examined thus far, this source is attributed not to Tannaim but to a Babylonian Amora. Rav, however, who tells the story, is an early Babylonian Amora trained in Palestine who transmits in his own name much Palestinian Tannaitic material.[91] Rav was a student of Rabbi, conventionally considered to be one of the latest Tannaim, and also a student of R. Ḥiyya, a figure transitional between the Tannaitic and Amoraic periods, who routinely quotes Tannaitic material. When Rav quotes a source (as opposed to stating his own view) the likelihood is great that the source is Tannaitic.[92] The fact that the source is introduced by the term *ma'aseh*, which often (but not always) introduces Tannaitic sources,[93] is further indication of the story's Tannaitic provenance. In particular, Rav transmits many stories, all in Hebrew, and many purportedly or demonstrably derive from pre-Amoraic Palestine.

What is at first glance a distinction between this usage of the phrase and other usages, therefore, is most likely a feature it shares with them. In addition, like most of the other cases examined in this chapter, the story has a parallel in the Yerushalmi[94] (although not in the Tosefta), and the story to which the sages respond involves only nonrabbis. And once again, the version in the Yerushalmi, unlike that of the Bavli, makes no mention of sages.

This usage of the phrase is atypical, however, in that (1) the parallel in the Yerushalmi is in a different tractate and in a different language (Aramaic rather than Hebrew); (2) while the main point of the story in the Palestinian and Babylonian compilations is the same,[95] there are more than the usual number of inconsequential plot differences; and (3) the story does not purport to be ancient. Any date within or prior to the Tannaitic period is possible.

Finally, in several respects, the use of the phrase in a Baraita in b. Eruvin 21b does not conform to the patterns observed thus far. The story upon which the sages comment involves R. Akiba rather than a nonsage; the story does not locate the action in the distant past; and the narrative has no parallels in other compilations.

4

Anxious Rabbis and Mocking Nonrabbis

This chapter examines traditions that depict rabbis as sensitive to the fact that their statements appear or might appear to nonrabbis to fly in the face of common sense or to contradict the everyday functioning of the world or the meaning of scripture. What happens when rabbinic sources acknowledge that a rabbi says or does something that was or might be construed as ludicrous or far-fetched? Is the rabbi ridiculed, and if so, what is his reaction? Does the ridicule provoke anxiety, defensiveness, and/or a desire for revenge?[1]

This chapter attempts to show that Palestinian rabbinic sources tended to be more attuned than Babylonian rabbinic sources to the reactions, whether real or anticipated, of nonrabbis to their statements.[2] Palestinian rabbis tended to be more aware than Babylonian rabbis that their actions and opinions could or did provoke ridicule among nonrabbis. In a significant number of cases, all having to do with the rabbis' worries about their status in the eyes of nonrabbis, and/or rabbinic self-consciousness about nonrabbinic reaction to their statements, Palestinian rabbis revealed their insecurity and discomfort and attempted to demonstrate the reliability of their opinions and interpretations in the face of nonrabbinic ridicule. As a result, Palestinian rabbis, more than their Babylonian counterparts, told stories that vindicated rabbis who were the objects of nonrabbinic ridicule and depicted their antagonists receiving their just desserts.[3]

I claimed in the introduction that (1) Palestinian rabbis interacted with nonrabbis more routinely and in more informal contexts than did their Babylonian counterparts, and that (2) Palestinian rabbis needed nonrabbis for economic support and social advancement. The stories considered here are easily explicable according to that theory, since in the pages that follow we encounter numerous Palestinian traditions, some discussed here in detail and many others cited in notes, that portray Palestinian rabbis as acutely sensitive to the reactions of nonrabbis to their statements, as interacting with them in informal contexts, and as killing nonrabbis in response to their mockery of the rabbis' statements. The Babylonian Talmudic parallels either lack or significantly downplay these preoccupations, typically transforming a narrative that in the Yerushalmi is a dramatic encounter between a rabbi and a nonrabbi into a clash between competing rabbis, or a morality tale about what happens to rabbinic disciples who treat their masters with insufficient respect.

To keep this chapter within manageable proportions and to simplify matters methodologically, I have confined the discussion to cases in which statements by and stories involving rabbis reveal defensiveness, concern for or self-consciousness about how they appear in the eyes of nonrabbis, and/or anxiety in the face of attacks by outsiders. It makes no difference for my purposes whether or not the encounter described really took place, or even that the story purports to depict face-to-face confrontations. It may, for example, depict a nonrabbi *thinking* that a rabbi's words are ridiculous, or untrue, or self-contradictory, without actually saying so to the rabbi's face or publicly humiliating him. It would certainly be worthwhile to examine a larger body of material, for example, all purported rabbinic interactions with nonrabbis,[4] since the overwhelming majority of these interactions conclude with the rabbi winning a debate, resolving an objection, and the like and are therefore of potential relevance to our inquiry. To examine all such cases, however, would require a separate monograph, and I thought it worthwhile to tackle only a portion of the material, at least preliminarily.[5]

We turn first to the issue of rabbinic sensitivity to mockery by nonrabbis. A story involving a Palestinian rabbi, R. Yoḥanan, for example, hammers home the point that even the most outrageous rabbinic statements, in this case an interpretation of scripture about the messianic future, are demonstrably true and are confirmed by eyewitness testimony of the most hardened skeptics. Different versions of the story are preserved in the Bavli and in a Palestinian compilation, but in both versions the message is basically the same. Ultimately, the story teaches, there is no need for verification of a rabbi's statements. The individual who in both versions doubts the rabbi is reduced to a pile of bones. The warning is clear to all those who demand proof: rabbis speak the truth, and those who doubt them are asking for trouble. This tradition reveals an intense concern on the part of the story's authors that their statements are or might be the subject of ridicule, and an intense desire to depict the rabbis as more than equal to the challenge.

The version of Pesikta de-Rav Kahana,[6] a Palestinian rabbinic compilation, is as follows:

> "[I will make]...your gates of precious stones" (Isa. 54:12)....
>
> R. Yoḥanan sat and expounded in the great synagogue of Sepphoris: "In the future the Holy One will make the eastern gate of the Temple, it and its two wickets, a single precious gem."

> A heretic who was a sailor was there. He said, "Even something the size of a turtledove's egg we don't find there; and this one sits here and says such a thing?"
>
> When [the sailor] set sail on the Mediterranean Sea, his ship sank into the sea and went down to the deepest depths, and he saw ministering angels chiseling, carving, and fastening.
>
> He said to them, "What is this?"
>
> They said to him, "This is the eastern gate of the Temple. It and its two wickets are a single precious stone."
>
> Immediately a miracle happened to him and [the sailor] came out of there unharmed.
>
> The next year he went and found R. Yoḥanan sitting and expounding this matter: "In the future the Holy One, blessed be He will make the eastern gate of the Temple, it and its two wickets, a single precious stone."
>
> [The sailor] said to him, "Old man, old man, whatever you can say, say. [Whatever you can] glorify, glorify. If I hadn't seen it with my own eyes I would not have believed it."
>
> [R. Yoḥanan] said to him, "If you hadn't seen it with your own eyes you wouldn't have believed the words of Torah that I speak?"
>
> He raised his eyes and looked at him and immediately he became a heap of bones.

The Bavli's version is as follows:[7]

> R. Yoḥanan sat and expounded: "In the future the Holy One, blessed be He, will bring forth precious stones and jewels that are 30 cubits by 30 cubits, and He will engrave in them an engraving of 10 or 20 cubits, and He will set them up as the gates of Jerusalem, as it is said, 'And I will make your battlements of rubies and your gates of precious stones'" (Isa. 54:12).
>
> A certain student mocked him. [The student] said, "Now we don't find anything the size of a turtledove's egg.[8] This much we will find?"
>
> After a while, [the student's] ship traveled to sea. He saw ministering angels cutting precious stones and jewels.
>
> [The student] said to them, "What are these for?"
>
> They said to him, "In the future the Holy One, blessed be He, will set them up as the gates of Jerusalem."
>
> When [the student] returned, he found R. Yoḥanan sitting and expounding scripture.
>
> [The student] said to him, "Rabbi, expound! It is good for you to expound! Just as you said, so I saw."
>
> [R. Yoḥanan] said to him, "Empty one! If you hadn't seen you wouldn't have believed? You are a mocker of the words of the rabbis!"
>
> [R. Yoḥanan] set his eyes upon him and made him a heap of bones.

In the Bavli's version, R. Yoḥanan "sits and expounds," but we are not told where he is at the time. Significantly, however, the only other human character in the Bavli's version is "a student," who ridicules R. Yoḥanan's interpretation of scripture, goes on a sea voyage, observes the angels, and returns to receive his comeuppance. The fact that he is a student does not require the assumption that the story's *Sitz im Leben* is a study house, but the Bavli's version of the story depicts an encounter between rabbis, or, more precisely, between a rabbi and a rabbi in training. The version in the Palestinian compilation, in contrast, takes place in a synagogue, where rabbis as well as nonrabbis gather together, and features a rabbi and a heretical sailor.

It bears mentioning that the Palestinian version, which identifies R. Yoḥanan's antagonist as a heretic, makes for a more effective story. In the Palestinian version, part of what motivates the storyteller's fury is the fact that the heretic contrasts the present ruined state of the Temple site in Jerusalem with Yoḥanan's depiction of its glorious future. At issue is not only scriptural interpretation but also the very nature of God's relationship with the Jewish people. It is tempting to view the heretic as a Christian; he could, however, belong to any one of a number of groups[9] who vied for superiority in Palestine and who used the destruction of the Temple as proof that God had abandoned the Jewish people. This point does not come through in the Bavli's version, according to which the dispute is an internal rabbinic affair, suggesting that the story originated in Palestine and lost something in the process of transfer from Palestine to Babylonia.

Other stories also attest to differing Babylonian and Palestinian rabbinic sensitivities to mockery by nonrabbis. Y. Shevi'it 9:1 (38d),[10] for example, reads as follows:

> R. Shimon bar Yoḥai hid in a cave for 13 years. [He ate] in the cave carobs of *terumah* until his flesh became scaly.
>
> After 13 years he said, "Should I not go out to find some information about the world?"
>
> He went out and was sitting at the mouth of the cave when he saw a hunter of birds spread a trap.
>
> [R. Shimon] heard a heavenly voice saying, "Reprieved!"[11] and the bird escaped.
>
> He thought, "If a mere bird, unless heaven wills it, cannot escape [its fate], how much the more a man cannot escape."
>
> When he saw the world around was tranquil he said, "Let us go down to inspect the baths of Tiberias."
>
> He said, "We should go and do something to better the world as our ancestors used to do. . . ."
>
> He said, "Let us purify Tiberias."
>
> He took lupines and cut them up and scattered them, and whenever there was a dead body, it floated up and he took it away.
>
> From above, a Samaritan was watching the events.

> [The Samaritan] thought, "Should I not go and ridicule this Jewish elder?"
>
> He took a corpse and hid it in a place that [R. Shimon] had already cleansed of corpses.
>
> He then came to R. Shimon bar Yoḥai and said to him, "Have you not purified that place? Nonetheless I can produce [a corpse] for you from there."
>
> R. Shimon bar Yoḥai saw through the holy spirit that [the Samaritan] had put it there himself.
>
> He said, "I decree that those above shall descend [i.e., the Samaritan will die] and those below [i.e., the corpse] will arise."
>
> And thus it happened.
>
> When he passed by Migdal, he heard the voice of a scribe[12] saying, "Here is bar Yoḥai, who purified Tiberias!"
>
> [R. Shimon] said to him, "I swear that I have heard that Tiberias would one day be purified. Yet you did not believe!"[13]
>
> Immediately [the scribe] became a pile of bones.

This version of the story contains two episodes that depict mockery of a rabbi. First, a Samaritan says explicitly that he wants to ridicule the rabbi, which he accomplishes by demonstrating that R. Shimon failed to do what he set out to do. Second, a scribe mocks the rabbi, apparently because he does not believe the tradition quoted by R. Shimon, and possibly (also?) because he does not believe that R. Shimon's actions in Tiberias were efficacious. Once again, for the reasons outlined above, a Palestinian source takes pains to demonstrate the reliability of a great rabbi's actions and/or traditions in the face of nonrabbinic ridicule.

A version of this story found in Kohelet Rabbah 10:8, like the Yerushalmi, relates both the first encounter between R. Shimon and the Samaritan, and the scene in which R. Shimon faults his second antagonist for not "believing" his tradition. These versions are thus strongly reminiscent of the story of R. Yoḥanan's clash with the heretical sailor (see above). Here as well, the story teaches that failure to believe a rabbi is wicked, and is punishable by death via a glance by the offended sage.[14]

Pesikta de-Rav Kahana, also a Palestinian compilation, preserves a third version.[15] It differs from the Yerushalmi and Kohelet Rabbah in a number of ways, but for my purposes the relevant differences are (1) there is no confrontation between R. Shimon and a Samaritan, and (2) the encounter with the scribe is as follows:

> When [R. Shimon] left [Tiberias], he passed by the synagogue of Minkai, scribe of Migdol, [who] said, "Here is bar Yoḥai, who purified Tiberias."
>
> [R. Shimon] said to him, "Did you not vote [among those who declared Tiberias clean]?"

> He raised his eyes, and immediately [the scribe] became a heap of bones.

The Pesikta's description of Minkai the scribe having participated in the vote regarding the ritual status of Tiberias may establish for the rabbinic authors of this story his identity as a rabbi. Perhaps the story, therefore, does not depict interaction between rabbis and nonrabbis. The Pesikta's version does not contradict my thesis, however, since it is not my claim that Palestinian sources do not depict rabbis concerned about their reputations in the eyes of other rabbis, sometimes with fatal consequences. Rather, my claim is that these sources tend, more so than Babylonian sources, to be preoccupied with this issue in narratives involving nonrabbis.

In a fourth Palestinian version, in Genesis Rabba,[16] the first encounter is between R. Shimon and a nonrabbi (an *am ha-areẓ*). The nonrabbi mocks the rabbi,[17] and R. Shimon makes him pay for his actions with his life. The second encounter, however, may pit two rabbis against each other, since Nika'ia the scribe took part in the vote about Tiberias's ritual status, and, as noted, the rabbinic story may assume that only rabbis could participate in this vote.

The Bavli's version of the story, in b. Shabbat 33b–34a, lacks the first encounter. In addition, the character of R. Shimon's antagonist as a rabbi is unambiguous in the Bavli. As noted, in Pesikta de-Rav Kahana and Genesis Rabba, the only indication of his rabbinic status is R. Shimon's question to him: "Did you not vote?" and in the Yerushalmi and Kohelet Rabbah, there is no hint that he might be a rabbi. In contrast, in the Bavli we find the following:

> Said [R. Shimon], "Since a miracle has occurred, let me go and emend something. . . . Is there anything that requires emending?"
>
> They said to him, "There is a place of doubtful uncleanness, and priests have the trouble of going around it."
>
> Said [R. Shimon], "Does any one know if there was a presumption of cleanliness here?"
>
> A certain elder replied, "Here ben Azzai cut down lupines of terumah." So [R. Shimon] did likewise. Wherever [the ground] was hard he declared it clean; where it was loose he marked it off.
>
> Said the elder, "Ben Yoḥai has purified a cemetery!"
>
> Said [R. Shimon], "Had you not been with us, or even if you had been with us but did not vote, you might have spoken well. But now that you were with us and voted with us, it will be said, '[Even] whores paint one another; how much the more so should sages [help one another].' "
>
> [R. Shimon] cast his eyes upon [the elder] and he died.

That the "elder" is a rabbi, according to the Bavli's version, is indicated not only by the fact that he was present for and took part in the vote (but see above) but also by the fact that (1) he cites a rabbinic precedent (that involving ben

Azzai), and (2) R. Shimon's comparison between whores and sages only makes sense if the elder is a sage. As noted, furthermore, the term "elder" often—but by no means always—is synonymous with "sage."

The issue of mockery of a rabbi by a nonrabbi, therefore, is prominent in three of the four Palestinian compilations that record this story. In two of the Palestinian compilations, a prominent issue might be mockery of a rabbi by another rabbi, but only in the Bavli's version is the character of R. Shimon's antagonist as a rabbi emphasized or even clear.

A narrative in y. Ma'aser Sheni 4:11 (55c) further attests to Palestinian efforts to drive home the point that nonrabbis pay dearly for disrespect toward a rabbi:

> A Samaritan said, "I will go and make fun of[18] that elder of the Jews [R. Yishmael bei R. Yosi]."
>
> [The Samaritan] went to him and said, "I saw in my dream four cedar trees and four sycamore trees, a bundle of reeds,[19] a barn,[20] a cow, and I[21] was sitting and treading.
>
> [R. Yishmael bei R. Yosi] said to him, "May your[22] spirit burst. This is not a dream. Even so, you will not leave empty-handed. The four cedars are the four posts of your bed. The four sycamores are the four legs of your bed. The bundle of reeds is the foot of your bed. The barn is a mattress of straw.[23] The cow is the leather bed coverings,[24] and you[25] sitting and treading is you lying in it neither alive nor dead."
>
> And thus it happened to him.

This story is one in a series that depicts Palestinian rabbis as reliable dream interpreters.[26] Dream interpretation was a controversial topic in the ancient world, with some holding it in high esteem and others viewing it as the stock in trade of charlatans. This series of rabbinic narratives considers dream interpretation an honorable profession, but Palestinian rabbis were sensitive to the fact that by plying this trade they exposed themselves to ridicule. The story before us depicts a nonrabbi attempting to confound a rabbi by going before him with a fabricated account of a dream. The Samaritan hopes to prove that R. Yosi is a fraud; any interpretation he offers will be unfounded, since the Samaritan is not reporting to him an actual dream. The rabbi recognizes the ruse and successfully proves that dream interpretation is legitimate and that he is a skilled practitioner. Once again a nonrabbi attempts to humiliate a rabbi, but the rabbi demonstrates his resourcefulness and expertise and inflicts on his antagonist a well-deserved punishment.

We find another example in y. Ta'anit 3:4 (66d), also involving a Samaritan, suggesting that the mocking Samaritan was a stock character in rabbinic stories:[27]

> R. Aḥa fasted 13 fasts but rain did not fall. While approaching, he met a Samaritan.
>
> [The Samaritan] said to him, "Rabbi, Rabbi, wring out the rain from your cloak!"[28]

[R. Aḥa] said to him, "By your life,[29] the heavens will perform miracles and the year will prosper, but you[30] will not live."
And the heavens performed miracles and the year prospered, but the Samaritan died.
And everyone said, "Come and see a Samaritan's bier."[31]

Further evidence of the difference between the Bavli and Palestinian corpora on this issue is provided by what purports to be a Baraita in b. Kiddushin 81b. This purported Baraita depicts a "student" mocking R. Tarfon for instructing unnamed listeners to "Warn me on account of my mother-in-law," that is, to remind him not to be alone with her lest he become involved in some sexual impropriety. R. Abahu follows with a quotation of another Tanna, R. Ḥanina ben Gamliel, according to which "It was not long before that student stumbled with his mother-in-law." That is, he had sexual relations or was involved in some sexual impropriety with his mother-in-law, proving that R. Tarfon was correct to be so scrupulous, and serving as fitting punishment for the student's crime of mocking a great rabbi. Once again, the Bavli records a purportedly Palestinian source expressing concern about mockery of a rabbi, but presents it as an internal rabbinic affair, as a matter of proper relations between a student and his teacher. As outlined in the introduction, despite the fact that this narrative involves a Palestinian rabbi, we should probably classify it as at least partially "Babylonian" because it contains a Babylonian twist on a Palestinian motif.[32]

It will be recalled that the R. Yoḥanan story that opened this chapter evinces awareness that nonrabbis view as peculiar some rabbinic interpretations of scripture. Kohelet Rabbah 1:1:9 further illustrates this Palestinian sensitivity:

"Only that shall happen, which has happened" (Eccles. 1:9). . . .
It happened that the kingdom [of Rome] sent to our rabbis and said to them, "Send us one of your torches."
They said to him, "They have so many torches and they ask us for one torch?"[33] It appears to us that they want someone who enlightens people with halakhah."
They sent to them R. Meir,[34] and they asked him and he answered, they asked him and he answered, until they finally asked him, "Why is [the pig, which for the rabbis was a symbol of Rome] called a *ḥazir*?"
He said to them, "In the future they will return [*yaḥaziru*] the kingdom to its [rightful] owners."
R. Meir also sat and expounded, "In the future the fox will be covered with a fleece of fine wool[35] and the dog with ermine fur."
They said to him, "Enough, R. Meir; 'And there is nothing new under the sun'" (Eccles. 1:9).

R. Meir is portrayed as a great man, the "torch" sent to the Romans to answer their questions. Most of the story is a conventional account of a great sage impressing foreign conquerors with his superior wisdom. In the conclusion, however, R. Meir, apparently still in the presence of Romans, expounds scripture in what the Romans regard (according to the story) as a far-fetched manner. According to R. Meir, Kohelet describes remarkable changes that will take place in the natural world some time in the future, prompting the Romans to ask him to desist, and to quote Kohelet's famous assertion "There is nothing new under the sun."[36] As noted, this narrative reveals self-consciousness about the reaction of nonrabbis to rabbinic statements, and sensitivity to how some nonrabbis might or in fact did respond to rabbinic interpretations of scripture. This and comparable forms of self-consciousness are missing from statements involving Babylonian rabbis (but see below).

A story in the Bavli about Rabban Gamliel, a Palestinian patriarch and rabbi, is strikingly similar to the conclusion of the story of R. Meir and the Romans.[37] It also resembles the stories examined above in that it depicts mockery of a great rabbi, but once again unlike the Palestinian accounts the Bavli's narrative describes an encounter between two rabbis:

> Rabban Gamliel sat and expounded, "In the future a woman will give birth every day, as it is written, 'She conceives and gives birth at the same time'" (Jer. 31:7).[38]
>
> A certain student mocked him. He said, "'There is nothing new under the sun'" (Eccles. 1:9).
>
> [Rabban Gamliel] said to him, "Come and I will show you its like in this world."
>
> He went out and showed him a hen.
>
> Again Rabban Gamliel sat and expounded, "In the future trees will bear fruit every day, as it is written, 'It shall bring forth branches and produce fruit' (Ezek. 17:23), just as a branch [grows] every day, so too fruit [grows] every day."
>
> A certain student mocked him. [The student] said to him, "Behold it is written, 'There is nothing new under the sun'" (Eccles. 1:9).
>
> [Rabban Gamliel] said to him, "Come and I will show you its like in this world."
>
> He went out and showed him a caper bush.
>
> Again Rabban Gamliel sat and expounded, "In the future the land of Israel will give forth loaves of bread and fine woolen garments, as it is said, 'Let abundant grain be in the land'" (Ps. 72:16).
>
> A certain student mocked him and said, "'There is nothing new under the sun'" (Eccles. 1:9).
>
> He went out and showed him mushrooms and truffles; and as to [something corresponding to] fine woolen garments, [he showed him] the bark of a young palm shoot.[39]

This story, like several others analyzed above, is intent upon demonstrating the truth even of the rabbis' most outrageous statements. And like the narrative of

R. Meir and the Romans, this story delivers its message in a comparatively lighthearted fashion. The story in the Bavli thus preserves intact motifs that appear to derive from Palestine. Like the Babylonian version of the R. Yoḥanan story with which we began this study, however, the Bavli delivers its message in a narrative involving a rabbi and his student. While the story apparently derives from Palestine, therefore, it has been partially Babylonianized, as we found to be the case with the other narratives analyzed above.[40]

Several other Palestinian rabbinic traditions are self-conscious about nonrabbinic reaction to idiosyncratic forms of rabbinic Bible exegesis. These narratives take it for granted that at least some exegetical techniques that convince rabbis will not suffice when rabbis debate heretics. As a result, some of these narratives depict Palestinian rabbis using radical, noncontextual methods of interpretation among themselves and less radical methods that adhere more closely to the biblical context when debating heretics.[41] These stories further exemplify my claim regarding the sensitivity of Palestinian rabbis to at least the possibility of unfavorable nonrabbinic reaction to their statements.

In y. Sanhedrin 1:4 (19b), for example:

> Agnatos[42] the general asked R. Yoḥanan be Zakkai, " 'The ox shall be stoned and its owner shall also die' " (Exod. 21:29). [What did the owner do to deserve to die?]
>
> [R. Yoḥanan] said to him, "The highwayman's partner is like the highwayman."
>
> When [R. Yoḥanan] left, his students said to him, "Rabbi, you pushed that one off with a reed. What can you answer us?"
>
> He said to them, "It is written, 'The ox shall be stoned and its owner shall also die' (Exod. 21:29). The death of the owner is like the death of the ox. [Scripture] juxtaposed the death of the owners to the death of the ox. Just as the death of the owners [is carried out only following] examination and investigation[43] [which must be done before a court of] 23 [judges], so too the death of the ox [is carried out only following examination and investigation of the witnesses before a court of] 23 [judges]."

The rabbi responds to the nonrabbi with "logic," but to his students he responds with a standard, but nonetheless radical, rabbinic exegetical method (*hekesh*) that ignores the context of the biblical verse. The text expresses the desirability of hiding from the nonrabbi the true, precious meaning of scripture, which he does not deserve to know because he will only abuse it. The rabbi's reticence is due, it would appear, to his contempt for the non-Jew, but it may also be in part a reaction to or anticipation of a hostile response to a radical rabbinic exegetical technique.

Similarly, in Pesikta de-Rav Kahana 4:7:[44]

> A non-Jew asked R. Yoḥanan ben Zakkai. He said to him, "The thing you [Jews] do appears to be a kind of sorcery. You bring a cow, slaugh-

> ter it, burn it, crush it to powder, and gather its ashes. When one of you gets defiled by a corpse you sprinkle on him two or three drops and you say to him, 'You are clean.' "
>
> [R. Yoḥanan ben Zakkai] said to him, "Has the spirit of madness ever seized you?"
>
> He said to him, "No."
>
> He said to him, "Have you ever seen someone seized by a spirit of madness?"
>
> He said to him, "Yes."
>
> [R. Yoḥanan] said to him, "What do you do?"
>
> He said to him, "We bring roots and make them smoke underneath him, and we sprinkle water upon him and [the spirit] flees."
>
> [R. Yoḥanan] said to him, "Don't your ears hear what your mouth is saying? So too this spirit is a spirit of uncleanness, as it is said, 'I will make [false] prophets as well as the unclean spirit [vanish from the land]' " (Zech. 13:2).
>
> And when [the non-Jew] left, his students said to him, "Master, you pushed this one off with a reed. What can you say to us?"
>
> He said to them, "By your lives, the dead do not cause impurity nor does the water cleanse. Rather, it is the decree of the Holy One, blessed be He. Said the Holy One, blessed be He, 'I have set down a statute; I have decreed a decree, and you are not permitted to transgress My decree. "This is the statute of the Torah" ' " (Num. 19:1).

In this case, the rabbi supplies an answer that appeals to the outsider, but to his students he asserts that the issue has no "reason" beyond the fact that it is divinely mandated.[45] Significantly, this dialogue form ("You have pushed them off with a reed. What can you say to us?"), which always involves a rabbi and his students commenting on a dialogue between the rabbi and heretics or non-Jews, is found exclusively in Palestinian compilations, further support for my claim regarding Palestinian rabbis.[46]

The closest Babylonian analogue to the type of self-consciousness exhibited above is found in an anonymous Babylonian editorial discussion in b. Sanhedrin 46b, which unambiguously expresses awareness of the likelihood that a rabbinic exegetical technique will fail to convince nonrabbis. The anonymous editors there discuss a dialogue between Rav Ḥama, a Babylonian Amora, and the Persian monarch, Shapur. Shapur asks Rav Ḥama what verse in the Torah mandates burial of the human body after death, and when Rav Ḥama fails to respond, the anonymous editors suggest that he should have answered with a midrashic interpretation of the verse "You shall surely bury him" (Deut. 21:23), which depends on the doubling of the verb "to bury." The anonymous editors respond to their own objection by observing that Shapur, a nonrabbi, would have found this standard (but nevertheless radical and noncontextual) midrashic technique to be unacceptable and unconvincing. In this case, therefore, the attitudes of Babylonian rabbis approximate those of their Palestinian counterparts.

It is significant, however, that this case involves a rabbi conversing with a Persian monarch. Babylonian rabbis had much to be anxious about, and much to gain from, contact with Persian royalty. As noted in the introduction, my conclusions regarding the insularity and relatively secure social position of Babylonian rabbis apply only to rabbis vis-à-vis their social subordinates. My earlier research revealed that portrayals of interactions between Babylonian rabbis and their social superiors (for example, Persian kings, government officials, and the Jewish exilarch and his entourage) follow different patterns from those between rabbis and their social inferiors.[47] We need not accept the historicity of this story's portrayal of a conversation between a Babylonian rabbi and a Persian king to understand why the anonymous editors would care about how such a king might react to a radical form of rabbinic scriptural exegesis, but not care when "lesser" individuals were involved.[48]

It is also possible that this case is an example, one of many, of statements by and stories involving later Babylonian rabbis departing from patterns observable in statements attributed to earlier Babylonians and conforming to patterns observable in traditions involving and attributed to Palestinian rabbis. As I have noted several times, the anonymous editorial layer of the Bavli is a relatively late layer of Babylonian rabbinic discourse. That the anonymous Babylonian editors follow what is otherwise a Palestinian pattern, therefore, is in keeping with later Babylonian trends observable throughout the Talmud, for reasons I touched on in the introduction and will explore further in the conclusion.

Finally, it would be surprising if in a literature as vast and variable as that of the rabbis of late antiquity we found no overlap whatsoever between Palestinian and Babylonian rabbis on the issues of concern here. As also noted in the introduction, matters are seldom unambiguous where culture and attitude are concerned. Typically, we find differing shades of gray rather than diametrically opposed categories of black and white, and we may be simply dealing here with the exception that proves the rule.[49]

A story about Rav Sheshet in b. Berakhot 58a sheds further light on Babylonian rabbinic tendencies. This story depicts (1) a "heretic–rabbinic disciple"[50] (*mina bar bei rav*)[51] serving as a Babylonian Amora's mocking antagonist; and (2) the Amora reducing the heretic to a pile of bones. While certainty on this issue is at present beyond our grasp, the ensuing discussion argues that this story about a Babylonian Amora illustrates the extent to which the Palestinian motif of a humiliating encounter between a rabbi and a nonrabbi was perceived as incongruous in a Babylonian setting.

The story, I will argue, may have originated in Palestine, but it served the didactic purposes of Babylonian rabbinic storytellers and/or editors to feature as its protagonist Rav Sheshet, the archetypical blind scholar. Once the story featured a Babylonian protagonist, the *mina* became a *mina bar bei rav* ("heretic–rabbinic disciple"), in accordance with the Babylonian tendency to depict the humiliation of rabbis as an internal rabbinic affair. This awkward designation "heretic–rabbinic disciple" (*mina bar bei rav*), found nowhere else in rabbinic literature, is one of several indications that the story may have had a complicated prehistory before it attained its present form.

This story teaches that the evidence of the senses alone is of little help in navigating one's way through the world.[52] What is really necessary is spiritual insight, which one derives from the study of Torah. The story features Rav Sheshet, a late third-, early fourth-century CE Babylonian rabbi, not because the events it describes "really happened" to him, but because he is the most appropriate protagonist of a story that emphasizes the impotence of physical sight alone, and the power of spiritual insight that comes from the correct interpretation of scripture. While the story's protagonist is a Babylonian Amora, therefore, the "historical" Rav Sheshet is not the story's concern, but rather Rav Sheshet the symbol of the scholar who knows the proper balance between tradition and the physical senses, and even of the Jewish people vis-à-vis their gentile oppressors. The Jewish people, this story teaches, are weak and powerless in comparison to their Persian and Roman overlords, but ultimately the tables will be turned. Like Rav Sheshet, the Jews will perceive the king before the wicked gentiles, and like the heretic, the gentiles will ultimately be discomfited.[53]

The story, in b. Berakhot 58a, is as follows:

> Rav Sheshet was blind. Everyone was going to greet the king and Rav Sheshet went with them. A heretic–rabbinic disciple found him and said, "Whole pitchers go to the river [for water]; where do broken ones go?"[54]
>
> [Rav Sheshet] said to him, "Come and see that I know more than you."
>
> A first troop of soldiers passed by, making a lot of noise.
>
> The heretic said to him, "The king has come."[55]
>
> Rav Sheshet said, "[The king] has not come."
>
> A second troop of soldiers passed by, making a lot of noise.
>
> The heretic said to him, "Now the king has come."
>
> Rav Sheshet said to him, "The king has not come."
>
> A third troop of soldiers passed by in silence.
>
> Rav Sheshet said to him, "Certainly now the king has come."
>
> The heretic said to him, "How do you know this?"
>
> [Rav Sheshet] said to him, "The earthly kingdom is like the heavenly kingdom, as it is written, 'Go out and stand on the mountain before God. And behold, God passed by. [There was] a great and mighty wind, splitting mountains and shattering apart rocks by the power of God; but God was not in the wind. After the wind, an earthquake; God was not in the earthquake. After the earthquake, fire; but God was not in the fire. After the fire, a soft murmuring sound'" (1 Kings 19:11–12).
>
> When the king came, Rav Sheshet opened and blessed him.
>
> The heretic said to him, "You are blessing someone that you do not see!"

> And what happened to the heretic? Some say Persian priests put out his eyes,[56] and some say Rav Sheshet cast his eyes on him and he became a pile of bones.

As noted, the blind Rav Sheshet is better able to "see" what really matters, and is better able to interpret the evidence of his senses than the sighted heretic. Rav Sheshet understands what he perceives because he has scripture and knows how to interpret it; the heretic relies on his physical senses alone, which leads him astray since he lacks the ability to interpret scripture.

It is likely that the "king" in this story stands for the messiah or God. Even though the king does eventually arrive at the story's conclusion, this is very likely a preview of the advent of the messianic period or the end of days, since, as noted, what happens to Rav Sheshet and the heretic is on one level to be understood as a forecast of things to come for the Jewish people and the gentiles.

The heretic berates Rav Sheshet for blessing someone he does not see, unmindful of the irony of his words. Rav Sheshet blesses the earthly king whom he does not see, just as it is appropriate to bless the heavenly king whom it is impossible to see. According to the first version of the story's ending the heretic is punished measure for measure. He mocked Rav Sheshet's blindness so he, too, becomes blind; now he is both spiritually and physically blind. According to the second version, Rav Sheshet again demonstrates the greater power of his vision, putting the heretic to death with his sightless eyes in a reversal of the common trope of the physically powerless blind man, and in conformity with the motif of the blind man who sees and understands.[57] Rav Sheshet's blind eyes are actually quite powerful after all.[58]

The story implies that the physical senses unaided by scripture are an extremely blunt instrument, but it stops short of saying that the evidence of one's senses is necessarily inimical to spiritual insight, that the two necessarily contradict. Rav Sheshet makes use of the limited senses he has, informed by the powerful tool of scripture, to come to correct conclusions about the world and about God. The story contrasts reliance on one's senses independent of scripture, which leads to the arrogance and error of the heretic, to reliance on one's physical senses informed by scripture, which leads to the wisdom, insight, and power displayed by Rav Sheshet.

It also bears mentioning that the Rav Sheshet story is one of only two cases in which a story depicts interaction between a Babylonian rabbi and a heretic (*min*).[59] As I have noted elsewhere, in the overwhelming majority of cases, the sources depict interaction between Palestinian rabbis and heretics.[60] In addition, the Rav Sheshet story is the only one I have discovered thus far that depicts a Babylonian rabbi reducing someone[61] to a pile of bones. The possibility cannot be excluded that the present story as well originated in Palestine, and when it traveled to Babylonia it preserved its original character as a dialogue between a rabbi and a heretic, but was partially Babylonianized, in that (1) the figure of Rav Sheshet, the blind scholar, became attached to it because he served as such a powerful symbol due to his character as the archetypical blind sage, and (2) an encounter between a rabbi and a nonrabbi (*mina*) became an encounter between two rabbis. The story's rather complicated (hypothesized) history may be indicated by the awkward *hapax legomenon*, "heretic–rabbinic disciple," which, if the above analysis is correct, bears witness to both its Palestinian and Babylonian heritage.

Many of the stories above were motivated in part by the rabbis' discomfort and self-consciousness about their status in the eyes of nonrabbis. I argued above that this discomfort appears to have been experienced more acutely in Palestine than in Babylonia, because Palestinian rabbis were more closely involved with nonrabbis. Real or anticipated attacks against Palestinian rabbis based on the absurdity or unreliability of their opinions, for example, provoked anxious and often ferocious literary counterattacks that depicted the sudden death of their nonrabbinic antagonists.

Such motifs are rare in traditions attributed to and stories involving Babylonian rabbis. When we found such traditions in the Bavli, including traditions that have explicit parallels in Palestinian compilations, those responsible for the mockery were not heretics, Samaritans, or *amei ha-areẓ*, but other rabbis or rabbis-in-training. For Babylonian rabbis, the prospect and no doubt the reality of mockery by students or colleagues in the presence of other rabbis was a major preoccupation; the prospect of humiliation by a nonrabbi hardly seems to have troubled them at all, (1) because they minimized their contact with nonrabbis to the extent possible, and (2) because they were socially secure and had little to fear from the community.

As noted, these conclusions do not require positing that the Palestinian rabbinic stories and statements under discussion are the result of actual encounters between rabbis and nonrabbis, but neither can we dismiss this possibility. In other words, it is possible that some of the traditions under discussion, edited, stylized, and designed to impart a polemical message though they certainly are, derive from actual encounters. For my present purposes, however, it is enough to say that in making these statements and in telling these stories, Palestinian rabbis anticipated the unfavorable reaction of nonrabbis to rabbinic interpretations of scripture, statements about the nature of the world, humanity, and God, rabbinic interpretations of dreams, and the like, and that the anticipation of these reactions was enough to motivate the creation of narratives in which the rabbis humiliated their antagonists as badly as they wished to humiliate the rabbis.

5

Idolatry in Late Antique Babylonia

I observed in the introduction that the tendency of Babylonian rabbis prior to the mid–fourth century to avoid informal contacts with nonrabbis, to refrain from marrying into their families and accepting them into the rabbinic movement on the basis of acquired merit, established Babylonian rabbis as more Persian than Roman. This chapter proceeds in the same direction, arguing that Persian attitudes and practices with regard to idols and idol worship also had a significant impact on Babylonia, constituting another respect in which Babylonia was more Persian than Roman during the period under discussion.

To be specific, I find that the Babylonian Talmud attests to a distinction between Parthian and Sasanian Babylonia that corresponds to and provides a measure of confirmation of scholarly claims regarding the different policies of the Parthian and Sasanian dynasties with respect to idols. Mary Boyce and others claim that the Sasanian Persians, in contrast to the Parthians who routinely worshipped idols, proscribed statues and raised reliefs used in cultic ceremonies, although they permitted rock reliefs, rock carvings, and drawing that were not the objects of cultic worship. Along the same lines, Philippe Gignoux writes of "the iconoclastic taboo of Sasanian Zoroastrianism." Michael Morony similarly documents the decline of public paganism and its survival in private contexts in Sasanian Persia. While firm conclusions are not possible due to the paucity of evidence, the one tradition in the Bavli that depicts Babylonian rabbis confronted with a pagan statue in a public place is set during the Parthian period; rabbis from the Sasanian period, judging from the evidence of the Bavli, encountered idols only when they went out of their way to find them.[1]

It bears emphasizing, however, that the Bavli's paucity of evidence does not mean that the conclusions of this chapter rest on a mere argument from silence. This is so because the Bavli is not silent when it comes to Palestine, but only (relatively speaking) when it comes to Babylonia. Why the difference? Why the selectivity, with idols portrayed as impinging regularly on the rabbis in Palestine but hardly at all in Babylonia? The answer of this chapter is that the literary differences reflect a difference in historical circumstance, a conclusion supported by modern scholarly theories regarding a basic distinction between idolatry in the Sasanian and Roman empires.

For this reason, I concentrate on traditions in the Bavli, both concerning Babylonia and Palestine.[2] Had I contrasted (1) portrayals of Palestine in the Yerushalmi, for example, with (2) portrayals of Babylonia in the Bavli, the differences might be attributable to differences between the two compilations and the types of material they include and exclude. However, since all of the portrayals derive from the Bavli (with numerous Palestinian parallels cited in the notes), the difference is more likely due to historical circumstances, given the corroboration provided by the non-Jewish Persian and Roman evidence.

In addition, this chapter takes issue with the conventional scholarly view that the rabbis of late antiquity were single-mindedly opposed to idol worship. I argue that at least some rabbis, both Palestinian and Babylonian, found idol worship far more attractive than scholars have heretofore imagined. The Talmud provides a record of late antique rabbinic anxiety about idolatry in part because the rabbis were struggling to convince themselves that idols were inefficacious and unreal and that idolatry was totally worthless.

This chapter, therefore, allows us to penetrate through the apparent confidence with which the rabbis rejected pagan culture, and permits, it is hoped, a more nuanced understanding of their attitudes toward that culture. This study complements an earlier study that argued that at least some rabbis of late antiquity were attracted to Christianity, and that several of their most fiercely polemical statements about it were attempts to suppress that attraction, for example by dramatizing the disasters that resulted when one indulged one's fascination with the forbidden "other."[3]

Finally, this chapter suggests that there may have been a basic disconnect between Babylonian rabbinic anxiety about idolatry on the one hand and historical reality on the other, according to which the actual threat of idolatry in late antique Persia was quite remote. This disconnect, I will argue, further supports my characterization of Babylonian rabbis as to a significant extent relating to the outside world through the medium of texts. In the texts they received from Palestine, idolatry was very much a live concern, a concern that fueled some very vivid expressions of anxiety on the part of Babylonian rabbis despite the remoteness of an actual threat in Sasanian Babylonia.

Purported Palestinian and Babylonian Rabbinic Contact with Idols

As noted, we find a clear distinction between traditions in the Bavli that purport to describe reality in Babylonia and those that purport to describe reality in

Palestine. Literary references to idols in Babylonian traditions are particularly scarce. Idols in Babylonia, to judge from the relatively meager literary evidence, did not impinge upon the rabbis unless the rabbis took the initiative and sought them out. For reasons noted above, and to be elaborated upon below, it is not unreasonable to conclude that the Bavli's literary portrayal is an accurate representation of historical reality in Sasanian Babylonia.

Several modern scholars agree that the archaeological and literary evidence from Roman Palestine presents a picture of relatively frequent Palestinian rabbinic contact with idols.[4] The following tradition, in b. Moed Katan 25b,[5] highlights the contrast between the situation in Palestine and Babylonia:[6]

> When R. Abahu died, the pillars of Caesarea shed tears. When R. Yosi died, the rainspouts of Sepphoris discharged blood. When R. Yaakov died, stars were seen during the daytime. When R. Asi died, all of the trees were uprooted. When R. Ḥiyya died, meteorites fell down from the sky. When R. Menaḥem son of R. Simai[7] died, all the statues were smoothed down and became like mats.[8] When R. Tanḥum bar Ḥiyya died, all of the statues[9] were cut down. When Rav Elyashiv died, 70 break-ins took place in Nehardea. When Rav Hamnuna died, hailstones fell down from the sky. When Rabbah and Rav Yosef died, the stones of the Euphrates River kissed one another. When Rav Mesharshya died, the date palms bore bad dates.[10]

This collection of traditions reports miracles that purportedly took place when prominent rabbis died. The lesson is that inanimate objects and cosmic phenomena publicly acknowledged the greatness of these rabbis at the time of their deaths. Only the accounts of events attending the deaths of Palestinian rabbis involve statues in public contexts; the accounts of Babylonian rabbis in the same collection do not.

R. Menaḥem son of R. Simai, one of the rabbis mentioned in this collection, is referred to elsewhere in rabbinic literature as an extreme opponent of pagan symbolism.[11] The objects that honor him after his death, therefore, are particularly appropriate. The point is evidently not that rabbinic and pagan culture are implacably opposed, and that the death of the rabbi was an appropriate occasion to demonstrate the inferiority of pagan culture, but rather that this particular rabbi, renowned as an especially zealous opponent of certain aspects of pagan culture, was honored in a fashion that befit the values he espoused during his lifetime. This is why R. Menaḥem son of R. Simai, a marginal figure about whom very little is known and from whom very little has been preserved, received this honor, rather than a rabbi such as R. Yoḥanan, whose deeds and statements fill the pages of both Talmuds.

M. Avodah Zarah 3:4[12] further attests the relatively wide diffusion of statues of the gods in Palestine:

> Proclus ben Philosophos[13] asked Rabban Gamliel, who was in Acco bathing in the bathhouse of Aphrodite, "It is written in your Torah, 'Let nothing that has been doomed [by its association with

> idolatry] stick to your hand' (Deut. 13:18). Why then do you bathe in Aphrodite's bathhouse?"
>
> He replied, "One does not reply in the bathhouse."
>
> When he had come out he said to him, "I did not enter into her domain, she entered into mine. One does not say, 'Let us make the bathhouse an ornament to Aphrodite; rather it is Aphrodite who is an ornament to the bathhouse.'"[14]

This story depicts a rabbi coming in contact with a statue of a prominent pagan goddess during the course of his daily life. Despite the story's claim to the contrary, pagan cultic activities took place even in bathhouses.[15] Still, the distinction between a statue that had been formally consecrated and one that had not served as an object of cultic worship was a familiar one in the Greco-Roman world.[16]

Another story, in b. Avodah Zarah 50a, similarly depicts the situation in Palestine:

> (1) The house of King Yannai was in ruins. Idol worshippers set up in it [stones for the worship of] Mercury [*Markolis*]. Other idol worshippers who did not worship Mercury took [the stones] and paved with them roads and streets. Some rabbis stayed away and other rabbis did not. Said R. Yoḥanan, "The son of the holy ones walks on them and we should stay away from them?"
>
> (2) And who is "the son of the holy ones?"
>
> (3) R. Menaḥem son of R. Simai.[17]

While it is unclear precisely when the roads and streets were supposedly paved with the stones of a Mercury, the question of whether or not to walk on these stones clearly is portrayed as a preoccupation of third-century rabbis, during the lifetime of R. Yoḥanan. An object of pagan worship intrudes upon the public space of Palestinian rabbis and demands a rabbinic response. The fact that the rabbis are permissive is not my concern, since their positions varied on this issue. What is constant is the fact that the sources depict the problem confronting them in Palestine but not in Babylonia.

Another brief narrative set in Palestine portrays an object of worship as a public nuisance:

> Rabbah bar bar Ḥanah said [that] R. Yehoshua ben Levi said, "One time I was walking on the road behind R. Elazar Hakapar Beribbi. He found there a ring on which was an engraving of a dragon. He found an idolater who was a child and he said nothing to him. He found an idolater who was an adult and he said to him, "Nullify it," but he didn't nullify it. He slapped him and he nullified it.[18]

If the rabbis did not consider the ring to be an object of pagan worship, there would have been no need to "nullify it." These few examples will suffice to illustrate my claim that in Palestine idols impinged on rabbis during the course of their daily lives. It would be a simple matter to provide additional examples, from Palestinian compilations as well as from the Bavli.

As noted, the Bavli's depiction of the situation in Babylonia is markedly different. Babylonian rabbis encounter idols only rarely, and these encounters do not come about during the routine interactions of daily life. In one tradition, for example, we find:

> Rav Menasheh went to Bei Torta.[19]
> They said to him, "An idol[20] stands here."
> He took a clod and threw it at it.
> They said to him, "It is a Mercury [*Markolis*, and by throwing the clod at it, you have worshipped it]."
> He said to them, "We learn [in a mishnah], 'One who throws a stone at a Markolis' [and I threw a clod]."[21]
> He went and asked in the study house.
> They said to him, "We learn [in a mishnah], 'One who throws a stone at a Markolis,' even though he intends to stone it."
> He said to them, "Shall I go and remove it?"
> They said to him, "One is liable whether one puts it there or one removes it. Each one [who removes it] leaves space for another [to place a new one there]."

This story, set in Babylonia, depicts the idol as something the rabbi goes out of his way to encounter, rather than as something that confronts him during the course of his everyday life.[22] Rav Menasheh encounters the idol only after being informed by unnamed interlocutors that "an idol stands here." It is not something that he notices on his own or that stands in the public domain, unlike the statues that publicly honor the Palestinian rabbis, R. Menaḥem son of R. Simai and R. Tanḥum bar Ḥiyya, or the Aphrodite that occupied the bathhouse in Acco (see above).

An idolatrous temple referred to in a Babylonian context in a narrative in b. Avodah Zarah 55a likewise does not directly impinge on the rabbis:

> Said Rava bar Rav Yizḥak to Rav Yehudah, "Behold there is a temple of an idol in our locality. When the world needs rain, [the idol] appears to them in a dream and says to them, 'Slaughter for me a man and I will bring rain.'[23] They slaughter for it a man and rain comes."

As in the previous example, and unlike several of the cases that purport to take place in Palestine, this idol does not have a specific name, but is simply a generic "idol." In addition, the rabbi says explicitly that the idol, or the god who dwells in the idol, appears "to them," that is, to the idolaters, "in a dream," making it clear that his report is not based on personal experience.

One reference to a statue in a public place in Babylonia is of enormous importance to my inquiry:[24]

> Behold the synagogue of Shaf ve-Yatev in Nehardea[25] in which they had set up a statue, and Abuha de-Shmuel and Levi[26] entered it and prayed in it and they did not worry about suspicion.[27]

Of crucial importance is the fact that the rabbis involved, Abuha de-Shmuel and Levi, flourished in Babylonia prior to the advent of the Sasanian dynasty, that is, prior to a period of intensive Persian opposition to and destruction of statues and images that were the objects of cultic worship.[28] If the rabbis featured in the story are reliable indicators of its chronology, then the story's depiction of a statue in a public place in Babylonia during the Parthian period supports my conclusions in this chapter regarding the place of Mesopotamia within the Persian orbit.

A narrative in b. Avodah Zarah 55a may also be relevant to my inquiry.[29] This narrative is a purported dialogue between R. Akiba and a certain Zunin, most of which is in Hebrew, except for an Aramaic introduction that is of primary concern to me here. Zunin asks, in Aramaic, why "men go [to the pagan temple] crippled and come back healed."[30] The Aramaic section of the story is either an editorial paraphrase of an earlier Hebrew version or a reconstruction of a portion of the narrative, which reached the editors in fragmentary condition. It is possible, therefore, that this source's reference to an idolatrous temple derives from and reflects reality in Babylonia, but once again, there is no indication that idols impinge on rabbis in the course of their daily lives.

All in all, therefore, the Bavli preserves a very minimal record of idols in Babylonia. While we must be wary about drawing far-reaching conclusions because of the paucity of evidence, as noted, none of the narratives portray these idols interfering with the everyday functioning of Jewish life in the public sphere. In addition, none of the narratives that feature rabbis who flourished during Sasanian rule place objects of pagan worship in the major centers of rabbinic settlement. One story is set in Bei Torta and involves Rav Menasheh, and another involves Rava bar Rav Yiẓḥak in his unnamed "locality." Both rabbis are extremely marginal in the Talmudic corpus, as is Bei Torta, and we have no basis whatsoever upon which to identify Rava bar Rav Yiẓḥak's place of residence.[31]

Rabbinic Anxiety about the Appeal of Idol Worship

Turning to rabbinic attitudes toward idols in the rabbinic present, we obtain what appears to be a markedly different result. Given the paucity of evidence for the existence of idols in Sasanian Babylonia, we would expect Babylonian rabbis to view the temptation to worship idols as a thing of the distant past, all but irresistible to biblical Israelites, but whose day has passed, such that in the rabbinic present it was only necessary to deal with idolatry, if at all, in its guise as a gentile practice.[32] Contrary to what we would expect, however, the Bavli provides a record of late antique rabbinic anxiety about idolatry, which would appear at first glance to lead to the conclusion that it remained a potent force in Sasanian Babylonia.

It is necessary, of course, to document this claim regarding Babylonian rabbinic attitudes, since earlier scholars have taken it for granted that the rabbis of late antiquity were single-mindedly opposed to idol worship. Ephraim Urbach,[33] for example, writes: "The prevailing view of the Sages in the third century [CE] was that the craving for idolatry had been uprooted and removed from Israel already at the beginning of the second Temple period."[34] Similarly, Saul Lieberman maintains: "Unlike the earlier Hellenistic Jews the Rabbis were no longer struggling with gentile paganism.... In the first centuries C.E. the Jews were so far removed from clear-cut idolatry that there was not the slightest need to argue and to preach against it."[35]

Lieberman writes further:

> A perusal of the *Letzanuta de-'Abodah Zarah* (ridiculing of the idols) found in early Talmudic sources will convince us that there is a great difference between the rabbinic and Christian attacks on idolatry. In rabbinic writings we possess only comparatively few scattered passages on this topic. The whole tractate of *'Abodah Zarah* which deals with idol worship and worshippers almost ignores this subject. It only records and discusses laws and precepts, but does not engage in refutations of principles of idol worship.[36]

Lieberman claims that "the Rabbis occasionally dramatize the abuse of the idols available in the Prophets" and asserts that "the rabbinic satire is only a literary elaboration of the Bible."[37] Urbach and Lieberman have no doubt that the rabbis were implacably and unproblematically opposed to idol worship,[38] while there was little to idolatry that even nonrabbinic Jews found attractive.[39]

The ensuing discussion analyzes a lengthy passage in the Bavli in an attempt to nuance this overly simplistic characterization of rabbinic attitudes,[40] although Lieberman is certainly correct that many rabbinic comments about idol worship are responses to or attempts to interpret the Bible. Perhaps the rabbis' anxiety was motivated by concern for the susceptibility of nonrabbinic Jews to the attractiveness of idolatry, but it is more likely that the Talmud, composed primarily of literature by rabbis and for rabbis, supplies evidence of attempts by rabbis to convince themselves or other rabbis of the inefficacy of idols.

This study may therefore lend weight from an unexpected source (the Babylonian Talmud) to scholarly claims of the continued vitality of paganism in the Roman Empire and, more surprisingly, even in Persian Babylonia, for centuries after the beginning of the common era.[41] Given the evidence surveyed above, however, which indicates the paucity of idols in Persia in general and Babylonia in particular, it appears that at least in Babylonia, this continued vitality was more in the minds of the rabbis than grounded in the realities of life in Sasanian Persia.

What is the evidence for the claim that the Bavli attests to rabbinic anxiety about the attractiveness of idols? It is not at all a simple matter to ferret out this evidence. In the description above of the miracles accompanying the deaths of great rabbis,[42] for example, are we to understand the apparent confidence with which the rabbis assert the idols' submissive gestures to the great rabbis, indeed, the very need of the rabbis to assert their superiority, as more or less transparent attempts on the rabbis' part to compensate for their anxieties? It is not enough for our purposes to point to statements that rule that idolatry is punishable by death, even the strictest form of execution, since such statements perhaps prove only that idol worship was the subject of intellectual interest, that the laws dealing with it were considered fitting subjects of Torah and therefore worthy of scrutiny by rabbis. One can make such statements without being motivated by some external stimulus, for example, Jewish involvement in or attraction to idol worship, or strong, vital, and very visible non-Jewish cultic activity. Similarly, one can make statements about the importance of idolatry to some biblical Israelites, and the heroic zeal with which other biblical figures opposed idol worship, and be motivated by nothing other than a desire to explicate the biblical text, or to embellish the biblical narrative in an attempt to improve upon the story,[43] or to rehabilitate a biblical character's reputation.[44]

One collection of stories, however, seems best explicable as evidence of rabbinic anxiety about phenomena that appear to support belief in the efficacy of idols.[45] For my purposes it is irrelevant whether or not the miracles, or even the phenomena interpreted as miracles, actually took place. What is important is that the rabbis took reports of these phenomena very seriously. Individual stories within the collection and, even more markedly, the stories as they play off and build upon one another, defuse the potentially explosive effect that arguments in favor of the efficacy of idols might have on the rabbis' audience.[46]

The compilation, found in b. Avodah Zarah 54b–55a, reads as follows:

> (1) Mishnah [First narrative:] They asked the elders in Rome, "If He [i.e., God] disapproves of idols,[47] why does He not nullify them?"[48]
>
> [The elders] said to them, "If they worshipped something that was of no use to the world, He would have nullified them. Behold they worship the sun, the moon, the stars, and the planets. Should He destroy His world because of lunatics?"
>
> They said to [the elders], "If so, let Him destroy things that the world has no use of, and leave alone things that the world needs."
>
> [The elders] said to them, "This would strengthen the hand of those who worship things [that the world needs], for they would say, 'Know that they are gods, for they were not nullified.'"
>
> (2) Talmud [First narrative:] Our rabbis taught [in a Tannaitic source]: Philosophers asked the elders in Rome, "If your God disapproves of idols, why does He not get rid of them?"

[The elders] said to them, "If they worshipped something that was of no use to the world, He would have gotten rid of them. They worship the sun, the moon, the stars, and the planets. Should He destroy His world because of lunatics? Rather the world proceeds in its customary fashion and lunatics that sin will give an accounting in the future." . . .

(3) [Second narrative:] A philosopher asked Rabban Gamliel, "It is written in your Torah, 'For the Lord your God is a consuming fire, an angry God' (Deut. 4:24). Why is He angry at those who worship idols but not at the idols themselves?"

[Rabban Gamliel] said to him, "I will tell you a parable: To what can the matter be compared? To a king of flesh and blood who had a son, and that son raised a dog and gave it the name of his father, and when he took an oath he said, 'By the life of Abba [i.e., Father] the dog.' When the king finds out, who is he angry at, the son or the dog? Surely he is angry at the son!"[49]

He said to him, "You call [the idol] a dog? Surely it has power!"

He said to him, "How do you know?"

He said to him, "One time fire fell on our city and burned the entire city, but its idolatrous temple was not burned."

He said to him, "I will tell you a parable: To what can the matter be compared? To a king of flesh and blood whose country rebelled against him. When he wages war, does he fight the living or the dead? Surely he fights the living!"

He said to him, "You call [the idol] a dog, you call it dead? If so, let him [i.e., your God] destroy it."

He said to him, "If they worshipped something that the world did not need, He would have gotten rid of it. They worship the sun, the moon, the stars, the planets, the springs, and the ravines. Should He destroy His world on account of lunatics?"

And thus it states, " 'Shall I sweep everything away from the face of the earth,' says the Lord; 'am I to sweep away man and beast; am I to sweep away the birds of the sky and the fish of the sea, the stumbling blocks of the wicked?' Because the wicked stumble over these things is He to destroy them from the world? Do they not worship humans also? So 'am I to destroy mankind from the face of the earth?' " (Zeph. 1:2–3).

(4) [Third narrative:] Agrippas the general asked Rabban Gamliel, "It is written in your Torah, 'For the Lord your God is a consuming fire, a jealous God' (Deut. 4:24).[50] Is a sage jealous of anyone but a sage, a hero of anyone but a hero, a rich man of anyone but a rich man?"

He said to him, "I will tell you a parable: To what can the matter be compared? To a man who married a woman in addition to his first wife. If she is of higher social standing, she is not jealous of her. If she is of lower social standing, she is jealous of her."

(5) [Fourth narrative:] Zunin said to R. Akiba, [Aramaic:] "You and I know that there is no reality to an idol. Yet we see men who go crippled and return healed. Why is this?"

He said to him, [Hebrew:] "I will tell you a parable: To what can the matter be compared? To a trusted man in a city. All the inhabitants of the city left deposits with him without witnesses. One man deposited with him with witnesses, but one time he forgot and deposited with him without witnesses. His wife said to him, 'Let us deny [that it was ever deposited with us].' He said to her, 'Because that lunatic acted improperly, we should destroy our reputation?' And so it is with sicknesses: When they send them upon a man, they make them swear that they will arrive on a certain day and will leave on a certain day and a certain time, by means of a certain man and a certain drug. When their time came to leave, the man went to an idolatrous temple. The sicknesses said, 'By rights we should not leave.' But then they say, 'Because this lunatic behaved improperly we should violate our oath?' "[51]

And this is [the same as] what R. Yoḥanan said, "What is [the meaning of] that which is written, 'Evil and trustworthy sicknesses' (Deut. 28:59)? Evil in their mission but trustworthy in their oath."

(6) [Fifth narrative:] Rava bar Rav Yiẓḥak said to Rav Yehudah, "There is a temple of an idol in our locality. When the world needs rain, it appears to them in a dream[52] and says to them, 'Slaughter a man for me and I will bring rain.' They slaughter [a man] for it and rain comes."

[Rav Yehudah] said to [Rava bar Rav Yiẓḥak], "If I were dead I could not have told you this statement by Rav: 'What is [the meaning of that] which is written, "Which the Lord your God has allotted [*ḥalak*] unto all peoples" (Deut. 4:19). This teaches that [God] causes them to slip [*heḥelik*] in their deeds in order to drive them from the world.' "

And this is similar to what R. Shimon ben Lakish said: "What is [the meaning of that] which is written, 'Surely He makes the scornful scorners [*la-leiẓim hu yaliẓ*],[53] but He gives grace to the lowly' (Prov. 3:34). If one wants to defile himself he is given the wherewithal to do so, and if he comes to purify himself support is given to him."

This collection of stories opens with a mishnaic account of a dialogue between "elders" (i.e., Jewish sages) and unnamed interlocutors, apparently non-Jews, in Rome. The first Talmudic story in the collection, purportedly a Baraita, is basically identical to the mishnaic account, although the elders' response is expanded slightly and the sages' interlocutors are referred to as "philosophers," and therefore certainly are intended to be non-Jews. The second Talmudic story involves a gentile philosopher in dialogue with Rabban Gamliel, who on numerous occasions is depicted as a spokesman for the Jews to non-Jews. No place is specified as the scene of their encounter, although given the conventions of rabbinic narrative, it is likely that we are to assume that it took place in Palestine, the locality of the rabbinic protagonist.

The fourth Talmudic story involves Zunin and R. Akiba, and once again we are probably to assume that the dialogue took place in Palestine. R. Akiba is the Palestinian rabbinic sage par excellence, the outstanding representative of the Tannaitic point of view, although it is unclear whether Zunin is supposed to be a Jew or a non-Jew. The fifth and final Talmudic story is the first in the collection that definitely involves two rabbis, and the scene has shifted to Babylonia.

I go into such detail about the characters and the locale because they provide important clues to the meaning of the stories and the purpose they serve in the larger collection. The opening mishnah and Baraita, which, as noted, are basically the same, feature unnamed philosophers and elders in Rome. Rome, of course, is the philosophers' home turf and the very center of pagan civilization. The objection by the philosophers is based on an apparent conflict between (1) observation of the normal functioning of the world, and (2) a rabbinic belief about God's attitude toward idolatry that is based on the Bible. The objection is based on God's inaction against idolatry, which the Bible and the rabbis claim He despises.

Given the nature of rabbinic literature as literature by rabbis for rabbis, this story is most likely not intended to convince non-Jews, but to satisfy Jews, and in fact to satisfy only rabbis, probably the sole intended audience of the story. From a rabbinic point of view, the objection is not a particularly serious or dangerous one, since it is based on observation of the ordinary rather than on miracles and the interpretation of texts, and the response, which is likewise not based on traditional texts, is all that the objection demands. Still, the very need to pose the question betrays at least a modicum of anxiety on the rabbis' part, and the sense that the opposition possesses arguments that must be responded to, even if only to make the rabbinic authors of the story feel more secure in their beliefs.

The main function of this collection, I argue, is to help the rabbis feel confident about their rejection of idol worship. The editors make their case in a rhetorically effective way, which they accomplish by shifting the scene from the least serious challenge in the most threatening environment (pagan Rome) to the most serious challenge in the least threatening environment (rabbinic Babylonia).[54] Arguments that the rabbinic audience of these tales can bear to hear expressed by rabbis among themselves in the relative safety of Babylonia, where idolatry is less of a threat than in Roman Palestine and certainly less than in Rome, would be intolerable were the locale and the participants different.

The second Talmudic narrative, as noted, is apparently set in Palestine and involves an unnamed philosopher in dialogue with Rabban Gamliel. By (1) choosing as his protagonist a rabbi customarily depicted as dealing with gentiles and representing Judaism before the Romans, and (2) by setting the dialogue in Palestine, the editor prepares his audience for a more difficult challenge. In this story, two objections are raised, the first of which is based on scripture,[55] which to a rabbinic audience is more serious than an objection based on observation of the world, and the second of which is based on a miracle that appears to attest to the efficacy of idols, on the fact that an entire town burned down with the exception of a pagan temple. Surely, it would appear, these are proofs that idols have efficacy and rabbinic beliefs are in error. But not to worry, for Rabban Gamliel's response both satisfies his gentile interlocutor and allays the fears of his rabbinic audience. The rabbi answers the gentile on his own terms, with parables that will engage the philosopher on logical rather than exegetical or dogmatic grounds, and the (Babylonian?) editor of the collection affixes a rabbinic interpretation of scripture to the end of the story, satisfying his rabbinic audience.

As noted, the fourth Talmudic narrative involves Zunin and R. Akiba and is also set in Palestine. While it is not clear whether Zunin is a gentile or a Jew,[56] the fact that Akiba answers him with a parable rather than a traditional text establishes beyond doubt that he is not a rabbi.[57] The fact that the rabbinic interlocutor is R. Akiba further allays the audience's fears, since R. Akiba typically fills the role of "the greatest rabbi who ever lived," for whom no question is too difficult. As soon as R. Akiba's name is mentioned, the audience knows it is in capable hands, and that no fundamental rabbinic principles will be undermined or even weakened as a result of this encounter.

Furthermore, Zunin's assertion at the outset, "You and I know that there is no reality to an idol," assures us immediately that any arguments raised on behalf of idolatry will fail to convince. The audience needs these assurances, because Zunin's objection is very serious, the most serious one raised thus far. As in the second narrative, Zunin's objection is based on a miracle, but while the second narrative's miracle was a one-time event that could be attributed easily to coincidence, Zunin's miracle happened repeatedly and is more difficult to explain away. Zunin does not explicitly say, furthermore, that *some* people enter the idolatrous shrine crippled and come out cured. His phraseology admits of a stronger interpretation, namely, that the miracle happens to everyone who enters the temple, with no exceptions at all.

Once again, the rabbi resolves the objection with a parable, aimed at demonstrating to the audience the rabbi's ability to convince his interlocutor. Appended to the story, not part of the story but a crucially important part of the collection, is a scriptural interpretation by no less an authority than R. Yoḥanan, which demonstrates to the rabbinic audience the truth of R. Akiba's arguments. In responding with a mere parable, R. Akiba may have "pushed Zunin off with a reed,"[58] that is, with an argument that would have sufficed to convince a nonrabbi; it would have failed, however, to convince a rabbinic audience. The statement of R. Yoḥanan, which consists of a proof from scripture, demonstrates to the rabbinic audience that Zunin's challenge has been fully met.

In the collection's final story, we move from Palestine to Babylonia, and from a dialogue between a rabbi and either (1) a gentile sage or (2) a nonrabbinic Jew to a dialogue between rabbis. The audience's fears are once again allayed at the outset, since nothing that rabbis say to one another will dramatically challenge rabbinic belief, and any doubts that rabbis express will remain safely within the confines of the rabbinic study house. No rabbi and no Jew will be humiliated; no Jewish dogma will be ridiculed or seriously undermined.

Adding to this feeling of security is the fact that the story is set in rabbinic Babylonia, where idolatry is absent from the public sphere, and where rabbis are more securely sheltered from the rest of humanity (i.e., nonrabbis) than are their counterparts in Palestine. In other words, it works rhetorically for the most difficult challenge to be placed in the mouth of one rabbi in dialogue with another, particularly one Babylonian rabbi in the presence of another. Had a nonrabbi posed the most serious challenge, it would have increased its effectiveness in the eyes of the audience. And the more effective the challenge, the more defensive the rabbi's response appears and the less rhetorically effective.

In formulating this challenge to Jewish belief, it appears that the final narrative goes out of its way to present the idol worshipper's point of view as effectively as possible, as if the rabbis can express their worst fears in the privacy of the study house. According to Rava bar Rav Yiẓḥak in the final narrative, *whenever there is drought*, the idol that inhabits the pagan temple in his locality appears to the priests of the temple and demands a human sacrifice, in return for which he promises rain. There is no effort to debunk the miracle; it is presented even more forcefully than the miracle described in the previous story as something that happens without exception. And the rabbi grants a shocking amount of reality to the idol, which appears to the priests in a dream and gives them explicit instructions. The idol is not mute or at work behind the scenes, but is given a speaking role.

And this final story presents the most serious problem, because we are no longer dealing, as in the mishnah and the first Talmudic narrative, with God's decision to refrain from action and to allow the world to operate according to its own laws; nor are we dealing, as in the second Talmudic narrative, with God's apparent decision to spare the pagan temple; nor, as in the fourth Talmudic narrative, with God's apparent decision to heal the sick despite their visit to a pagan shrine. Rather, in this final narrative pagans kill human beings, which runs counter to everything that rabbis allow themselves to imagine the Jewish God tolerating. And yet the pagan murderers are rewarded, apparently by the idol that inhabits the temple and demands the human sacrifices.

And only in this last story, a dialogue between rabbis, is the author of the objection answered with scripture and scripture alone. Only this last story contains no proverbs, because scripture alone, as interpreted by the rabbis to other rabbis, is in need of no additional support. The rabbi's response is buttressed by a scriptural interpretation drawn from a rabbinic statement originating in a different context, perhaps to say that it is not only in the heat of debate that this interpretation is valid, plucked out of midair to respond to an extremely vexing problem. Another rabbi interpreted scripture in precisely the same manner in an entirely unpolemical context.

The seriousness of the final objection calls for a correspondingly fierce portrayal of God's hatred of idols and idolaters. In the final story, God is so violently opposed to idolatry that He creates opportunities for idolaters to sin further, even going out of His way to make idolatry more and more irresistible to them. Such a depiction of God's hatred of idolatry and idolaters is satisfying to an audience listening in on a dialogue between rabbis. In depicting such a dialogue, the storyteller can vent his anger and frustration over the fact that reality fails to refute pagans and paganism, by attributing precisely the same sentiments to God. In depicting dialogues between rabbis and nonrabbis, particularly non-Jewish idolaters, the (Babylonian?) editor of the collection and/or the authors of the individual stories depict the rabbis as more discreet in their depiction of God. Apparently, these authors and editors are uncomfortable about depicting rabbis who are so impolitic and so foolhardy that they would unleash the full force of their fury on a believing pagan. In addition, the challenges posed prior to this final story have not warranted such fury in response.

Babylonian rabbis, therefore, viewed idol worship as a significant threat, and arguments in its favor provoked rabbinic anxiety and demanded refutation. Even though my survey of literary evidence for direct Babylonian rabbinic contact with idols turned up very little, the above discussion suggests that this evidence does not tell the whole story. Dramatic stories depicting the power of idols circulated in Babylonia, some deriving from Babylonia itself but others deriving from the Greco-Roman world or from times and places in the Persian Empire unaffected by the Sasanian destruction of idols, fueled in all likelihood by the Bible's profound obsession with idolatry, and by the tendency of any group to exaggerate the menace posed by outsiders.

It must be admitted that at present it is difficult to determine the extent to which this collection reflects rabbinic attitudes in Babylonia. It is possible that a significant portion of it reached Babylonia from Palestine, although we saw above that the last story is Babylonian from start to finish, and a crucial part of the penultimate story was Babylonian as well, at least in its present formulation. As noted, Zunin's opening pronouncement is in Aramaic while the rest of the story is in Hebrew, making it clear that anonymous Babylonian editors or storytellers are responsible for at least the current formulation of Zunin's statement, and perhaps for its content as well.

I have established, in any event, that at least for some Babylonian rabbis, the issue of the efficacy of idols and idol worship remained a live one until some time between (1) the mid– to late third century, when the dialogue between Rav Yehudah and Rava bar Rav Yiẓḥak purportedly took place; and (2) the sixth or seventh centuries CE, the time of the Bavli's final editing and therefore the latest possible date for the compilation of this collection.[59]

More Rabbinic Anxiety about Idols

Two traditions in the Bavli further demonstrate that despite the apparent rarity with which Babylonian rabbis encountered idols, they occupied a significant place in their consciousness. Unlike the stories analyzed above, however, the issue in these stories is not the danger that Jews will be attracted to idols, but rather that they will be tripped up by their very zeal to show their contempt.

B. Sanhedrin 64a,[60] for example, contains the following story.

> Our rabbis taught [in a Tannaitic tradition]: It happened that Sabta ben Elem rented his donkey to a gentile woman. When she reached Pe'or [the name of an idol], she said to him, "Wait until I go and come back." When she came back, he said to her, "You also wait until I go and come back."
>
> She said to him, "Aren't you a Jew?"
>
> He said to her, "What do you care?"
>
> He entered, uncovered himself [i.e., defecated] before [the idol], and wiped himself on [the idol's] nose. The priests of the idol praised him and said, "No one has ever worshipped him that way before."

This story, Palestinian in origin,[61] is a rabbinic burlesque of gentiles who the rabbis imagined would consider the most disgusting forms of idol worship to be the highest forms of piety.[62] For our purposes, the story is important because it warns Jews to stay away from idols, demonstrating that even when one treats an idol with the utmost contempt, one can never be certain what the outcome of that encounter will be. The Jew in the story unwittingly devised a new form of worship that won the enthusiastic endorsement of the pagan priests.

The same concern is reflected in a story, also in b. Sanhedrin 64a, involving Rav Menasheh, a Babylonian rabbi, in a Babylonian locality. I examined this story earlier in this chapter; due to its significance for my inquiry, I reproduce the translation here:

> Rav Menasheh went to Bei Torta.
>
> They said to him, "An idol stands here."
>
> He took a clod and threw it at it.
>
> They said to him, "It is a Mercury [Markolis, and by throwing the clod at it, you have worshipped it]."
>
> He said to them, "We learn [in a mishnah], 'One who throws a stone at a Markolis' [and I threw a clod]."
>
> He went and asked in the study house.
>
> They said to him, "We learn [in a mishnah], 'One who throws a stone at a Markolis,' even though he intends to stone it."
>
> He said to them, "Shall I go and remove it?"
>
> They said to him, "One is liable whether one puts it there or one removes it. Each one [who removes it] leaves space for another [to place a new one there]."

Unlike the stories in the lengthy narrative chain examined above, this narrative betrays no concern about the attractions of idol worship. Instead, it warns against any form of Jewish involvement in idolatry, even if one thinks that the conduct is "safe" and "rabbinically approved." There is no such thing as a safe encounter with an idol, argues this tradition, and all contact is forbidden contact. Once again, it appears that traditions in the Bavli manifest a preoccupation with idolatry out of proportion to the threat it posed in Sasanian Babylonia.

Rabbinic Polemics against Idolatry

A story about Rav Sheshet, in b. Berakhot 58a, may further support this claim. This story, analyzed in detail in chapter 4, expresses rabbinic anger toward idolatry and idol worshippers, but in contrast to the collection of narratives examined in the preceding section, it betrays no clear anxiety about the power of idols and the attractiveness of idol worship to Jews. It is also not clear from this story whether the concern of the rabbis is with the worship of statues per se, or with the worship of "things that the eyes can see" in general, irrespective of whether they are idols, human beings (such as emperors), or objects in nature (such as the sun or the moon).

It is not entirely clear, furthermore, precisely how much of this story reflects Babylonian attitudes, since, as noted in chapter 4, it is likely that the story originated in Palestine but was subjected after the fact to Babylonian manipulation. In Palestine, the story obviously would have had relevance as a protest against the emperor cult, which many scholars believe to have been the most important and widely diffused cult in the Roman Empire in late antiquity. To the extent that the story is Babylonian, it may be valuable contemporary evidence of an emperor cult in Sasanian Persia as well.[63]

Another story in the Bavli with a dual Palestinian-Babylonian heritage polemicizes against idolatry, although this story as well expresses anger, but no clear-cut anxiety about the attractiveness of idolatry.[64] Recognizable forms of the story are recorded in 2 Maccabees 7 and 4 Maccabees 8:1–18:23,[65] and thus predate the rabbinic version by several centuries. In these versions, the issue is the Jewish heroes' refusal to eat the flesh of a pig sacrificed to a god. Only in the rabbinic versions, therefore, which apparently reached their present form centuries after the purported "death" of the idolatrous impulse in Israel, is the story an angry polemic against the worship of idols.

This story may be quoted in the Bavli for no other purpose than to glorify the heroism of the martyrs of old, such that the principle for which they give their lives is less important than the portrayal of Jews who are willing to die for their beliefs. The conclusion above that idolatry was an important preoccupation of Babylonian rabbis, however, increases the likelihood that the specific issue of idol worship also motivates the Bavli's interest in the story.[66] Apparently the rabbis are not motivated by an antiquarian concern nor are they repeating a stereotypical diatribe. Rather, the rabbis repeated and perhaps altered this story because it delivered a message that the rabbis and their audience still found meaningful.

To reiterate, Palestinian rabbis confronted the problem of how to live their lives normally while maintaining distance between themselves and forbidden objects of pagan worship. Clear evidence that they wrestled with this problem is preserved in the sources, and is almost totally absent from the traditions about Babylonian rabbis, because (1) idolatry and idols in Babylonia tended to be confined to temples, and (2) rabbinic settlements in Babylonia tended to be exclusively Jewish, as opposed to the mixed pagan/Jewish character of rabbinic settlements in Palestine.[67] In this respect, then, the literary sources of the rabbis provide invaluable contemporary evidence of historical reality in Sasanian Babylonia, the archaeological record of which has yet to be fully exploited, and the literary record of which is notoriously problematic, since much of the literary evidence survives in texts that were written centuries after the period they purport to describe, often in Arabic by Muslims who were hostile to their Zoroastrian predecessors.

As noted, furthermore, my findings shed light on the question of the extent to which Mesopotamia, the home of Babylonian rabbinic settlements, was within the cultural orbit of Persia. Scholars of ancient Persia argue that the Sasanians attempted to suppress statue cults and to destroy image shrines throughout their empire,[68] although Mary Boyce remarks sensibly that "many generations evidently lived and died before the long-established use of images was wholly suppressed,"[69] if, in fact, it ever was wholly suppressed. If the literary record of the Bavli is any indication, the policy of the Sasanians had repercussions in Babylonia, contributing to the paucity of idols there.

With regard to Armenia, another western Sasanian province, James Russell observes that "the Armenians generally, though not universally, opposed the . . . reforms" of the Sasanians.[70] An important reason for the difference between Armenia and Babylonia would have been the fact, noted in the introduction, that rabbinic Babylonia was situated closer to the heart of the Sasanian Empire,[71] while Armenia to an even greater extent was a border province, whose close cultural and political ties with Persia[72] were often contested by Rome, and which for centuries formed a major battleground between the two world powers.[73] The Armenians tended to drift away from Iran during the Sasanian period, never reconciling themselves to the end of the Arsacid dynasty (being themselves Arsacids) and the advent of the Sasanians, and the Zoroastrianism that survived in Armenia even after its conversion to Christianity was closely linked to more ancient forms of the religion.[74]

It is also likely that the rabbis' frequent assertions that idol worship is among the most heinous crimes a Jew can commit[75] had practical implications and served a polemical purpose in Roman Palestine and Persian Babylonia of late antiquity. These denunciations were not just formulaic repetitions of stereotypical slogans nor were they merely "to deter Jews from falling victim to [idol worship] under duress or for lucrative reasons."[76] Rather, they were designed to deter Jews, and the rabbis themselves, from engaging in idol worship when times were normal and because of sincere fascination. Given the paucity of idols in Babylonia, the rabbinic anxiety surveyed in this chapter may be another example of the puzzling disconnect between reality "on the ground" in Sasanian Babylonia and the rabbis' experience of the world.[77]

Perhaps this disconnect is further evidence in favor of my description of Babylonian rabbis as intensely inward-looking. Their experience of the world depended as much on the texts they learned and discussed as on observed reality. And many of these texts—the Bible, the Mishnah, Baraitot, and rabbinic discussions based on these texts—derived from the land of Israel and thus presupposed a world in which idol-worshippers were very much a reality and a menace. Babylonian rabbis tended to look at the world around them through the prism of these texts, such that the finer points of the behavior of non-Jews often mattered little to them in determining their interactions and their descriptions of those interactions.

6

Persian Persecutions of the Jews

As noted in the previous chapter, modern scholars writing the history of the Jews in Sasanian Babylonia are forced to rely heavily on literary evidence, due to the well-known scarcity and inaccessibility of material remains. In addition, these scholars are forced to rely heavily on literary evidence preserved in Jewish sources, specifically the Babylonian Talmud, due to the scarcity of written Persian evidence from Sasanian Babylonia, and the problematic nature of (1) post-Sasanian materials in Arabic and Persian, and (2) post-Talmudic Jewish literature, composed centuries after the period in question and therefore suspect as anachronistic.

In this chapter, I hope to exemplify my contention in the introduction that significant aspects of the history of the Jews of late antiquity will have to be rewritten once the latest developments in Talmud text criticism are taken into account. These developments greatly complicate the historian's task, but they add depth and subtlety to the historian's arguments and ensure that conclusions rest on a firmer literary foundation. Among the more significant of my findings will be the discovery that there is less reason than earlier scholars thought to view early Babylonian rabbis as important players in the Jewish community's interactions with the Persian government. While it would be a mistake to conclude that the same held true for all Babylonian rabbis at all times,[1] the findings of this chapter strengthen and add subtlety to one of the central arguments of this book: that the Babylonian Talmud tends to portray Babylonian rabbis as inward-looking, with the study house to a significant extent the sum total of their experience, even in situations where it had been the consensus of earlier scholarship that they served as the preeminent leaders of the Jewish community.

I will also attempt to show that the transition from Parthian to Sasanian Persian rule was not perceived by the rabbis to be a watershed in Jewish history. Earlier scholars have tended to portray the Parthians as tolerant of religious minorities within their empire, as strongly Hellenized and relatively lukewarm in their adherence to Zoroastrianism. The Sasanians, in contrast, are portrayed as returning to the zealous orthodoxy of their Achaemenid Persian forebears, whether out of conviction or as part of a political attempt to unify their empire, or both. Religious minorities within the empire suffered under the Sasanians, according to this scholarly account, and the period following the accession of the first Sasanian emperor, Ardashir I, as well as the advent of Kerdir, a fanatical Zoroastrian priest, later in the third century, were particularly problematic periods. My analysis of the Talmudic evidence purporting to depict Sasanian treatment of the Jews in the third century will yield a strikingly different picture.[2] The rabbis who were Ardashir's and Kerdir's contemporaries, I will argue, did not look back longingly at the golden age they experienced under the Parthians, nor did they view the Sasanians with disapproval or trepidation. They did not engage with one another in a lively debate over the proper way to respond to the new Sasanian menace, apparently because they did not view the new dynasty as a significant departure from the old. This conclusion has implications for study of Persian history, since it is possible that the experience of the Jews in third-century Iran was typical of religious minorities during the period in question, and perhaps scholars need to reevaluate the extent to which the advent of the Sasanians marked a new era even for the Persian majority.[3]

A discussion in b. Yoma 10a, which has played a crucial role in modern scholarly descriptions of the vicissitudes in the relationship between the Persians and the Jews, will illustrate these points. The discussion is as follows:

> (A) Said R. Yehoshua ben Levi said Rabbi [Yehudah Hanasi], "In the future the Romans will fall into the hands of the Persians, as it is said, 'Hear, then, the plan which the Lord has devised against Edom, and what He has purposed against the inhabitants of Teman: "Surely the young of the flock will drag them away; surely the pasture shall be aghast because of them"'" (Jer. 49:20).
>
> (B) Rabbah bar Ulla objected against [Rabbi Yehudah Hanasi's opinion], "What is the basis [for the view] that 'the young of the flock' [refers to] Persia, as it is written, 'The two-horned ram that you saw [signifies] the kings of Media and Persia' (Dan. 8:20). Say [rather that it refers to] Greece, as it is written, 'And the buck, the he-goat, the king of Greece'" (Dan. 8:21).
>
> (C) When Rav Ḥaviva bar Surmaki ascended [to the land of Israel], he reported [this objection] to a certain rabbi. [The latter] said to him, "One who does not know how to interpret verses objected against Rabbi [Yehudah Hanasi]? What [is the meaning of] 'the young of the flock'? The youngest of the brothers, as Rav Yosef taught [in a

Baraita], ' "Tiras" [in the verse "The descendants of Japeth: Gomer, Magog, Madai, Javan, Tubal, Meshech, and Tiras" (Gen. 10:2)],[4] this is Persia.' "[5]

(D) Said Rabbah bar bar Ḥanah said R. Yoḥanan in the name of R. Yehudah b'R. Ilai, "In the future the Romans will fall into the hands of the Persians. It is an a fortiori argument: The first Temple, which was built by descendants of Shem [i.e., Jews] and destroyed by Chaldeans [i.e., Babylonians], the Chaldeans fell into the hands of the Persians; the second Temple, which was built by Persians and destroyed by Romans, how much the more so will the Romans fall into the hands of the Persians?"

(E) Said Rav [Hebrew:], "In the future the Persians will fall into the hands of the Romans."[6]

(F) Rav Kahana and Rav Asi said to Rav [Aramaic:], "Builders [will fall] into the hands of destroyers?"

(G) [Rav] said to them [Hebrew:],[7] "It is a decree of the King."

(H) There are some who [report Rav's response to them as follows]:

(I) He said to them [Aramaic:],[8] "They also destroy synagogues."

(J) It is also taught thus [in a Baraita] [Hebrew:], In the future the Persians will fall into the hands of the Romans. [Aramaic:] First, because they destroy synagogues,[9] [Hebrew:] and also, it is a decree of the King that builders should fall into the hand of destroyers.

(K) For[10] said Rav Yehudah said Rav, "The son of David [i.e., the Messiah] will not come until the kingdom of Rome extends throughout the entire world for nine months, as it is said ['And you, O Bethlehem of Ephrath, least among the clans of Judah, from you one shall come forth to rule Israel for Me . . .]; Truly He will leave them [helpless] until she who is to bear has borne; then the rest of his brothers shall return . . . For lo, he shall wax great to the ends of the earth' " (Mic. 5:1-3).

The most thorough historical treatment of this passage is that of Isaiah Gafni.[11] According to Gafni, this passage attests to "a reevaluation" of the Persians by the rabbis in response to the Sasanians replacing the Parthians as the dominant Persian dynasty. R. Yehudah b'R. Ilai, quoted in part D, experienced firsthand the tremendous suffering the Romans caused the Jews in the wake of the Bar Kokhba revolt. This rabbi looks forward to Rome's defeat at the hands of the Persians, which during his time meant the Parthians. Two generations later, after the rise of the Sasanian dynasty in Persia, Rav disagrees and looks forward to the opposite.

As support for his reading of Rav's statement, Gafni cites b. Baba Kamma 117a, according to which Rav alludes to the Persian dynastic changes, and refers to the Parthians as "Greeks, who were not particular about bloodshed," and to the Sasanians as "Persians, who are particular about bloodshed." He also cites b. Avodah Zarah 10b, where Rav is quoted as crying out in grief "The bond is severed," when hearing of the death of Artaban, the last Parthian king.

Obviously Gafni's arguments are strengthened by the multiplication of traditions all pointing toward the same conclusion, since theories based on the exegesis of a small number of ancient texts are always suspect. This is so particularly because of problems in textual transmission and interpretive ambiguities, not to mention the fact that typically there is no corroborating evidence in sources external to rabbinic literature. In this instance, b. Baba Kamma 117a has been the subject of an extensive literature, with scholars pointing out the numerous additions that have been made at a number of different stages to the text of this lengthy story, and to the difficulty in using it as evidence regarding the Amoraic protagonists of the tale.[12] In addition, the statement attributed to Rav in Baba Kamma expresses a sense that something important changed with the advent of the "Persians," but, as Gafni is well aware, that "something" is not described as a difference between the Jews' former ability to live in peace and their being forced now to endure persecution. In fact, it seems to me that a religious minority such as the Jews in the Persian Empire would have good reason to prefer a government that was "particular about bloodshed" to one that was not.

Similarly, the conventional scholarly interpretation of b. Avodah Zarah 10b depends on reading Rav's exclamation as not only an expression of grief upon hearing of the death of the Persian king but also as an expression of worry about the new dynasty in the process of taking power. However, while Rav[13] is apparently expressing grief about the death of Artaban, it is not at all clear that he is anxiously contemplating the new Persian dynasty.

In our evaluation of Gafni's arguments, therefore, much depends on our interpretation of b. Yoma 10a. How clearly does it support Gafni's conclusions regarding changing rabbinic attitudes toward the Persians as a result of the advent of a new ruling dynasty? The major question posed by this source is: Does its reference to the destruction of synagogues reflect (1) the troubles attendant upon the advent of the new dynasty in 226 CE; (2) the persecutions of religious minorities instituted by Kerdir toward the end of the third century CE; (3) the Persian persecutions of the Jews mentioned in post-Talmudic and post-Sasanian gaonic and Arabic sources; or (4) none of these? What impact did these events have on the Jewish community and on the rabbis in particular? Are these events mentioned in the Talmud, and can the Talmud be used to corroborate Persian and Christian sources? Are we to consider Kerdir's claim to have persecuted religious minorities throughout Persia to be idle boasting or are we to accept it as trustworthy? Are we to view Christian martyrologies as historically accurate, albeit distorted and melodramatic, or are we to view them as fabrications? Virtually all sources of late antiquity are tendentious; if literature deriving from one group attests to a phenomenon described in the same terms by another group, it is obviously more likely to reflect historical reality.

As the discussion now stands, there are two versions of Rav's response to the objection of Rav Kahana and Rav Asi (part G: "It is a decree of the King";

part I: "They also destroy synagogues"). According to the first version, there is no logical explanation for Rav's view that "the builders [of the second Temple, i.e., the Persians]" will be defeated by "the destroyers [of the second Temple, i.e., the Romans]." It is simply "a decree of the King," that is, the will of God as expressed in scripture.

This version of Rav's response has much to recommend it. First, the discussion continues with another statement attributed to Rav himself, in which he derives from scripture that the entire world, presumably including Persia, will eventually fall to Rome (part K: "The son of David [i.e., the Messiah] will not come until the kingdom of Rome extends throughout the entire world for nine months, as it is said"). That is, a statement attributed to Rav himself supports the first version of Rav's response.[14]

It also bears mentioning that the assertion that it is "a decree of the King" that Persia will fall to Rome is an effective response to the objection of Rav Kahana and Rav Asi (part F: "Builders [will fall] into the hands of destroyers?"). Convincing scriptural proof always trumps logic according to the rabbis,[15] and it is easy to see why Rav would prefer scripture to the logical argument of Rav Kahana and Rav Asi.[16]

There are strong arguments, therefore, in support of the first version of Rav's response. There are reasons to doubt, furthermore, the second version of his response. What are those reasons?[17] One argument I offer tentatively is that the second version of Rav's response (part I: "They also destroy synagogues") does not counter the objection of Rav's interlocutors as effectively as the first version does. Rav Kahana and Rav Asi, it will be recalled, object that it is illogical and unjust to say that the Persians, the builders of the second Temple, will be conquered by the Romans, who destroyed the second Temple. According to the second version of Rav's response (part I), the Persians are also destroyers, since they have destroyed synagogues (or, according to some versions, they have destroyed "a synagogue").[18] This response is less than fully satisfactory, however, since it means that the Persians are both builders and destroyers, while the Romans are only destroyers. The second version of Rav's response does not fully solve the problem, since it remains the case that the Romans are worse than the Persians, and it is unfair that the Romans should be the Persians' conquerors.[19]

A particularly important argument in favor of the first version being original is the fact that immediately after Rav's dialogue with Rav Kahana and Rav Asi, the discussion continues with part J:

> It is also taught thus [in a Baraita] [Hebrew:], In the future the Persians will fall into the hands of the Romans. [Aramaic:] First, because they destroy synagogues, [Hebrew:] and also, it is a decree of the King that builders should fall into the hand of destroyers.

As currently formulated, this Baraita contains two reasons why in the future Persia will fall into the hands of Rome, one corresponding to the first version of Rav's response and the other to the second version. The phrase in Aramaic, however ("First, because they destroy synagogues"), is an obvious interpolation, since Baraitot, almost without exception, are formulated exclusively in Hebrew, and even the few exceptional cases incorporate Aramaic phrases only for a small number of very specific reasons.[20] Without the interpolation, the Baraita supports only the first version of Rav's response (part G: "It is a decree of the King").

In addition, the second version of Rav's response renders problematic the phrase (part J) "It is also taught thus [in a Baraita]," which is found in all versions of the discussion and which works perfectly well according to the first version of Rav's response. In other words, the phrase "It is also taught in a Baraita" is inappropriate when the Baraita only supports one of two versions of a statement. We would expect the Baraita to be used as an objection against one version and as a support for the other.[21]

These arguments are even more compelling according to a version of the above discussion preserved in ms. JTS Rab. 218 (EMC 270).[22] According to this manuscript, the passage reads:

> (A) He said to them [i.e., Rav said to Rav Kahana and Rav Asi], "It is a decree of the King."
>
> (B) It is also taught thus [in a Baraita]: In the future, Persia will fall into the hands of Rome. It is a decree of the King that builders should fall into the hands of destroyers.

According to this reading, the passage originally said nothing at all about the Persians destroying synagogues, neither in a second version of Rav's response (in this manuscript there is no second version of Rav's response) nor in the Baraita. If this manuscript is preferable to the reading of the printed edition, then the discussion originally made no mention of the Persians tearing down synagogues. This claim about the Persians would have been added by a later editor, storyteller, or scribe, in all likelihood after the time of the final redaction of the Talmud in the sixth or seventh centuries CE.[23]

Which is to be preferred, the reading of ms. JTS Rab. 218[24] or the reading of the printed edition and all other manuscripts? The reading of the JTS manuscript is preferable because it solves the problems mentioned above. First, there is no Aramaic interpolation into the Baraita; second, the Baraita, minus the interpolation, supports the one and only response by Rav. A third difficulty avoided by the reading of the JTS manuscript is the fact, noted above, that the second response was not fully satisfactory as a resolution of the difficulty posed by Rav Kahana and Rav Asi.[25] This alternative reading, which lacks the second response entirely, is therefore precisely the same as the reading of the printed edition with the difficult passages removed; namely, (1) the Aramaic phrase in the Baraita, and (2) the second version of Rav's response.

Originally, therefore, Rav offered no logical justification for his opinion whatsoever, but rather asserted that he is doing nothing more than stating the unfathomable divine will. And, as several scholars have warned, when rabbis claim to be basing their opinions on the interpretation of scripture, it is often wise to take them at their word.[26] It is likely, in other words, that Rav's opinion here is precisely what it purports to be, namely, exegesis of scripture, with no provocation from historical reality. His scriptural interpretation is perfectly in accordance with the canons of rabbinic Bible exegesis, and I see no compelling reason to claim that this interpretation was motivated by anything other than an attempt to make sense of scripture. In other words, Rav is not looking to scripture to prove that the foreign power that torments him the most will fall to the power he harbors less hatred for.

I am well aware that this is a difficult argument to prove, since the scriptural sources quoted here admit of more than a single interpretation, and the rabbis were free to choose which verses to emphasize and which to ignore. For example, it is possible that Rav's experience of the Persians led him to base his opinion on one set of verses, which he interpreted in a way he found personally satisfying.

My conclusion above, however, that originally Rav[27] explicitly claimed that his opinion was based on scripture and scripture alone ("It is a decree of the King") and that Rav explicitly rejected a logical argument based on the Jews' experience of the Persian and Roman empires ("Builders will fall into the hands of destroyers?") suggests strongly that Rav accepts the premise that the Persians are preferable to the Romans, contrary to the depiction of Rav vis-à-vis the Persians in modern scholarly literature. Rav accepts, in other words, that the Persians are builders and the Romans destroyers, but he thinks that this reality does not determine how we interpret what scripture has to say about their future fates just prior to the coming of the Messiah. Rav[28] tells us explicitly, in other words, that in this particular case we are to read the Bible without the interference of historical experience, logic, or justice. It goes without saying, however that we can never be absolutely certain that an ancient figure who purports to base an opinion on the interpretation of scripture bases this opinion entirely on scripture divorced from historical or personal experience. The individual himself, after all, may be influenced subconsciously by historical or personal factors, so how can we, almost two millennia after the fact, confidently assert that such considerations play no role?

Whoever added the second version of Rav's response, however, had historical experience very much on his mind. Who was the author of this later addition? E. S. Rosenthal believes that it derives from the period of Kerdir in the late third century CE. He bases his belief primarily on what he views as the strong similarity between Kerdir's account of his persecutions and the claim of b. Yoma 10a that the Persians destroyed synagogues.[29] A glance at the text of Kerdir's boastful inscription, however, shows that Rosenthal's reading of the evidence is possible, but by no means fully convincing, and we will see that another context is preferable. The relevant portions of Kerdir's inscription are as follows:

> And Jews and Buddhists and Hindus and Nazarenes and Christians and Baptists and Manichaeans[30] were smitten in the empire, and

> idols were destroyed and the abodes of the demons disrupted and made into thrones and seats of the gods.[31]

Rosenthal understands Kerdir to be referring here to the destruction of synagogues, and he believes that the reference of b. Yoma 10a to the destruction of synagogues was added in response to Kerdir's persecution. It is not at all clear, however, that Kerdir refers to the destruction of synagogues.[32] And Rosenthal presumably believes that the additions to the dialogue between Rav and his interlocutors, as well as to the Baraita, were made around the time of Kerdir himself in response to events of the time. It is extremely unexpected, according to this reconstruction of the text's development, that we should be in possession of a manuscript that lacks the later addition. As noted several times throughout this book, manuscript variation tends to be characteristic of relatively late, anonymous editorial passages in the Talmud,[33] and it is surprising, to say the least, that a passage added to the text in the third century should be the subject of such a significant textual variant.

Moshe Beer, in contrast, argues that the activity referred to in the second version of Rav's statement most likely took place during the time of Rav himself, which he portrays as a period of upheaval brought about by the religious fanaticism of an ascendant Zoroastrian priesthood, fostered by Ardashir (226–42 CE), the founder of the Sasanian dynasty, and his son, Shapur I, during the early days of his reign (242–72 CE).[34] Beer cites as proof several statements attributed to Rav that he believes reflect Rav's reaction to the religious upheaval taking place in Persia during the first half of the third century, which had a profoundly negative impact on the Jews in Babylonia.[35] While I cannot deal in detail with all of Beer's claims in this discussion, his argument based on the second version of Rav's statement is extremely unlikely, given my conclusion above that this second version is a later addition to the text and is not part of the original dialogue between Rav and his interlocutors.

A more likely source of the second version of Rav's statement is *Igeret Rav Sherira Gaon* or *Seder Tannaim ve-Amoraim*. In Rav Sherira's description of the persecutions inflicted upon the Jews by the Persians toward the end of the fifth century CE, he informs us: "In the year 474, when Rabbah Tosfa'ah died, all of the synagogues of Babylonia were closed [*itasru*]."[36] The word translated as "closed" (*itasru*) might have been misread, misunderstood, or misremembered by a scribe or an oral performer and taken to mean "were destroyed" (*istaru*) by means of the unintentional reversal of the order of two letters.[37] Interestingly, the ninth-century-CE gaonic chronicle *Seder Tannaim ve-Amoraim* mentions the destruction of "houses of study" (*bei midrasha*) at the time of the death of the same Rabbah Tosfa'ah.[38]

I am aware, of course, that it is possible that the second version of Rav's statement in the Bavli was the source for the statement in *Seder Tannaim ve-Amoraim* or *Igeret Rav Sherira*. I prefer, however, to view the gaonic chronicles as the Bavli's source, since there is no question that the description of the Persians' activity in persecuting the Jews is an integral part of the chronicles, while we saw abundant reason to doubt that the second version of Rav's statement is an integral part of the Bavli. It therefore makes most sense to conclude that copyists of the Talmud added to the text on the basis of Rav Sherira rather than vice versa, according to which the second version of Rav's statement, at the very earliest, dates from the ninth or tenth century CE.

To summarize the conclusions of this section, we find that according to the "original" version of this discussion,[39] Rav is portrayed as an exegete of scriptural texts. Rav's "foreign policy statements," to use an obviously anachronistic term, are apparently based on the scholarly interpretation of texts uttered in the presence of fellow rabbis and are apparently intended for internal consumption alone.

In addition, there is no proof from b. Yoma 10a for the common scholarly view that Rav viewed the advent of the Sasanian dynasty as a catastrophe in the making. Rather, the narrative examined above depicts Rav as a firm supporter of the Persians, accepting their characterization as "builders" and therefore much to be preferred to the Romans, the "destroyers." The evidence for such activity on the Persians' part derives from the ninth or tenth century and refers to persecutions that ostensibly took place during the fifth century. Were we to accept the reference to the destruction of synagogues in b. Yoma 10a as an integral part of the text, we could perhaps begin to formulate a theory of Persian policy toward the Jews. Instead, we are left with the account in the gaonic chronicles, written five centuries after the purported events, plus a dubious reference in Kerdir's inscription.[40]

It is important to emphasize that my conclusions do not depend on regarding the report in the gaonic chronicles as fictional due to the time gap between the chronicles and the event they purportedly describe. For the purposes of this study, I am not particularly interested in the question of whether or not the Persians persecuted Babylonian Jews during the fifth century. Rather, my primary concern is to show (1) that Rav's statement in b. Yoma 10a, despite modern scholarly claims to the contrary, is not an expression of third-century Amoraic consternation in response to the advent of the Sasanian dynasty; and (2) that there is less reason than we thought previously to view third-century Babylonian Amoraim as preoccupied with the pressing political issues of their day and as the leaders of substantial segments of the Babylonian Jewish community in their dealings with the Persian government.

In evaluating the gaonic chronicles' account of the fifth-century persecutions, however, it is important to bear in mind that a Persian chronicle written after the demise of the Sasanian Empire also describes fifth-century Persian persecutions of the Jews. This chronicle describes the persecutions as limited to the city of Isfahan, in contrast to the gaonic accounts, which describe persecutions that affected the Babylonian Jewish community as a whole.[41] Even if we accept that the medieval chronicles constitute reliable evidence that "something happened," therefore, the precise nature and scope of this "something" is not entirely clear.

Other Talmudic traditions have been misinterpreted by modern scholars, who have taken them to be serious formulations of rabbinic political calculation rather than academic exercises in the reconciliation of logical contradictions. In addition, other Talmudic traditions have been enlisted, without success, I will argue, in support of the modern scholarly claim that the change from Parthian to Sasanian rule, and/or the advent of persecutions during the time of Kerdir, was perceived by third-century rabbis as a turning point in Babylonian Jewish history. In b. Gittin 16b–17a, for example, we find the following:

> (A) Rabbah bar bar Ḥanah was ill. Rav Yehudah and the rabbis[42] entered to ask him a question.
> (B) They asked him, "Two who brought a writ of divorce from a far-off place, do they have to say, 'It was written in our presence and it was signed in our presence,' or not?"
> (C) He said to them, "They don't have to. . . ."
> (D) In the meantime, a magian priest [*ḥabara*][43] came and took the oil lamp from before them.
> (E) [Rabbah bar bar Ḥanah] said, "Merciful One, either in Your shade or in the shade of the son of Esau [Rome]."
> (F) Is this to say that the Romans are better than the Persians? Behold, R. Ḥiyya taught, "What [is the meaning of] what is written, 'God understands the way to [Wisdom; i.e., Torah]; He knows its source' (Job 28:23)? God knows that Israel cannot stand the decree of the Romans; [therefore] he exiled them to Babylonia."
> (G) It is not difficult. This [part F] [was said] before the magian priests [*ḥabarei*] came to Babylonia; this [parts A–E] [took place] after the magian priests came to Babylonia.

Modern scholars observe that we are dealing here with a routine Jewish practice (lighting a lamp in a home for light) that offends basic Zoroastrian religious sensibilities. Zoroastrians consider fire to be a manifestation of Ahura Mazda, the divinity, and are concerned that it not be rendered impure. Zoroastrian priests who tend the central fire wear masks so as not to pollute it with their breath, and nonbelievers who come in contact with fire will certainly render it impure. The Persian priest who burst into the home of Rabbah bar bar Ḥanah was simply serving the Zoroastrian deity.[44]

Modern scholars have accepted the anonymous editorial claim (part F) that the story involving Rabbah bar bar Ḥanah and the tradition of R. Ḥiyya are contradictory. They have accepted as well the anonymous editors' answer to the objection (part G) according to which R. Ḥiyya, who flourished in the early third century CE, predates the magian priests and therefore prefers the Persians to the Romans, while Rabbah bar bar Ḥanah lived after the *ḥabarei* came to Babylonia and therefore prefers the Romans.

As noted several times, however, the Talmud's anonymous argumentation is generally considered by scholars to constitute a relatively late layer of Talmudic discourse. While it is possible that the authors of this anonymous commentary correctly interpret statements of third-century rabbis, who may predate them by centuries, it is also possible that they retroject onto earlier rabbis the events of a later time.

In addition, it needs to be borne in mind that these anonymous editors are exegetes rather than historians. Their primary task is to interpret traditions, to make and resolve objections, and to do so they strive primarily for logical rather than historical cogency. The chronological distinction made here serves their exegetical purposes; its historical accuracy is at best of secondary importance.

Perhaps it will be argued that while it is true that the anonymous editors' primary concern is not history, they resolved the objection in this particular fashion on the basis of a tradition to the effect that the advent of magian priests in the mid–third century had a profoundly negative impact on Babylonian Jewish life. While that tradition is found only in the later editorial layer of the Bavli, the argument might proceed, it cannot be dismissed out of hand, and perhaps it has a historical foundation.

I would argue in response that it is likely that a discussion in b. Yevamot 63b, to be discussed in detail below, is the source of the anonymous editorial "tradition" about the advent of magian priests. And this discussion, I will argue, refers to the magian priests as problematic, but ultimately controllable. Their appearance on the scene is a source of consternation, but because "they accept bribes," the danger they pose will not get out of hand. The "tradition" at the basis of the anonymous editorial response in b. Gittin 16b–17a, therefore, is b. Yevamot 63b, and this tradition has been reworked in order to perform the exegetical task that the editors of b. Gittin set for themselves.

Finally, it bears emphasizing that the anonymous editorial objection itself is artificial. This objection depends on reading the Rabbah bar bar Ḥanah story as an expression of the view that the Persians are worse than the Romans. The anonymous editors tend to read stories in a hyperliteral fashion, and consistently fail, perhaps out of ignorance, to appreciate them as stories.[45] Against the anonymous editors, it is possible, perhaps preferable, to read Rabbah bar bar Ḥanah's exclamation as an expression of momentary irritation. Nothing bothers us more than the hardship we are undergoing at the moment, and the story may have no interest in formulating a rule, based on the apparently isolated experience of one rabbi, about the relative merits of the Persian and Roman empires.

It is likely, furthermore, that the story's audience would have been familiar with Rav Yehudah's depiction as a Babylonian rabbi who strongly discouraged scholars from leaving Babylonia for Israel, and who, in fact, is said to have considered it a crime to leave Babylonia, the place of greater Torah scholarship (from the Babylonian rabbinic perspective), for Israel, the place of lesser Torah scholarship.[46] The audience would likewise have known that Rabbah bar bar Ḥanah did, in fact, leave Babylonia for Israel, and part of the story's raison d'être may have been to show that Rabbah bar bar Ḥanah left Babylonia for a trivial reason. The Persian priest took a lamp, an inconvenience that pales in comparison to the crimes that the rabbis routinely attribute to the Romans. Certainly the aggravation endured by Rabbah bar bar

Ḥanah is trivial in comparison to what Israel had to endure at the hands of the Romans.[47]

According to the discussion above, therefore, it is difficult to use b. Gittin 16b–17a as support for the modern scholarly claim that the third century CE marked a pivotal turning point in Persian-Jewish relations, and that Babylonian rabbis played a pivotal role in formulating the Jewish community's response to the new dynasty. The modern scholarly use of this passage is based on the acceptance as historical evidence of argumentation by the Talmud's anonymous editors, despite the generally ahistorical nature of the editors' concerns.

A discussion in b. Yevamot 63b, discussed preliminarily above, further exemplifies my claim regarding the surprisingly meager evidence in support of the claim that third-century Amoraim viewed the advent of the Sasanian dynasty as a disaster in the making.[48] Most scholars have correctly characterized this discussion as a sermon, based on the interpretation of texts and the explanation of Persian mistreatment of Jews as the result of divine measure for measure punishment of Jewish wrongdoing. The text is as follows:

> (A) "I'll . . . vex [Israel] with a nation of fools" (Deut. 32:21).
>
> (B) Said R. Yoḥanan, "These are the magian priests [*ḥabarei*]." . . .
>
> (C) [Aramaic:] They said to R. Yoḥanan, "The magian priests have come to Babylonia."
>
> He bent over and fell.[49]
>
> They said to [R. Yoḥanan], "They accept bribes."
>
> He sat up straight.
>
> (D) [Hebrew:] They decreed about three [things] because of three [things]. They decreed about meat because of [the priestly] gifts; they decreed about bathhouses because of [ritual] immersion; [Aramaic:] they disinter the dead [Hebrew:] because they rejoice on the day of their festivals[50] (as it is said),[51]
>
> (E) "The hand of God will strike you and your fathers" (1 Sam. 12:15).
>
> Said Rabbah bar Shmuel, "This is the disinterring of the dead, as the master said, 'On account of the sin of the living the dead are disinterred.' "

As earlier scholars have noted, at several points these traditions are unclear. The ensuing discussion focuses on the following points: First, who does the story portray as responsible for the decrees listed in part D? Second, what are the decrees and what motivated them? Third, what is the relationship between the various parts of the discussion? To be specific, is part D the continuation of the dialogue in part C, or does a new speaker intervene?[52] Similarly, is part E the continuation of part D, or is it a separate tradition? Fourth, how do we account for the shift from Hebrew to Aramaic and back again to Hebrew in part D, ostensibly a unified tradition? Fifth, what are we to make of the Bavli's attribution to R. Yoḥanan of intense interest in details about Persian priests and how they impinged on Babylonian Jewry, given the fact that Palestinian compilations preserve no evidence of such interest on the part of R. Yoḥanan or any other Palestinian rabbi? Sixth, do any sources external to the Talmud shed light on the events described?[53]

With regard to the first question, I accept the claim of several modern commentators that the story in part D attributes the decrees to the Persians.[54] This interpretation is supported (1) by the context, which deals with Persians and the problems they cause the Babylonian Jewish community, and (2) by the fact that the third punishment, "disinterring the dead," can only be interpreted as something the Persians do to the Jews.[55] To anticipate my conclusions, part D builds on the statement quoted by Rabbah bar Shmuel ("On account of the sin of the living the dead are disinterred")[56] by identifying the specific sin that causes God to exploit the Persians as His agents in punishing Babylonian Jews.[57]

Part D, furthermore, understands God, via the unwitting agency of the Persians, to be punishing Babylonian Jews for their failure to observe specific commandments.[58] At first glance, this interpretation appears to require reading too much into the simple statement "They decreed about bathhouses because of immersion," such that it means "God, using the Persians as His unwitting agents, decreed that Jews were forbidden to use bathhouses as punishment for their failure to zealously fulfill the commandment of ritual immersion." We find a close structural parallel, however, in b. Avodah Zarah 17b–18a, where the meaning is unambiguous. We read there: "Immediately [the Romans] decreed that [R. Ḥaninah ben Teradion be executed by] burning...because he pronounced [God's] name with the letters in which it is written." Here as well we have a decree by non-Jews,[59] acting unwittingly on behalf of God by inflicting punishment on a Jew for committing a sin. As in the case of the Babylonian Jews in b. Yevamot 63b, the Jew in b. Avodah Zarah deserves punishment in the eyes of the non-Jews for violating their laws, in addition to his sin against God. In b. Avodah Zarah 17b–18a, the Romans execute R. Ḥaninah ben Teradion by burning for violating their ban against Torah study, and his execution is simultaneously divine punishment for the sin of pronouncing God's name. In b. Yevamot 63b, Persians harass Babylonian Jews by forbidding them to use bathhouses, a prohibition that is simultaneously divine punishment for their failure to perform the commandment of ritual immersion.

In the case of the Persians in b. Yevamot, each of the punishments are, in purely human terms, Persian responses to Jewish practices that violate Persian ritual law, and that offend Persian sensitivities because they violate basic Zoroastrian principles. The practices that offend the Persians are unnamed in b. Yevamot, but modern scholars convincingly argue that the Persians "disinterred the dead" because they considered it a serious sin to defile the holy earth by burying the dead rather than exposing their flesh to birds and wild animals. Similarly, the Persians forbade bathhouses because they were offended by Jewish women defiling the sacred element, water, by purifying themselves of menstrual impurity through ritual immersion. The decree against meat is more obscure, but it may refer, as Geoffrey Herman has argued, to Zoroastrian opposition to Jews' eating the meat of animals slaughtered according to Jewish law. Slaughtering according to Jewish law, whereby the animal's throat is cut, may have offended the Persians because the animal's blood, considered by Zoroastrians to be food for demons, would fall to the ground and contaminate the pure earth, just as a corpse would. Herman observes that Zoroastrians practiced ritual slaughter through stunning and strangulation, making efforts not to let the blood leave the animal upon slaughtering.[60]

In addition, many commentators correctly understand that the decrees are "measure-for-measure" punishments. As is so often the case in rabbinic literature, in other words, the divine punishment fits the crime. Bathhouses are closed, therefore, to punish Babylonian Jews for their failure to observe with sufficient zeal the commandment of ritual immersion. Babylonian Jews are forbidden to eat meat (?) as punishment for their failure to give the priests the appropriate parts of a slaughtered animal. The dead are disinterred, causing sadness and mourning to Babylonian Jews, as punishment for the crime of rejoicing on Persian festivals.[61]

Part D is problematic, however, since the phrase "they disinter the dead" is in Aramaic, while the rest of part D (i.e., the remaining two punishments and all three crimes) are in Hebrew. As I have noted numerous times, Shamma Friedman argues convincingly that a change of language in a Talmudic passage is often a mark of a later addition.[62] It also bears mentioning that the first two punishments ("cattle" and "bathhouses") are phrased as decrees prohibiting the Jews from performing certain actions ("They decreed about X on account of Y"), while "they disinter the dead" is phrased as an action performed by the Persians themselves. Only in the third case, the only one in Aramaic, is the language of "they decreed" not employed.[63]

It is likely, therefore, that the third punishment, "they disinter the dead," is a later addition to part D.[64] What motivated the ancient rabbis to add to this discussion in precisely this manner? It is likely that part D originally[65] lacked the introductory mention of three decrees/sins, and consisted only of the first two pairs ([1] meat/gifts; [2] bathhouses/ritual immersion) with no introduction. The third pair ([3] they disinter the dead/they rejoice on the days of their festivals) was added on the basis of Rabbah bar Shmuel's statement (in Aramaic, incidentally), according to which the Persians act as unwitting agents of God by "disinterring the dead," which is simultaneously a divine punishment of the "sins of the living." The final editors of part D, who inherited knowledge of a third punishment from Rabbah bar Shmuel, sought an appropriate transgression, which would also involve the Persians and would yield a convincing measure-for-measure punishment. They therefore created the crime of "rejoicing on the day of their festivals," unattested elsewhere in the Bavli, a lacuna rendered all the more problematic due to the rabbis' intense concern for the related issue of doing business with idolaters on, before, and after the days of their festivals.[66] The Meiri and several medieval anthologists appear to be aware of this anomaly when they "interpret" the third crime as a reference not only to rejoicing with idolaters on the days of their festivals but also to doing business with them on these days.[67] Why, these anthologists appear to wonder, does the Talmud refer to a "new" Jewish transgression and omit mention of one that is extremely well attested? The explanation, I argue, is that the Talmud in b. Yevamot seeks a crime that will serve as an appropriate measure-for-measure match for the punishment they inherited from the past, in the form of the punishment mentioned by Rabbah bar Shmuel, who refers to some unspecified sin.

The number 3 plays a crucial role in the literature of widely diverse cultures, including the literature of the ancient rabbis.[68] Confining ourselves to rabbinic literature, countless statements, sections within larger discussions, and complete discussions are arranged in groups of three.[69] It is likely that this fact played a role in the incorporation of a third element into the discussion, and that the introductory phrase "They decreed three on account of three" was added to the discussion along with or shortly after the incorporation of the third pair of decree/transgression. The status of the introductory phrase as a later addition is indicated by the large number of variants preserved in manuscripts and medieval testimonia, as well as the change of Hebrew terminology from *bishvil* in the introductory phrase to *mipenei* in the description.[70]

We turn now to the third question posed above, namely the issue of whether or not part D ("They decreed about three [punishments] on account of three [sins]") is the continuation of the dialogue between R. Yoḥanan and his interlocutors in part C. It is difficult to view parts C and D as a unity, since part C is in Aramaic and part D, with the exception of one phrase, is entirely in Hebrew (see above). Supporting this conclusion is the fact that while part C is a dialogue, part D does not work as the words of either of the interlocutors. To be specific, part C portrays R. Yoḥanan as uninformed about the behavior of Persian priests, and it is peculiar that in the very next breath (in part D) he should be portrayed as imparting information about them ("They decreed about three [punishments] on account of three [sins]"). It is also difficult to view part D as the words of R. Yoḥanan's interlocutors,[71] since it is strange, given what we know of rabbinic etiquette and the hierarchical relationships between rabbis,[72] that R. Yoḥanan's subordinates in part C[73] would behave in the very next scene as his teachers, listing the Persian decrees and explaining the Jewish sins that induced God to inflict them on Babylonian Jewry.[74]

Most likely, therefore, part D is not the continuation of part C.[75] This conclusion is significant because of the critically important role this tradition has played in modern scholarly discussions of Persian treatment of the Jews, in particular claims that Talmudic and Persian sources tell the same story and mutually shed light on one another. Once we divorce part D from part C, the Talmud no longer necessarily reveals the chronological and geographical source of the tradition about the three Persian decrees. We remove the need to view it as a record of events that took place when "the *ḥabarei* came to Babylonia," which most modern scholars view as a reference to the advent of

Sasanian rule in 226 CE. Moshe Beer, for example, is not necessarily justified in using the traditions in part D to characterize Persian treatment of the Jews during the first few decades of Sasanian rule.[76] We also remove the need to date the traditions in part D to the time of R. Yoḥanan, the main protagonist of part C, which weakens the claim of E. S. Rosenthal that part D refers to the persecutions of Kerdir in the final decades of the third century CE.[77]

When we view part D in isolation from part C, with the later additions removed, we are left with the following Hebrew tradition without attribution:

> They decreed about meat because of [the priestly] gifts; they decreed about bathhouses because of [ritual] immersion.

Such a tradition is an anomaly in the Babylonian Talmud because (1) most unattributed statements in the Bavli are in Aramaic, and (2) the overwhelming majority of such statements are argumentational,[78] while part D is declarative. While certainty on this subject is not possible, part D may originally have been the continuation of R. Yoḥanan's interpretation of Deuteronomy 22:21 (see parts A and B), yielding the following:

> (A) "I'll . . . vex [Israel] with a nation of fools" (Deut. 32:21).
> (B) Said R. Yoḥanan, "These are the magian priests [*ḥabarei*].
> They decreed about meat because of [the priestly] gifts; they decreed about bathhouses because of [ritual] immersion."

In other words, it is possible that R. Yoḥanan continues his previous statement, briefly explaining why he disapproves of Persian priests.

In evaluating this hypothesis, it needs to be borne in mind that I am dealing with the issue of what the tradition purports to be, and not the issue of what it actually is, that is, from where and when it actually derives. I am claiming only that the tradition originally may have been the continuation of a statement attributed to R. Yoḥanan; it could actually derive from Babylonia and have been composed any time prior to the Talmud's final redaction (see below).

Part E, furthermore, is also of very limited help in resolving the issue of the chronological provenance of part D. Part E, it will be recalled, consists of the following:

> (as it is said,)[79]
> "The hand of God will strike you and your fathers" (1 Sam. 12:15).
> Said Rabbah bar Shmuel, "This is the disinterring of the dead, as the master said, 'On account of the sin of the living the dead are disinterred.' "

This tradition appears to be connected to part D by means of the phrase "as it is said," according to which the authors of part D quote Rabbah bar Shmuel, a mid-fourth-century Babylonian Amora, to support their claim that the Persian practice of disinterring the dead is divine punishment for the sins of Babylonian Jews. With this connecting phrase, the authors of part D appear to postdate Rabbah bar Shmuel, whom they apparently quote in support of their view. Most manuscripts and medieval testimonia, however, lack the linking phrase "as it is said,"[80] according to which part E is likewise an independent tradition. And the reading without the linking phrase is preferable to that of the printed edition, since the statement by Rabbah bar Shmuel serves rather poorly as proof for the third of the punishment/sin pairings in part D. Part D asserts, it will be recalled, that the Persians disinter the dead because Babylonian Jews rejoice on Persian festivals, while part E merely claims that the Persians disinter the dead as punishment for some unspecified sin of the living.

Understood as an independent tradition not quoted by the authors of part D, however, Rabbah bar Shmuel's statement does permit us to determine roughly when the Aramaic phrase "they disinter the dead" was added to part D, together with its accompanying transgression, "they rejoice on the day of their festivals." According to my conclusions above, the third section of part D, that is, the third punishment/transgression pair, was added some time after or contemporary with the mid-fourth-century Amora Rabbah bar Shmuel, since it bases itself on his statement. Greater precision than this, unfortunately, as well as the provenance of the rest of the statement, is at present beyond our grasp. We have yet to decide whether part D reflects on the one extreme (1) an early rabbinic perspective on events in Babylonia; (2) a late Babylonian rabbinic account on the other; or (3) one of several possibilities in between these two extremes.

While the tradition's chronology is a mystery, its geography is less so. To be specific, we can rule out Palestine as part D's point of origin, for although the Bavli several times depicts Palestinian rabbis as preoccupied with the fate of Babylonian Jewry at the hands of the Persians, as noted, no Palestinian rabbinic compilation preserves the slightest hint of such a preoccupation. The Bavli is intensely concerned with (1) the actions and statements of Palestinian rabbis; (2) Palestinian rabbinic attitudes toward Babylonians and Babylonia; and (3) the status, learning, and genealogy of the former compared to the latter. Palestine and Palestinians captured the imaginations of Babylonian rabbis and formed an essential part of their self-definition. To judge from the evidence of the Palestinian compilations, however, Palestinian rabbis tended to be less fascinated with the fate of Babylonian rabbis. Palestinian rabbis quote the statements of and tell stories about Babylonian rabbis (although much less so than Babylonians do vis-à-vis Palestinians), but the experience of Babylonian rabbis in Babylonia did not preoccupy Palestinian rabbis to a significant degree.[81] It is unlikely, although not out of the question, that Palestinian rabbis would use stories describing the fate of Babylonian rabbis in Persia to teach a lesson about divine justice.

As noted, earlier scholars maintained that the decrees mentioned in b. Yevamot 63b date from the first or second half of the third-century, primarily based on the assumption that the Talmud intended part D to correspond chronologically to part C. Once we raise the possibility of pseudepigraphic authorship, however, other chronologies are equally plausible, since we find close parallels between the Talmud's three decrees and descriptions of Persian attitudes and actions in a variety of late antique and early medieval non-Jewish sources.

What does the Christian and Persian evidence reveal? As noted, the second decree, "bathhouses," was apparently a prohibition of Jewish use of water. The Persians regarded water as holy, and we find evidence of Persian preoccupation with non-Zoroastrian use of water throughout the Sasanian period. I observed above that Kerdir, in the late third century, boasts of having benefited water throughout the empire. In addition, during the persecution of the Christians in the mid–fifth century, Yazdegird II (438–57 CE) decreed that Christians, like Persians, must wash their hands in cow urine so as not to impurify water.[82] In the fourth century, Shapur II (309–79 CE) complained that the Christians do not honor water,[83] and it is well documented that the Mazdaeans detested several groups, such as Manichees, who practiced baptism.[84] Any one of these might have provided the context for a Persian prohibition of the use of bathhouses; taken together, they suggest, in fact, that any time during the Sasanian period could have provided such a context.

The same is true of the Zoroastrian attitude toward burial. Christian martyrologies relate that Bahram V (421–39 CE) ordered that Christians be removed from their graves, and claimed that this order remained in force for five years.[85] The same sources relate Yazdegird II's reproach of the Christians for impurifying the earth by burying the dead,[86] and report that when Khusrau Anosharwan and Justinian signed a peace treaty in 563 CE, the Persian king granted the Christians religious freedom, which included the right to bury their dead.[87] The evidence of both rabbinic and nonrabbinic sources, therefore, leads to the conclusion that the Persians could have harassed the Jews in this fashion at virtually any point during the Sasanian period, although Kerdir's inscription and the Christian martyrologies perhaps point to the late third or the mid–fifth to mid–sixth centuries CE as the most likely time.[88]

In conclusion to the discussion of this text, it is crucially important to note that the Bavli in this context does not depict the advent of the *ḥabarei* as a disaster. Even if we accept the attribution of these statements and stories to R. Yoḥanan and his circle, the texts tell us that the *ḥabarei* decreed two decrees against the Babylonian Jews (the third decree clearly being a tradition that postdates R. Yoḥanan), and that news of their arrival in Babylonia provoked consternation in R. Yoḥanan, until he heard that they accept bribes. While the *ḥabarei* are not greeted with enthusiasm, therefore, neither is their arrival on the scene considered significant enough to constitute the dividing line between two eras in Jewish history.

Still another Talmudic discussion dealing with Persian persecutions of Jews demonstrates the fragility of historical reconstructions of the era based on rabbinic literary evidence. This Talmudic discussion has been crucial to modern scholarly claims that Rav and Shmuel were leaders of the Babylonian Jewish community who disagreed about the best strategy to employ in response to the advent of the Sasanians. According to this scholarly picture, Shmuel counseled accommodation, while Rav remained stubbornly opposed to the new dynasty. I have dealt in detail with the fragility of the evidence in favor of portraying Rav in this fashion, and the ensuing discussion challenges this portrayal of Shmuel.

We read in b. Moed Katan 25b–26a:

> (A) (Our rabbis taught [in a Baraita:])[89] Which are the tearings [done as a sign of mourning] that are not repaired? One who tears for his father and his mother and for his master who taught him Torah and for the patriarch and for the *av beit din* and for bad news.... And what is the [scriptural] source [that one tears] for the patriarch and for the *av beit din* and for bad news?[90] As is written,[91] "David took hold of his clothes and rent them, and so did all the men with him. They lamented and wept, and they fasted until evening for Saul and his son Jonathan, and for the soldiers of the Lord and the House of Israel who had fallen by the sword" (2 Sam. 1:11–12)....
>
> (B) [Aramaic:] And do we rend [garments upon hearing] bad news? Behold,
>
> (C) [Aramaic:] They said to Shmuel,[92] "Shapur the [Persian] king killed 12,000 Jews in Caesarea Mazaca," and he did not rend [his garments].
>
> (D) [Hebrew:] They only said [that one rends one's garments upon hearing bad news] in the case of the majority of the community in conformity with what happened [to Saul, Jonathan, the soldiers of the Lord, and the House of Israel].
>
> (E) [Aramaic:] And did Shapur the king kill Jews? Behold
>
> (F) [Aramaic:] Shapur the King said to Shmuel, "May evil befall me if I have ever killed Jews."
>
> (G) [Aramaic:] In that case they brought it upon themselves.
>
> (H) [Aramaic:] For
>
> (I) [Aramaic:] R. Ami said, "From the noise of the bows of Caesarea Mazaca the wall of Laodicea collapsed."

The discussion as it presently stands is structured as follows: (1) part A is a Baraita, to which (2) the anonymous editors object in part B by quoting a brief story (part C) involving the mid-third-century-CE Amora, Shmuel, and his interlocutors. The anonymous editors resolve their own objection (part D), but follow with another objection (part E), which bases itself on a brief statement by King Shapur in the presence of the same figure, Shmuel (part F). In part G, the anonymous editors resolve their objection, and support it by quoting a statement by a somewhat later Amora, R. Ami. The anonymous editors, therefore, have Amoraic and Tannaitic material at their disposal (parts A, C, F, and H), which they use to construct a typical *sugya*, that is, a flowing discourse comprised of objections followed by responses, the standard stuff of anonymous editorial discourse throughout the Talmud.

For a variety of reasons, however, this understanding of the discussion is problematic. First, once again, we are faced with a change of language, this time from Aramaic to Hebrew. Specifically, the anonymous editors object in Aramaic (part B), but phrase their response to the objection (part D) in Hebrew. In fact, with the exception of part D, all of the statements by the anonymous editors in this passage (parts B, E, and G) are in Aramaic. Even more important, throughout the Talmud anonymous editorial discourse is overwhelmingly, virtually without exception, Aramaic, particularly where argumentation is concerned, so much so that the fact that part D is in Hebrew virtually guarantees that this statement does not derive from the anonymous editors. If the anonymous editors did not author part D, however, then who did?

Before we answer this question, another difficulty with the above division of the discussion needs to be pointed out. I refer to the fact that the second response (part G: "In that case they brought it upon themselves") could have served equally well as an effective response to the first objection (part B: "And do we rend garments upon hearing bad news?").[93] In other words, based upon the standards of Talmudic give and take encountered on virtually every page of the Bavli, the above discussion is anomalous. Based on Talmudic give and take elsewhere, we would expect the ebb and flow of the discussion to be different, with both objections resolved simultaneously by part G (the second response), thereby eliminating entirely the need for part D (the first response).[94]

Once again, we see that a change of language is accompanied by other factors that undermine the place of the linguistically problematic statement in the ebb and flow of the discussion.

Also of relevance is the fact that according to the above understanding of the discussion, part C ("They said to Shmuel, 'Shapur the [Persian] King killed 12,000 Jews in Caesarea Mazaca,' and he did not rend [his garments]") and part F ("Shapur the king said to Shmuel, 'May evil befall me if I have ever killed Jews' ") contradict each other. According to the above understanding, therefore, these two traditions obviously are to be understood as deriving from diverse sources, which the anonymous editors juxtapose to one another and reconcile.[95] We moderns are trained to be skeptical of such later editorial resolutions, however, and our inclination is to reject the editorial response as artificial, as a device by the anonymous editors to get themselves out of an embarrassing hermeneutical situation. More likely, our tendency is to conclude, we simply have two contradictory traditions regarding Shapur's treatment of the Jews. According to one tradition (part C), he killed great numbers of them, perhaps because they were in his way during the course of his numerous incursions against Rome, or perhaps because the Jews of Cappadocia sided with Rome against the Persians; according to the other tradition (part F), he behaved in exemplary fashion toward them throughout his reign. Our inclination, furthermore, is to treat the first tradition (part C) as more trustworthy, since it corresponds to the behavior we expect of ancient emperors and their subject peoples, as well as the behavior of the religious leaders of these subject peoples who often needed to behave in public in a politically expedient fashion. Shmuel may have thought it was atrocious that Shapur had murdered Jews, but publicly he had to support the king, whose favor was so important for the welfare of the Jews of Babylonia. According to this understanding, the fate of the Jews of Asia Minor, while lamentable, was not Shmuel's most pressing concern.

This understanding of the relationship between the two parts of the discussion is problematic, however, since parts C and F are so similar linguistically, structurally, and thematically that it is difficult to believe that they derive from different sources. Their similarity can perhaps be illustrated by observing that part C consists of 13 words and part F of 11 words, and seven of the words are identical, or are the same word but in a different form (e.g., *amru*, "they said," as opposed to *amar*, "he said").[96]

In addition, the two brief stories do not really contradict, despite the Talmud's claim that they do. The first story, related by an omniscient narrator, asserts that Shapur killed 12,000 Jews in Caesarea Mazaca. The second story consists of Shapur's claim of innocence. Why does Shapur's claim of innocence, however, contradict the omniscient narrators' claim that he killed large numbers of Jews? There is a contradiction only if we assume that Shapur is telling the truth, and heads of state, ancient as well as modern, are wont to lie.

If we structure the discussion differently, however, and take into account manuscript variants, we resolve all of these objections and arrive at a much different understanding of the history of these traditions and of the work of later editorial harmonizers versus that of the storytellers themselves. This rereading changes our evaluation of these sources as historical evidence, and shows that we are dealing to a larger extent than we originally thought with a narrative that purports to derive from the time of Shmuel himself, that is, the early to mid–third century CE, rather than with a rather thin layer of story read, or rather misread, by later editors. It is important to reiterate that a story about an early Amora can be later (although it need not be), and that an early story can be fictitious while a later story can be true.[97] It is important, in other words, not to exaggerate the importance of our findings. Still, here as elsewhere, historical reconstructions of the evidence will be profoundly affected by decisions regarding what was contributed by the editors on the one hand and by the storytellers on the other.

In understanding the discussion in this new fashion, it is not necessary to emend in the slightest. According to my reevaluation, the anonymous editors interrupt the flow of a single tradition, doing so with a minimum of invasiveness. They convert what were originally declarative statements and dialogue within a story into responses to objections, unmindful or unconcerned about the incongruities created in the process. The editors convert narrative, a combination of actions and dialogue, into standard Talmudic give and take.

Before the later editors tampered with the discussion, it was a single, unified story, based on the Baraita (part A), as follows:

> (A) (Our rabbis taught [in a Baraita:]) Which are the tearings [done as a sign of mourning] that are not repaired? One who tears for his father and his mother and for his master who taught him Torah and for the patriarch and for the *av beit din* and for bad news. . . . And what is the [scriptural] source [that one tears] for the patriarch, the *av beit din* and bad news? As is written, "David took hold of his clothes and rent them, and so did all the men with him. They lamented and wept, and they fasted until evening for Saul and his son Jonathan, and for the soldiers of the Lord and the House of Israel who had fallen by the sword" (2 Sam. 1:11–12). . . .
>
> (C) [Aramaic:] They said to Shmuel, "Shapur the [Persian] king killed 12,000 Jews in Caesarea Mazaca," and he did not rend [his garments].
>
> (D) [Hebrew:] [Shmuel said to them],[98] "They only said [that one rends one's garments upon hearing bad news] in the case of the majority of the community in conformity with what happened" [to Saul, Jonathan, the soldiers of the Lord, and the House of Israel].
>
> (F) [Aramaic:] Shapur the king said to Shmuel, "May evil befall me if I have ever killed Jews."

This narrative differs from the previous version of the discussion primarily in that we have omitted from the discussion part B ("And do we rend [garments upon hearing] bad news? Behold"); and part E ("And did Shapur the king kill Jews? Behold"), both of which are objections added by the later editors that serve to convert the preexisting narrative into Talmudic give and take. We have also omitted part G ("In that case they brought it upon themselves"), which is apparently the anonymous editors' response to their own objection.[99] Finally, we have eliminated parts H and I (For R. Ami said, "From the noise of the bows of Caesarea Mazaca the wall of Laodicea collapsed"), since it is difficult to see how the statement by R. Ami makes the point it is supposedly invoked to make.[100] For, as Saul Lieberman notes, R. Ami's statement means: "From the noise of the [Persian] bows of Caesarea Mazaca the wall of Laodicea collapsed."[101] The Persians were renowned archers, and the statement most likely refers to Persian bows, in which case it is a mystery how the statement supports the claim that the Jews of Caesarea Mazaca are responsible for their own fate. And even if we admit of the possibility that Jewish archers are referred to, the statement says nothing about the Jews initiating military action, or precludes the possibility of the Jews having acted in self-defense. It should also be noted that a close parallel to this statement is preserved in y. Baba Batra 2:3 (13b) as well as in a Persian source,[102] where Persian bows and different cities are referred to. Evidently the anonymous editors have taken a statement that was "in circulation" in various parts of the ancient world about a variety of different cities, and have quoted it in connection with a discussion about Caesarea Mazaca, making only a minimal effort to link it to its new context.

According to my reconstruction, furthermore, the original story opens with unnamed interlocutors informing Shmuel that "Shapur the king killed 12,000 Jews in Caesarea Mazaca." Shmuel responds by refraining from rending his garments, explaining that the Baraita that mandates rending the garments upon hearing bad news only applies to evil tidings about "the majority of the community in accordance with the story of 'Saul, Jonathan, and the entire House of Israel.' "[103] The story concludes with Shapur swearing to Shmuel that he never killed Jews.

This rereading of the story and the role of the anonymous editors solves all of the problems raised above. For example, the news that "Shapur the King killed 12,000 Jews" and Shapur's own claim that he "never killed Jews" do not derive from contradictory sources. These two statements are part of a seamless narrative, with Shapur's claim not to have killed Jews an attempt on the king's part (imagined by the rabbinic authors of the story) to improve his standing in the eyes of Shmuel. We also eliminate the problem of the anonymous editors speaking Hebrew, since according to my reconstruction above, the statement in question is Shmuel's response to his interlocutors rather than a response by the anonymous editors.[104] Finally, even though the response to the second objection ("In that case they brought it upon themselves") works to explain why Shmuel did not rend his garments, Shmuel did not invoke this argument at the first available opportunity because it derives from the later anonymous editors, who had before them Shmuel's response (part D) as an integral part of the story.

How does this rereading of the Talmudic discussion change the way we should evaluate the historicity of this passage? First, we see that more of the passage than we originally thought purports to describe events and conversations that took place during the mid–third century CE. As noted, this fact does not guarantee that the story is true or that it derives from the period it purports to describe. Still, we are dealing to a lesser extent with ad hoc, artificial, and after-the-fact explanations by later editors, and to a greater extent than we originally thought with a single, unified story. The number 12,000 is without a doubt a round number and simply means that many Jews died, and it is unlikely that Shmuel had this or any other conversation with Shapur. Part F ("Shapur the king said to Shmuel, 'May evil befall me if I have ever killed Jews' ") is an attempt on the storyteller's part to glorify Shmuel, to show how the great Persian monarch, the king of kings, found it necessary to appear before a rabbi and respond to the accusation against him. It is not at all uncommon for the rabbis to tell stories featuring non-Jewish personages for the purpose of self-aggrandizement.

Of greatest importance, however, is the conclusion that part D purports to be the words of Shmuel himself rather than the anonymous editors' response to their own objection.

> [Shmuel said to them], "They only said [that one rends one's garments upon hearing bad news] in the case of the majority of the

> community in conformity with what happened" [to Saul, Jonathan, the soldiers of the Lord, and the House of Israel].

Viewing the statement as the words of the anonymous editors virtually guarantees that we understand it as an artificial, scholastic attempt by professional reconcilers to mask the subtle, sophisticated political maneuver of Shmuel to avoid antagonizing the Persian monarch, whose friendship he cultivated because he knew the fate of Babylonian Jewry rested in Shapur's hands and he had no choice but to accommodate himself to the harsh political realities of the age.[105] The Sasanians were in Babylonia to stay, and, in part based on the discussion before us, Shmuel is routinely portrayed in modern scholarly literature as a hardheaded pragmatist in his dealings with the Persians.[106] Shmuel, in fact, is seen as an important early architect of what was to become standard Jewish strategy in dealing with the majority culture on whose good graces they depended for survival.

Viewing part D as the words of Shmuel himself, however, or at least as words that the storyteller attributed to Shmuel, increases the likelihood that the explanation he offers for his failure to rend his garments in response to the "evil tidings" is not artificial. It increases the likelihood that the hermeneutical explanation is in fact correct, that Shmuel (or whoever put these words into his mouth) really believes that the requirement to rend the garments only applies to a case that resembles that described in 1 Samuel, which is, after all, the basis upon which the Tannaitic source (part A) derives the requirement in the first place. Once again, we must avoid the temptation to view the Talmud's hermeneutical explanations as so much window dressing and pious talk, as cautious attempts by savvy politicians to avoid revealing the true reasons for their actions. As I have noted throughout this book, the Babylonian Talmud, particularly that part of it that derives from Babylonia, is primarily literature by rabbis and for rabbis.[107] Neither the Persian government nor nonrabbinic Jews would have access to it, and the Talmud contains numerous unambiguous criticisms of Persians and Persian kings, as well as of nonrabbinic Jews. Why would the rabbis be so secretive here when in so many other instances they exhibit no hesitation whatsoever about giving voice to opinions their competitors and enemies in Babylonia would have found offensive?[108] This consideration does not guarantee that the response attributed to Shmuel here reflects the "real" reason for his behavior, but simply suggests that according to my conclusions above, the likelihood that it does so is increased.

The editors' motive from start to finish may have been the creation of argumentation out of the earlier Amoraic material at their disposal. According to this explanation, the editors blame the Jews of Caesarea Mazaca for bringing upon themselves the wrath of the Persians because doing so enables them to resolve an objection by bringing R. Ami's statement into the discussion. Rather than a briefer discussion and a freestanding statement, or a story and a freestanding statement with virtually no argumentation, the editors have created a lengthier discussion that finds a place for what were at an earlier stage independent elements. The editors' motive, here as in so many places, is *lehagdil Torah u-leha'adirah*, to increase the length, complexity, and lavishness of the Talmud's argumentation rather than to make a political, historical, or theological statement.[109]

It has not been my intention in this chapter to minimize the tremendous advances in our understanding of ancient Jewish culture and society that have resulted from the efforts of historians in recent decades. The insights of the historian are too often ignored by the text critic, whose work suffers greatly as a result. Gafni's work, in particular, the finest synthetic study of the history of the ancient Jews in Babylonia, hardly stands or falls on the conclusions of this chapter. I hope to have illustrated merely that historians of the period need to pay closer attention to the latest developments in the field of Talmud text criticism, which result in important revisions in our understanding of the history and culture of the Jews of late antiquity. There is less reason than earlier scholars thought to view Rav and Shmuel, the most important Babylonian rabbis active during the transition from Parthian to Sasanian rule, as having taken strong, opposing stands about the rival Persian dynasties. There is less reason than we thought previously to view the rabbis' opinions about the Persians as of interest to the larger Jewish community, and to view the rabbis, at least those of the early to mid–third century, as anything other than teachers stating their opinions in the presence of their students. There is also less reason than we thought previously to view the advent of the Sasanian dynasty as an event of major significance to one important minority in the Persian Empire. Perhaps this conclusion will stimulate scholars to reexamine the consequences of this change of regime for other minorities within the empire, and perhaps for the Persian majority as well.

Appendix 1: Rabbinic Responses to the Advent of the Sasanian Dynasty

Other traditions cited by scholars as proof for the claim that the advent of a new Persian dynasty was a turning point in the Jewish experience in Babylonia are equally unpersuasive. B. Shabbat 45a will serve as an example:

> (A) And does Rav accept the opinion of R. Yehudah? Behold,
>
> (B) They asked Rav, "What [is the law with regard] to moving a Hanukah lamp from before a magian priest [*ḥabar*] on Shabbat?"
>
> (C) [Rav] said to them, "It is well."
>
> (D) A time of emergency is different, for behold
>
> (E) Rav Kahana and Rav Asi said to Rav, "This is the law?"
>
> (F) [Rav] said to them, "R. Shimon can be relied upon in a time of emergency."

It is possible that the expression "a time of emergency" is not a reference to the period after the *ḥabarei* come to Babylonia as distinct from the period before their arrival, but to the period when one becomes aware of the approach of the magian priests as distinct from periods of quiet, when the priests were not in the vicinity and posed no threat.[110] Understood in this fashion, this tradition reveals nothing about rabbinic responses to the danger posed to the Jews by the new Sasanian dynasty.

A Baraita in b. Shabbat 21b may also be relevant:

> (A) Our rabbis taught [in a Baraita]: A Hanukah lamp, it is a mizvah to leave it at the entrance to his house on the outside.
>
> (B) If he lived in an upper story, he places it in the window near the public domain.
>
> (C) In a time of danger, he leaves it on his table and it is sufficient.

Here the reference is to "a time of danger," which some commentators claim refers to the situation in Persia.[111] However, as noted in chapter 1, other scholars have noted that the term "a time of danger" elsewhere refers to the Roman persecutions of the Bar Kokhba period.[112] While it is possible that we are dealing with a "Babylonian Baraita," therefore, the fact that in the discussion in b. Shabbat 45a involving Rav, Persian interference with the performance of the mizvah[113] is referred to as *sha'at ha-dehak* ("a time of emergency") rather than *sha'at ha-sakanah* ("a time of danger") suggests, in the absence of evidence to the contrary, that the scene contemplated by this Baraita is Israel under Rome rather than Babylonia under Persia.

Appendix 2

The Talmud has a variety of ways in which it typically constructs discussions in which a single rejoinder responds to more than one objection. According to one possibility, the two objections could have been placed one right after the other, for example, as follows:

> (B) And do we rend [garments upon hearing] bad news? Behold
>
> (C) They said to Shmuel, "Shapur the [Persian] King killed 12,000 Jews in Caesarea Mazaca," and he did not rend [his garments].
>
> (E) And did Shapur the king kill Jews? Behold
>
> (F) Shapur the king said to Shmuel, "May evil befall me if I have ever killed Jews.

This structure would have eliminated the need for and the usefulness of part D, and part G ("In that case they brought it upon themselves") would have followed as a response to both objections. According to another possibility, the discussion could have remained as at present, that is, with part D, but at the end of the discussion the anonymous editors could have explicitly informed us that "Now that we have come this far (*hashta de-atit le-hakhi*), it is possible to resolve the first objection in the same way as the second." The latter type of footnote to a discussion is used, apparently, when a later editor adds to a discussion already commented upon by an earlier editor, and the later editor responds in a fashion that he feels renders the response of the earlier editor superfluous.[114]

7

Josephus in Sasanian Babylonia

As noted in the introduction, Ẓvi Dor first observed decades ago that statements by and stories involving mid-fourth-century-CE Babylonian rabbis frequently depict them (1) commenting on the opinions of Palestinian rabbis; and (2) expressing opinions and performing actions characteristic of Palestinian rabbis.[1] Dor's observation has been confirmed by more recent studies, all of which point to the fourth century as a period when the literature and behavior of Babylonian Amoraim, as well as the traditions deemed worthy of their study, exhibited a marked Palestinian character.[2]

The next two chapters further document the influx of Palestinian traditions into Babylonia, and the susceptibility of fourth-century Babylonian rabbis to Palestinian modes of thought and behavior. This chapter shows that Josephus or Josephus-like traditions[3] deriving from the west, whether from Roman Palestine or from somewhere in the Roman Empire outside of Palestine, reached Persian-controlled Mesopotamia and found a receptive rabbinic audience there. Once again, my conclusion will be that Babylonian rabbis were motivated not by events, trends, or personalities in the larger, nonrabbinic Jewish society, but by literature, which produced a significant change in Babylonian rabbinic literature. As noted in the introduction, however, this conclusion should not be construed as a claim on my part that Babylonian rabbis were always motivated by literature and never by "current events."

This chapter is based on comparison between rabbinic and Josephan traditions about the Sadducees.[4] I will attempt to show that traditions in the Bavli tend to be hostile toward the Sadducees, while traditions in Palestinian compilations tend to reflect a more neutral perspective.[5] The Palestinian traditions acknowledge, or even revel in, the existence of individual Sadducees who are wicked, but these individuals are always quickly punished with death by God for their evil deeds, and the Sadducees as a group are harmless, obedient, in fact, to the rulings of the Pharisees. I will also demonstrate that since it is a fundamental tenet of rabbinic thought that the rabbis possessed traditions that were authoritative despite their independence from scripture, the introduction into Babylonia of traditions that portray the Sadducees as accepting only scripture and rejecting traditions external to the Bible[6] motivated these hostile Babylonian portrayals. I will argue that the Bavli's portrayal of the Sadducees as a group that accepts only scripture[7] derives either from (1) Josephus, or (2) traditions drawn upon independently by both Josephus and the rabbis.[8] Both the harsh criticisms of the Sadducees and their portrayal as rejecting extrabiblical traditions can be shown to have been incorporated into the Bavli at approximately the same time (the mid–fourth century) and apparently by the same individuals or the same group of people, supporting my claim that a close relationship exists between these two phenomena.

In one important case, chronological and geographical markers will allow me to approximate when a portrayal of the Sadducees made its way into Babylonian rabbinic circles, and to describe the subtle shifts in this portrayal throughout the rabbinic period. In other words, sometimes the layered nature of Talmudic discourse permits us to write the history of an idea or an institution, but sometimes the process of editorial homogenization erases all or most evidence of such developments, which is precisely what we would expect to find in a literature as vast and variegated as that of the Babylonian Talmud.[9]

Rabbinic Traditions about the Sadducees

Support for my claim regarding the Bavli's unique tendency to denigrate the Sadducees[10] is found in b. Yoma 4a, which contains the following presumably Tannaitic text:

> (A) [Hebrew:] Aaron separated himself for seven days and he served [as high priest] for one day, and Moses sent to him all seven days in order to instruct him regarding the [sacrificial] service. And even in future generations the high priest separates himself for seven days and serves for one day, and two disciples of the sages from among the disciples of Moses—
>
> (B) [Aramaic:]—to exclude Sadducees—
>
> (A) [Hebrew:]—send to him all seven days in order to instruct him regarding the [sacrificial] service.

Section B, an obvious Aramaic interpolation into an earlier Hebrew tradition (A), interprets the curious phrase "two disciples of the sages from among the disciples of Moses"[11] to exclude Sadducees. By asserting that Sadducees are not "disciples of Moses," the author of this interpolation reveals extreme antipathy toward them. Elsewhere in rabbinic literature, the claim that a group[12] denies Moses as its rabbi serves to brand its members as heretics, who deny the authority of Moses. This brief interpolation is perhaps the most extreme expression of disapproval of the Sadducees found in any ancient rabbinic text.[13]

B. Yoma 19b also records a negative portrayal of the Sadducees that goes beyond what we encounter in Palestinian compilations:

> (A) Mishnah: We [the priests] adjure you [the high priest] in [the name of] Him who dwells in this house [the Temple] that you will not change anything we told you [i.e., that you will perform the ritual exactly as we instructed you]. [The high priest] separates himself and cries and they separate themselves and cry.[14]
>
> (B) Talmud: [The high priest] separates himself and cries, because they suspected him of being a Sadducee. And they separate themselves and cry, for
>
> (C) R. Yehoshua ben Levi said, "Whoever suspects those who are worthy suffers bodily harm."

The high priest weeps because he is "suspected" of being a Sadducee, which to provoke such consternation must be a serious charge. As utilized here by the Talmud's anonymous editors, furthermore, R. Yehoshua ben Levi's statement implies that if the high priest is a Sadducee he is not worthy. The priests weep out of concern that they are suspicious of someone who has done nothing wrong. The fact that he may be a Sadducee makes the risk worth taking.

In another brief but telling comment, b. Eruvin 68b contains a purportedly Tannaitic tradition that quotes Rabban Gamliel referring to a Sadducee as an "abomination." This statement is parallel to m. Eruvin 6:2, a Palestinian source, and Rabban Gamliel's comment there lacks the pejorative epithet.

Along the same lines, b. Baba Batra 115b–116a depicts the Sadducees in bitter conflict with sages, and describes them in harshly negative terms unprecedented in traditions found in Palestinian compilations. The story, most likely a post-Tannaitic, Babylonian creation, since it is derived from and modeled after a tradition in b. Menaḥot 65a–b,[15] is as follows:[16]

> (A) Said Rav Huna said Rav, "Anyone, even a prince of Israel, who says that a daughter is to inherit with the daughter of a son, must not be obeyed, for such [a ruling] is only the practice of the Sadducees."
>
> (B) As it was taught [in a Tannaitic statement] [Aramaic:] On the twenty-fourth of Tevet we returned to our [own] law. [Hebrew:] For the Sadducees maintained [that] a daughter inherited with the daughter of the son.
>
> Rabban Yoḥanan ben Zakkai joined issue with them.
>
> He said to them, "Fools! From where do you derive this?"

Not one of them answered, except for an old man who babbled at him,[17] saying, "If the daughter of his son, who comes [to inherit] by virtue of his son's right, is heir to him, how much more so his daughter, who derives her right from himself?"

[Rabban Yoḥanan ben Zakkai] applied to him the verse, " 'These are the sons of Seir the Horite, the inhabitants of the land: Lotan and Shobal and Zibeon and Anah' (Gen. 36:20), and [lower down] it is written, 'And these are the children of Zibeon: Aiah and Anah' (Gen. 36:24). [But this] teaches that Zibeon had intercourse with his mother and fathered Anah."

(C) Is it not possible that there were two [called] Anah?

(D) Rabbah said, ". . . Scripture says, 'This is Anah,' [implying] the same Anah that was [mentioned] before."

(B) [The Sadducee] said to [Rabban Yoḥanan ben Zakkai], "Rabbi, do you dismiss me with such [a feeble reply]?"

[Rabban Yoḥanan ben Zakkai] said to [the Sadducee], "Fool! Is not our perfect Torah as good as your worthless talk? A son's daughter [has a right of inheritance] because her claim is valid where there are brothers, but can the same be said of the [deceased's] daughter whose right [of inheritance] is impaired where there are brothers?"

Thus they were defeated. And that day was declared a festive day.

According to this narrative, the Sadducees are "fools," such that no one among them is able to respond to Rabban Yoḥanan ben Zakkai's challenge, except for an "old man"[18] who "babbles" at the rabbi and who is himself a "fool." Moreover, the "perfect Torah" of the rabbis is in stark contrast to the "worthless talk" of the Sadducees. Only when the Sadducee explicitly acknowledges Rabban Yoḥanan ben Zakkai's superiority, referring to him as "Rabbi," does Rabban Yoḥanan ben Zakkai reveal to him the true reason for the sages' opinion. Only after his submission is the Sadducee, though still a "fool" and still the purveyor of "worthless talk," worthy of knowing the true scriptural proof.

Significantly, this halakhic dispute is recorded in two Palestinian compilations, and in neither of the parallels is there the slightest hint of contempt for or criticism of the Sadducees or their opinion, although it goes without saying that the rabbis consider the Sadducean opinion to be incorrect.[19]

In addition, b. Berakhot 29a is more critical of the Sadducees than is a parallel discussion in Pesikta de-Rav Kahana, a Palestinian compilation.[20] The Bavli's discussion is as follows:

(A) Abaye said, "I have a tradition that a good person does not become bad."

(B) No? Behold it is written, "If a righteous person turns away from his righteousness and does wrong" (Ezek. 18:24).

(C) [The text from Ezekiel] refers to someone who was originally wicked [and then became righteous. He may return and become wicked again.] But someone who was originally righteous, no [i.e., he will not become wicked].

(D) No? Behold

(E) We taught [in a Tannaitic tradition],[21] "Do not trust yourself until the day of your death, for Yoḥanan the High Priest served in the office of high priest for 80 years and in the end he became a Sadducee."

(F) Said Abaye, "[King] Yannai and Yoḥanan [the High Priest] are one [and the same person]."

According to this discussion, late in life Yoḥanan the High Priest became wicked, a transformation proven by the fact that he became a Sadducee.

The second half of part E is closely paralleled in a Palestinian compilation, Pesikta de-Rav Kahana,[22] where the comment is found in the context of a discussion of the evil inclination. In its context in the Pesikta, the statement "They said about Yoḥanan the High Priest that he served in [the office of] the high priesthood for 80 years and in the end became a Sadducee" implies that there is something anomalous about Yoḥanan becoming a Sadducee after so many years of faithful service to God, and the anomaly is evidence of the power of the evil inclination. While the Pesikta clearly views Yoḥanan the High Priest's "conversion" to Sadduceeism with disfavor, it is less forceful than the Bavli's unqualified characterization of him as "wicked."

In addition, Abaye's second statement in the Bavli (part F) also distinguishes the Babylonian attitude toward the Sadducees from that expressed in the Pesikta. Abaye declares that Yoḥanan the High Priest is none other than the Hasmonean king Yannai, the subject of numerous stories in the Bavli that describe his depravity. As noted in chapter 2, Babylonian rabbis routinely depict the Hasmoneans in a bad light, with King Yannai usually made to play the role of the evil Hasmonean monarch.[23] For reasons to be expanded on below, it is likely that Abaye has at least some of this background in mind when he identifies King Yannai and Yoḥanan the High Priest.

Detailed examination of a story in b. Kiddushin 66a, together with its Amoraic and anonymous commentary, will further support my claim regarding the tendency of the Bavli to depict the Sadducees negatively (see below).[24] Turning first to an examination of the scanty evidence of negative attitudes toward the Sadducees in Palestinian compilations, we find a substantially different picture.[25] In y. Eruvin 1:1 (18c) we find the following:

[The rabbis] said to [R. Meir], "If so, let the enemies of R. Yoḥanan be like a Sadducee vis-à-vis the occupants of the courtyard and let the occupants of the courtyard be forbidden [to carry within the courtyard]."

The Yerushalmi here employs a circumlocution ("let the enemies of R. Yoḥanan be like a Sadducee"), adding the phrase "the enemies of" to the text to avoid the suggestion that R. Yoḥanan himself was like a Sadducee. The statement implies nothing whatsoever about R. Yoḥanan's ethical character, his obedience to the sages, or his observance of halakhah, but the thought of associating R. Yoḥanan and Sadducees was so disturbing that the phrase "the enemies of" was added to the text so that anyone reading or repeating it would associate R. Yoḥanan's enemies, rather than R. Yoḥanan, with the hated Sadducees. The phrase is not an integral part of the discussion, however, and very late, post-Talmudic copyists may have added it, since other than in this one easily detachable comment, the Yerushalmi nowhere expresses disapproval of the Sadducees.

A second negative statement, in Sifrei Numbers,[26] may also be a later addition to the text. We read there:

> "'For he despised the word of the Lord' (Num. 15:31), this is a Sadducee.
> 'And he broke his commandments' (Num. 15:31), this is an Epikoros."

Clearly this tradition is harshly critical of Sadducees. Once again, however, it is uncertain whether or not the negative attitude is an integral part of the text, since the passage cited above is missing from two versions of the Sifrei.[27] This tradition may have been added long after the Sifrei's final editing, when the term "Sadducee" was routinely substituted for the term *min* (heretic), and negative judgments about heretics were routinely associated with Sadducees.[28]

Both quantitatively and qualitatively, therefore, traditions in Palestinian compilations are less harshly critical of and hostile to the Sadducees than are traditions in the Bavli.[29] Significantly, whenever I found parallels between Palestinian and Babylonian sources, the latter were always more hostile toward the Sadducees than were the Palestinian parallels. This phenomenon calls out for explanation, although our conclusions must remain tentative due to the paucity of relevant data.

How might we explain these curious facts? We cannot argue that the larger number of negative traditions is simply a function of the larger number of relevant traditions of any sort, since Sadducees are mentioned about as frequently in Palestinian compilations as in the Bavli.[30] Furthermore, according to this explanation, the greater hostility of Babylonian traditions remains unaccounted for.

We also cannot account for the difference purely on the basis of genre, explaining that the Bavli is richer in narratives than are Palestinian compilations, and narratives are more apt to depict conflict and hatred between the protagonists. This explanation fails, since only one of the Babylonian traditions examined above criticizes the Sadducees in the context of a narrative that has no close parallel in a Palestinian compilation.[31] In addition, as noted, there are elaborate narratives about the Sadducees in both Babylonian and Palestinian compilations, but it is primarily in the Bavli that we find harsh criticisms of the Sadducees. While in general the greater narrativity of the Bavli is an indisputable fact, it does not account for the greater negativity of the Bavli's traditions in this context.

How else might we account for these phenomena?[32] In an earlier study, I examined rabbinic traditions about the Hasmoneans and found that Babylonian traditions tend to be critical of Hasmoneans while Palestinian traditions tend to be neutral or even positive toward them, similar to the distinction noted here.[33] It is possible that Babylonian rabbis may have used these unflattering stories and statements to criticize Babylonian contemporaries who claimed Hasmonean descent.[34] Perhaps, therefore, Babylonian rabbis were competing against contemporary Jews who referred to themselves as Sadducees or who exhibited Sadducean traits.[35]

Who or what might such a group or such individuals have been like? What might have marked one as a Sadducee in third- to seventh-century Babylonia? Several traditions in the Bavli, as well as Josephus, characterize Sadducees as a group that accepts only scripture and rejects the traditions of the Pharisees or the sages.[36] In this guise they bear a striking resemblance to Karaites,[37] who originated in Persia and only subsequently moved to Israel.[38] Early Karaites were often referred to by their medieval rabbanite contemporaries and opponents as Sadducees, in part because one of the fundamental tenets of Karaism is the denial of the rabbinic tradition and the claim to be reliant on the authority of the Bible alone.[39] While the Karaite movement "coalesced only about the end of the ninth or beginning of the tenth century,"[40] it is theoretically possible that Karaite tendencies percolated in the Babylonian Jewish community for centuries prior to Karaism's crystallization as a movement. Perhaps third- to seventh-century Babylonian rabbis were aware of some proto-Karaite groups or individuals in Jewish society, and perhaps they polemicized against them or took literary vengeance on them by telling stories that portrayed ancient Sadducean characters as villains.

Several factors, however, militate against this explanation. First, in my earlier study of the Hasmoneans, I found evidence that Babylonian rabbis competed with contemporary Jews who claimed Hasmonean descent. One story, for example, features a character who opposes a prominent Babylonian rabbi while claiming Hasmonean descent.[41] I found no evidence, however, of Babylonian Jews of the third to seventh centuries claiming Sadducean descent, or of Babylonian rabbis responding to Sadducee-like groups as a continued presence during the rabbis' own era. We have no evidence before the ninth or tenth centuries of actual groups or individuals in Babylonia who were referred to as Sadducees or who exhibited Sadducean tendencies. The advent of the Karaite movement in ninth- or tenth-century Persia still leaves a gap of at least two centuries between the Talmudic and the post-Talmudic evidence. The findings of this study, therefore, appear to call for a different explanation from that offered in my earlier work. Finally, it is strange, although not impossible, that the rabbis would attack proto-Karaites only by tampering with stories about first-century (or earlier) Sadducees. As I have noted several times, Babylonian rabbis were not at all shy about criticizing their opponents directly, for example by means of stories depicting the misdeeds of their contemporaries.[42]

We avoid these problems if we adopt an explanation based on two closely related literary phenomena: the incorporation into the Bavli of Josephus or Josephus-like traditions, and the influx into Babylonia of traditions from Roman Palestine, especially beginning in the mid–fourth century CE. To be specific, I will attempt to show that the introduction of Josephus or Josephus-like traditions into mid-fourth-century Babylonia motivated the Bavli's tendency to portray the Sadducees in negative terms. Josephus, or the Josephus-like traditions mentioned above, had relatively little impact on Palestinian compilations (as is shown by the simple fact that parallels between Josephus and traditions in Palestinian compilations are relatively rare), which explains the tendency of traditions in Palestinian documents to depict the Sadducees in relatively neutral fashion.

As noted, this conclusion does not preclude the possibility that Babylonian rabbis were also reacting to the existence of proto-Karaites in their midst. In fact, the presence of such groups or individuals would help explain why Babylonian rabbis were receptive to Josephus or Josephus-like traditions and incorporated them into their developing compilation. Alternatively, the rabbis were perhaps receptive to these traditions because they afforded them opportunities to retell Jewish history in a way that glorified the rabbis and emphasized the indispensable role they played in rescuing Judaism from those who would destroy it. It remains the case, furthermore, that no positive evidence has yet been found for the existence of such groups or individuals in Sasanian Babylonia, and the arguments raised above against this possibility establish it as rather unlikely, although not impossible.

The Portrayal of Sadducees as a Group That Accepts Only Scripture

What is the basis for the claim that Josephus or Josephus-like traditions motivated the Bavli's negative portrayals of Sadducees? The answer is that in the Bavli we find descriptions and portrayals of the Sadducees that are strikingly similar to those found in Josephus, and unlike anything found in Palestinian compilations. Moreover, it is easy to see why people portrayed with such characteristics would be anathema to the rabbis, and the negative portrayals of Sadducees and the portrayals of them as a group that accepted only scripture are known to the same Babylonian rabbis, attested beginning in the mid–fourth century CE.

To establish this claim, however, it is necessary to engage in the close reading of several Babylonian rabbinic texts. In b. Horayot 4a we find the following:

> (A) Said Rav Yehudah said Shmuel, "A court [that issues an incorrect opinion, causing the community to sin inadvertently] is not obligated [to bring a sacrifice] until it rules on a matter with which the Sadducees disagree. But if it is a matter with which the Sadducees agree, the court is exempt [from bringing a sacrifice]."

(B) What is the reason?

(C) It is a matter of "Go and read in [the children's] schoolhouse [*zil karei bei rav*]."

According to this brief discussion, and according to a strikingly similar but independent discussion in b. Sanhedrin 33b,[43] the expression "a matter with which the Sadducees agree" is synonymous with scripture, since scripture is what is "read in [the children's] schoolhouse."[44] The term *bei rav* often refers to a school for children, and the usage here of the term *karei*, "read," to denote what goes on there supports this understanding, since every curriculum of children's study mentioned in classical rabbinic literature specifies scripture as the one and only thing that children learned to read.[45] According to this discussion, the Sadducees accepted scripture but rejected rabbinic learning in toto.

We have yet to determine, however, approximately when this conception of the Sadducees is first attested in Babylonia. As noted, it is important to decide this question because it is crucial for making my case that Josephus or Josephus-like traditions motivated the Bavli's negative portrayals of the Sadducees. As noted in the introduction, chronology is crucial in establishing this link, since we will find that both phenomena, both the Bavli's negative portrayals of the Sadducees and its portrayal of them as accepting only scripture, are attested for the first time in Babylonia by rabbis who flourished during the mid–fourth century CE.

Based on the attribution of the statement examined above to Shmuel, it would appear that the earliest attestation in the Bavli of the portrayal of Sadducees as accepting only scripture is from the beginning of the Amoraic period, in the first half of the third century CE. Closer examination, however, reveals that only part C of the statement attests to this portrayal, and part C most likely derives from the Bavli's anonymous editors rather than from the early Amora.

What is the evidence for this claim? Part A of the discussion is in Hebrew, and parts B and C are in Aramaic, and as I have remarked many times, a change of language often indicates a change of speaker.[46] It is likely, therefore, that the statement by Shmuel as quoted by Rav Yehudah originally[47] consisted of part A alone. Supporting this conclusion is the strangeness, which is by no means the impossibility, of a single individual making a statement in Hebrew and then asking "What is the reason?" in Aramaic, with the latter question based on his own statement.[48] Finally, why would Shmuel (or whomever attributed the statement to Shmuel) use the ambiguous phraseology "a matter with which the Sadducees disagree," which cries out for further clarification, rather than the much clearer locution "something not written in scripture," which would eliminate the need for further clarification?

I belabor this point because it is only according to part C that the Sadducees are clearly conceived of as accepting only scripture and as rejecting rabbinic tradition. If we confine ourselves to part A alone, that is, to the original core of the statement,[49] then this statement need not imply a strict division between scripture and rabbinic tradition. Rather, the early to mid-third-century-CE Babylonian Amoraim (Shmuel and Rav Yehudah) may be saying that if a court issues a ruling that even the Sadducees accept, it may be assumed that the ruling is common knowledge and/or practice,[50] agreed on by all, since the issues on which the Sadducees and the sages agreed represent the bare minimum that every Jew, even a Sadducee, could be assumed to share in common. And if a matter is common knowledge or practice, the court is not obligated to bring a sacrifice, since they have not caused the community to sin. In other words, it may be a matter of indifference to the early Amoraim, with respect to the issue of determining the court's liability to bring a sacrifice, whether or not a particular law or practice is present in the Bible. The important variable may be whether or not the law or practice in question is a matter of common knowledge or agreed upon by every Jew, independent of its provenance.

According to my conclusions above, therefore, it is the anonymous authors of part C who are the first to assert that the Sadducees accept only scripture and reject rabbinic tradition. It would appear that this notion entered the Talmud some time between the early third century (when Shmuel flourished) and the early seventh century (after the Muslim conquest of Babylonia, when the Talmud as a recognizable book was almost certainly complete). Since the anonymous portions of the Talmud are among its latest layers,[51] it is likely that this anonymous commentary was added to the Talmud some time during the latter part of this period.

A statement in b. Horayot 4b provides perhaps the strongest support for my claim regarding the early Amoraic conception of the Sadducees. That is, during the early Amoraic period, the Sadducees were not portrayed in Babylonia as a group that accepted only scripture. This portrayal is not attested until the mid–fourth century, which we will see below is the time when the negative portrayals of Sadducees as accepting only scripture are first attested in the Bavli.

We read in b. Horayot 4b:

> Said Rav Sheshet, and so [it was] taught [in] the house of R. Yishmael, "Why did they say, '[If the court] rules concerning a matter with which the Sadducees agree, [the members of the court] are exempt [from bringing a sacrifice]?' Because [the community] should have learned [what the proper ruling is] and they did not learn."[52]

This statement is entirely in Hebrew, and is apparently Amoraic from start to finish. Rav Sheshet is a late third-, early fourth-century Babylonian Amora, and Ḥanokh Albeck has demonstrated that the phrase "the house of R. Yishmael" introduces a statement of Amoraic authority.[53] Unlike the statement examined previously,[54] where it was necessary to hypothesize the existence of an earlier Amoraic core to which was added anonymous commentary, here we have an unadorned Amoraic statement, and it conforms to my claim above regarding the Amoraic versus the anonymous editorial parts of the statement. As I argued above, this Amoraic statement does not explicitly credit Sadducees with the rejection of rabbinic tradition and with the acceptance of scripture alone. As noted, there is no reason to assume that the expression "a matter with which the Sadducees agree" refers to scripture. The phrase apparently refers to the fundamentals of Jewish law, whatever their source or mode of derivation.

We must once again be wary of drawing far-reaching conclusions on the basis of a small number of cases. Rav Sheshet's statement, however, supports my claim above that the Aramaic section of the statement in b. Horayot 4a[55] is an anonymous editorial addition to a statement by an Amora. The Amoraim (at least the early Amoraim; see the discussion below) do not define "what the Sadducees agree with" as acceptance by the Sadducees of scripture and scripture alone.

Analysis of another set of traditions may enable us to fix with greater precision when, prior to the anonymous editors, the conception of the Sadducees as accepting only scripture made its first appearance in the Bavli. The ensuing discussion argues that this took place during or shortly after the mid–fourth century, in the form of statements attributed to Abaye and Rav Naḥman bar Yiẓḥak, both mid-fourth-century Babylonian Amoraim. As noted, this conclusion is essential to my argument, because we will find that the rabbis who present the Sadducees as accepting only scripture are the same rabbis who cite traditions that depict the Sadducees negatively, supporting my claim that the two phenomena are linked. It is therefore likely that not only the few rabbinic traditions that explicitly characterize the Sadducees as accepting only scripture betray the influence of Josephan or Josephus-like traditions; the traditions in the Bavli that are sharply negative toward the Sadducees do so as well. Dating these two phenomena to the mid–fourth century CE allows us, therefore, to add to the growing body of evidence indicating that this era witnessed the literary crystallization of cultural processes accelerated by the events of the third century in Syria and Mesopotamia (see the conclusion). It supports my characterization of this period as one of Babylonian receptivity to Jewish traditions deriving from the Roman Empire, perhaps from Roman Palestine, adding depth and perspective to our understanding of Jewish culture in late antiquity.

It is important to note that the conclusion that the conception of the Sadducees as accepting only scripture manifested itself in Babylonia in the mid–fourth century depends on accepting the attribution of statements to Abaye and Rav Naḥman bar Yiẓḥak as indicative at least of the approximate period during which the statements were made. The fact that earlier Amoraic traditions attest to one conception of the Sadducees, and later traditions, both anonymous and Amoraic, attest to another, supports this methodology, a point I will develop below. The findings of this chapter are thus an illustration of the argument developed in the introduction regarding the importance of taking the Talmud's attributions seriously, rather than rejecting them outright, as is the practice of many modern scholars.

The first of Abaye's relevant statements is in b. Berakhot 29a, examined preliminarily above:

> (A) We taught [in a Tannaitic tradition]: Do not trust yourself until the day of your death, for Yoḥanan the High Priest served in the office of the high priesthood for 80 years and in the end he became a Sadducee.
>
> (B) Said Abaye, "[King] Yannai and Yoḥanan [the High Priest] are one [and the same person]."

At first blush Abaye's statement is strange. What induces him to equate King Yannai and Yoḥanan the High Priest, given the obvious fact that they have different names and are portrayed so differently throughout rabbinic literature?

For reasons to be spelled out in detail below, it is likely that a lengthy narrative, quoted by Abaye in b. Kiddushin 66a, helps answer this question.[56] We read there:

> (A) Abaye said, "What is the basis for [my opinion]?
>
> (B) It is taught [in a Tannaitic teaching]: Yannai the king went to Koḥlit in the desert and conquered 60 cities. When he returned, he rejoiced greatly and called to all of the sages of Israel.
>
> [He] said to them, 'Our ancestors ate mallows when they built the Temple, so too we shall eat mallows in memory of our ancestors.'
>
> They placed mallows on golden tables and ate. And there was an elder there, a scoffing, evil, worthless man named Elazar ben Po'erah.
>
> And Elazar ben Po'erah said to Yannai the king, 'Yannai the king, the hearts of the Pharisees are against you.'
>
> [Yannai] said to him, 'What shall I do?'
>
> [Elazar] said to him, 'Make them swear an oath by the frontlet between your eyes.'
>
> [Yannai] made them swear an oath by the frontlet between his eyes. There was an elder there and Yehudah ben Gedidi'ah was his name.
>
> And Yehudah ben Gedidi'ah said to Yannai the king, 'Yannai the king, the crown of kingship is enough for you, leave the crown of priesthood to the seed of Aaron.'
>
> For people had said, 'His mother had been taken captive in Modi'im.'
>
> The matter was investigated but not confirmed, and the sages departed in anger.
>
> And Elazar ben Po'erah said to Yannai the king, 'Yannai the king, such is the law for a commoner in Israel. For you who are king and high priest should such be the law?'
>
> [Yannai said to him], 'What shall I do?'
>
> [Elazar said to Yannai], 'If you listen to my advice, trample them.'
>
> [Yannai said to Elazar], 'And what will become of the Torah?'

> [Elazar said to Yannai], 'It is bound up and lying[57] in a corner. Whoever wants to learn it, let him come and learn.' "
>
> (C) Said Rav Naḥman bar Yiẓḥak, "Immediately heresy was cast into him."
>
> (D) For [Yannai] should have said, "It is well [with regard to] the written Torah. What about the oral Torah?"
>
> (B) "Immediately the evil sprouted forth as a result of Elazar ben Po'erah [and as a result of Yehudah ben Gedidi'ah], and all of the sages were killed, and the world was desolate until Shimon ben Shetach came and restored the Torah as of old."

This narrative makes no explicit mention of Sadducees, but as noted in chapter 2, it closely parallels an account in Josephus, which identifies the opponents of the Pharisees as Sadducees.[58] It will be helpful to quote again the relevant passage from Josephus:

> As for Hyrcanus, the envy of the Jews was aroused against him by his own successes and those of his sons; particularly hostile to him were the Pharisees, who are one of the Jewish schools, as we have related above. And so great is their influence with the masses that even when they speak against a king or high priest, they immediately gain credence. Hyrcanus too was a disciple of theirs, and was greatly loved by them.
>
> And once he invited them to a feast and entertained them hospitably, and when he saw that they were having a very good time, he began by saying that they knew he wished to be righteous and in everything he did tried to please God and them—for the Pharisees profess such beliefs; at the same time he begged them, if they observed him doing anything wrong or straying from the right path, to lead him back to it and correct him. But they testified to his being altogether virtuous, and he was delighted with their praise.
>
> However, one of the guests, named Eleazar, who had an evil nature and took pleasure in dissension, said, "Since you have asked to be told the truth, if you wish to be righteous, give up the high-priesthood and be content with governing the people."
>
> And when Hyrcanus asked him for what reason he should give up the high-priesthood, he replied, "Because we have heard from our elders that your mother was a captive in the reign of Antiochus Epiphanes."
>
> But the story was false, and Hyrcanus was furious with the man, while all the Pharisees were very indignant.
>
> Then a certain Jonathan, one of Hyrcanus's close friends, belonging to the school of the Sadducees, who hold opinions opposed to those of the Pharisees, said that it had been with the general approval of all the Pharisees that Eleazar had made his slanderous

> statement; and this, he added, would be clear to Hyrcanus if he inquired of them what punishment he deserved—for, he said, he would be convinced that the slanderous statement had not been made with their approval if they fixed a penalty commensurate with the crime—, and they replied that Eleazar deserved stripes and chains; for they did not think it right to sentence a man to death for calumny, and anyway the Pharisees are naturally lenient in the matter of punishments. At this Hyrcanus became very angry and began to believe that the fellow had slandered him with their approval. And Jonathan in particular inflamed his anger, and so worked upon him that he brought him to join the Sadducean party and desert the Pharisees, and to abrogate the regulations which they had established for the people, and punish those who observed them. Out of this, of course, grew the hatred of the masses for him and his sons, but of this we shall speak hereafter.
>
> For the present I wish merely to explain that the Pharisees had passed on to the people certain regulations handed down by former generations and not recorded in the Laws of Moses, for which reason they are rejected by the Sadducean group, who hold that only those regulations should be considered valid which were written down, and those which had been handed down by former generations need not be observed. And concerning these matters the two parties came to have controversies and serious differences, the Sadducees having the confidence of the wealthy alone but no following among the populace, while the Pharisees have the support of the masses. But of these two schools and of the Essenes a detailed account has been given in the second book of my *Judaica*.
>
> And so Hyrcanus quieted the outbreak, and lived happily thereafter; and when he died after administering the government excellently for 31 years, he left five sons. Now he was accounted by God worthy of three of the greatest privileges, the rule of the nation, the office of high priest, and the gift of prophecy; for the Deity was with him and enabled him to foresee and foretell the future; so, for example, he foretold of his two elder sons that they would not remain masters of the state. And the story of their downfall is worth relating, to show how far they were from having their father's good fortune.

As noted, Abaye, the author of the strange statement identifying Yannai and Yoḥanan the High Priest in b. Berakhot 29a, quotes the story about Yannai's conflict with the Pharisees in b. Kiddushin 66a. As also noted, the story in Kiddushin motivates, at least in part, Abaye's peculiar statement in Berakhot, since the story can easily be read (and in fact is read by Rav Naḥman bar Yiẓḥak, Abaye's younger contemporary; see below) as depicting King Yannai's adoption of a heresy that bears a striking resemblance to Josephus's description of a fundamental tenet of Sadduceeism,[59] as well as to a belief attributed to the Sadducees by the Bavli's anonymous editors in b. Horayot 4a and b. Sanhedrin 33b (see above). While the Kiddushin story nowhere mentions the term "Sadducee," Abaye in Berakhot easily could have inferred that Yannai became a Sadducee according to Kiddushin had he known Josephus or a Josephus-like source, or had he known or shared the anonymous editorial description of them in Horayot and Sanhedrin. Furthermore, the role of Yannai in Kiddushin is played by John Hyrcanus (the rabbis' Yoḥanan the High Priest) in Josephus, and by Yoḥanan the High Priest in Berakhot.[60]

In other words, Abaye in Berakhot asserts that Yoḥanan the High Priest, who became a Sadducee after 80 years of service as high priest, is the same as Yannai in Kiddushin, who consistently follows the advice of Elazar ben Po'erah. And Elazar ben Po'erah clearly shows himself to be a Sadducee, as described by Josephus and the anonymous editors of the Bavli, when he has the following exchange with King Yannai in the story in Kiddushin:

> [Elazar said to Yannai], "If you listen to my advice, trample them" [i.e., have all of the sages killed]."
>
> [Yannai said to Elazar], "And what will become of the Torah?"
>
> [Elazar said to Yannai], "It is bound up and lying in a corner. Whoever wants to learn it, let him come and learn." . . .
>
> Immediately the evil sprouted forth as a result of Elazar ben Po'erah [and as a result of Yehudah ben Gedidi'ah], and all of the sages were killed.

Since this story portrays Yannai as totally dependent on Elazar ben Po'erah and as following all of his advice, it is not much of a leap to conclude that Yannai comes to accept Elazar's claim that all of the Torah is contained in scripture, and killing the sages does not diminish or endanger the Torah in the slightest. When Abaye asserts in Berakhot that Yoḥanan the High Priest and King Yannai are one and the same, he is in effect saying that the belief shared by Yannai and Elazar according to this plausible reading of Kiddushin is a tenet of Sadduceeism. Abaye's two statements taken together yield the earliest rabbinic expression of the notion that the Sadducees accept scripture alone, and reject rabbinic tradition.

It is possible, of course, that the attributions to Abaye of the statements in Berakhot and Kiddushin are pseudepigraphical, in which case we have no evidence regarding mid-fourth-century Babylonian Amoraic conceptions of Sadducees. It strains credulity, however, to claim that Abaye's statements do not derive from a single individual, or at least from a single school or group. For if they are pseudepigraphical, and/or they derive from different schools, then we render incoherent the claim in b. Berakhot 29a that "[King] Yannai and Yoḥanan [the High Priest] are one [and the same person]." It is understandable why a single person or group would make this statement in combination with the statement on b. Kiddushin 66a. We need posit only (as I posited above) that the person or group who identified Yannai and Yoḥanan the High Priest in b. Berakhot 29a also knew the story in b. Kiddushin 66a, which features Yannai the king, and knew as well that the story describes the king's conversion to

Sadduceeism, as is clear from Josephus's version of the story and as is deducible from the anonymous Babylonian texts discussed above.

If the attributions are pseudepigraphical, then the same pseudepigraphers knew all of this information, and for some unknown reason attributed all of it to Abaye, and also attributed it to Abaye's younger contemporary, Rav Naḥman bar Yiẓḥak (see below). The same pseudepigraphers, presumably, attributed a different conception of the Sadducees to pre-mid-fourth-century Amoraim, creating the illusion of chronological development (why, we cannot say), and arranged as well for conceptions about the Sadducees in anonymous editorial additions to conform to those of the later Amoraim, striving as they were for chronological verisimilitude.

It is much more likely, as noted, that the attributions in this case are trustworthy, or at least are indicative of the approximate time period when the statements were made. It is important to emphasize that this is not an argument in favor of trusting ancient rabbinic attributions in general; it is simply to say that in the cases under consideration here it makes sense to do so. My conclusions certainly increase the likelihood that other rabbinic attributions are reliable, but we have no idea how many, nor can we be confident that this is the case (or is not the case!) regarding any statement in the absence of concrete proof.

Be that as it may, if we accept on the basis of his statement in b. Berakhot 29a that Abaye believes the story in b. Kiddushin 66a is about Sadducees, and also accept the attribution to Abaye of the quotation of the story in b. Kiddushin 66a, we have proof that some time between Rav Sheshet and Abaye, between the third and fourth Babylonian Amoraic generations, that is, some time during the mid–fourth century CE, the Josephan characterization of the Sadducees as a group that accepted only scripture and rejected rabbinic traditions became known to and accepted by at least one Babylonian rabbi.

This conclusion is strengthened by the fact that Rav Naḥman bar Yiẓḥak, also a mid-fourth-century Babylonian Amora, comments on the story in b. Kiddushin 66a and apparently shares Abaye's characterization of the Sadducees. Rav Naḥman bar Yiẓḥak's comment and the immediate context are worth examining in greater detail:

> And Elazar ben Po'erah said to Yannai the king, "Yannai the king, such is the law for a commoner in Israel. For you who are king and high priest should such be the law?"
>
> [Yannai said to him], "What shall I do?"
>
> [Elazar said to Yannai], "If you listen to my advice, trample them."
>
> [Yannai said to Elazar], "And what will become of the Torah?"
>
> [Elazar said to Yannai], "It is bound up and lying in a corner. Whoever wants to learn it, let him come and learn."
>
> Said Rav Naḥman bar Yiẓḥak, "Immediately heresy was cast into him." For [Yannai] should have said, "It is well [with regard to] the written Torah. What about the oral Torah?"

In this crucial section of the story, Yannai worries about the fate of the Torah should the sages be disposed of, implying that he at least entertains the possibility that the sages are custodians or teachers of the Torah, and perhaps that their wisdom, independent of scripture, has the status of Torah. When Elazar ben Po'erah says "It is bound up and lying in a corner," he asserts that the Torah consists of scripture alone, and the loss of the sages will not affect it in the slightest.

To understand more fully the significance of Rav Naḥman bar Yiẓḥak's comment, it is important to note that his statement is divisible into two parts. The first part is in Hebrew and is apparently Amoraic, and the second part is in Aramaic and is apparently later, anonymous commentary based on the earlier Amoraic core.[61] The Hebrew core of the statement consists of the phrase "Immediately heresy was cast into him," and most likely the "him" referred to is Yannai, who allows the sages to be murdered because he is convinced by Elazar ben Po'erah's argument. According to Rav Naḥman bar Yiẓḥak, therefore, Yannai accepts Elazar ben Po'erah's claim that "the Torah" and "scripture" are synonymous, thereby accepting the Sadducean heresy as described by Josephus and as reflected in the statements of Abaye and the Bavli's anonymous editors. The fact that both Abaye and Rav Naḥman bar Yiẓḥak share this conception, but earlier Amoraim share a subtly but demonstrably different idea, allows us to approximate when the Josephan portrayal of the Sadducees reached or at least found acceptance in rabbinic Babylonia. This took place after the time of Rav Sheshet and during or shortly after the fourth generation of Babylonian Amoraim, approximately midway through the fourth century CE.

What do we make of the Aramaic continuation ("He should have said, 'It is well [with regard to] the written Torah. What about the oral Torah?' "), which I argued above was most likely an anonymous addition to Rav Naḥman bar Yiẓḥak's statement? According to this anonymous addition, Yannai's heresy was his denial of the oral Torah, his refusal to consider as Torah anything but the written scroll.

This characterization of Yannai's heresy is similar but not identical to the characterization of Sadducean doctrine that I attributed above to the fourth generation Amoraim and the anonymous editors of b. Horayot 4a.[62] The anonymous editors grafted onto Rav Naḥman bar Yiẓḥak's statement concern for the distinction between the oral and the written Torah. For Rav Naḥman bar Yiẓḥak, the salient part of Yannai's heresy was his denial of the proposition that the sages' learning was Torah; for the author of the anonymous addition it was Yannai's denial that the Torah was divisible into two parts, distinguishable above all by their mode of transmission.[63]

Interestingly, modern scholars differ over the question of whether or not the Sadducees portrayed by Josephus reject nonscriptural traditions because these traditions are oral or because they are not part of the Bible. The modern scholarly debate revolves around opposing interpretations of Josephus's description of the Sadducees in the lengthy account cited above, as follows:

> The Pharisees had passed on to the people certain regulations handed down by former generations and not recorded in the Laws of Moses, for which reason they are rejected by the Sadducean group, who hold that only those regulations should be considered valid which were written down, and these which had been handed down by former generations need not be observed.

This modern scholarly debate may have an ancient analogue in the different emphases of Rav Naḥman bar Yiẓḥak, and the anonymous commentators who added to his statement. Some modern scholars, in other words, have interpreted Josephus's Sadducees as accepting the written Torah and rejecting Pharisaic oral tradition, and it is not out of the question that the anonymous commentators who added to Rav Naḥman bar Yiẓḥak's statement in b. Kiddushin 66a interpreted Josephus, or Josephus's source, in precisely this fashion. Along these same lines, it is possible that Rav Naḥman bar Yiẓḥak minus the anonymous addition to his statement interpreted Josephus to be saying that the Sadducees rejected the Pharisees' traditions because they are nonscriptural and not because they are oral.

It bears mentioning that to date, the most comprehensive analysis of this controversial passage from Josephus is that of Steve Mason, who explains it in accordance with the interpretation of Abaye and Rav Naḥman bar Yiẓḥak. Mason translates the passage as follows:

> [T]he Pharisees passed on to the people certain ordinances from a succession of fathers, which are not written down in the laws of Moses. For this reason the party of the Sadducees dismisses these ordinances, averring that one need only recognize the written ordinances, whereas those from the tradition of the fathers need not be observed.[64]

Mason claims that this passage "says nothing whatsoever about the question whether the Pharisees actually transmitted their teachings orally or in writing. . . . Josephus has nothing to say about the matter. His point is that the Pharisaic ordinances were not part of the written Law of Moses and that for this reason they were rejected by the Sadducees."[65]

To summarize the unfortunately convoluted arguments above, I started my discussion with the observation that statements and stories in the Bavli tend to be more harshly negative toward the Sadducees than statements and stories in Palestinian compilations. There is uncertainty why this should be the case, however, since I found no indication that any Babylonian Jews referred to themselves as Sadducees or exhibited Sadducean traits, such that the Babylonian rabbis would be polemicizing against them by telling nasty stories about their ancient namesakes or counterparts, as I found to be the case in an earlier study of rabbinic traditions about the Hasmoneans.

The traditions analyzed above suggest that the introduction into Babylonia of the writings of Josephus, or of traditions used by Josephus,[66] during the mid-fourth century may provide a key to solving this puzzle. For, as noted, apparently during the fourth Amoraic generation, the Josephan characterization of the Sadducees achieved currency in Babylonia. Abaye and Rav Naḥman bar Yiẓḥak, both mid-fourth-century Amoraim, knew the story in b. Kiddushin 66a that depicts a pernicious heresy, which we know Abaye considered to be Sadducean on the basis of his statement in b. Berakhot 29a. The heresy Abaye attested to is strikingly similar to Josephus's depiction of the Sadducees in his version of the same story.

Whether the Babylonians received this portrayal from Josephus himself or from a source similar to Josephus is at present a moot point. Also unclear is why Babylonians should have been receptive to such a portrayal, unless (1) its presence in an ancient source is explanation enough, or (2) it presented Babylonian rabbis with yet another opportunity to emphasize the importance of sages as a source of Torah, at the expense of the murderous (not to mention incompetent) Hasmonean monarch, King Yannai. This portrayal, namely of the Sadducees as accepting only the Bible and rejecting the traditions of the sages (or the Pharisees),[67] induced Babylonian rabbis to alter the image of the Sadducees in the texts they inherited from Palestine, or, to be more precise, to bring out the theme of the Sadducees' wickedness, only a minor theme in Palestinian texts, and make it more prominent in their retelling of the stories.[68]

Appendix 1: Josephus or Josephus's Source?

I have maintained the distinction throughout between "Josephus" and "Josephus's source" since, as noted, it is not entirely clear whether the rabbis of the Bavli received these traditions directly from Josephus, or whether Josephus and the rabbis drew upon a common fund of traditions. This issue confronts scholars of rabbinic literature, and in fact of any ancient literature, in a variety of ways. I dealt in chapters 2 and 3, for example, with traditions preserved in the Tosefta and the Bavli, albeit with significant changes. I repeatedly confronted the question of whether (1) the tradition existed in an ur-form prior to both the Tosefta and the Bavli, from where it was taken up and modified to a greater or lesser extent by both later compilations, or (2) the Bavli took the tradition directly from the Tosefta, such that all or most of the differences between the two traditions are the work of Babylonian editors.

This question is extremely difficult to answer in most cases, but one important consideration with regard to the relationship between Josephus and the Bavli suggests that we may be dealing with an ur-text incorporated into two later compilations. I refer to the fact that in a large proportion of the cases in which Josephus and the Bavli share traditions, the tradition in question is missing from Josephus's earlier work, *The Jewish War,* and is found only in his later work, *Antiquities,* where its connection to Josephus's larger discussion is tenuous.[69] It is peculiar that the Babylonian rabbis should exhibit a preference for Josephan materials that fit only loosely into Josephus's larger discussion and that he discovered between the composition of his earlier and later works. It is likely, although far from certain, that both Josephus and the rabbis are drawing on a common body of traditions that they altered and/or that had undergone development during the 150 to 500 years between the time Josephus incorporated them into his work and the time the Babylonian rabbis incorporated them into the developing Talmud.

Appendix 2: Sadducees and Boethusians

The above discussion focused on stories and statements about the Sadducees in rabbinic literature. No such discussion, however, can ignore the rabbinic depiction of the Boethusians,[70] since several scholars have shown that rabbinic portrayals of these two groups are sometimes indistinguishable,[71] and parallel traditions in different compilations sometimes disagree about whether a particular narrative features Sadducees or Boethusians.[72]

Although, as noted, we should be cautious about drawing far-reaching conclusions on the basis of a small corpus of traditions, it appears that attention paid to the level and type of criticism directed at these groups in rabbinic sources yields one answer to the longstanding question of how or even whether the ancient rabbis distinguished between them.[73]

To be specific, my research revealed that the rabbis did draw such a distinction, in cases where parallel versions in the various compilations agree that a story is about Boethusians. For in contrast to most Palestinian stories about Sadducees, in the small number of cases in which the reading "Boethusian" is stable from compilation to compilation, Palestinian stories depict them as guilty of serious legal and ethical offenses.

In such cases, (1) the Boethusians are implicated en bloc in despicable schemes to sabotage the sages' attempts to observe the halakhah, and (2) common people ally themselves with the sages, helping them foil the Boethusians' schemes.[74] In contrast, several traditions in the Bavli and in Palestinian compilations depict the Sadducees as obedient to or fearful of the sages, with the exception of a single zealot who defies them and is swiftly and justly killed by heaven as a result.[75] In addition, no stories depict the common people as the sages' allies against the wicked Sadducees.

A story about the Boethusians in t. Rosh Hashanah 1:15 will illustrate several of these points:[76]

> At first they accepted testimony [regarding the new moon] from every man.
>
> One time the Boethusians hired two witnesses to come and cause the sages to err, since the Boethusians think that Shavuot should always fall after the Sabbath.
>
> One witness came, gave his testimony, and left, and the second [witness] came and said, "I was ascending Ma'aleh Adumim and I saw [the moon] crouching between two rocks. Its head resembled a calf's, its ears resembled a kid's, its horns resembled a

> gazelle's. I saw it and was startled and I fell backwards and behold, 200 zuz were tied to my belt."
>
> [The sages] said to him, "The coins are yours as a gift and those who hired you shall come and be lashed. Why did you get mixed up in this business?"
>
> He said to them, "Because I heard that the Boethusians wanted to come and cause the sages to err. I said, 'It is good that I go and inform the sages.' "

The Boethusians hire false witnesses and attempt to cause Israel to sanctify the new moon at the wrong time. Clearly this story depicts Boethusians as guilty of an extremely serious transgression.

A parallel to the above narrative, in y. Rosh Hashanah 2:1 (57d), tells basically the same story. The Yerushalmi's version is based on m. Rosh Hashanah 2:1:

> (A) Mishnah: At first they accepted testimony [regarding the] new moon from every man. After the heretics [*minim*] sinned, they ordained that they should only accept [testimony] from [people they] recognized.
>
> (B) Yerushalmi: It happened that the Boethusians hired two false witnesses to testify that the new moon had been sanctified. One of them came and gave his testimony and left.
>
> The other came and said, "I was ascending Ma'aleh Adumim and I saw [the moon] crouching between two rocks. Its head resembled a calf's and its ears resembled a kid's. I saw it and was startled and sprang backward, and behold 200 zuz were tied to my belt."
>
> They said to him, "Behold the 200 zuz are yours as a gift, and those who sent you shall come and be lashed. Why did you get mixed up in all of this?"
>
> He said to them, "I saw that they wanted to cause the sages to err. I said, 'It will be good if I go and inform the sages.' "

In both Palestinian versions of this story, the Boethusians are guilty of extremely serious offenses, and no distinction is drawn between "good Boethusians" and "bad Boethusians." The same is true of the Bavli's version, likewise based on m. Rosh Hashanah 2:1:

> Our rabbis taught [in a Baraita]: How did the Boethusians sin?
>
> One time the Boethusians wanted to cause the sages to err. They hired two people with 400 zuz, one of ours [i.e., a member of the sages' party] and one of theirs [i.e., a member of the Boethusian party]. Theirs testified and left.
>
> They said to [ours], "Say how you saw the moon."
>
> He said to them, "I was ascending Ma'aleh Adumim and I saw [the moon] crouching between two rocks. Its head resembled a calf's

and its ears resembled a kid's, its horns resembled a gazelle's, and its tail was between its legs. I looked at it and was startled and fell backward. And if you don't believe me, here are 200 zuz that were wrapped in my neckerchief."

They said to him, "What caused you to get mixed up in this?"

He said to them, "I heard that the Boethusians wanted to cause the sages to err. I said, 'I will go and inform them lest unworthy people come and cause the sages to err.'"

They said to him, "The 200 zuz are yours as a gift, and he who hired you will be stretched on the pillar."

At that time they ordained that testimony is only accepted from [people that one] recognizes.

The portrayal of Boethusians, therefore, is quite stable from one compilation to the next. The Boethusians portrayed in these texts bear little or no resemblance to rabbinic portrayals of Sadducees, which supports my claim that the rabbis sometimes distinguished clearly between the two groups.

Another relevant case is found in t. Sukkah 3:1. We read there:

[The requirement of] the lulav overrides the Sabbath at the beginning [of the holiday], and [that of] the willow [overrides the Sabbath] at the end [of the holiday]. It happened that the Boethusians pressed large rocks over [the willows] on the eve of the Sabbath. The common people [*amei ha-areẓ*] saw them and came and dragged[77] [the willows] out from underneath the rocks on the Sabbath, since the Boethusians do not agree that [the ceremony of] beating the willow overrides the Sabbath.

A parallel to this tradition in b. Sukkah 43b shows that once again the reading "Boethusians" is stable from one compilation to the next, and once again the depiction of Boethusians is clearly distinguishable from that of the Sadducees. In this case as well, the Boethusians attempt to sabotage the sages' observance of the law; there is no distinction between "good Boethusians" and "bad Boethusians"; and nonrabbis come to the sages' aid and foil the Boethusians' plot.

The paucity of sources makes firm conclusions impossible at present, but it would appear that we find preserved in rabbinic texts narratives about two distinct groups referred to by distinct names and depicted in diverse ways, which, however, have merged significantly during the course of transmission.[78] One example of this amalgamation bears examining in detail, since the variation in terminology may be attributable to the fact that the story depicts neither a "typical" Boethusian nor a "typical" Sadducean as I described them above. I refer to the following story in t. Sukkah 3:16:

It already happened that a Boethusian poured the [water] libation onto his feet and all of the people pelted him with their citrons. The horn of the altar was damaged, and the [sacrificial] service was nullified on that very day, until they brought a clump of salt and put it on [the horn of the altar] in order that the altar not appear to be damaged, for every altar that lacks a horn, a ramp, and a base is unfit.[79]

This story is paralleled in b. Sukkah 49a. For my present purposes, the only notable distinction between the two versions is that the Bavli's version features a Sadducee instead of a Boethusian.[80] This story depicts an individual sinner acting in defiance of the sages (characteristic of stories about Sadducees), the sinner surviving his act of defiance of the sages (characteristic of stories about Boethusians), and the common people acting in opposition to the nonrabbinic protagonist (also characteristic of stories about Boethusians). This story, therefore, does not consistently follow either the Boethusian or the Sadducean story patterns described above, and it is perhaps for this reason that the story's terminology is not consistent in all of the parallels.

Appendix 3

B. Baba Batra 115b–116a's derivative character vis-à-vis b. Menaḥot 65a–b is evident both from the reason the Sadducee provides for his opinion and Rabban Yoḥanan ben Zakkai's mocking application of a biblical verse to the Sadducee. The problem with both of these motifs in Baba Batra is that there is nothing at all objectionable or foolish, from a rabbinic perspective, about the Sadducee's proof, and yet Rabban Yoḥanan ben Zakkai responds, as in Menaḥot, by insulting the Sadducees' foolishness and "worthless talk." The Sadducee bases himself on a *kol ve-ḥomer*,[81] an a fortiori argument: "If the daughter of one's son inherits [property] on the strength of the son's [claim], is it not all the more so that one's daughter [inherits], since her claim derives directly from the father?" Comparable arguments are found throughout rabbinic literature; from a rabbinic perspective this is a perfectly fine argument, an assessment supported by the fact that precisely the same halakhic argument is used by the Sadducees elsewhere in Palestinian literature,[82] and nowhere else do the Sadducees' interlocutors ridicule them or express even a hint of contempt.

In addition, the derivative nature of the Baba Batra narrative is indicated by the fact that the discussion based on the Sadducee's argument has nothing to do with that argument. In response to the Sadducee, Rabban Yoḥanan ben Zakkai ostensibly quotes a verse or verses from Genesis 36, one of which describes Anah as the brother of Zibeon and another of which describes Anah as Zibeon's father; neither these verses nor the Amoraic responses that follow have anything to do with the halakhic dispute at hand: whether or not a daughter inherits along with the daughter of a son. In contrast, in the Menaḥot narrative Rabban Yoḥanan ben Zakkai answers the Sadducee on the latter's own terms, by means of an argument that directly contradicts the Sadducee's and that bases itself on what is from a rabbinic point of view the Sadducee's faulty logic (see below). Finally, in the Baba Batra narrative, the discussion based on the Sadducee's argument contains a series of Amoraic responses, clear indication that we are dealing with a later interpolation into an originally Tannaitic narrative.[83]

In contrast, the rabbinic audience of the story in b. Menaḥot 65a–b would readily assent to the story's characterization of the Boethusian's teaching as "worthless talk," given his outrageous claim that the fixed celebration of Shavuot after Shabbat was determined by Moses rather than God ("Moses our rabbi loved Israel and knew that Shavuot lasts only one day. He therefore ordained that it come after Shabbat so that Israel would celebrate for two days"). According to the Boethusian, an important feature of the Jewish calendar is of human rather than divine origin, an absurd, heretical notion from a rabbinic perspective.[84]

The Boethusian's feeble attempt at a response leads Rabban Yoḥanan ben Zakkai to respond in kind with a deliberately feeble argument of his own. The rabbi answers the Boethusian with an argument that replicates the latter's foolish claim that Moses rather than God is in control of Israel's destiny: "And if Moses our rabbi loved Israel, why did he detain them in the desert for forty years?"

The story in Baba Batra, therefore, is a later editorial reworking (just how late is not clear) of an earlier story (just how early is also not clear), but it remains the case that the editors who reworked the story saw fit to retain from the model narrative strikingly negative portrayals and evaluations of the Sadducees, yielding a story that expresses a level of contempt for the Sadducees that is unparalleled in Palestinian compilations.

Conclusion

We have seen that in several respects, Babylonian Jewish society between the third and seventh centuries CE conformed to Persian models. At no time, however, was it sealed off from influences from the west, most recognizably in the form of traditions deriving from Palestinian rabbis, but also in the form of nonrabbinic and non-Jewish traditions deriving from Palestine, and perhaps from elsewhere in the Roman Empire. Mid-fourth-century Babylonia, however, appears to have witnessed the literary crystallization of processes accelerated by events of the mid–third century in Syria and Mesopotamia, with literature,[1] literary forms, and modes of behavior deriving from the west attributed in the Bavli to Babylonian rabbis, perhaps to a greater degree than had been the case previously (see below).

In chapter 5, I characterized as Persian the paucity of statues of the gods in rabbinic Babylonia, particularly in public contexts in the major areas of Jewish settlement. The only possible exception involved rabbis who flourished under the Parthians, who ruled Persia prior to the advent of the Sasanians in the third decade of the third century CE.[2] The Talmudic record, therefore, conforms to developments in Persia, since the Sasanians, unlike their predecessors, appear to have systematically destroyed idols in cultic contexts throughout their empire, albeit with varying degrees of success.

I also characterized as Persian the tendency of Babylonian rabbis to remain aloof from their social inferiors, and to interact to the extent possible with other rabbis in the privacy of their study houses. Chapter 6 further advanced this argument by demonstrating that early Babylonian rabbis were not the important politicians that earlier scholars portrayed them to be. The Babylonian Jewish community did not wait with bated breath for these rabbis to state their opinions about the burning political questions of the day: are the Persians preferable to the Romans or vice versa; is the Persian king wicked or not; and so on? Rather, I argued, the very stories earlier scholars used as the basis of their portrayal of these rabbis as the political leaders of the Jewish community actually buttress my claims regarding their insularity. Although certainty is beyond our grasp, it is likely that these stories depict them talking among themselves in the privacy of their study houses rather than interacting with or expressing opinions of vital importance to the larger Jewish community. Talmudic traditions that have frequently been interpreted as examples of Babylonian rabbinic "foreign policy" statements concerning the Persian government turn out to be equally or better explicable as routine interactions between rabbis and their disciples involving the interpretation of texts. Similarly, in chapter 7, I argued that Babylonian rabbinic attitudes toward the Sadducees were responses to literary traditions depicting Sadducees as espousing views they found obnoxious rather than to the existence of actual Sadducee-like groups, such as proto-Karaites, in their midst.

Palestinian rabbis told stories to allay their anxieties about their standing in the eyes of nonrabbis; Babylonian rabbis told the same stories about rabbis vis-à-vis other rabbis.[3] Palestinian rabbis told stories depicting kings and priests possessing power and authority in the distant past; Babylonians told the same stories, but transformed the protagonists into sages or gave sages the final word.[4] Babylonian rabbis lived, thought, and dreamed primarily in the study house, which hindered them from visualizing a world, past or present, dominated by anyone other than sages.

It bears emphasizing that the characterization of Babylonian rabbis as Persian does not imply that Persian society was monolithic. As noted in the introduction, Babylonian rabbis flourished in Mesopotamia, a border province subject to considerable western influence even prior to the fourth century. My claim throughout this book has not been that Palestine and Babylonia were diametrically opposed, with Babylonia unproblematically Persian, or that Persia and Rome were diametrically opposed. Rather, my claim is (1) that in late antiquity the rudiments of a partly shared elite culture may have been emerging in Syria and Mesopotamia, perhaps a refinement of a rudimentary shared nonelite culture that had existed earlier, and (2) that we may find modest evidence for the emergence of this shared culture in the pages of the Bavli, in the form of the mid-fourth-century "Palestinianization" of Babylonian rabbis.[5]

It is also important to emphasize that my claim regarding the depiction of Babylonian rabbis as Palestinian in the mid–fourth century is not meant to exclude Persian influence, but rather to add nuance to our understanding of Babylonia between the two empires. The fate of Babylonia during this time was similar to that of Armenia, which remained Persian in numerous respects even after its conversion to Christianity in the early fourth century.

As noted, the evidence surveyed in chapter 7, together with the conclusions of several earlier studies,[6] pointed to the mid–fourth century as an important period when this shared culture between the empires began to manifest itself in Babylonian rabbinic literature, and, I will argue, in changing rabbinic behavior as well. As noted several times, Ẓvi Dor copiously documented and described Palestinian rabbinic learning in mid-fourth-century and later Babylonia,[7] and his findings have been accepted by the overwhelming majority of modern scholars of rabbinics.[8]

It would be absurd to attempt to recapitulate the details of Dor's arguments in the present context, and I will instead confine the discussion to reviewing some of the proofs offered by scholars other than Dor. For example, Christine Hayes writes:[9]

> With the possible exception of one text... statements and stories that assert the value of scholarship over genealogical fitness can be attributed to Palestinian *tannaim* and *amoraim*.... It is not until the mid–fourth century that Babylonian sages, perhaps increasingly aware of or susceptible to Palestinian teachings on the matter, voice criticism of the preservation of hierarchical distinctions based on genealogy rather than learning.... The evidence of the sources suggests that pedigree was trumped by learning at an early stage in Palestine but only later in Babylonia. The difference between the two rabbinic communities may be a reflection of trends in the larger cultural environment.

Along the same lines, Isaiah Gafni surveys the Palestinian and Babylonian rabbinic evidence for the existence of Jewish communal support for public education. He finds that Palestinian rabbinic sources attest to the existence of such support in Jewish Palestine of late antiquity, but that it is virtually unattested in Babylonian rabbinic sources. "Among all of the Babylonian Amoraim," writes Gafni, "only Rava [who flourished during the mid–fourth century] is connected with more extensive communal involvement" with education.[10]

The historicity of the Palestinian rabbinic evidence is open to question, since elsewhere in the Greco-Roman world of antiquity the burden fell on the individual family, and the community played no role. Even if we are purely in the realm of wishful thinking, however, the correspondence between later Babylonia and earlier Palestine is once again striking.

Along the same lines:

> The Bavli and Yerushalmi preserve several stories in which early Palestinian Amoraim witness improper halachic practices in outlying areas and either protest or remain silent. A superior sage hears what transpired... and passes judgment on the action of his inferiors....
>
> Examination of both Talmuds reveals no comparable stories involving early (i.e., first- through third-generation) Babylonian Amoraim. We do find a similar story involving Rava, a fourth-generation [i.e., mid-fourth-century] Babylonian.[11]

The same is true even regarding minute details of formal expression:

> The . . . technical formula: *Amar Rav X: Ba'i*[12] *Rav Y* ("Said Rav X: Asked Rav Y") . . . indicates that Rav X cites a question authored by Rav Y. The question introduced by the term *ba'i* ("he asked") serves as the first link in a quotation chain. . . . Examination of the entire Bavli reveals a total of 11 or 12 cases in which a question introduced by *ba'i* is the first link in a quotation chain (*Amar Rav X: Ba'i Rav Y*). The tradent (Rav X) is Palestinian in 9 or 10 cases, and is Babylonian in only two cases. Rava is involved in one case, and a student of Rava is involved in the other.[13] . . . According to the Bavli, therefore, this quotation chain is primarily a Palestinian phenomenon, a conclusion supported by the Yerushalmi, where this quotation form is relatively common.[14]

In an earlier study, furthermore, I documented cases of the preference of later Babylonians for the authority of earlier Palestinians, even over that of the greatest early Babylonian sages:[15]

> Some later [Babylonian] Amoraim . . . consider R. Yohanan to be more authoritative than Rav or Shmuel, but never express the view that Rav is more authoritative than Shmuel, or vice versa. On Eruvin 47b, for example, Ravina, a fifth-generation subordinate of Rava, objects to a statement by Rava on the basis of a halachic principle which favors the halachic opinion of R. Yohanan over that of Shmuel. Apparently in response to Ravina's objection, Rava revises his position. Similarly, on Beizah 4a–b Rav Papa, also a fifth-generation subordinate of Rava, refers to a halachic principle which favors the halachic opinion of R. Yohanan over that of Rav. On Beizah 4a, Rav Ada bar Ahava, likewise a fifth-generation subordinate of Rava, invokes the same principle. Rava and his school, therefore, are credited with the view that R. Yohanan is more authoritative than Rav and Shmuel, but neither Rava nor any other later Amoraim consider Rav to be more authoritative than Shmuel, or vice versa.[16]

Comparison of the Bavli's transmission of statements by Shmuel and R. Yoḥanan yields the same conclusions:

> Early Amoraim tend to comment only on statements by one or the other of the two rabbis, with early Babylonians commenting almost exclusively on statements by Shmuel. Later Amoraim, however, in particular the most prominent Babylonian Amoraim, tend to comment both on statements by Shmuel and on statements by Yohanan.[17]

In other words, the mid–fourth century witnesses the integration of R. Yoḥanan's statements into the mainstream of Babylonian learning, with Abaye and Rava commenting on statements by Shmuel and R. Yoḥanan to almost exactly the same degree. Any generalizations we make regarding the fifth and seventh generations of Babylonian Amoraim are of limited value, due to the relative paucity of material attributed to these rabbis, but regarding the sixth generation, that is, the late fourth, early fifth century CE, we again find Babylonian rabbis commenting on statements by Shmuel and Yoḥanan to roughly the same extent.

Traditions dealing with the issue of whether or not idolatry is a thing of the past conform to similar chronological patterns. The book of Judith, apparently composed in Palestine in the second century BCE,[18] states unambiguously:

> For there has not been in our generation, nor is there among us today a tribe or family, a rural area or town that worships man-made gods, as was the case in former times.[19]

Song of Songs Rabbah 7:8, also a Palestinian source, expresses the same idea, as does t. Menaḥot 13:22:

> The first Temple, why was it destroyed? Because of idolatry, forbidden sexual acts, and bloodshed. . . . But later on, we know that they devoted themselves to Torah and were careful about tithing, why were they exiled? Because they loved money and hated one another, which teaches you that God despises hatred of one person for another, and scripture equates it to idolatry, forbidden sexual acts, and bloodshed.

According to this Toseftan passage, idolatry reached epidemic proportions among the ancient Israelites and was one of the primary causes of the destruction of the first Temple.[20] Some time afterward, however, it lost its position of preeminence among Israelite sins.

This Palestinian view is also attributed to a Palestinian rabbi in b. Sanhedrin 93b:

> (A) "And some of your sons, your own issue, whom you will have fathered, will be taken to serve as *sarisim* in the palace of the king of Babylon" (2 Kings 20:18).
>
> (B) What is [the meaning of] *sarisim*?
>
> (C) Rav said, "Literally, eunuchs."
>
> (D) R. Ḥanina said, "That idol worship was castrated in their time" [i.e., in the days of Hezekiah].

Rav (part C), an early Babylonian Amora, may know the Palestinian view (expressed by R. Ḥanina, a Palestinian Amora)[21] but reject it.[22] In the continuation, however, Rav Naḥman bar Yiẓḥak, a later Babylonian Amora, resolves an objection against R. Ḥanina's opinion, suggesting that he supports it. We therefore appear to be confronted with another case in which an opinion found only in Palestinian traditions prior to the mid–fourth century achieves currency among later Babylonian Amoraim.

This conclusion is strengthened by the fact that the same view is attributed to Rav Ashi, a late fourth-, early fifth-century Babylonian Amora, in b. Sanhedrin 102b:

> Rav Ashi stopped [the lesson] at [the mishnah that lists] the three kings [who have no portion in the world to come] (m. Sanhedrin 10:2).
> He said, "Tomorrow we will begin [the lesson by discussing] our colleagues."
> Manasseh came and appeared to him in a dream.
> He said, "You call us your colleague and your father's colleagues?
> Where should you [break off a piece of bread from the loaf when you] begin *Ha-motzi* [the blessing one recites before eating bread]?"
> [Rav Ashi] said to [Manasseh], "I don't know."
> He said to him, "You don't know where you should begin *Ha-motzi*, and you call me your colleague?"
> He said to him, "Teach me, and tomorrow I will expound in your name in a public lecture."
> He said to him, "From where the baking forms a crust."
> He said to him, "Since you are so wise, why did you worship idols?"
> He said to him, "If you had been there, you would have picked up the hem of your garment and run after me."
> The next day, [Rav Ashi] said to the rabbis, "Let us begin with our teachers."

This story expresses bewilderment over the behavior of biblical Israelites, who for some inexplicable reason found idolatry irresistible. Clearly, the story implies, human nature profoundly changed between the time of the Bible and the time of the rabbis to make idolatry lose its appeal, although this story does not explain the nature of this change or why it took place.

While we cannot date this story with certainty, the fact that it involves Rav Ashi places it in Babylonia and makes it clear that it derives from a late stratum of the Talmud.[23] In b. Beiẓah 39a and b. Arakhin 32b, finally, the anonymous editors, who, as noted throughout this book, probably derive from the later strata of the Bavli, express precisely the same view.[24]

Earlier research revealed a variety of other respects, crucially important for my purposes, in which later Babylonian sages depart from earlier Babylonian rabbinic patterns and are portrayed or behave like Palestinian rabbis. To be specific, I found that Babylonian rabbis after the mid–fourth century, like Palestinian rabbis but unlike earlier Babylonian rabbis, (1) idealize and promote nonrabbinic support of sages;[25] (2) express approval of marriage between rabbis and nonrabbis;[26] (3) tolerate violations of their personal space by nonrabbis;[27] (4) tell stories and make statements that presuppose or imply that nonrabbis can become rabbis;[28] (5) emphasize the importance of giving charity directly to the poor;[29] and (6) advocate discretion in matters of genealogy, including the genealogical blemishes of nonrabbis.[30] These modes of thought and behavior are in keeping with Roman society's tendency toward hierarchical flexibility.[31] As noted in the introduction, late antique Roman society was more upwardly mobile than that of contemporary Persia, and the evidence of the Talmud suggests that some time during the mid–fourth century Jewish society in Babylonia began to exhibit a similar pattern.

Stories about rabbis giving charity directly to the poor clearly illustrate these claims. A story in b. Ketubot 67b, for example, relates the following:

> A certain man came before Rava.
>
> He said to him, "What do you eat [i.e., what food should I give you as charity]?"
>
> [The man said to Rava], "Fattened hen and aged wine [both of which are expensive delicacies]."
>
> [Rava] said to him, "Aren't you concerned about the financial pressure on the public?"
>
> [He said to Rava], "Do I eat from what is theirs? I eat from what is God's, as is taught [in a Baraita], 'The eyes of all look to You expectantly, and You give them their food in his time'[32] (Ps. 145:15). It is not said 'In their time,' but 'in his time.' This teaches that God gives sustenance to every single person in the proper time."

According to this narrative, a later Babylonian Amora gives charity directly to a poor man, evidence of a (depiction of a) breakdown of social barriers without precedent in stories involving earlier Babylonians. A story about later Amoraim in b. Baba Batra 10a yields the same picture:

> Rav Papa ascended a ladder. His foot slipped and he almost fell.
>
> He said, "Now, then, I would have been punished[33] like those who have violated the Sabbath and worshipped idols."
>
> Ḥiyya bar Rav Midifti said to Rav Papa, "Perhaps a poor person came your way and you did not sustain him, as is taught [in a Baraita], 'R. Yehoshua ben Korḥa says, "All who hide their eyes from [an opportunity to give] charity, it is as if they worship idols."'"

The historicity of the story is of no concern to us. What is of concern is the story's attribution to Ḥiyya bar Rav Midifti, a later Babylonian Amora, of the lesson that it is important to give charity directly to the poor when the opportunity presents itself.[34]

Stories in Palestinian compilations take it for granted that Palestinian rabbis give charity directly to the poor. For example, y. Shabbat 6:9 (8d) reads as follows:

> Two students of R. Ḥanina went out to cut wood. A certain astrologer saw them.
>
> [The astrologer] said, "These two will go out but not return."

> When they went out they came upon a certain old man.
> [The old man] said to them, "Give me charity, for it has been three days since I have tasted anything."
> They had a loaf of bread. They cut it in half and gave it to him. He ate and prayed for them.
> He said to them, "May your lives be preserved this day just as you have preserved my life for me this day."
> They went out safely and came back safely.

Along the same lines, y. Peah 8:8 (21b) reads as follows:

> It happened that R. Yoḥanan and R. Shimon ben Lakish went in to bathe in the bathhouse in Tiberias. A poor man encountered them.
> He said to them, "Acquire merit through me [by giving me charity]."
> They said to him, "When we return."
> When they returned, they found him dead.
> They said, "Since we did not acquire merit through him in his lifetime, let us take care of him in death."
> As they took care of him, they found a purse of money hanging from him [proving that he did not really need charity].
> They said, "This is [the meaning of] what R. Abahu said [that] R. Lazar said,[35] 'We need to thank the deceitful among [those who beg for charity], for were it not for the deceitful among them, if one of them demanded charity from a person and he did not give it to him, he would immediately be punished.'"

The story's attempt to limit the obligation to give charity directly to the poor is necessary precisely because the obligation is so important.[36] It is necessary to balance the responsibility to give charity with the realities of everyday life, which requires compromise and flexibility.

B. Baba Meẓia 22a further depicts the breakdown of social barriers between later Babylonian rabbis and nonrabbis:

> Amemar, Mar Zutra, and Rav Ashi happened upon the garden of Mari bar Isak. [Mari bar Isak's] sharecropper brought them dates and pomegranates and placed them before [the rabbis].[37] Amemar and Rav Ashi ate; Mar Zutra did not eat.
> In the meantime, Mari bar Isak came and found them and said to his sharecropper, "Why didn't you give this beautiful [fruit] to the rabbis?" Amemar and Rav Ashi said to Mar Zutra, "Why don't you eat [the fruit] now?"

Similarly, a story in y. Peah 7:4 (20a) relates:

> It happened that R. Abahu and R. Yosi ben Ḥanina and R. Shimon ben Lakish passed through the vineyard of Doron.[38] The share-

cropper brought them a peach. They and their colleagues ate it and there was some left over, and they estimated that it was the size of a pot from Kefar Ḥananya, which holds a *se'ah* of lentils.

A few days later they passed through there [again]. [The sharecropper] brought them two or three [peaches] in his hand.

They said to him, "We want to eat from the tree [that we ate from before]."

He said to them, "It is from the same tree."

They applied to him the verse "The fruitful land has become a salt marsh because of the wickedness of its inhabitants" (Ps. 107:34).[39]

Here as well a story involving late fourth- and early fifth-century Babylonians has a close parallel in a Palestinian rabbinic source. Analysis of traditions about early Babylonians yields no comparable accounts.

Stories about physical contact between rabbis and nonrabbis yield the same results. For example, b. Sanhedrin 27a–b reads as follows:

(A) Bar Ḥama killed a man.

(B) The exilarch said to Rav Abba bar Yaakov, "Go out and examine this case. If he did kill [someone], put out his eye."[40]

(C) Two witnesses came and testified about him that he killed [someone]. [Bar Ḥama] went and brought two witnesses. They testified about one of the [other two witnesses].

One said, "In my presence he stole a *kav* of barley."[41]

The other said, "In my presence he stole the handle of a spear."[42]

(D) He said to him,[43] "What is your opinion? [Do you hold] like R. Meir? [When it is a case of] R. Meir versus R. Yosi [as it is here], the law follows R. Yosi, and R. Yosi says, 'If he is unfit to be a witness in a monetary case, he is fit to be a witness in a capital case.'"

Rav Papi said to him, "These words [namely, that the law follows R. Yosi when he disagrees with R. Meir] [apply] when the anonymous mishnah does not follow R. Meir. Here, the anonymous mishnah follows R. Meir." . . .

Bar Ḥama arose, kissed [Rav Papi's] feet, and accepted upon himself payment of his poll tax[44] for the entire year.

This story depicts a late-fourth-century Babylonian Amora, Rav Papi, tolerating a violation of his personal space by a nonrabbi, one of many small pieces of evidence indicating (or depicting) the loosening of barriers separating rabbis from nonrabbis during this time.

Once again a story depicts the same form of interaction in a Palestinian rabbinic source, y. Kiddushin 1:7 (61c):

R. Yannai and R. Yonatan were sitting. A man came and kissed the feet of R. Yonatan.

> R. Yannai said to [R. Yonatan], "What favor is he repaying you for?"
> [R. Yonatan said to R. Yannai], "One time he complained to me that his son was not supporting him, and I said to him, 'Go, shut the synagogue on him and humiliate him.' "

Portrayals of direct contact between rabbis and nonrabbis are not encountered in stories involving earlier Babylonian rabbis.[45]

In addition, it is difficult to dismiss as mere coincidence the fact that Babylonian Amoraim of the mid–fourth century and later express opinions that run counter to the tendency of earlier Babylonians to emphasize (1) the importance of genealogical purity, and (2) the genealogical superiority of Babylonia to other lands. To be specific, several later Babylonian rabbis exhibit the more relaxed attitude of Palestinian rabbis to genealogical purity, and deny earlier Babylonian claims of superiority. The early Babylonian obsession with genealogical purity can be interpreted as an important motivation for their desire to avoid informal contact with nonrabbinic Jews. The fact that this obsession becomes the subject of controversy in later Babylonian literature is therefore significant.

B. Kiddushin 71a, for example, contains the following discussion:

> For R. Yiẓḥak said, "A family [of tainted genealogy that becomes] hidden [i.e., its genealogical defects are no longer publicly known], remains hidden."
> Abaye said, "We also learn the same [in a mishnah]: 'The family of Beit ha-Ẓerifah was in the Transjordan, and Ben Ẓion declared it genealogically unfit[46] by force. [Families] like these, Elijah will come to declare impure or pure, to declare genealogically fit or unfit.'[47] [Families] like these, where we know [whether they are fit or unfit, Elijah will declare impure or pure], but a family [of tainted genealogy which becomes] hidden, remains hidden."

Palestinian rabbis routinely look the other way in cases of suspected genealogical blemishes. They adopt (or are depicted adopting) a policy of benign neglect in situations where Babylonian rabbis prior to the mid–fourth century advocate zealotry.[48] Abaye, however, a later Babylonian, quotes a mishnah in support of the Palestinian view, suggesting strongly that he agrees with it.

A second statement attributed to a later Babylonian rabbi in b. Kiddushin 71a expresses the same view:

> (A) It is taught [in a Baraita], "There was another [family of doubtful lineage] and the sages did not want to reveal it [publicly], but the sages transmit [the information] to their sons and to their students once every seven years. And some say twice every seven years."
> (B) Rav Naḥman bar Yiẓḥak said, "It makes sense according to the one who said, 'Once every seven years,' as it is taught [in a Baraita], '[If one said], "I will be a nazir if I do not reveal [the genealogical

> blemishes of] families," he should become a nazir and not reveal [the genealogical blemishes of] families.' "[49]

Like his older contemporary, Abaye, Rav Naḥman bar Yiẓḥak prefers discretion to zealotry in matters of genealogical purity.

Along the same lines, b. Kiddushin 72b records the following:

> (A) Said Rav Yehudah said Shmuel, "These are the words of R. Meir [i.e., the mishnah, according to which Babylonia is genealogically spotless,[50] is a minority opinion], but the sages say, 'All lands are presumed to be genealogically fit' " [i.e., since the mishnah is only a minority opinion, it is not authoritative. The halakhah is in accordance with the majority view].
>
> (B) Amemar permitted Rav Huna bar Natan to marry a woman of Maḥoza.[51]
>
> (C) Rav Ashi said to him, "What is your opinion? [Do you hold like Rav Yehudah in the name of Shmuel], for Rav Yehudah said Shmuel said, 'These are the words of R. Meir, but the sages say, "All lands are presumed to be genealogically fit?" ' But behold, the house of Rav Kahana does not teach the tradition in this fashion, and the house of Rav Papa does not teach the tradition in this fashion, and the house of Rav Zevid does not teach the tradition in this fashion."
>
> (D) Even so, [Amemar] did not accept this [opposing opinion] from [Rav Ashi], since he heard [the above version] from Rav Zevid Minehardea.

We see, therefore, that the firmly held position regarding Babylonia's genealogical superiority, so well attested in traditions attributed to earlier Babylonian Amoraim, is the subject of controversy later on. It is striking that Rav Zevid Minehardea and Amemar attribute to Rav Yehudah the view that all lands are genealogically fit, indicating that they reject several traditions that attribute to the same Rav Yehudah the most extreme advocacy of Babylonian genealogical superiority.[52]

Further evidence that later Babylonian rabbis behaved, or are depicted as behaving, like Palestinian rabbis is found in b. Baba Batra 149a:

> Isur the convert had 12,000 zuz in the house of Rava. Rav Mari, [Isur's] son, was born after his father converted but was conceived before his father converted,[53] and he was in the study house. Said Rava, "How shall Rav Mari acquire these zuzim?"

Apparently, we encounter the same characters in b. Yevamot 49b:

> Rava pronounced Rav Mari bar Rachel fit and appointed him to an important position of authority in [the city of] Babylon.[54] And even though the master said, " 'You shall surely place a king over yourselves [. . . one of your brothers you shall place over you as king. You

> may not appoint a foreign man over you, who is not your brother]' (Deut. 17:15), all of the appointments which you make shall only be from among your brothers"; this one, because his mother is Jewish, we apply to him the verse '... one of your brothers.'[55]

In other words, Rav Mari bar Rachel's father was not Jewish at the time of Rav Mari's conception, a fact that the Talmud indicates by referring to him by his mother's name, Rachel, and suppressing the name of his father. Despite Rav Mari's tainted lineage, Rava accepts him into the rabbinic fold and even appoints him to an important position of authority.

No traditions about earlier Babylonian rabbis depict the rabbinic movement as open to men of nonrabbinic extraction, particularly those of suspect lineage. The motif is common, by contrast, in stories about Palestinian rabbis.[56]

In b. Shabbat 23b, furthermore, a later Babylonian Amora expresses approval of marriage between rabbis and nonrabbis, echoing a sentiment attributed elsewhere only to Palestinian rabbis:[57]

> Said Rava, "One who loves rabbis will have children who are rabbis. One who honors rabbis will have sons-in-law who are rabbis. One who fears rabbis will himself become a rabbi.[58] And if he is not fit [to be a rabbi], then his words will be obeyed as if he were a rabbi."

It is unlikely that Rava has to convince rabbis of the importance of "loving" and "honoring rabbis," or that the promise that one "will himself become a rabbi" will serve as much of an incentive to one who is already a rabbi. It is likely, therefore, that Rava is speaking about nonrabbis, and the fact that he promises those who honor rabbis that they will have "sons-in-law who are rabbis" shows his approval of marriage between rabbis and nonrabbis.[59] The fact that Rava promises one who respects rabbis that "he himself will become a rabbi" further indicates that later Babylonians admit, or approve of admitting, nonrabbis into their ranks.[60]

Promoting marriage between rabbis and nonrabbis is motivated in part by the desire to persuade wealthy nonrabbis to support less wealthy rabbis. Numerous Palestinian traditions encourage, or favorably depict, nonrabbis supporting rabbis in business and giving them charity, as well as encouraging or permitting rabbis to accept such gifts.[61] Once again a story about a later Babylonian rabbi, in b. Ta'anit 21b–22a, clearly parallels the Palestinian traditions:

> Abba the bloodletter received greetings from heaven every day.
>
> Abaye received them every Sabbath.... Abaye was despondent on account of Abba the bloodletter.
>
> They said to him, "You are not able to do what he does."
>
> What did Abba the bloodletter do?... When a rabbi[62] visited him, he took no payment from him. When [the rabbi] was done [with his treatment, Abba] would give him coins and say to him, "Go and heal yourself."

> One day, Abaye sent a pair of rabbis to examine him [to see if he really was so righteous]. [Abba] sat them down, fed them, gave them something to drink, and lay down mattresses for them at night.

The motif of the unlearned but pious man whose status in the eyes of heaven is superior to that of a sage is widely attested in Palestinian rabbinic literature. To the best of my knowledge, this motif is not found in traditions about Babylonians prior to the mid–fourth century.[63] Significantly, Peter Brown observes that the same motif, *mutatis mutandis,* is found frequently in Byzantine Christian literature:

> The eastern Church had entered on to what came to strike early medieval western observers as a baffling "crisis of overproduction" of the holy. More men were accepted as bearers or agents of the supernatural on earth, and in a far greater variety of situations, than came to be tolerated in Western Europe. . . . For at any time, the man who enjoyed most favour with God in Heaven might be, not St. Anthony, but a doctor in Alexandria, not St. Macanus, but a farmer in an Egyptian village, and even, who knows, an imperial inspector of brothels in Alexandria. The paradox of sanctity enabled the holy to scatter itself widely throughout Byzantine society. . . . At the bottom, it fell heavily on prostitutes as it never fell on the equally whore-laden towns of Italy.[64]

In other words, my claim regarding a striking feature of Palestinian literature is confirmed by independent analysis of Christian literature of the same time and place (the eastern Mediterranean world). The story of Abaye and Abba the bloodletter shows once again that later Babylonian rabbinic literature conforms to western models.

Also relevant is a tradition in b. Berakhot 10b, which may attribute to a later Babylonian rabbi[65] the view that individual scholars may decide for themselves whether to follow Elisha's example and accept support from nonrabbis (2 Kings 4:8–37) or to follow Samuel's example and refuse support:

> Said Abaye, and some say R. Yiẓḥak, "He who wishes to derive benefit may derive benefit, like Elisha, and he who does not wish to derive benefit should not derive benefit, like Samuel of Ramah, as it is said, 'Then he would return to Ramah, for his home was there' (1 Sam. 7:17), and R. Yoḥanan said, 'Every place he went, his home was there with him.' "[66]

Some tradents transmit this statement in the name of a later Babylonian (Abaye),[67] others in the name of a Palestinian Amora (R. Yiẓḥak). The frequency of transmissional confusion between Palestinian and later Babylonian Amoraim is an additional fact pointing to the close connection between them.[68]

The Palestinianization of Babylonian rabbis described above should not be taken for granted—dismissed, for example, by the assertion that all of the individuals involved are rabbis, so of course they were influenced by one another. I insist upon this point because the movement of literature and/or behavior described in this chapter was one-way, from west to east, from Palestine (and perhaps beyond) to Babylonia, and not vice versa. We find no comparable reliance upon and usage of Babylonian rabbinic traditions in the later strata of the Yerushalmi,[69] and modern scholarship is almost unanimous in accepting as a methodological given the movement of fourth-century and later traditions from Palestine to Babylonia, and the need to understand the former as representing an earlier stage in the development of traditions than those found in the latter.[70] If only a fraction of the evidence that Alyssa Gray, Jeffrey Rubenstein, and Daniel Boyarin adduce proves the reworking of Palestinian rabbinic sources by sixth-century and later Babylonian Talmudic editors, I have further support for my thesis, since the fourth-century trends described in this book will have continued and perhaps expanded for centuries, probably until the advent of the Muslims in the seventh century.[71] The *naḥotei* were not sufficient, it seems, to alter learning and behavior in Palestine in other than ad hoc or episodic respects, and the fourth-century "spike" I have tentatively identified in rabbinic Babylonia vis-à-vis the west may be part of a larger process affecting the entire region: Armenia, Georgia, Osrhoene, eastern Syria, and western Persia, at approximately the same time, involving Jew and non-Jew alike. As Fergus Millar observes, "in terms of influences, pagan, Jewish, and Christian, there are clearer indications that Mesopotamia and Babylonia were affected by various currents and changes in the Roman Near East than the other way around."[72]

In deriving these historical conclusions, it was necessary to argue, in contrast to many modern scholars, that it is sometimes possible to make the leap from literature to history "on the ground." I am well aware that it is possible to attribute all or much of the evidence adduced above as proof of the appearance of western *traditions* in Babylonia rather than to actual changes in Babylonian rabbinic *behavior*. It is possible to attribute the evidence to the adoption of western literary motifs rather than to Babylonian rabbis in the mid–fourth century behaving more like Palestinians. I myself have adopted that explanation at times, notably in chapter 7.[73] The fact, however, that throughout the region, the *behavior* and not just the literature of non-Jews was changing, to wit, large numbers of people were converting to Christianity, and that we may be able to explain in part why these shifts of behavior took place at precisely this time and locality, leads me tentatively to prefer an explanation of at least some of the Jewish evidence along similar lines, namely as evidence of changes in behavior rather than of literature alone.

Hopefully this book will stimulate additional studies of the place of Jewish Babylonia within its larger cultural context, as well as the recognition by non-Talmudists of the importance of rabbinic literature for a more fully rounded picture of the ancient world. As numerous earlier studies have shown, there can be no doubt that many aspects of rabbinic literature of late antiquity are better understood when examined in the light of contemporary cultures, and it is hoped that I have succeeded in showing that the opposite is sometimes true as well.

Notes

PREFACE

1. Isaiah M. Gafni, *Yehudei Bavel bi-Tekufat ha-Talmud* (Jerusalem: Merkaz Zalman Shazar le-Toldot Yisrael, 1990), pp. 68–91.

2. Shamma Friedman, *Talmud Arukh*, vol. 2, *Ha-Perushim* (Jerusalem: Jewish Theological Seminary, 1996), pp. 22–23; and Robert Brody, "Stam ha-Talmud ve-Divrei ha-Amoraim," paper delivered at the July 31–August 4, 2005, World Congress of Jewish Studies, Jerusalem.

3. David Halivni, *Mekorot u-Mesorot: Yoma-Ḥagigah* (Jerusalem: Jewish Theological Seminary, 1975), pp. 1–12; Shamma Friedman, "Al Derekh Ḥeker ha-Sugya," in *Perek ha-Ishah Rabbah ba-Bavli* (Jerusalem: Jewish Theological Seminary, 1978), pp. 7–13 and 17–25; David Goodblatt, "The Babylonian Talmud," in *Aufstieg und Niedergang der römischen Welt* 2:19/2 (1979), reprinted in *The Study of Ancient Judaism: The Palestinian and Babylonian Talmuds*, ed. Jacob Neusner (New York: Ktav, 1981), vol. 2, pp. 154–64 and 177–81.

4. See William Scott Green, "Palestinian Holy Men: Charismatic Leadership and Rabbinic Tradition," in *Aufstieg und Niedergang der römischen Welt* 2:19/2 (1979), pp. 619–47; and chapters 1, 2, 3, and 7.

5. See David Rosenthal, "Arikhot Kedumot ba-Talmud ha-Bavli," in *Meḥkerei Talmud*, ed. Yaakov Sussmann and David Rosenthal (Jerusalem: Magnes Press, 1990), vol. 1, pp. 155–204.

6. Jacob Neusner, *Judaism, The Classical Statement: The Evidence of the Bavli* (Chicago: University of Chicago Press, 1986), pp. 94–114 and 211–40.

7. Avraham Goldberg, "The Babylonian Talmud," in *The Literature of the Sages*, pt. 1, *Oral Torah, Halakha, Mishna, Tosefta, Talmud, External Tractates*. Compendia Rerum Iudaicarum ad Novum Testamentum, sec. 2, vol. 3, The Literature of the Jewish People in the Period of the Second Temple and the Talmud, ed. Shmuel Safrai (Assen: Van Gorcum, 1987), p. 336; and Richard Kalmin, *The Sage in Jewish Society of Late Antiquity* (London: Routledge, 1999), pp. 112–13.

8. See Yoḥanan Breuer, "Gadol mei-Rav Rabbi, Gadol mei-Rabbi Rabban, Gadol mei-Rabban Shemo," *Tarbiẓ* 66, no. 1 (1997), pp. 41–59, especially pp. 53–56. Breuer argues that the distinction between "Rav" and "Rabbi" was one of phonetics and dialect alone, wherein Eastern Aramaic dialects tended to drop vowels at the end of words (hence: Rav) whereas Western Aramaic retained them. The names of some rabbis, such as Shmuel, lack an introductory honorific, and the names of other rabbis, such as Rava, are formed via the contraction of the honorofic, Rav, and the personal name, Abba. As a rule of thumb, however, the honorifics cited here suffice for my purposes.

INTRODUCTION

1. The precise significance of the term "western" will be elaborated on later. Regarding the border between Persia and Rome and its impact on Jewish history, see also Mauricio Bubis, "Am Yisrael bein Paras le-Romi: Ha-Imut bein Malkhut Paras ve-ha-Keisarut ha-Romit, ve-Hashpa'atah al Ḥayyei ha-Yehudim bi-Tekufat ha-Talmud" (Ph.D. diss., Hebrew University, 1990).

2. Kalmin, *The Sage in Jewish Society*, pp. 1–14. See also Yaakov Elman, "The Suffering of the Righteous in Palestinian and Babylonian Sources," *Jewish Quarterly Review* 80, nos. 3–4 (1990), pp. 315–39, especially p. 338; and "How Should a Talmudic Intellectual History Be Written? A Response to David Kraemer's *Responses*," *Jewish Quarterly Review* 89, nos. 3–4 (1999), p. 370; and Eliezer Segal, *The Babylonian Esther Midrash* (Atlanta: Scholars Press, 1994), vol. 1, pp. 2–12; vol. 3, pp. 220–34.

3. See, for example, Anait Perikhanian, "Iranian Society and Law," in *The Cambridge History of Iran*, vol. 3, pt. 2, *The Seleucid, Parthian and Sasanian Periods*, ed. Ehsan Yarshater (Cambridge: Cambridge University Press, 1983), pp. 632–33; Ehsan Yarshater, "Iranian National History," in *The Cambridge History of Iran*, vol. 3, pt. 1, *The Seleucid, Parthian and Sasanian Periods*, ed. Ehsan Yarshater (Cambridge: Cambridge University Press, 1983), p. 406; Richard N. Frye, *The History of Ancient Iran* (Munich: Beck, 1984), pp. 218–21, 315–16, 329, and 334; and Michael G. Morony, *Iraq after the Muslim Conquest* (Princeton: Princeton University Press, 1984), pp. 280–81 and 296–97.

4. See chapters 1–4, and A. H. M. Jones, "The Social Background of the Struggle between Paganism and Christianity," in *The Conflict between Paganism and Christianity in the Fourth Century*, ed. Arnaldo Momigliano (Oxford: Clarendon Press, 1963), pp. 34–37; Ramsey Macmullen, "Social Mobility and the Theodosian Code," *Journal of Roman Studies* 54 (1964), pp. 49–53; and *Roman Social Relations, 50 B.C. to A.D. 284* (New Haven: Yale University Press, 1974); Peter Brown, "The Rise and Function of the Holy Man in Late Antiquity," *Journal of Roman Studies* 62 (1971), p. 99 (reprinted, with additions, in *Society and the Holy in Late Antiquity* [Berkeley: University of California Press, 1982], pp. 148–49); and Gafni, *Yehudei Bavel*, pp. 126–29. See also William V. Harris, "On the Applicability of the Concept of Class in Roman History," in *Forms of Control and Subordination in Antiquity*, ed. Toru Yuge and Masaoki Doi (Leiden: Brill, 1988), pp. 598–610.

5. Frye, *The History of Ancient Iran*, pp. 207–8; and Nina G. Garsoïan, "Prolegomena to a Study of the Iranian Aspects of Arsacid Armenia," *Zeitschrift für armenische Philologie* 90 (1976), pp. 177–234 (reprinted in *Armenia between Byzantium and the Sasanians* [London: Variorum Reprints, 1985], pp. 9–11, 19–34, and 41–43. See also Garsoïan's contrast between Armenia and the Greco-Roman world, pp. 21–25). Regarding the attitudes of Babylonian rabbis toward genealogy, see, for example,

Aharon Oppenheimer, "Taharat ha-Yiḥus be-Bavel ha-Talmudit," in *Eros, Erusin ve-Isurim*, ed. Israel Bartal and Isaiah Gafni (Jerusalem: Merkaz Zalman Shazar le-Toldot Yisrael, 1998), pp. 71–82.

6. Isaiah Gafni, "Ḥiburim Nestorianim ki-Makor le-Toldot Yeshivot Bavel," *Tarbiẓ* 51, no. 4 (1981–82), pp. 567–76.

7. Gafni, however, believes that this characteristic of the Christian academy distinguishes it from the rabbinic academy. See Gafni, "Ḥiburim Nestorianim," pp. 575–76. For documentation of the Christian school's inner-directed character, see also Arthur Vööbus, *The Statutes of the School of Nisibis* (Stockholm: Estonian Theological Society in Exile, 1962), pp. 77, 97, and 99. See also Adam Becker, "Devotional Study: The School of Nisibis and the Development of 'Scholastic' Culture in Late Antique Mesopotamia" (Ph.D. diss., Princeton University, 2004), pp. 10–14 and 60–70. Becker concentrates primarily on a text dating from the late sixth century, but he documents similar preoccupation with pedagogy, institutions of learning, and the master-disciple relationship in Syriac literature composed in the fourth century and even earlier.

8. See, for example, J. N. Epstein, *Mavo le-Nusaḥ ha-Mishnah*, 2nd ed. (Jerusalem: Magnes Press, 1964), pp. 353–493; Yaakov Sussmann, "Sugyot Bavli'ot li-Sedarim Zera'im ve-Tohorot" (Ph.D. diss., Hebrew University, 1969), pp. 20–28, 30–30e, 110–11, 128–39, 161–62, 177–226, and 245–90; David Goodblatt, *Rabbinic Instruction in Sasanian Babylonia* (Leiden: Brill, 1975), pp. 4–5 and 63–196; and "Towards the Rehabilitation of Talmudic History," in *History of Judaism: The Next Ten Years*, ed. Baruch M. Bokser (Chico, Calif.: Scholars Press, 1980), pp. 31–44; Baruch M. Bokser, *Post Mishnaic Judaism in Transition: Samuel on Berakhot and the Beginnings of Gemara* (Chico, Calif.: Scholars Press, 1980), pp. 3 and 9; E. S. Rosenthal, "Mashehu al Toldot ha-Nusaḥ shel Masekhet Pesaḥim (Bavli)," in *Talmud Bavli, Masekhet Pesaḥim: Ketav-Yad Sason-Lunzer u-Mekomo be-Masoret ha-Nusaḥ* (London: Valmadona Library, 1985), 5–59; David C. Kraemer, "On the Reliability of Attributions in the Babylonian Talmud," *Hebrew Union College Annual* 60 (1989), pp. 175–90; Gafni, *Yehudei Bavel*, pp. 11–16, 137–48, 187–90, 210–2, and 224–6; Richard Kalmin, *Sages, Stories, Authors, and Editors in Rabbinic Babylonia* (Atlanta: Scholars Press, 1994), pp. 2–3 and 10–13; Christine E. Hayes, *Between the Babylonian and Palestinian Talmuds: Accounting for Halakhic Difference in Selected Sugyot from Tractate Avodah Zarah* (Oxford: Oxford University Press, 1997), pp. 9–17; Shaye J. D. Cohen, ed., *The Synoptic Problem in Rabbinic Literature* (Providence, R.I.: Brown Judaic Studies, 2000); and Alyssa Gray, *A Talmud in Exile: The Influence of Yerushalmi Avodah Zarah on the Formation of Bavli Avodah Zarah* (Providence, R.I.: Brown Judaic Studies, 2005).

9. See, for example, William Scott Green, "What's in a Name? The Problematic of Rabbinic 'Biography,'" in *Approaches to Ancient Judaism: Theory and Practice*, ed. Green, pp. 77–96; Sacha Stern, "Attribution and Authorship in the Babylonian Talmud," *Journal of Jewish Studies* 45, no. 1 (1994), pp. 28–51; Günter Stemberger, *Introduction to Talmud and Midrash*, trans. Markus Bockmühl, 2nd ed. (Edinburgh: T and T Clark, 1995), pp. 57–59 (on p. 59, Stemberger summarizes: "Dating according to rabbis' names certainly involves numerous problems. Apart from the problem of pseudepigraphy . . . such factors of uncertainty are to be seen most of all in the transmission of names." Stemberger is certainly correct that there are problems, but it is important to note that in numerous instances they can be overcome); and review of Cohen, *The Synoptic Problem in Rabbinic Literature*, *Journal for the Study of Judaism* 33, no. 3 (2002), pp. 324–25 (on p. 325, Stemberger remarks: "One should be very careful not to return to the traditional method of grouping texts by the names of rabbis instead of considering first of all the document in which a saying or story occurs"); and

Robert Goldenberg, *The Nations That Know Thee Not: Ancient Jewish Attitudes toward Other Religions* (New York: New York University Press, 1998), pp. 5–6, 81–83, and 110, nn. 10–11. Regarding the work of Jeffrey Rubenstein and Jacob Neusner, see the discussion below.

10. See note 1 of the conclusion. Chapter 7 traces the history of the portrayal in Babylonia of the Sadducees as a group that denies the authority of traditions transmitted orally, an issue of enormous importance to Babylonian rabbis, who held that rabbinic teachings constituted an oral Torah, the authority of which rivaled or equaled that of the written Torah.

11. The fact that these traditions are not mentioned in Palestinian rabbinic literature raises the possibility that they reached Babylonia from Rome itself, where Josephus wrote, or from somewhere in the Roman Empire other than Palestine, although my conclusions in no way depend on ruling out Roman Palestine as the source of these traditions. It bears mentioning that Eusebius, the late third-, early fourth-century Church historian, relies heavily on Josephus both in the *Chronicles* and in the *Praeparatio Evangelica*. Since Eusebius lived and worked in Caesarea in Palestine, it seems most likely that he encountered Josephus's works there. In addition, Josephus, *The Jewish War* 1.1–6, mentions Babylonia and other eastern provinces as destinations for his work, although he makes no such claim regarding *Antiquities*, and most of the Babylonian rabbinic parallels to Josephus are found in the latter work. See, however, t. Pesahim 4:15; b. Pesahim 64b; and Josephus, *Jewish War* 6.422–27; and Seth Schwartz, *Josephus and Judaean Politics* (Leiden: Brill, 1990), pp. 166–67.

12. See, for example, Matthew 5:14–17; and b. Shabbat 116b; and the discussion of Burton L. Visotzky, "Overturning the Lamp," in *Fathers of the World: Essays in Rabbinic and Patristic Literatures* (Tübingen: Mohr/Siebeck, 1995), pp. 81–83.

13. Ẓvi Dor, *Torat Ereẓ Yisrael be-Bavel* (Tel Aviv: Devir, 1971), for example, pp. 11–84.

14. Regarding the date of the Armenian conversion to Christianity, see Kyriakos Savvidis, "Armenia," in *Der Neue Pauly: Enzyklopädie der Antike*, ed. Hubert Cancik and Helmuth Schneider (Stuttgart: Metzler, 1997), vol. 2, p. 11.

15. See, for example, Garsoïan, "Prolegomena," pp. 4–5, n. 9. This is not to suggest that Christianity immediately achieved universal acceptance throughout Armenia. See, for example, Robert W. Thomson, "The Formation of the Armenian Literary Tradition," in *East of Byzantium: Syria and Armenia in the Formative Period*, ed. Nina G. Garsoïan et al. (Washington, D.C.: Dumbarton Oaks, 1982), p. 137, and p. 148, n. 12.

16. Territories within Armenia and Babylonia alternated between Roman and Persian rule throughout late antiquity. See Nina G. Garsoïan, "Armenia in the Fourth Century: An Attempt to Redefine the Concepts 'Armenia' and 'Loyalty,'" *Revue des etudes arméniennes* 8 (1971) (reprinted in *Armenia between Byzantium and the Sasanians*, pp. 343–45); and James R. Russell, *Zoroastrianism in Armenia* (Cambridge, Mass.: Harvard University, Department of Near Eastern Languages and Civilizations, 1987), p. 515.

17. See, for example, Richard N. Frye, *The Golden Age of Persia: The Arabs in the East* (New York: Harper & Row, 1975), p. 8; Aharon Oppenheimer, *Babylonia Judaica in the Talmudic Period* (Wiesbaden: Ludwig Reichert, 1983), pp. 21; 23; 177; 186; 189–91 (see b. Megillah 26b, where Rava judges a case involving the Yehudai Romai synagogue); 203; 205; 212–14; 219–20; 224–34; 328–31; and 378–81; and T. D. Barnes, "Constantine and the Christians of Persia," *Journal of Roman Studies* 75 (1985),

pp. 131–32. Yaakov Elman, "Middle Persian Culture and Babylonian Sages: Accommodation and Resistance in the Shaping of Rabbinic Legal Traditions," in *Cambridge Companion to Rabbinic Literature,* ed. Charlotte E. Fonrobert and Martin S. Jaffee (Cambridge: Cambridge University Press, forthcoming), writes: "Mesopotamia was both the breadbasket of the [Persian] Empire and the province most vulnerable to Roman invasion." I thank Professor Elman for providing me with a copy of his article in advance of its publication.

18. See J.-M. Fiey, "Topographie chrétienne de Mahoze," *L'Orient Syrien* 12 (1967), pp. 397–420; and Oppenheimer, *Babylonia Judaica in the Talmudic Period,* pp. 179–235.

19. See Peter Brown, "The Diffusion of Manichaeism in the Roman Empire," *Journal of Roman Studies* 59 (1969), pp. 92–103.

20. See Garth Fowden, *Empire to Commonwealth: Consequences of Monotheism in Late Antiquity* (Princeton: Princeton University Press, 1993), pp. 12–36; and Maurice Sartre, *The Middle East under Rome,* trans. Catherine Porter and Elizabeth Rawlings (Cambridge, Mass.: Harvard University Press, 2005), for example, pp. 318 and 365–66. See also Brown, "The Diffusion of Manichaeism," pp. 92–93; and J. B. Ward-Perkins, "The Roman West and the Parthian East," *Proceedings of the British Academy* 51 (1985), pp. 174–99. Compare Fergus Millar, *The Roman Near East, 31 BC–AD 337* (Cambridge, Mass.: Harvard University Press, 1993), pp. 492–93.

21. See Ian Gillman and Hans-Joachim Klimkeit, *Christians in Asia before 1500* (Richmond, England: Curzon Press, 1999), pp. 91–92 and 95. See also Barnes, "Constantine and the Christians of Persia," p. 132.

22. David Bundy, "Christianity in Syria," in *The Anchor Bible Dictionary,* ed. David Noel Freedman (New York: Doubleday, 1992), vol. 1, p. 971.

23. Gillman and Klimkeit, *Christians in Asia,* p. 148. J.-M. Fiey, "Aones, Awun et Awgin (Eugène). Aux origins du monachisme mésopotamien," *Analecta Bollandiana* 80 (1962), pp. 52–81, however, theorizes that the Mar Awgin tradition derives from a later period.

24. Jes P. Asmussen, "Christians in Iran," in *The Cambridge History of Iran,* ed. Yarshater, vol. 3, pt. 2, pp. 931–33 and 940; and Gillman and Klimkeit, *Christians in Asia,* p. 146.

25. Asmussen, "Christians in Iran," p. 941; Gillman and Klimkeit, *Christians in Asia,* pp. 113–14 and 116; and James R. Russell, "Christianity in Pre-Islamic Persia: Literary Sources," in *Encyclopaedia Iranica,* ed. Ehsan Yarshater (Costa Mesa, Calif.: Mazda, 1992), vol. 5, p. 525.

26. Sebastian P. Brock, "Christians in the Sasanian Empire: A Case of Divided Loyalties," in *Religion and National Identity: Studies in Church History,* ed. Stuart Mews (Oxford: Blackwell, 1982), p. 3.

27. Bundy, "Christianity in Syria," p. 976. See also Robert Murray, "The Characteristics of the Earliest Syriac Christianity," in *East of Byzantium,* ed. Garsoïan et al., pp. 3–16; Lucas van Rompay, "The Christian Syriac Tradition of Interpretation," in *Hebrew Bible/Old Testament: The History of Its Interpretation,* ed. Magne Saebo (Göttingen: Vandenhoeck and Ruprecht, 1996), vol. 1, pt. 1, p. 640. See also Stephen Gero, "The See of Peter in Babylon: Western Influences on the Ecclesiology of Early Persian Christianity," in *East of Byzantium,* ed. Garsoïan et al., pp. 45–48; and Marlia M. Mango, "The Continuity of the Classical Tradition in the Art and Architecture of Northern Mesopotamia," in *East of Byzantium,* ed. Garsoïan et al., pp. 119–22 and 128–29.

28. Sebastian Brock, "Eusebius and Syriac Christianity," in *Eusebius, Christianity, and Judaism*, ed. Harold W. Attridge and Gohei Hata (Detroit, Mich.: Wayne State University Press, 1992), pp. 212–34.

29. Bundy, "Christianity in Syria," pp. 975–76.

30. Sebastian Brock, "From Antagonism to Assimilation: Syriac Attitudes to Greek Learning," in *East of Byzantium*, ed. Garsoïan et al., pp. 17–34. See also Jeffrey L. Rubenstein, *The Culture of the Babylonian Talmud* (Baltimore, Md.: Johns Hopkins University Press, 2003), pp. 35–38.

31. Van Rompay, "The Christian Syriac Tradition of Interpretation," pp. 617 and 640.

32. Murray, "Earliest Syriac Christianity," p. 9. Similarly, on p. 10: "With the prose of Aphrahat and Ephrem we can really speak of Syriac *Kunstprosa*... but if we want to look for antecedents, we have to look in Greek"; see also pp. 11–12; Hans Drijvers, "The Persistence of Pagan Cults and Practices in Christian Syria," and Mango, "The Continuity of the Classical Tradition in the Art and Architecture of Northern Mesopotamia," in *East of Byzantium*, ed. Garsoïan et al., pp. 37 and 115–34, respectively.

33. Van Rompay, "The Christian Syriac Tradition," p. 621.

34. Ibid., p. 622.

35. In an inscription on the Ka'ba-i Zardusht at Naqsh-i Rustam near Persepolis, Shapur I refers to "the people we displaced from the Roman empire, from Aniran [areas outside of Iran], those we settled in the empire of Iran, in Persis, in Parthia, in Susiana, in Mesopotamia and in all other provinces in which we, our father and our ancestors and forefathers possessed crown domains." The translation is that of Josef Wiesehöfer, *Ancient Persia from 550 BC to 650 AD* (London: Tauris, 1996), p. 155; see also pp. 160–62. See also the translation of Frye, *The History of Ancient Iran*, pp. 371–73. Regarding the dating of Shapur's conquests, see Michael I. Rostovtzeff, "*Res Gestae Divi Saporis* and Dura," *Berytus* 8, fasc. 1 (1943), pp. 17–60; Barnes, "Constantine and the Christians of Persia," pp. 126–36; Erich Kettenhofen, *Die römisch-persischen Kriege des 3. Jahrhunderts n. Chr.* (Wiesbaden: Ludwig Reichert, 1982); Pat Southern, *The Roman Empire from Severus to Constantine* (London: Routledge, 2001), pp. 234–40 and 358–60; and the literature cited by Gafni, *Yehudei Bavel*, pp. 259–64.

36. See Wiesehöfer, *Ancient Persia*, pp. 190 and 192–93.

37. Wiesehöfer asserts that "several hundred thousand mostly Christian" inhabitants of Roman Syria, Cilicia, and Cappadocia were deported, although it is unclear how he arrives at this number of deportees, or how he knows that they were "mostly Christian."

38. Glanville Downey, *A History of Antioch in Syria: From Seleucus to the Arab Conquest* (Princeton: Princeton University Press, 1961), pp. 592–93, n. 24, dates this chronicle to the mid–eleventh century. Frye, *History of Ancient Iran*, p. 288, dates it to the thirteenth century. Its reliability as a source for events of the third century, therefore, is certainly open to question.

39. *Ancient Persia*, p. 201. See also Rostovtzeff, "*Res Gestae Divi Saporis* and Dura," p. 21, n. 9; and pp. 30, 35, and 37–42; Brown, "The Diffusion of Manichaeism," pp. 94–96, and Downey, *History of Antioch in Syria*, pp. 258–61. For a different explanation, see Barnes, "Constantine and the Christians of Persia," p. 131.

40. Theodor Nöldeke, ed., *Geschichte der Perser und Araber zur Zeit des Sasaniden, Aus der arabischen Chronik des Tabari* (1897; reprint, Leiden: Brill, 1973), pp. 32–33 and 40–41.

41. Frye, *History of Ancient Iran*, pp. 296–303, especially p. 298. See also Richard N. Frye, *The Heritage of Persia* (Cleveland: World, 1963), p. 204; and Zeev Rubin, "The Roman Empire in the *Res Gestae Divi Saporis*: The Mediterranean World in Sasanian Propaganda," in *Ancient Iran in the Mediterranean World: Proceedings of an International Conference in Honour of Professor Józef Wolski held at the Jagiellonian University, Cracow, in September, 1996*, ed. Edward Dąbrowa (Cracow: Jagiellonian University Press, 1998) (*Electrum: Studies in Ancient History*), pp. 179–80.

42. Bei Lapat in the Bavli. See Oppenheimer, *Babylonia Judaica*, pp. 86–90.

43. Wiesehöfer, *Ancient Persia*, pp. 162, 204, and 218–19.

44. Persian Christians had officially accepted this doctrine in a synod at Seleucia-Ctesiphon in 410.

45. See the detailed survey by Downey, *History of Antioch in Syria*, pp. 252–71 and 587–95 (especially the references to Libanius, Ammianus Marcellinus, and Malalas, all of whom lived in Antioch); and the sources cited in Michael H. Dodgeon and Samuel N. C. Lieu, eds., *The Roman Eastern Frontier and the Persian Wars (AD 226–363): A Documentary History* (London: Routledge, 1991), pp. 34–65 and 354–69. The thirteenth book of the Sibylline Oracles seems to refer to the Persian conquest of Antioch, which also appears to be confirmed by numismatic evidence. See also the Roman literature surveyed by Fowden, *Empire to Commonwealth*, pp. 27–36.

46. See, for example, W. B. Henning, "The Great Inscription of Sapur I," *Bulletin of the School of Oriental Studies* 9 (1939), p. 827; Rostovtzeff, "*Res Gestae Divi Saporis* and Dura," pp. 23–30, 35, 39, 45, and 54; Kettenhofen, *Die römisch-persischen Kriege*, pp. 68–73; Millar, *The Roman Near East*, pp. 160 and 308–9; Georgina Hermann, "Naqsh-i Rustam 6: The Roman Victory of Shapur I and The Bust and Inscription of Kerdir," p. 20; and D. N. Mackenzie, "Kerdir's Inscription," pp. 43–44 (synoptic text in transliteration), 55 (transcription), 58 (translation), and 65 (commentary), both in *Iranische Denkmäler*, fasc. 13, "The Sasanian Rock Reliefs at Naqsh-i Rustam" (Berlin: Dietrich Reimer, 1989).

47. Ammianus Marcellinus 20.6.7; Procopius, *Persian Wars* 2.9.15–16 and 2.14.1–4; and Theophylact Simocatta (see *The History of Theophylact Simocatta: An English Translation with Introduction and Notes*, ed. and trans. Michael Witby and Mary Witby [Oxford: Clarendon Press, 1986], p. 140, and n. 26, there); and Dodgeon and Lieu, *The Roman Eastern Frontier*, pp. 34–65 and 354–65. See also Nina G. Garsoïan, "Byzantium and the Sasanians," in *The Cambridge History of Iran*, ed. Yarshater, vol. 3, pt. 1, p. 570; and Millar, *The Roman Near East*, pp. 159–67.

48. See Wiesehöfer, *Ancient Persia*, pp. 218–19.

49. See, for example, Wayne A. Meeks, *Jews and Christians in Antioch in the First Four Centuries* (Missoula, Mont.: Scholars Press, 1978).

50. Notable exceptions are Gafni, *Yehudei Bavel*, pp. 149–76; and Yaakov Elman, "Marriage and Marital Property in Rabbinic and Sasanian Law," in *Rabbinic Law in Its Roman and Near Eastern Context*, ed. Catherine Hezser (Tübingen: Mohr/Siebeck, 2003), pp. 227–76; and "Acculturation to Elite Persian Norms and Modes of Thought in the Babylonian Jewish Community of Late Antiquity," in *Netiot LeDavid: Jubilee Volume for David Weiss Halivni*, ed. Ephraim Halivni et al. (Jerusalem: Orhot Press, 2004), pp. 31–56. See also Jacob Neusner, "How Much Iranian in Jewish Babylonia?" in *Talmudic Judaism in Sasanian Babylonia: Essays and Studies* (Leiden: Brill, 1976), pp. 139–47.

51. Elman, "Acculturation to Elite Persian Norms," pp. 31–34; and the literature cited there.

52. Elman, "Middle Persian Culture and Babylonian Sages," citing b. Kiddushin 70a–b.

53. Kalmin, *The Sage in Jewish Society*, p. 6.

54. See, for example, Brown, "The Rise and Function of the Holy Man," pp. 80–101; Garth Fowden, "The Pagan Holy Man in Late Antique Society," *Journal of Hellenic Studies* 102 (1982), pp. 33–59; Philip Rousseau, *Ascetics, Authority and the Church in the Age of Jerome and Cassian* (Oxford: Oxford University Press, 1978), pp. 56–67, 126, 149–51, and 161–65; and "Ascetics as Mediators and as Teachers," in *The Cult of Saints in Late Antiquity and the Early Middle Ages*, ed. James Howard-Johnston and Paul A. Hayward (Oxford: Oxford University Press, 1999), pp. 45–59; James E. Goehring, "The Origins of Monasticism," in Attridge and Hata, *Eusebius, Christianity, and Judaism*, pp. 235–55; and "Withdrawing into the Desert: Pachomius and the Development of Village Monasticism in Upper Egypt," *Harvard Theological Review* 89 (1996), pp. 267–85; Alan Cameron, *The Mediterranean World in Late Antiquity* AD *395–600* (London: Routledge, 1993), pp. 73–75; and David Brakke, *Athanasius and the Politics of Asceticism* (Oxford: Clarendon Press, 1995), pp. 4, 9–10, 82–110, and 324.

55. Compare Elman, "Acculturation to Elite Persian Norms," pp. 31–56. It goes without saying that the terms "texts" and "literature" need not imply writing.

56. See Russell, *Zoroastrianism in Armenia*.

57. See, for example, chapter 6.

58. An especially radical theory of the Talmud's formation is that of Jacob Neusner. See, for example, Jacob Neusner, *Making the Classics in Judaism* (Atlanta: Scholars Press, 1989), pp. 1–13 and 19–44. See also the literature cited in note 9. Many scholars have critiqued Neusner's theories in detail elsewhere (see, for example, Kalmin, *Sages, Stories, Authors, and Editors*, pp. 2–3 and 10–13; and Hayes, *Between the Babylonian and Palestinian Talmuds*, pp. 9–17), and I will therefore discuss them only briefly here. Neusner acknowledges that the Talmud contains preredactional traditions, but claims that for the most part these earlier traditions cannot be identified. Little purpose is served, according to Neusner, in identifying the Bavli's component sources, since for the most part, such source criticism yields trivialities. Generally speaking, Neusner argues, the Talmud is the statement of its final editors, since it contains primarily (1) material authored or molded beyond recognition by these editors; or (2) preredactional material that the final editors saw fit to transmit to future generations because it corresponded to their worldview and intended message. Neusner's theory has been convincingly refuted, however, since, as noted, it is frequently possible to divide the Talmud into its constituent layers and reach significant conclusions about the literature, personalities, and institutions of the rabbis who flourished prior to the Talmud's final redaction. Material attributed to early rabbis often differs from that attributed to later rabbis; early material is at times even antithetical to the standards and norms of later generations. It is not true, in other words, that the Talmud's later editors retained only or even primarily sources that conformed to their own sentiments. Later tradents and editors often retained earlier material for the simple reason that it was traditional. As such, it could no longer be excised from the text. I am not arguing, it is important to emphasize, that later generations slavishly transmitted everything they received from earlier generations. Countless examples, many of which will be adduced throughout this study, prove that later generations often had great freedom to emend sources in response to real or perceived difficulties. See also, for example, David Halivni, *Mekorot u-Mesorot: Shabbat* (Jerusalem: Jewish Theological Seminary, 1982), pp. 5–16; and *Midrash, Mishnah, and Gemara: The Jewish Predilection for Justified Law* (Cambridge, Mass.: Harvard University Press, 1986),

pp. 76–84; Goldberg, "The Babylonian Talmud," pp. 333–34; Yaakov Sussmann, "Shuv al Yerushalmi Nezikin," in Rosenthal and Sussmann, *Meḥkerei Talmud*, vol. 1, pp. 106–14; Shamma Friedman, "Al ha-Aggadah ha-Historit ba-Talmud ha-Bavli," in *Sefer Zikaron le-R. Shaul Lieberman*, ed. Shamma Friedman (Jerusalem: Saul Lieberman Institute for Talmudic Research, 1993), pp. 119–64; *Talmud Arukh*, vol. 2, *Ha-Perushim*, pp. 7–23; and "Ha-Baraitot ba-Talmud ha-Bavli ve-Yaḥasam le-Makbiloteihen she-ba-Tosefta," in *Atarah le-Ḥayim: Meḥkarim be-Sifrut ha-Talmudit ve-ha-Rabbanit li-Kevod Professor Ḥayim Zalman Dimitrovsky*, ed. Daniel Boyarin et al. (Jerusalem: Magnes Press, 2000), pp. 163–201. I am simply claiming that we encounter the opposite phenomenon as well: cases in which later generations acted with great restraint toward received traditions, preserving them intact despite the obstacles they posed. For further development of these arguments, see Richard Kalmin, "The Formation and Character of the Babylonian Talmud," in *The Cambridge History of Judaism*, vol. 4, *The Late Roman-Rabbinic Period* (Cambridge: Cambridge University Press, 2006), pp. 843–52.

59. Rubenstein, *Culture*, p. 11, says: "One can neither accept all attributions as reliable indicators of Amoraic tradition nor reject them *in toto*," a claim with which I am in complete agreement.

60. See Jeffrey L. Rubenstein, "The Thematization of Dialectics in Bavli Aggada," *Journal of Jewish Studies* 53, no. 2 (2002), p. 2; and *Culture*, pp. 2–9 and 31–35. Rubenstein, *Culture*, p. 10, contrasts his approach with that of scholars who "ignore attributions" and "accept them completely." It is clear, however, that there are many possible approaches within the two extremes. I would argue that Rubenstein and I occupy this middle ground, and that we are attempting to decide on a case-by-case basis whether or the extent to which attributions provide usable information. Phrased simply, we disagree about the extent to which the Bavli was composed by later Babylonian editors, and the standards of proof necessary to state confidently that a given tradition in the Bavli derives from later Babylonian editors. Rubenstein requires relatively little (in my opinion, insufficient) proof, and I require much more. Rubenstein's attempt (p. 165, n. 25) to place me in the camp that "accepts [attributions] completely" (which he later softens to "accepts attributions as reliable indicators of earlier traditions") is inappropriate. See the discussion below.

61. See the references cited in note 8.

62. Rubenstein, *Culture*, p. 11, appears to acknowledge the relative weakness of his arguments in support of a late date for the distinctions he describes, when he claims: "For those who reject my methodology, this study still has value in demonstrating general differences between the rabbinic cultures of Babylonia and Palestine, although not specifically Stammatic culture." I can sometimes agree with Rubenstein's less radical claim, but unfortunately, his arguments regarding the *significance* of the differences between Palestine and Babylonia depend on acceptance of his dating of the traditions to the fifth and sixth centuries.

63. See, for example, Daniel Boyarin, *Border Lines: The Partition of Judaeo-Christianity* (Philadelphia: University of Pennsylvania Press, 2004), p. 5.

64. Hayim Lapin, review of Kalmin, *The Sage in Jewish Society in Late Antiquity*, paper presented at the conference of the American Academy of Religion/Society of Biblical Literature, Nashville, Tennessee, November 19, 2000.

65. See chapters 2, 3, and 7; and Shaye J. D. Cohen, "Parallel Traditions in Josephus and Rabbinic Literature," in *Proceedings of the Ninth World Congress of Jewish Studies* (Jerusalem: World Union of Jewish Studies, 1986), div. B, vol. 1, pp. 7–14.

66. Jacob Neusner, *A History of the Jews in Babylonia* (Leiden: Brill, 1968–69), vol. 3, p. 317; vol. 4, pp. 254–55. Shaye J. D. Cohen, "The Place of the Rabbi in Jewish Society of the Second Century," in *The Galilee in Late Antiquity*, ed. Lee I. Levine (New York: Jewish Theological Seminary, 1992), pp. 157–73, found the same to be true of rabbis portrayed as adjudicating actual cases in the Mishnah and Tosefta.

67. Jeffrey L. Rubenstein, *Talmudic Stories: Narrative Art, Composition, and Culture* (Baltimore, Md.: Johns Hopkins University Press, 1999), pp. 281–82 and 405–6.

68. See chapters 1, 2, and 3.

69. Perhaps it will be claimed that the theory of audience does not commit itself to any one narrative of Babylonian Jewish social history. It is possible, therefore, even according to this theory, that Babylonian Jewish society resembled the dominant Persian society. Were this the case, however, discourse and reality would correspond in this instance, a remarkable coincidence that would appear to render the theory superfluous.

70. I am grateful to Avigdor Shinan, who raised this objection in a conversation on June 20, 2002.

71. This should not be construed as a denial on my part that it is possible to know anything at all about individual rabbis. The final word on this important issue has yet to be written. For two very different perspectives, see Green, "What's in a Name?" pp. 77–96; and Yaakov Elman, "Righteousness as Its Own Reward: An Inquiry into the Theologies of the Stam," *Proceedings of the American Academy of Jewish Research* 57 (1991), pp. 35–67.

72. For precisely this misunderstanding of my position, see Adiel Schremer, review of Kalmin, *The Sage in Jewish Society of Late Antiquity*, *Ẓion* 60, no. 2 (2000), pp. 229–35.

73. Countless modern scholars have emphasized this point. See, for example, Goodblatt, "The Babylonian Talmud," pp. 148–51; Daniel Boyarin, *Carnal Israel: Reading Sex in Talmudic Culture* (Berkeley: University of California Press, 1993), pp. 134–66.

74. With the possible exception of statements by Rav, who spent time in both Palestine and Babylonia and whose statements sometimes reflect Palestinian, other times Babylonian, points of view. See Aharon Hyman, *Toldot Tannaim ve-Amoraim* (1910; reprint, Jerusalem: Makhon Peri ha-Areẓ, 1987), pp. 15–42.

75. The same is true of statements attributed to and stories involving Babylonian rabbis in the Palestinian Talmud. My methodological approach to such stories and statements is the same as that regarding statements and stories involving Palestinian rabbis in the Bavli.

CHAPTER 1

1. See my comments in the introduction.

2. The one exception is probably the prohibition of circumcision. See the discussion below. See Peter Schäfer, *Der Bar Kokhba-Aufstand: Studien zum zweiten jüdische Krieg gegen Rom* (Tübingen: Mohr/Siebeck, 1981); and "Hadrian's Policy in Judaea and the Bar Kokhba Revolt: A Reassessment," in *A Tribute to Geza Vermes: Essays on Jewish and Christian Literature*, ed. Philip R. Davies and Richard T. White (Sheffield, England: Sheffield Academic Press, 1990), pp. 281–303 (*Journal for the Study of the Old Testament* series 100). For other detailed treatments of rabbinic sources about Bar Kokhba, see, for example, Yiẓḥhak Halevy, *Dorot ha-Rishonim* (1897–1939; reprint, Jerusalem: n.p., 1967), vol. 4, pp. 579–85, 605–6, 640–72, 706–45, and

775–81; Gedalya Alon, *Toldot ha-Yehudim be-Ereẓ Yisrael bi-Tekufat ha-Mishnah ve-ha-Talmud* (Tel Aviv: Ha-Kibuẓ ha-Me'uḥad, 1958), vol. 2, pp. 43–47, 56–57, and 60–61; Saul Lieberman, "The Martyrs of Caesarea," *Annuaire de l'Institut de philologie et d'histoire orientales et slaves* 7 (1939–44), pp. 395–446; and "Redifat Dat Yisrael," in *Sefer Yovel li-Kevod Shalom Baron*, vol. 3, ed. Saul Lieberman and Arthur Hyman (Jerusalem: American Academy for Jewish Research, 1975), pp. 213–45; Yehoshua Efron, "Milḥemet Bar-Kokhba le-Or ha-Masoret ha-Talmudit ha-Ereẓ-Yisre'elit ke-Neged ha-Bavlit," in *Mered Bar-Kokhba: Meḥkarim Ḥadashim*, ed. Aharon Oppenheimer and Uriel Rapaport (Jerusalem: Yad Yiẓḥak Ben-Ẓvi, 1984), pp. 47–105; and Peter Schäfer, ed., *The Bar Kokhba War Reconsidered: New Perspectives on the Second Jewish Revolt against Rome* (Tübingen: Mohr/Siebeck, 2003).

3. Regarding the tendency of rabbinic compilations, especially the Bavli, to rabbinize traditions, see the introduction and chapters 2, 3, and 4; Green, "Palestinian Holy Men," pp. 619–47; Baruch M. Bokser, "Wonder-Working and the Rabbinic Tradition: The Case of Hanina ben Dosa," *Journal for the Study of Judaism* 16, no. 1 (1985), pp. 42–92; and Richard Kalmin, "Rabbinic Portrayals of Biblical and Post-Biblical Heroes," in *The Synoptic Problem in Rabbinic Literature*, ed. Shaye J. D. Cohen (Providence, R.I.: Brown Judaic Studies, 2000), pp. 119–41.

4. Compare Benjamin Isaac and Aharon Oppenheimer, "The Revolt of Bar Kokhba, Ideology and Modern Scholarship," in Benjamin Isaac, *The Near East under Roman Rule: Selected Papers* (Leiden: Brill, 1998), pp. 250–51, who claim that the tendency of the Romans "was not the suppression of Jewish religion as such. Their tendency was to suppress those elements in the Jewish religion which were of national significance and to abolish the autonomy of the Jewish people." See also Lieberman, "The Martyrs of Caesarea," pp. 426, 428, and 531–32; and "Redifat Dat Yisrael," pp. 214–18 and 227; and M. D. Herr, "Persecutions and Martyrdom in Hadrian's Days," *Scripta Hierosolymitana* 23 (1972), pp. 94–102.

5. Schäfer argued, for example, that several traditions that earlier scholars assigned to the Bar Kokhba era (regarding this term, see the discussion below) might refer to the Jewish rebellion during the reign of Trajan, which is often described by modern scholars as a diaspora rebellion but may have involved the Jews of Palestine as well. Compare Millar, *The Roman Near East*, p. 103, who writes: "There is as yet no concrete evidence of a Jewish revolt in Judaea, parallel to that in Egypt, Cyrene, and Cyprus." See also M. D. Herr, "The Participation of Galilee in the 'War of Qitus' or in the 'Bar Kosba Revolt,'" *Katedra* 4 (1971), pp. 67–73; Lieberman, "Redifat Dat Yisrael," pp. 213–14; E. Mary Smallwood, *The Jews under Roman Rule: From Pompey to Diocletian* (Leiden: Brill, 1976), pp. 421–27; Glen W. Bowersock, "A Roman Perspective on the Bar Kokhba Revolt," in *Approaches to Ancient Judaism*, vol. 2, ed. William Scott Green (Chico, Calif.: Scholars Press, 1980), pp. 132–34; and Isaac and Oppenheimer, "The Revolt of Bar Kokhba," p. 239–41, especially the sources cited in n. 10 there.

6. In an earlier version of this chapter, "Rabbinic Traditions about Roman Persecutions of the Jews: A Reconsideration," *Journal of Jewish Studies* 54, no. 1 (2003), pp. 21–50, I examined whether or not certain key terms (*shemad*, "persecution," and *sakanah*, "danger") are technical terms for events that storytellers want us to believe took place during the Bar Kokhba period. Lieberman ("The Martyrs of Ceasarea," pp. 427–28; and "Redifat Dat Yisrael," pp. 228–29) and Herr ("Persecutions and Martyrdoms," pp. 97–101, 112, and 117) argue that they are, but Schäfer (*Der Bar Kokhba-Aufstand*, pp. 195–235) raised serious questions about their methodological presuppositions. My earlier article examined the evidence afresh and concluded that on this issue, Lieberman and Herr are most likely correct. See the discussion there. Compare the lists

compiled by Herr, "Persecutions and Martydom," pp. 94–98; and Lieberman, "Redifat Dat Yisrael," pp. 214–15. See the critical evaluation in Schäfer, *Der Bar Kokhba-Aufstand*, pp. 194–235. I do not discuss several traditions mentioned by Herr and Lieberman because I am persuaded by Schäfer's arguments against their relevance to our topic. See, for example, t. Megillah 3(4):30; y. Megillah 4:12 (75c); b. Menaḥot 32b; Schäfer, *Der Bar Kokhba-Aufstand*, pp. 202–3; and Isaac and Oppenheimer, "The Revolt of Bar Kokhba," p. 251. See also Yosef Geiger, "Ha-Gezerah al ha-Milah u-Mered Bar-Kokhba," *Ẓion* 41, nos. 3–4 (1976), pp. 143–44.

7. See, for example, m. Shabbat 19:1.

8. See also the parallel in b. Ta'anit 18a. For further discussion of this story, see Halevy, *Dorot ha-Rishonim*, vol. 4, pp. 729–38; Alon, *Toldot ha-Yehudim*, vol. 2, p. 58, n. 36, and pp. 60–61; and Herr, "Persecutions and Martyrdom," pp. 85–87. All translations of rabbinic texts in this book are my own. All of the translations of biblical texts are based on *Tanakh, The Holy Scriptures: The New Jewish Publication Society Translation According to the Traditional Hebrew Text* (Philadelphia: Jewish Publication Society, 1988).

9. *Dikdukei Soferim*, ed. Rafael Rabbinovicz (1868–97; reprint, Jerusalem: Ma'ayan ha-Ḥokhmah, 1960), n. *yud*, on b. Rosh Hashanah 19a, records several versions reading "The evil kingdom decreed a persecution [*shemad*] against Israel." The London manuscript reads "the evil Greek kingdom," but the word "Greek" is apparently a mistake, given the reference to "all the greats of Rome" later on in the story. Vered Noam, "Le-Nusaḥav shel ha-'Skolion' le-Megillat Ta'anit," *Tarbiẓ* 62, no. 1 (1993), pp. 80–83; and *Megillat Ta'anit: Ha-Nusaḥim, Pesharam, Toldoteihem, be-Ẓeruf Mahadurah Bikortit* (Jerusalem: Yad Yiẓḥak Ben-Ẓvi, 2003), pp. 128–30 and 312–15 (see also pp. 20–21, there), records several versions (see below) that read "the Greek kingdom decreed" or "the wicked Greek kingdom decreed," and argues persuasively that the Oxford manuscript made no mention of the Romans or the story involving Yehudah ben Shamua. According to this version, she claims, the scholion to Megillat Ta'anit dates the wonderful event that occurred on the eighteenth of Adar to pre-Roman times, and in all probability refers to the suspension of the decrees of Antiochus IV. Throughout this book, I discuss variant readings only when they directly bear on my argument or when the text is difficult without some reference to them.

10. Samuel Krauss, *Paras ve-Romi ba-Talmud u-va-Midrashim* (Jerusalem: Mosad ha-Rav Kuk, 1948), pp. 120–22 and 128, claims that the term "the greats of Rome" (*gedolei Romi*) sometimes refers to Roman aristocrats living in the land of Israel.

11. Noam, "Le-Nusaḥav," pp. 55–99; and *Megillat Ta'anit*, pp. 22–27 and 370–82. She concludes that the Oxford manuscript is the other relatively early and reliable version of Megillat Ta'anit. See, however, chapter 3 for a comparison between the various degrees of "Babylonianization" undergone by the Oxford and Parma manuscripts.

12. See Noam, *Megillat Ta'anit*, pp. 19–27, and literature cited in pp. 28–36, there.

13. See also ibid., p. 314. The Oxford manuscript of the scholion understands the decree as a prohibition of public reading of the Torah.

14. Regarding the term "the Bar Kokhba period," see the discussion above.

15. See note 9.

16. The parallel in t. Kelim Baba Batra 7:9 also has Yehudah ben Shamua quoting R. Meir.

17. See, for example, b. Sanhedrin 13b–14a, and the parallel tradition on b. Avodah Zarah 8b.

18. See Ernst Bammel, "Der Achtundzwanzigster Adar," *Hebrew Union College Annual* 28 (1957), pp. 109–13; and Schäfer, *Der Bar Kokhba-Aufstand*, p. 211.

19. Compare Lieberman, "The Martyrs of Ceasarea," pp. 418–20. See also Daniel Boyarin, *Dying for God: Martyrdom and the Making of Christianity and Judaism* (Stanford: Stanford University Press, 1999), pp. 50–59.

20. Regarding the obscure term "the House of Avidan," see Michael Sokoloff, *A Dictionary of Jewish Babylonian Aramaic of the Talmudic and Geonic Periods* (Ramat-Gan, Israel: Bar Ilan University Press, 2002), p. 209; Boyarin, *Dying for God*, pp. 54 and 167, n. 44; *Arukh ha-Shalem*, ed. Alexander Kohut (1878–92; reprint, Vienna: Menorah, 1926), vol. 2, pp. 45–46; Marcus Jastrow, *A Dictionary of the Targumim, Talmud Babli, Yerushalmi, and Midrashic Literature* (1886–1903; reprint, New York: Judaica Press, 1971), p. 5; and Jacob Levy, *Neuhebräisches und Chaldäisches Wörterbuch über die Talmudim und Midraschim*, 2nd rev. ed., Lazarus Goldschmidt (Berlin: Benjamin Harz, 1924), vol. 1, p. 9.

21. See *Dikdukei Soferim*, ed. Rabbinovicz, n. *yud*.

22. Boyarin, *Dying for God*, p. 57, notes that part D and part B present two accounts of Ḥanina ben Teradion's arrest.

23. Ed. Louis Finkelstein (1939; reprint, New York: Jewish Theological Seminary, 1969), p. 346.

24. According to a second, less likely interpretation, part B correctly explains part A, according to which part A really intends to say that Ḥanina ben Teradion was arrested because of his Torah study, and Elazar ben Perata was arrested because of his Torah study and performance of deeds of lovingkindness. I consider this interpretation less likely, first because nowhere else in rabbinic literature do we find the theme of the Romans arresting someone for performing deeds of lovingkindness, and second, because according to this interpretation, part A states that Elazar ben Perata was arrested because of "five matters" and immediately goes on to specify that he was arrested because he occupied himself with "Torah and deeds of lovingkindness." This peculiar equivalency disturbs the smooth flow of the story, forcing the audience to ask how "Torah" plus "deeds of lovingkindness" equals "five matters." Would it not be preferable for the story to say that Elazar was arrested for "two matters?" According to the first interpretation, however, part A does not explain the expressions "one matter" and "five matters." These missing explanations do not disturb the smooth flow of the narrative, but instead raise expectations that the "matters" will be identified, expectations that are met in part B (see below).

25. See, for example, the sources cited in note 3 of the preface.

26. It is not entirely clear how "robbery" is a good deed. Perhaps the meaning is that when committed against the wicked Romans, robbery is a good deed, whereas in the eyes of the Romans it was an offense punishable by death. In addition, the term *bei avidan* (see above) is unclear, so it is difficult to know how this is a "good deed." See Maharsha, s.v. *Ashrekha*.

27. To be specific, part D twice informs us why the Romans executed Ḥanina ben Teradion. The first time, according to our present versions, it is because Ḥanina "sits and busies himself with Torah [study] [and gathers crowds in public] with a Torah scroll resting in his lap." According to ms. New York JTS 44830, ed. Shraga Abramson, however, Ḥanina "gathers crowds in public with a Torah scroll resting in his lap, and sits and expounds." In other words, according to the printed editions as well as ms. New York, Ḥanina ben Teradion is involved with the study of Torah, but (1) the former mention only his Torah study (*yoshev ve-osek ba-Torah*) while the latter uses different phraseology to describe his Torah study and/or teaching (*ve-yoshev ve-doresh*),

and (2) the former place Torah study first while the latter places Torah teaching third. Furthermore, according to H. G. Enelow's edition of Menorat ha-Ma'or, Ḥanina "gathers crowds in public with a Torah scroll resting in his lap." While Menorat ha-Ma'or describes R. Yosi ben Kisma as rebuking R. Ḥanina ben Teradion for endangering himself by studying (or teaching) Torah in public, Menorat ha-Maor's quotation of the text of the Talmud itself makes no mention of Torah study (or teaching). See R. Israel Ibn Al-Nakawa, *Menorat ha-Ma'or*, ed. H. G. Enelow (New York: Bloch, 1931), pt. 3, p. 401. It is conceivable, therefore, that the text originally made no reference to Torah study, and later scribes added the phrase on the basis of the preceding, Babylonian Amoraic discussion (part B), which, as noted, states explicitly that the Romans executed Ḥanina ben Teradion because he "occupied himself with Torah [study]."

28. Friedman, "Al Derekh Ḥeker ha-Sugya," p. 30.

29. The story features Tannaim, is entirely in Hebrew, and is introduced by a technical term indicative of Tannaitic provenance.

30. For earlier discussion of this story, see Boyarin, *Dying for God*, pp. 102–5.

31. *Dikdukei Soferim*, ed. Rabbinovicz, n. *bet*, records that the Paris manuscript and Beit Natan read "sitting and expounding, and gathering crowds in public with a Torah scroll in his lap," and that the same basic reading is found in ms. Munich. In addition, *Menorat ha-Ma'or*, ed. Yehudah Ḥorev and Moshe Katsenelenbogen (Jerusalem: Mosad ha-Rav Kuk, 1961), p. 526; Aggadot ha-Talmud; Sefer ha-Musar; and Ein Ya'akov read: "He gathered crowds in public, and expounded [*ve-darash*]." See also the discussion of b. Avodah Zarah 17b–18a, above.

32. In addition, in both cases the terms used to describe their activity are not uniform in the various versions. In some versions in both stories the term is "sitting and expounding (*yoshev ve-doresh*)," and in other versions the term is "sitting and engaging in Torah study (*yoshev ve-osek ba-Torah*)," although in the Avodah Zarah story, one version omits mention of Torah study altogether, while I found no versions of the R. Akiba story that make no mention of Torah study.

33. Lieberman, "The Martyrs of Ceasarea," pp. 425–26; and "Redifat Dat Yisrael," pp. 361 and 363; Herr, "Persecutions and Martyrdom," pp. 95–96; Schäfer, *Der Bar Kokhba-Aufstand*, p. 214 (although he doubts the historicity of this crime); and Boyarin, *Dying for God*, pp. 195–96, n. 40.

34. This tradition is entirely in Hebrew and is probably a Baraita, even though it lacks a technical term.

35. See, for example, Maharsha, s.v. *Le-Yoḥai*; and Herr, "Persecutions and Martyrdom," p. 95, n. 32.

36. The nature of the threatened denunciation is not clear. Would Yoḥai charge Akiba with continuing to teach Torah, even while in prison, or would he invent another charge? For our purposes, it does not matter.

37. Compare *Arukh ha-Shalem*, ed. Kohut, vol. 3, pp. 448–49; Halevy, *Dorot ha-Rishonim*, vol. 4, pp. 659–64; Lieberman, "Redifat Dat Yisrael," pp. 365–66; and Peter Schäfer, "R. Aqiva und Bar Kokhba," in *Studien zur Geschichte und Theologie des rabbinischen Judentums* (Leiden: Brill, 1978), pp. 101–8.

38. The statement is entirely in Hebrew and is identified as a Tannaitic source.

39. See also the statement attributed to Rav, quoted by Rav Yehudah, in b. Yevamot 105b, as well as the discussion of the parallel source in y. Yevamot 12:6 (12d), below.

40. Lieberman, "Martyrs of Ceasarea," p. 424; and Herr, "Persecutions and Martyrdom," pp. 96 and 100–101.

41. Lieberman, "Redifat Dat Yisrael," p. 215. See, however, n. 22 there.

42. The discussion, much of which is in Hebrew, features Tannaitic rabbis, but is not introduced by a technical term indicative of a Baraita.

43. The story of R. Reuven is linked to the Bar Kokhba period by virtue of the terminology used to introduce the Roman persecution ("the [Roman] government decreed a persecution" (*gazru shemad*). The printed edition of b. Me'ilah 17a reads "the kingdom decreed a decree" (*gazar gezerah*). However, mss. Munich 95 and Vatican 120 read "the wicked kingdom decreed a persecution." In addition, the word *sha'ah* in ms. Oxford 726 is most likely an error for *shemad*. For a literary analysis of the story, see Kalmin, "Rabbinic Traditions about Roman Persecutions of the Jews," pp. 33–38.

44. B. Berakhot 61a; b. Pesaḥim 112a–b; b. Avodah Zarah 17b–18a; and possibly b. Rosh Hashanah 19a (and parallel) and b. Yevamot 108b.

45. B. Shabbat 130a (twice); b. Rosh Hashanah 19a (and parallel); and b. Me'ilah 17a–b.

46. B. Rosh Hashanah 19a (and parallel) and b. Me'ilah 17a–b.

47. B. Shabbat 130a (a statement attributed to R. Shimon ben Elazar, a student of R. Meir); and possibly b. Shabbat 130a (and parallel) (a story about Elisha Ba'al Kenafayim).

48. B. Eruvin 91a.

49. B. Baba Batra 60b. The printed edition adds: "and some say, 'for the salvation of the son.'" See *Dikdukei Soferim*, ed. Rabbinovicz, n. *taf*; and Epstein, *Mavo le-Nusaḥ ha-Mishnah*, p. 691. According to this tradition, R. Yishmael ben Elisha asserts that the "evil decrees" issued by the Romans "nullify from us Torah and commandments [*miẓvot*]," vague references that indicate that the Romans made the free observance of Judaism impossible. The only specific observance mentioned, "the week of the child," is interpreted by most commentators to refer to circumcision, but Saul Lieberman, *Tosefta ki-Feshutah* (Jerusalem: Jewish Theological Seminary, 1973), vol. 8, pp. 771–72, argues convincingly that the reference is to celebrations held during the week following the birth of a baby boy or girl.

50. B. Sukkah 14b.

51. B. Ketubot 3b.

52. B. Shabbat 130a.

53. B. Shabbat 21b.

54. B. Sanhedrin 13b–14a (and parallel). This tradition is reported by Rav, quoted by Rav Yehudah, early Babylonian Amoraim who transmit much Palestinian Tannaitic material.

55. B. Avodah Zarah 17b–18a.

56. B. Me'ilah 17a–b.

57. B. Yevamot 122a. See also b. Gittin 66a and Kalmin, "Rabbinic Traditions about Roman Persecutions," pp. 39–40.

58. See Menaḥem Stern, *Greek and Latin Authors on Jews and Judaism* (Jerusalem: Israel Academy of Arts and Sciences, 1974–80), especially vol. 2, p. 619 (Scriptores Historiae Augustae), and Stern's discussion on pp. 619–21. See also vol. 1, pp. 296, 300, 312 (Strabo); 415 (Apion); 442 (Petronius); 525–26 (Martial); vol. 2, pp. 19, 26 (Tacitus); 102–3 (Juvenal); and 662–63 (Rutilius Namatianus).

59. See, for example, Alon, *Toldot ha-Yehudim*, vol. 2, pp. 10–13; Herr, "Persecutions and Martyrdom," pp. 93–94 and 98; Smallwood, *The Jews under Roman Rule*, pp. 428–31, 437–38, and 464–65; Bowersock, "Roman Perspective," pp. 135, 138, and 140–41, n. 28; Schäfer, *Der Bar Kokhba-Aufstand*, p. 234, n. 159; and "Hadrian's Policy in Judaea and the Bar Kokhba Revolt," pp. 281 and 298, n. 3; Lieberman, "Redifat Dat

Yisrael," pp. 214 and 228, especially the references cited in n. 4, there; Geiger, "Ha-Gezerah al ha-Milah," pp. 139–47; Stern, *Greek and Latin Authors*, vol. 2, pp. 619–21; Alfredo Mordechai Rabello, "Gezerat ha-Milah ke-Eḥad ha-Gormim le-Mered Bar-Kokhba," in Oppenheimer and Rapaport, *Mered Bar-Kokhba: Meḥkarim Ḥadashim*, pp. 27–46; and "The Ban on Circumcision as a Cause for Bar Kokhba's Rebellion," *Israel Law Review* 29 (1995), pp. 176–213, especially the bibliography cited on pp. 187–88, n. 37; and Isaac and Oppenheimer, "The Revolt of Bar Kokhba," pp. 234–36, and the secondary literature cited there.

60. See also b. Yoma 11a (Abaye; having a mezuzah in public); b. Gittin 64a (Rav; a divorce bill); and b. Ḥullin 101b (Rava, Rabin, and "all who go down to the sea"), where Amoraim, motivated at least in part by exegetical concerns, claim that Tannaitic statements describe a practice that was done differently because of "danger" or "persecution."

61. See also Lieberman, "Redifat Dat Yisrael," p. 227.

62. Schäfer, *Der Bar Kokhba-Aufstand*, p. 200.

63. See Goodblatt, *Rabbinic Instruction in Sasanian Babylonia*, pp. 199–238; especially p. 221, n. 1; Gafni, *Yehudei Bavel*, pp. 200–203 and 274–79, especially p. 200, nn. 99–101; and Kalmin, *Sages, Stories, Authors, and Editors*, pp. 193–212 and 303–4.

64. Similar examples can be found throughout this book. See also Friedman, "Al Derekh Ḥeker ha-Sugya," pp. 7–45; and Halivni, *Mekorot u-Mesorot: Shabbat*, pp. 5–27. For a similar case involving a story affixed to a prescriptive statement in the Tosefta, which ostensibly serves to establish a precedent for the prescriptive statement but in its original context referred to an entirely different issue, see chapter 3.

65. Mekhilta de-R. Yishmael, ed. Ḥ. S. Horowitz and I. A. Rabin (1931; reprint, Jerusalem: Wahrmann Books, 1966), p. 227.

66. Surprisingly, Lieberman, "Redifat Dat Yisrael," p. 216, does not distinguish between Torah study and public reading of the Torah.

67. The statement is entirely in Hebrew. In all likelihood it is (or purports to be) a Baraita, even though it is not introduced by a term indicative of Tannaitic provenance. As is well known, technical terminology is scarce in the Yerushalmi. See, for example, Baruch M. Bokser, "An Annotated Guide to the Study of the Palestinian Talmud," in *Aufstieg und Niedergang der römischen Welt* 2:19/2 (1979), pp. 53–55 and 70 (reprinted in *The Study of Ancient Judaism*, vol. 2, *The Palestinian and Babylonain Talmuds*, ed. Jacob Neusner [New York: Ktav, 1981]).

68. The ceremony of removing the levir's shoe, which releases the childless widow from her levirate obligation and permits her to marry someone other than her dead husband's brother.

69. Lieberman, "Redifat Dat Yisrael," pp. 230–34.

70. In an earlier part of the statement, not translated here, Rabban Shimon ben Gamliel refers to the destruction of the Temple. The first Shimon ben Gamliel is most likely not intended as the author, therefore, because according to all available evidence, he did not survive the destruction. The only other Rabban Shimon ben Gamliel whose statements have survived flourished after the Bar Kokhba war. See Hyman, *Toldot Tannaim ve-Amoraim*, pp. 1162–71; and David Goodblatt, *The Monarchic Principle: Studies in Jewish Self-Government in Antiquity* (Tübingen: Mohr/Siebeck, 1994), pp. 143–44, and the references cited in n. 53 there.

71. See Lieberman, *Tosefta ki-Feshutah*, vol. 8, pp. 771–72.

72. *Der Bar Kokhba-Aufstand*, p. 199. Schäfer suggests that the Vienna manuscript may have been altered by scribes in conformity with b. Baba Batra 60b (see

above), but it is also possible that the Erfurt manuscript was changed by a scribe who interpreted Vienna's vague reference to "uprooting the Torah" as a specific reference to Torah study. I have already observed this phenomenon in my discussion of the citation from Megillat Ta'anit. Compare the phrase "cease from the Torah" in the Aramaic substratum (designated as "A" in the discussion above) in b. Rosh Hashanah 19a (and parallel), and in Megillat Ta'anit, with the specific interpretation of this phrase found in the Hebrew scholion (designated as "B"). Lieberman, *Tosefta ki-Feshutah*, vol. 8, p. 771, overstates matters when he claims that it is "nearly certain" that the Vienna manuscript is correct and that the Erfurt manuscript is the result of emendation by scribes who "did not understand" this version. Regarding the complex issue of the relationship between the Erfurt and Vienna manuscripts of the Tosefta on the one hand and the Talmuds on the other, see Yaakov Sussmann, "'Ha-Yerushalmi Ketav-Yad Ashkenazi,' ve-'Sefer Yerushalmi,'" *Tarbiẓ* 65, no. 1 (1996), pp. 61–63, n. 166; and Adiel Schremer, "Li-Mesorot Nusaḥ ha-Tosefta: Iyun Rishoni be-Ikvot Shaul Lieberman," *Jewish Studies: An Internet Journal* 1 (2002), p. 14, n. 10; p. 15, n. 15; and p. 35, n. 130. Schremer tentatively concludes that the Erfurt manuscript reflects an ancient Palestinian version of the Tosefta, while other scholars conclude that the Erfurt manuscript tends to preserve emendations based on the Bavli. The case before us, according to my interpretation, conforms to the latter view, although even Schremer acknowledges (p. 36, and pp. 36–37, n. 134) that there are exceptional cases. The case under discussion is easily explicable according to Schremer's view that the Erfurt and Vienna manuscripts are two ancient recensions of the Tosefta, although it provides no unambiguous support.

73. Mekhilta de-R. Yishmael, ed. Horowitz and Rabin, p. 227; y. Avodah Zarah 3:1 (42c); Leviticus Rabbah 32:1, ed. Mordechai Margaliot (1956–58; reprint, New York: Jewish Theological Seminary, 1993), p. 735; and Kohelet Rabbah 2:16. See also t. Shabbat 15 (16):19. Regarding the date of Kohelet Rabbah's redaction, see Yonah Fraenkel, *Darkhei ha-Aggadah ve-ha-Midrash* (Givatayim, Israel: Yad la-Talmud, 1991), vol. 1, p. 8; and Herman Strack and Günter Stemberger, *Introduction to the Talmud and Midrash* (1991; reprint, Minneapolis: Fortress Press, 1992), p. 345.

74. T. Eruvin 5:24; Mekhilta de-R. Yishmael, ed. Horowitz and Rabin, p. 227; and y. Eruvin 9:1 (25c).

75. Y. Ḥagigah 2:1 (77b); Leviticus Rabbah 32:1, ed. Margaliot, p. 735; and Kohelet Rabbah 2:16.

76. T. Ketubot 1:1 (see Saul Lieberman, *Tosefta ki-Feshutah* [New York: Jewish Theological Seminary, 1967], vol. 6, pp. 186–87. The reading "they ordained" is an obvious mistake); and y. Ketubot 1:1 (24d).

77. Mekhilta de-R. Yishmael, ed. Horowitz and Rabin, p. 227; and Leviticus Rabbah, ed. Margaliot, p. 735.

78. T. Sukkah 1:7; and Leviticus Rabbah 32:1, ed. Margaliot, p. 735.

79. T. Baba Meẓi'a 2:17; and y. Baba Meẓi'a 2:7 (8c). Compare, however, the version in b. Baba Meẓi'a 28b.

80. Mekhilta de-R. Yishnael, ed. Horowitz and Rabin, p. 227; and Leviticus Rabbah, ed. Margaliot, p. 735.

81. Leviticus Rabbah 32:1, ed. Margaliot, p. 735.

82. T. Berakhot 2:13.

83. Leviticus Rabbah 32:1, ed. Margaliot, p. 735.

84. T. Megillah 2:4.

85. M. Ma'aser Sheni 4:11.

86. T. Ketubot 9:6.

87. Y. Ketubot 1:5 (25c).

88. T. Sotah 15:10; and y. Yevamot 12:6 (12d). See the discussion above.

89. T. Berakhot 2:13; and y. Yevamot 12:6 (12d). See the discussion above.

90. It bears mentioning that in his letters, Bar Kokhba insisted on the observance of the Sabbath, tithing, and the sabbatical year. He also gave instructions regarding the supply of the four species for the *mizvah* of lulav. In addition, archaeological discoveries in the caves of the Judaean desert attest to the observance of the *mizvah* of *tsitsit* and *shatnez* (the prohibition of garments made of linen and flax). See Aharon Oppenheimer, "Bar-Kokhba ve-Kiyum ha-Mizvot," in Oppenheimer and Rapaport, *Mered Bar Kokhba: Mehkarim Hadashim*, pp. 140–46.

91. Regarding the issue of genre as a factor helping to explain differences between versions of traditions preserved in different rabbinic compilations, see the introduction and chapter 7. Peter Schäfer noted differences in the terminology used by the various rabbinic compilations to refer to Roman persecutions, with the Mishnah and Tosefta favoring the term "in the time of danger" (*be-sha'at ha-sakanah*), and the Bavli and Yerushalmi favoring the term "in the time of persecution" (*be-sha'at ha-shemad*). At present, however, I see no reason to view this and other terminological differences as evidence of anything other than a linguistic development, devoid of any larger significance.

92. For example, the order *Kodashim* prescribes rules for the conduct of the sacrificial system that the Mishnah claims were in force when the Temple was in existence, and, presumably, that will again be in force when the Temple will be rebuilt.

CHAPTER 2

1. In addition to comparisons between Palestinian and Babylonian rabbinic versions of narratives, this chapter includes a comparison between b. Kiddushin 66a and its parallel in Josephus, *Antiquities* 13.288–300 (see the discussion below). Josephus wrote in Rome, but as noted in the introduction, it is unclear if the Bavli's source for the story is Josephus or some compilation drawn upon independently by Josephus and the rabbis. Comparison of the story's versions in Josephus and the Bavli contributes to the argument of this chapter, however, since Josephus's version is "western" vis-à-vis the Bavli's, as are the Palestinian rabbinic versions vis-à-vis those of the Bavli. See also chapter 7.

2. Compare Rubenstein, *Culture*, cited in note 60 of the introduction, and see chapter 7.

3. See, for example, Shaye J. D. Cohen, *From the Maccabees to the Mishnah* (Philadelphia: Westminster Press, 1987), p. 23.

4. See also chapter 3; and Pinhas Mandel, "Aggadot ha-Hurban: Bein Bavel le-Erez Yisrael," in *Merkaz u-Tefuzah: Erez Yisrael ve-ha-Tefuzot bi-Yemei Bayit Sheni, ha-Mishnah ve-ha-Talmud*, ed. Isaiah Gafni (Jerusalem: Merkaz Zalman Shazar le-Toldot Yisrael, 2004), pp. 141–42, and the literature cited there.

5. Friedman, "Ha-Baraitot ba-Talmud ha-Bavli ve-Yahasan le-Makbiloteihen she-ba-Tosefta," pp. 163–201, especially pp. 183–201 and the literature cited there. Compare Yaakov Elman, *Authority and Tradition: Toseftan Baraitot in Talmudic Babylonia* (Hoboken, N.J.: Ktav, 1994), pp. 1–46 (and the literature cited there) and 205–81.

6. See also the parallel in b. Megillah 9b, and the discussion of b. Horayot 12b, below.

7. The printed edition of b. Yoma 12b reads "Yosef ben Elem *in* Sepphoris," but the continuation establishes clearly that the event purportedly took place in Jerusalem.

The reading in the other contexts is "*from* Sepphoris," which is certainly correct. See also *Dikdukei Soferim*, ed. Rabbinovicz, n. *khaf*, on Yoma 12b.

8. R. Yosah is the same person referred to in the Bavli's version of this Baraita as R. Yosi. Yosi and Yosah are alternate forms of the same name. Yosef ben Ilim is also the same as the person referred to as Yosef ben Elem in the Bavli's version and as ben Ilem in the Yerushalmi's version (see below).

9. See also the parallels in y. Megillah 1:10 (72a) and y. Horayot 3:3 (47d). See Saul Lieberman, *Tosefta ki-Feshutah* (New York: Jewish Theological Seminary, 1962), vol. 4, pp. 725–26.

10. Regarding the version in b. Horayot, see the discussion immediately below.

11. Regarding the variant versions of this name in rabbinic sources, see note 8.

12. Josephus, *Antiquities*, 17.165–67.

13. Gedalya Alon, "Parirtin: Le-Toldot ha-Kehunah ha-Gedolah be-Sof Yemei Bayit Sheni," in *Meḥkarim be-Toldot Yisrael bi-Yemei Bayit Sheni u-bi-Tekufat ha-Mishnah ve-ha-Talmud* (Tel Aviv: Ha-Kibuẓ ha-Me'uḥad, 1957), vol. 1, p. 62.

14. In the Yerushalmi's version, anonymous editors quote the story as proof for the halakhic opinion that the original high priest and not the substitute high priest must supply the animals for the Yom Kippur sacrifice. The Yerushalmi does not use the story as support for R. Yosah's opinion, and does not credit R. Yosah with having quoted the story.

15. See also the story of the cruel, unnamed king in b. Keritut 28a–b (the name Yannai there is certainly a later addition to the story) (and b. Pesaḥim 57a–b); and the story about the civil war between Hasmonean claimants to the throne in b. Sotah 49b (and b. Baba Kamma 82b and b. Menaḥot 64b; compare the parallel in y. Berakhot 4:1 [7b], which makes no mention of Jewish kings).

16. See Piskei Rid and *Dikdukei Soferim ha-Shalem: Yevamot*, ed. Avraham Liss (Jerusalem: Makhon ha-Talmud ha-Yisre'eli ha-Shalem, 1986), pp. 370–71, n. 57.

17. See also Lamentations Rabbah, ed. Solomon Buber (1899; reprint, Hildesheim: G. Olms, 1967), p. 86.

18. See also b. Yoma 18a, according to which Rav Yosef quotes the statement by Rav Asi in response to a different unattributed objection. It is unclear whether Yevamot or Yoma is the original context of Yosef's remark (in all likelihood, his comment is based directly on the mishnah, and the anonymous objections are later attempts to reconstruct the impetus of his remark), but this uncertainty has no effect on my argument. It bears noting that it is uncertain exactly whom Rav Yosef quotes. He may be quoting the mid-third-century Babylonian Amora Rav Asi, but he may also be quoting the later third-century Palestinian Amora R. Asi, who began his career in Babylonia but subsequently moved to Palestine. (See also *Dikdukei Soferim*, ed. Rabbinovicz, n. *hei*, on b. Yoma 18a.) It is uncertain, therefore, whether or not Rav Asi's (or R. Asi's) statement itself further supports my argument. Significantly, however, Asi's statement is found only in the Bavli, raising the possibility that even if a Palestinian Amora is referred to, his statement has been Babylonianized.

19. Literally, the text reads "That man is the enemy of that man," employing circumlocutions to avoid negative direct speech.

20. See Mandel, "Aggadot ha-Ḥurban," p. 151, and n. 34, regarding this reading of the text.

21. The choicest sacrifice possible.

22. These are possible translations of the Hebrew, *anvetanuto*. See the discussion below.

23. See, for example, Gedalya Alon, *Toldot ha-Yehudim be-Ereẓ Yisrael bi-Tekufat ha-Mishnah ve-ha-Talmud* (Tel Aviv: Ha-Kibuẓ ha-Me'uḥad, 1952), vol. 1, p. 57; and "Nesi'uto shel Rabban Yoḥanan ben Zakkai," in *Meḥkarim be-Toldot Yisrael*, vol. 1, pp. 266–67, n. 63; Menaḥem Stern, "Aspects of Jewish Society: The Priesthood and Other Classes," in *The Jewish People in the First Century: Historical Geography, Political History, Social, Cultural and Religious Life and Institutions*. Compendia Rerum Iudaicarum ad Novum Testamentum, sec. 1, vol. 2, ed. Shmuel Safrai and Menaḥem Stern (Assen: Van Gorcum, 1976), pp. 578–79; Yiẓḥak Baer, "Yerushalayim bi-Yemei ha-Mered ha-Gadol," *Ẓion* 36, nos. 3–4 (1971), pp. 170–71; David Rokeaḥ, "Zekhariah ben Avkulas: Anvetanut O Kana'ut?" *Ẓion* 53, no. 1 (1988), pp. 53–56; and "Be-Khol Zot Misḥak Milim: Teguvah," *Ẓion* 53, no. 3 (1988), pp. 317–22; Daniel Schwartz, "Od li-She'elat 'Zekhariah ben Avkulas: Anvetanut O Kana'ut?' " *Ẓion* 53, no. 3 (1988), pp. 313–16; Anat Yisraeli-Taran, *Aggadot ha-Ḥurban* (Tel Aviv: Ha-Kibuẓ ha-Me'uḥad, 1997), pp. 12–23 and 104–6; Rubenstein, *Talmudic Stories*, pp. 139–75 and 345–62; and Mandel, "Aggadot ha-Ḥurban," pp. 141–58.

24. See Jastrow, *Dictionary*, pp. 1092–93, who records other meanings that are equally inappropriate in this context. See also *Arukh ha-Shalem*, ed. Kohut, vol. 6, p. 224; and Levy, *Wörterbuch*, vol. 3, p. 668.

25. Saul Lieberman, *Tosefta ki-Feshutah* (New York: Jewish Theological Seminary, 1962), vol. 3, pp. 268–69; Baer, "Yerushalayim bi-Yemei ha-Mered ha-Gadol," p. 170; Schwartz, "Od li-She'elat 'Zekhariah ben Avkulas: Anvetanut O Kana'ut?' " pp. 314–15; Kalmin, *Sages, Stories, Authors, and Editors*, p. 149. See also the references cited in the preceding and in the following notes. Rubenstein, *Talmudic Stories*, p. 150, comments, "I know of no other example of *'anvetan* used in a negative sense in all of rabbinic literature." He claims there that "R. Yoḥanan registers a protest against excessive *'anvetanut*." Rubenstein's need to add the word "excessive" to make sense of Yoḥanan's use of the word, however, highlights the problematic nature of the term in this context.

26. Baer, "Yerushalayim bi-Yemei ha-Mered ha-Gadol," pp. 170–71; and Rokeaḥ, "Zekhariah ben Avkulas," p. 56.

27. Louis Ginzberg, "He'arot le-Arukh ha-Shalem," in *Additamenta ad Librum Aruch Completum*, ed. Samuel Krauss (Vienna: Alexander Kohut Foundation, 1937), p. 418; and Mandel, "Aggadot ha-Ḥurban," p. 143, no. 12.

28. See H. Z. Reiness, *Be-Ohalei Shem* (Jerusalem: M. Newman, 1963), p. 201.

29. See Maharam Shif, s.v. *Gemara: Anvetanuto shel R. Zekhariah*.

30. Regarding the issue of language change in the Lamentations Rabbah text, see Mandel, "Aggadot ha-Ḥurban," p. 148, especially n. 29.

31. See, for example, Lieberman, *Tosefta ki-Feshutah*, vol. 3, pp. 268–69; and Schwartz, "Od li-She'elat 'Zekhariah ben Avkulas: Anvetanut O Kana'ut?' " pp. 313–16. Compare Baer, "Yerushalayim bi-Yemei ha-Mered ha-Gadol," pp. 170–71; and Mandel, "Aggadot ha-Ḥurban," p. 145.

32. Rokeaḥ, "Zekhariah ben Avkulas," p. 56.

33. Ibid., pp. 54–55.

34. See, for example, Strack and Stemberger, *Introduction to the Talmud and Midrash*, pp. 308–12. Compare Mandel, "Aggadot ha-Ḥurban," p. 142.

35. *Ginzei Midrash*, ed. Ẓvi Moshe Rabinovitz (Tel Aviv: University of Tel Aviv, 1977), pp. 152–54.

36. Mandel, "Aggadot ha-Ḥurban," pp. 145–47. Mandel bases his rendering on a photograph of the Genizah text. See his discussion of the manuscript variants.

37. For variants of this name, see Mandel, "Aggadot ha-Ḥurban," p. 147, n. 27.

38. It should be noted that the first time Zekhariah ben Avkulas is mentioned, the Tosefta does not refer to him as "Rabbi." As noted in the preface, however, the absence of the honorific title "Rabbi" is no guarantee that an individual cited or portrayed in rabbinic sources is not considered a rabbi.

39. See note 3 in chapter 1.

40. Kalmin, *The Sage in Jewish Society*, pp. 83–93 and 101–9.

41. See the introduction.

42. Mandel, "Aggadot ha-Ḥurban," pp 149–50.

43. Ibid., pp. 152–53.

44. A. A. Halevi, *Sha'arei ha-Aggadah* (Tel Aviv: A. Armony, 1963), p. 208, n. 28.

45. Schwartz, "Od li-She'elat 'Zekhariah ben Avkulas–Anvetanut O Kana'ut?' " p. 313.

46. Unfortunately, Schwartz's own interpretation of the meaning of R. Yoḥanan's statement in the Bavli is equally unconvincing.

47. With the exception of the story's opening line. See Mandel, "Aggadot ha-Ḥurban," p. 148, especially n. 29.

48. It is likely that the three versions of the author of the statement (Yosah, Yoḥanan, and Yosi bar R. Abun) are differing expansions of an earlier reading that indicated the name of the author only by his first initial, *yud*.

49. Josephus, *Jewish War* 4.225. See also *Jewish War* 2.409 for another detail paralleled strikingly in the Bavli's account. See also Mandel, "Aggadot ha-Ḥurban," p. 143, and the literature cited in n. 11, there.

50. Joseph Derenbourg, *Essai sur l'histoire et la géographie de la Palestine* (Paris, 1867), p. 267. See Josephus, *Life* 9.33. According to Josephus, however, Campsos son of Campsos argued in favor of loyalty to Rome.

51. Yiẓḥak Heinemann, *Darkhei ha-Aggadah* (Jerusalem: Magnes Press, 1970), p. 28.

52. For earlier scholarly discussion of this story, see Halevi, *Sha'arei ha-Aggadah*, pp. 180–88; and *Ha-Aggadah ha-Historit-Biografit le-Or Mekorot Yevani'im ve-Latini'im* (Tel Aviv: A. Armony, 1975), pp. 102–9; Z. W. Rabinowitz, *Sha'arei Torat Bavel* (Jerusalem: Jewish Theological Seminary, 1961), pp. 312–13; J. N. Epstein, *Mevo'ot le-Sifrut ha-Amoraim* (Jerusalem: Magnes Press, 1962), pp. 197–99; Ephraim E. Urbach, *Ḥazal: Pirkei Emunot ve-De'ot*, 2nd ed. (Jerusalem: Magnes Press, 1971), pp. 517–18; and Joachim Jeremias, *Jerusalem in the Time of Jesus* (Philadelphia: Fortress Press, 1969), pp. 190 and 331–32. See also B. Z. Luria, "Hordos ha-Melekh," in *Sefer Shmuel Yeivin: Meḥkarim ba-Mikra, Arkiologiah, Lashon, ve-Toldot Yisrael*, ed. Shmuel Abramski et al. (Jerusalem: Kiryat Sefer, 1970), pp. 512–13; and Daniel Schwartz, "Hordos ba-Mekorot ha-Yehudim," in *Ha-Melekh Hordos u-Tekufato*, ed. Mordechai Naor (Jerusalem: Yad Yiẓḥak Ben-Ẓvi, 1984), pp. 39–40.

53. Literally, "he set his eyes on..." See b. Gittin 58a, where the same expression is used, with precisely the same negative connotation.

54. See Epstein, *Mevo'ot*, p. 198; and *Dikdukei Soferim*, ed. Rabbinovicz, n. *reish*.

55. The Escorial manuscript lacks the phrase "but left [alive] the girl." See the discussion below.

56. Yad Ramah and the Munich and Florence manuscripts do not quote the phrase "When this girl saw that [Herod] wanted to marry her." In the Munich and Florence manuscripts, however, the verb *nasav* is used later in the story to help explain Herod's reason for preserving the girl in honey after her death. See also Yalkut Hamakhiri (Berlin, 1894), pp. 20–21.

57. Literally, "The only one left of them is that girl." See note 19.

58. "That girl."

59. See b. Kiddushin 70b and Epstein, *Mevo'ot*, p. 198. There is obviously no necessity to assign this part of the aggadah to Shmuel (early third-century Babylonia), since it is possible that Shmuel in Kiddushin is making use of an older source.

60. See Epstein, *Mevo'ot*, p. 198; and Halevi, *Sha'arei ha-Aggadah*, p.181, n. 6.

61. *Shiarei* is the reading in Yad Ramah, Yalkut Hamakhiri, pp. 20–21; and the Florence and Munich manuscripts. The Escorial and Rome manuscripts read *shavkei*, "he left [alive]." See the discussion below.

62. *Lemisav* is the reading of the Florence, Rome, Escorial, and Munich manuscripts. The printed edition and Yalkut Hamakhiri, pp. 20–21, read *lemishkal*.

63. Sokoloff, *Dictionary of Jewish Babylonian Aramaic*, pp. 533–34. Compare *Arukh ha-Shalem*, ed. Kohut, vol. 4, p. 128; Jastrow, *Dictionary*, p. 576; and Levy, *Wörterbuch*, vol. 2, p. 238.

64. The printed text is confused. See Yad Ramah and Epstein, *Mevo'ot*, p. 198.

65. The reading *ẓanitu* ("they are discreet," "modest") is found in Yad Ramah and the Rome, Florence, Munich, and Escorial manuscripts. The printed edition reads *zaharei*, "careful."

66. "That man's." See note 19.

67. "He."

68. See *Dikdukei Soferim*, ed. Rabbinovicz, n. *khaf*. The bracketed words are also found in the Escorial manuscript.

69. See *Dikdukei Soferim*, ed. Rabbinovicz, n. *nun*. The bracketed words are also in the Escorial manuscript.

70. See also Epstein, *Mevo'ot*, p. 198. I have translated according to the midrashic meaning. The Jewish Publication Society translates "And all the nations shall gaze upon it in joy."

71. The alternative verses quoted by Baba according to the printed text are missing in Yad Ramah and Yalkut Hamakhiri, pp. 20–21.

72. See Epstein, *Mevo'ot*, p. 199.

73. Regarding the text and meaning of this concluding phrase, see *Dikdukei Soferim*, ed. Rabbinovicz, n. *ayin*; *Arukh ha-Shalem*, ed. Kohut, vol. 3, p. 287; vol. 6, p. 45; and vol. 7, pp. 109 and 274; Jastrow, *Dictionary*, p. 1379; and Levy, *Wörterbuch*, vol. 4, pp. 312–13.

74. See Josephus, *Jewish War* 1.431–44; and *Antiquities* 15.62–87 and 202–42.

75. See Sifrei Deuteronomy, ed. Finkelstein, p. 271. See also Midrash Tannaim, ed. David Ẓvi Hoffman (1908–9; reprint, Jerusalem: Books Export Enterprises, 1984), p. 142.

76. Some of the linguistic parallels are in most, but not all, versions of the story. See notes 55–56 and 61–62.

77. See Boyarin, *Dying for God*, pp. 67–92, for earlier scholarly discussion of the phenomenon of rabbis (as well as church fathers) depicting themselves as feminized.

78. I am not claiming that only women are described as *ẓanitu*, but simply that it is more often a character trait associated with female behavior.

79. See Boyarin, *Dying for God*, pp. 77–78 and p. 184, n. 79.

80. There may be some residue of historical fact here. Not long after the building of the Temple and Herod's death, Judea lost its monarchical status and became a province. While Herod himself died as king, his son Archelaus was removed from that office by the Romans.

81. For more on the priesthood in Babylonia, see Kalmin, *The Sage in Jewish Society*, pp. 61–67; and Geoffrey Herman, "Ha-Kohanim be-Bavel bi-Tekufat

ha-Talmud" (master's thesis, Hebrew University, 1998), especially pp. 13–15, 61–67, 115–16, and 135–38. For studies of the priesthood in late antique Palestine, see, for example, Daliah Ben-Ḥayyim-Trifon, "Ha-Reka ha-Politi ha-Penimi shel Mered Bar-Kokhba," and David Goodblatt, "Ha-To'ar 'Nasi' ve-ha-Reka ha-Dati-Ideologi shel ha-Mered ha-Sheni," in Oppenheimer and Rapaport, *Mered Bar-Kokhba: Meḥkarim Ḥadashim*, pp. 13–26 and 113–32, respectively; Reuven Kimelman, "Ha-Oligarkiah ha-Kohanit ve-Talmidei ha-Ḥakhamim bi-Tekufat ha-Talmud," *Ẓion* 48, no. 2 (1983), pp. 135–47; Daliah Ben-Ḥayyim-Trifon, "Ha-Kohanim mei-Ḥurban Bayit Sheni ve-ad Aliyat ha-Noẓrut" (Ph.D. diss., University of Tel Aviv, 1985); Schwartz, *Josephus and Judaean Politics*, pp. 77–109 and 200–208; Yosef Yahalom, *Az be-Ein Kol: Seder ha-Avodah ha-Ereẓ-Yisre'elit ha-Kadum le-Yom ha-Kippurim* (Jerusalem: Magnes Press, 1996), pp. 56–57; and Oded Irshai, " 'Ateret Rosho ke-Hod ha-Melukhah Ẓanuf Ẓefirat Shesh le-Kavod u-le-Tiferet': Li-Mekomah shel ha-Kehunah be-Ḥevrat ha-Yehudit shel Shilhei ha-Et ha-Atikah," in *Reẓef u-Temurah: Yehudim ve-Yahadut be-Ereẓ Yisrael ha-Bizantit-Noẓrit*, ed. Lee I. Levine (Jerusalem: Merkaz Dinur le-Ḥeker Toldot Yisrael, 2004), pp. 67–106.

82. Or "western" vis-à-vis Babylonia. See note 1.

83. For further discussion of this rabbinic story and its relationship to the account in Josephus, see, for example, Markham J. Geller, "Alexander Jannaeus and the Pharisee Rift," *Journal of Jewish Studies* 30, no. 3 (1979), pp. 202–11; Lee I. Levine, "Ha-Ma'avak ha-Politi bein ha-Perushim li-Ẓedukim bi-Tekufat ha-Ḥashmona'it," in *Perakim be-Toldot Yerushalayim bi-Yemei Bayit Sheni: Sefer Zikaron le-Avraham Shalit*, ed. Aharon Oppenheimer et al. (Jerusalem: Yad Yiẓḥak Ben-Ẓvi, 1980), pp. 70–73; Albert I. Baumgarten, "Rabbinic Literature as a Source for the History of Jewish Sectarianism in the Second Temple Period," *Dead Sea Discoveries* 2, no. 1 (1995), pp. 36–52, and the references cited at p. 36, n. 81; Martin S. Jaffee, *Torah in the Mouth: Writing and Oral Tradition in Palestinian Judaism, 200 BCE–400 CE* (Oxford: Oxford University Press, 2001), pp. 53–55; and Steve Mason, *Flavius Josephus on the Pharisees: A Composition-Critical Study* (1991; reprint, Boston: Brill Academic, 2001), pp. 215–45.

84. Regarding the meaning of this term, see Saul Lieberman, *Tosefta ki-Feshutah* (New York: Jewish Theological Seminary, 1967), vol. 7, p. 397, n. 14.

85. Here the text changes from Hebrew to Aramaic, suggesting that the following phrase is not the continuation of Rav Naḥman bar Yiẓḥak's statement, but is commentary on his statement. See chapter 7, where I greatly expand upon this point.

86. Rav Naḥman bar Yiẓḥak's statement is not part of the story, but is Babylonian Amoraic (and anonymous; see note 85) commentary on it.

87. The phrase in brackets is missing from the printed texts but is found in mss. Munich 95, Oxford 842, and Vatican 111.

88. Josephus, *Antiquities* 13.288–300.

89. See, for example, Cohen, "Parallel Historical Traditions in Josephus and Rabbinic Literature," pp. 13–14. With respect to the narrative under discussion, see Josephus, *Jewish War* 1.61–70; and Mason, *Flavius Josephus on the Pharisees*, pp. 213–45. See also chapter 7, especially appendix 1. The complex issue of how best to distinguish between Josephus's sources and the contribution of Josephus himself, i.e., the degree to which Josephus was an author as opposed to a mechanical compiler, cannot be discussed in detail here. For a review of the literature on this issue, see Mason, *Flavius Josephus on the Pharisees*, pp. 18–39. For a discussion of the relationship between Josephus's *Jewish War* and *Antiquities*, see Shaye J. D. Cohen, *Josephus in Galilee and Rome: His Vita and Development as a Historian* (Leiden: Brill, 1979), pp. 48–66; and Mason, *Flavius Josephus on the Pharisees*, pp. 186–308.

90. Even Mason, *Flavius Josephus on the Pharisees*, p. 219, who tends to be skeptical of arguments in favor of Josephus's reliance on diverse sources (see, however, pp. 279–80), acknowledges that in this instance, the solution to the problems noted by scholars "is to be sought in Josephus's (or an intermediate author's) imperfect redactions of disparate sources. A virtual consensus obtains that the main body of the story originated in Jewish tradition, whether that tradition be understood as a chronicle of Hyrcanus's reign, an extensive written narrative, or an orally transmitted legend. The Jewish character of the tradition is usually surmised from (a) its favourable presentation of both Hyrcanus and the Pharisees and (b) a parallel story in the Babylonian Talmud." See also pp. 219–27.

91. See Mason, *Flavius Josephus on the Pharisees*, for a detailed examination of Josephus's attitudes toward the Pharisees. On p. 175, Mason summarizes: "Although Josephus agreed with the Pharisees on major philosophical issues, because they represented 'affirmative' mainstream position, he is very far from unrestrained enthusiasm for the group. He acknowledges their role as the foremost Jewish sect, but he hardly exults over it."

92. See also, for example, Levine, "Ha-Ma'avak ha-Politi bein ha-Perushim li-Ẓedukim," pp. 70–72.

93. See also chapter 7, especially appendix 1, and the literature cited in note 89.

94. It is not important for my purposes to determine whether the "tendency to glorify John Hyrcanus" is an accurate reflection of Josephus's own views, or is instead the view of sources quoted by Josephus. With regard to this question, see Mason, *Flavius Josephus on the Pharisees*, pp. 213–45.

95. Kalmin, *The Sage in Late Antiquity*, pp. 61–67 and 135–38. See also the discussion of b. Baba Batra 3b–4a, above, where I conclude that the first of the twin narratives, which depicts the Hasmoneans as ineffectual but not villainous, has roots in Josephus.

96. Josephus, *Antiquities* 13.288.

97. Mason, *Flavius Josephus on the Pharisees*, p. 229, refers to Josephus's "anti-Pharisaic animus," which he contrasts to the positive attitude of the body of the story of John Hyrcanus's rift with the Pharisees.

98. Mason, *Flavius Josephus on the Pharisees*, p. 218, observes that "the Elazar who utters the slander is not identified as a Pharisee but merely as 'one of the guests.'" See also pp. 229–30.

99. See note 98.

100. See, for example, M. H. Segal, *A Grammar of Mishnaic Hebrew* (1927; corrected reprint, Oxford: Clarendon Books, 1970), p. 71.

101. See also Philip Kieval, "The Talmudic View of the Hasmonean and Early Herodian Periods in Jewish History" (Ph.D. diss., Brandeis University, 1970), p. 51; Jacob Neusner, *Rabbinic Traditions about the Pharisees before 70*, pt. 3 (1971; reprint, Atlanta: Scholars Press, 1999), p. 250; and Yehoshua Efron, *Ḥikrei ha-Tekufah ha-Ḥashmona'it* (Tel Aviv: Ha-Kibuẓ ha-Me'uḥad, 1980), p. 153, for another argument in favor of the antiquity of the rabbinic story. I am not convinced, however, by their claim that Elazar ben Po'erah's comment to Yannai, "Yannai the king, such is the law for a commoner in Israel. Is this the law for you, a king and high priest?" is based on Josephus's version of the story.

102. Such as is *not* done, for example, by Yonah Fraenkel, *Darkhei ha-Aggadah ve-ha-Midrash* (Givatayim, Israel: Yad la-Talmud, 1991), for example, vol. 1, pp. 235–38. See Richard Kalmin, "The Modern Study of Ancient Rabbinic Literature: Yonah Fraenkel's *Darkhei ha'aggadah veha midrash*," *Prooftexts* 14 (1994), pp. 194–97.

103. See, for example, Albert I. Baumgarten, "Rabbi Judah I and his Opponents," *Journal for the Study of Judaism* 12, no. 2 (1981), pp. 141–42, and the literature cited in n. 28, there; and "Rabbinic Literature as a Source for the History of Jewish Sectarianism in the Second Temple Period," pp. 14–57.

104. See also Kalmin, *Sages, Stories, Authors, and Editors*, p. 39.

CHAPTER 3

1. For further confirmation of this point, see the previous chapter's discussion of b. Kiddushin 66a and the parallel in Josephus.

2. Regarding "rings" in the Temple, see m. Tamid 4:1 and m. Middot 3:5; y. Ma'aser Sheni 5:9 (56d) and y. Sotah 9:11 (24a); b. Sotah 48a; and *Arukh ha-Shalem*, ed. Kohut, vol. 2, p. 94, and the references cited there, and vol. 4, p. 12. For interpretations of the phrase "her window is shut," see Ḥanokh Albeck, *Shishah Sidrei Mishnah: Moed* (Jerusalem: Mosad Bialik, 1957), p. 479. See also Judith Hauptman, *Rereading the Mishnah: A New Approach to Ancient Jewish Texts* (Tübingen: Mohr/Siebeck, 2005), pp. 150–52.

3. Mss. London 5508, Munich 140, and Oxford 51 read *nishtamdah*. For discussion of this term, see Shlomo Pines, "He'arot al Tikbolet ha-Kayemet bein Munaḥim Suri'im u-vein Munaḥim shel Lashon Ḥazal," in *Sefer Zikaron le-Yaakov Friedman*, ed. Shlomo Pines (Jerusalem: Ha-Makhon le-Mada'ei Yahadut, 1974), pp. 209–11.

4. Jastrow, *Dictionary*, p. 1023; and *Arukh ha-Shalem*, ed. Kohut, vol. 6, p. 133.

5. The feminine pronoun is used here and in several other contexts to refer to the priestly division, Bilga. The sources before us, apparently because of scribal error, are not uniform in this regard. Sometimes they refer to Bilga the priestly division as masculine. To avoid confusion, I have not translated the feminine and masculine pronouns as "her" and "him" or "hers" and "his."

6. The word *imo*, "with him," found in the printed editions, is an obvious mistake. See Lieberman, *Tosefta ki-Feshutah*, vol. 4, p. 909, n. 49.

7. See note 3.

8. See note 3.

9. Or "to Him," i.e., to God.

10. For these dates, see R. D. Milns, "Alexander the Great," and Tessa Rajak, "Hasmonean Dynasty," in Freedman, *The Anchor Bible Dictionary*, vol. 1, p. 149; and vol. 3, p. 67, respectively. These dates do not correspond precisely to ancient rabbinic conceptions of the chronology of the period, but they convey a sense of the purported antiquity of the events described in the story.

11. Halivni, *Mekorot u-Mesorot: Yoma-Ḥagigah*, p. 384, n. 1. For the same understanding of the term, see Adolf Büchler, *Ha-Sanhedrin bi-Yerushalayim u-Veit ha-Din ha-Gadol she-be-Lishkat ha-Gazit* (Jerusalem: Mosad ha-Rav Kuk, 1974), pp. 85–86 (*Das Synedrin in Jerusalem und das grosse Beth-din in der Quaderkammer des jerusalemischen Tempels*); and Daniel Schwartz, *Studies in the Jewish Background of Christianity* (Tübingen: Mohr/Siebeck, 1992), pp. 47–48 and p. 48, n. 21.

12. Avraham Aderet, *Mei-Ḥurban li-Tekumah: Derekh Yavneh be-Shikum ha-Umah* (Jerusalem: Magnes Press, 1990), pp. 227–28. Aderet is writing about b. Eruvin 21b, which uses the same term.

13. See Martin Hengel, *Judaism and Hellenism* (Philadelphia: Fortress Press, 1974), vol. 1, p. 279, and vol. 2, p. 185. Compare Daniel Schwartz, *Sefer Makabim Bet: Mavo, Targum, Perush* (Jerusalem: Yad Yiẓḥak Ben-Ẓvi, 2004), pp. 64 and 103, who prefers the reading "Benjamin" to that of "Bilga."

14. See 1 Kings 2:26 and 4:2; and Hengel, *Judaism and Hellenism*, vol. 1, pp. 278–79, and vol. 2, p. 185.

15. Hengel, *Judaism and Hellenism*, vol. 1, pp. 279 and 293. See also the original German volume: Martin Hengel, *Judentum und Hellenismus: Studien zu ihrer Begegnung unter besonderer Berücksichtigung Palästinas bis zur Mitte des 2. Jhs. v. Chr.* (Tübingen: Mohr, 1969), pp. 508–9. See also Fausto Parente, "Onias III' Death and the Founding of the Temple of Leontopolis," in *Josephus and the History of the Greco-Roman Period: Essays in Memory of Morton Smith*, ed. F. Parente and J. Sievers (Leiden: Brill, 1994), p. 70; and Stern, "Aspects of Jewish Society: The Priesthood and Other Classes," pp. 565–66 and 591–94.

16. See also Shmuel Klein, "Die Baraita des Vierundzwanzig Priestabteilhungen" (Ph.D. diss., University of Heidelberg, 1909), pp. 70–72; and review of *Masoreten des Westens*, by P. Kahle, *Monatschrift für die Geschichte und Wissenschaft des Judentums* 73, nos. 1–2 (1929), p. 73.

17. See chapter 2.

18. Mss. London 5508, Munich 95, and JTS 1608 read: "The wicked Greek kingdom decreed a persecution (*shemad*) against Israel." Mss. Munich 140 and Oxford 23 read: "The wicked kingdom decreed a persecution against Israel."

19. See *Dikdukei Soferim*, ed. Rabbinovicz, n. *alef*; and Günter Stemberger, "The Maccabees in Rabbinic Tradition," in *The Scriptures and the Scrolls: Studies in Honour of A. S. Van der Woude on the Occasion of his Sixty-fifth Birthday*, ed. F. Garcia Martinez et al. (Leiden: Brill, 1992), p. 198, n. 3.

20. See Goodblatt, *The Monarchic Principle*, pp. 52–53.

21. For further discussion of this tradition, see Noam, "Le-Nusaḥav shel ha-'Skolion' le-Megillat Ta'anit," pp. 64, 83–84, 89, and 94; "Shetei Eduyot al Netiv ha-Mesirah shel Megillat Ta'anit ve-al Moẓ'a'o shel Nusaḥ ha-Kilayim le-Bei'urah," *Tarbiẓ* 65, no. 3 (1996), pp. 392–93 and 402; and *Megillat Ta'anit*, pp. 94–95 and 235–48. See also Solomon Zeitlin, "Megillat Ta'anit as a Source for Jewish Chronology and History in the Hellenistic and Roman Periods," *Jewish Quarterly Review*, n.s. 9 (1918–19), pp. 71–102, and 10 (1919–20), pp. 49–80 and 237–90; David Flusser, "Ha-Hishkiḥah Am Yisrael et ha-Ḥashmona'im bi-Yemei ha-Beina'im," *Katedra* 75 (1995), pp. 38–39; Ido Hampel, "Megillat Ta'anit" (Ph.D. diss., Tel Aviv University, 1976); Ephraim E. Urbach, *Ha-Halakhah: Mekoroteha ve-Hitpatḥutah* (Givatayim, Israel: Yad la-Talmud, 1984), pp. 44–45 and 248; and Yaakov Sussmann, "Ḥeker Toldot ha-Halakhah u-Megillot Midbar Yehudah: Hirhurim Talmudi'im Rishonim la-Or Megillat 'Mikẓat Ma'asei ha-Torah,'" *Tarbiẓ* 59, no. 1 (1989–90), p. 43, n. 139.

22. The text literally, and euphemistically, reads: "for the enemies of Israel."

23. See Noam, *Megillat Ta'anit*, p. 94, nn. on l. 12, for medieval testimonia reading "Yoḥanan the High Priest" or "Yoḥanan the priest."

24. Noam, *Megillat Ta'anit*, pp. 24–25.

25. Urbach, *Ha-Halakhah*, p. 247, n. 28, also thinks that the statement of the sages is a later addition to the story. See also Tashbaẓ (Teshuvot R. Shimshon ben Ẓadok) (Jerusalem: Kolel Taharat Yom Tov, 1973), pt. 1, *siman* 5. This usage, incidentally, is distinguishable from other sources examined in this chapter, in that the Baraita is unparalleled in the Tosefta and the Yerushalmi, and has a parallel only in Megillat Ta'anit.

26. See Noam, *Megillat Ta'anit*, pp. 57–140.

27. See the traditions cited by Noam, *Megillat Ta'anit*, pp. 141–58 and 354–55. See also pp. 355–82.

28. Regarding the frequency of this term in the scholion of Megillat Ta'anit and the various formulae used there to convey this meaning, see Stemberger, "The Maccabees in Rabbinic Tradition," pp. 200–201.

29. The text before us adds "for praise and thanksgiving." See Rashi.

30. Rashi, s.v. *Be-Telata be-Tishrei*. See also the different explanation offered by Maharsha, s.v. *Kakh*.

31. As noted, the Parma manuscript of Megillat Ta'anit reads "the sages of blessed memory [*zikharonam li-verakhah*] said."

32. See Joseph A. Fitzmayer and Daniel J. Harrington, *A Manual of Palestinian Aramaic Texts* (Rome: Biblical Institute Press, 1978), p. 187, who attempt to explain the Aramaic clause independent of the Hebrew scholion.

33. As noted, the Oxford manuscript of Megillat Ta'anit makes no explicit mention of sages. The "court" mentioned in this manuscript is not necessarily a rabbinic court.

34. Compare Noam, *Megillat Ta'anit*, p. 355, n. 168.

35. See Ḥanokh Albeck, *Mavo la-Talmudim* (Tel Aviv: Devir, 1969), p. 356.

36. See Ḥanokh Albeck, *Shishah Sidrei Mishnah: Tohorot* (Tel Aviv: Devir, 1959), pp. 486–87 and 610, n. 1. The alternative reading "A Galilean Sadducee" is most likely the result of scribal censorship. See chapter 7.

37. See Zeitlin, "Megillat Ta'anit as a Source for Jewish Chronology and History," pp. 271–72, n. 269; and Albeck, *Sishah Sidrei Mishnah: Tohorot*, p. 487.

38. Apparently the Galilean heretic does so as well, since he objects only to writing the ruler's name together with God's name, not to writing God's name in documents per se.

39. Josephus, *Antiquities* 16.6.2. See Goodblatt, *The Monarchic Principle*, pp. 52–55.

40. It is possible, although unlikely, that the scholion knew of the designation of John Hyrcanus as "Yoḥanan the high priest of the Most High God" through Josephus, in which case this proof for the relative antiquity of the scholion is less than fully probative.

41. For another example of supererogatory behavior, see b. Avodah Zarah 50a and chapter 5. Is the name R. Menaḥem be-R. Simai in the latter context a coincidence?

42. *Dikdukei Soferim*, ed. Rabbinovicz, n. *taf*, records several versions that identify Yosef ben Simai as *Rabbi* Yosef ben Simai *of* Shiḥin. The Oxford manuscript and many medieval commentators render the name *Yosi* ben Simai. As noted in the previous chapter, variation between the names Yosi and Yosef is common in ancient rabbinic texts. See also the Tosefta and the Yerushalmi, below.

43. *Gastra*, according to our printed texts. See *Dikdukei Soferim*, ed. Rabbinovicz, n. *alef*, who records the reading *kastaria* or *kistra*, which more closely resembles the reading of the Tosefta (*kaztra*) and the Yerushalmi (*kiztra*) and is a closer rendering of the Latin *kastra*.

44. See also the parallels in y. Yoma 8:5 (45b) and y. Nedarim 4:9 (38d). See also Deuteronomy Rabbah, ed. Saul Lieberman, 2nd ed. (Jerusalem: Shalem, 1992), p. 70.

45. See note 42.

46. See also Hyman, *Toldot Tannaim ve-Amoraim*, pp. 752–53 and 891–92.

47. See Lieberman, *Tosefta ki-Feshutah*, vol. 3, p. 213. Lieberman links this source to a Baraita in b. Sukkah 27a, which ostensibly records a dialogue between R. Eliezer and "the guardian of Agrippa the king." The two references to a guardian of the king, Lieberman argues, are to one and the same person, further strengthening

the claim that b. Shabbat 121a describes events of the Herodian period. Lieberman argues further that a certain Abba Yosi ben Simai, mentioned on b. Yevamot 115a as a contemporary of Rabbi Yehudah Hanasi (late second century to early third century CE) is not the same as the Yosef (or Yosi) ben Simai referred to on b. Shabbat 121a. Lieberman, in other words, thinks that Yosef ben Simai derives from a much earlier period than does the Abba Yosi ben Simai referred to in Yevamot. This may be so, and Lieberman may be correct that the "guardian of the king" referred to in Bavli Shabbat is the same guardian of the king referred to in Bavli Sukkah. It does not follow, however, that Bavli Shabbat's reference to "the guardian of the king" is reliable evidence of the source's antiquity. For Lieberman ignores the fact that the parallels to b. Shabbat 121a in the Tosefta and Yerushalmi make no reference to Yosef ben Simai as "guardian of the king," making it likely that the reference is a later addition to the Baraita. Apparently, the author of the addition found it difficult to believe that relations between the Roman occupying army and a Jew could be as cordial as this Baraita depicts them. Such cordial relations, according to the author of the addition, were possible because of Yosef ben Simai's ties to the government. It would be worthwhile examining other Babylonian Talmudic accounts of relations between Palestinian Jews and their Roman overlords. Do we find a general tendency for the Bavli to depict Roman-Palestinian Jewish relations as worse than they are depicted in Palestinian compilations such as the Yerushalmi or Leviticus Rabbah? If so, what might account for these differing portrayals? Such an examination, however, falls outside the purview of this book.

48. Agrippa II was the last member of the Herodian dynasty with a royal title. The Herodians remained important, but as Roman officials, down to the mid–second century, after which we lose sight of them.

49. B. Baba Meẓi'a 59a–b.

50. I doubt that the point of the story is to instill in the audience a feeling of unease, or that the story reflects unconscious tensions in the author's own mind. I have already established that the phrase "When the sages heard about the matter" tends to introduce later additions to a narrative; given the poor fit between the sages' concluding remark and the narrative prior to that point, it is likely that in this case as well the phrase introduced by this term is also a later addition.

51. More precisely, the most original version of the story we can reconstruct.

52. Friedman, "Al Derekh Ḥeker ha-Sugya," pp. 29–30.

53. For earlier discussion of the rabbinic texts about Ḥonio (Onias), see S. A. Hirsch, "The Temple of Onias," in *Jews' College Jubilee Volume* (London: Luzac, 1906), pp. 39–80; H. Tchernowitz, "Ha-Zugot u-Veit Ḥonio," in *Sefer ha-Yovel li-Khevod Levi Ginzberg* (New York: American Academy for Jewish Research, 1946), pp. 232–47; Shmuel Safrai, *Ha-Aliyah le-Regel bi-Yemei Bayit Sheni* (Tel Aviv: Am ha-Sefer, 1965), pp. 62–63 and 82–83; Neusner, *The Rabbinic Traditions about the Pharisees before 70*, pt. 1, pp. 54–57; Rafael Yankelevitch, "Neḥunion Aḥia: Li-She'elat Zehuto be-Ma'aseh Ḥananyah ben Aḥiv shel Rabbi Yehoshua," in *Milet: Meḥkerei ha-Universitah ha-Petuḥah be-Toldot Yisrael ve-Tarbuto*, vol. 2, ed. Shmuel Ettinger et al. (Tel Aviv: Ha-Universitah ha-Petuḥah, 1984), pp. 137–41; and "Mikdash Ḥonio: Meẓi'ut ve-Halakhah," in *Yehudim ve-Yahadut bi-Yemei Bayit Sheni, ha-Mishnah, ve-ha-Talmud*, ed. Aharon Oppenheimer et al. (Jerusalem: Yad Yiẓḥak Ben-Ẓvi, 1993), pp. 107–15; Cohen, "Parallel Historical Traditions in Josephus and Rabbinic Literature," p. 10; Parente, "Onias III' Death and the Founding of the Temple of Leontopolis," pp. 77, 81–82, and 96; James C. VanderKam, "Simon the Just: Simon I or Simon II," in *Pomegranates and*

Golden Bells: Studies in Biblical, Jewish, and Near-Eastern Ritual, Law, and Literature in Honor of Jacob Milgrom, ed. David P. Wright et al. (Winona Lake, Ind.: Eisenbrauns, 1995), pp. 303–18; and Günter Stemberger, "Narrative Baraitot in the Yerushalmi," and Peter Schäfer, "'From Jerusalem the Great to Alexandria the Small': The Relationship between Palestine and Egypt in the Graeco-Roman Period," in *The Talmud Yerushalmi and Graeco-Roman Culture*, vol. 1, ed. Peter Schäfer (Tübingen: Mohr/Siebeck, 1998), pp. 67–69 and 129–40, respectively. See also the literature concerning the accounts in 2 Maccabees and Josephus, cited below, some of which also discusses the rabbinic evidence.

54. The text literally reads "he." See above.

55. See Lieberman, *Tosefta ki-Feshutah*, vol. 8, p. 746.

56. See Samuel Krauss, *Griechische und lateinische Lehnwörter im Talmud, Midrasch und Targum* (1899; reprint, Hildesheim: G. Olms, 1964), vol. 2, p. 23.

57. Jastrow, *Dictionary*, pp. 1285–86; and Levy, *Wörterbuch*, vol. 4, pp. 195–96.

58. Literally, "he serves." See above.

59. The words "and so on, as above," are a very late, post-Talmudic abbreviation of the story, informing the reader that R. Yehudah's version continues on as did R. Meir's. The abbreviation is not entirely accurate, however, since the narrative flow demands that there be some differences.

60. For modern scholarly treatment of this episode, see Victor A. Tcherikover and Alexander Fuks, *Corpus Papyrorum Iudaicarum* (Cambridge, Mass.: Harvard University Press, 1957), pp. 2–3; 13; 20–21; 44–46; 52; and 80; and Victor A. Tcherikover, *Hellenistic Civilization and the Jews* (Philadelphia: Jewish Publication Society, 1966), pp. 275–81; M. Delcor, "Le temple d'Onias en Égypte: Réexamen d'un vieux problème," *Revue Biblique* 75 (1968), pp. 188–203; Bezalel Porton, *Archives from Elephantine: The Life of an Ancient Jewish Military Colony* (Berkeley: University of California Press, 1968), pp. 116–21; Hengel, *Judaism and Hellenism*, vol. 1, pp. 271–83, and vol. 2, p. 185; Stern, *Greek and Latin Authors*, vol. 1, pp. 403–6; Robert Hayward, "The Jewish Temple of Leontopolis: A Reconsideration," *Journal of Jewish Studies* 33, nos. 1–2 (1982), pp. 429–43; Arye Kasher, *The Jews in Hellenistic and Roman Egypt* (Tübingen: Mohr/Siebeck, 1985), pp. 119–34; Parente, "Onias III' Death and the Founding of the Temple of Leontopolis," pp. 69–98; Joseph Meleze Modrzejewski, *The Jews of Egypt: From Rameses II to Emperor Hadrian*, trans. Robert Coraman (Philadelphia: Jewish Publication Society, 1995), pp. 121–33 and the sources cited on pp. 252–53; Gideon Bohak, *Joseph and Aseneth and the Jewish Temple in Heliopolis* (Atlanta: Scholars Press, 1996); and "CPJ III, 520: The Egyptian Reaction to Onias' Temple," *Journal for the Study of Judaism* 26, no. 1 (1995), pp. 32–41; Erich S. Gruen, "The Origins and Objectives of Onias' Temple," in *Studies in Memory of Abraham Wasserstein*, ed. H. M. Cotton et al., vol. 2, pp. 47–70 (*Scripta Classica Israelica* 16 [1997]); Daniel Schwartz, "Yehudei Miẓra'im bein Mikdash Ḥonio le-Mikdash Yerushalayim u-le-Shamayim," *Ẓion* 62, no. 1 (1997), pp. 7–22 (a revised version of this article was published in *Merkaz u-Tefuẓah: Ereẓ Yisrael ve-ha-Tefuẓot bi-Yemei Bayit Sheni, ha-Mishnah ve-ha-Talmud*, ed. Isaiah Gafni [Jerusalem: Merkaz Zalman Shazar le-Toldot Yisrael, 2004], pp. 37–55); and Schäfer, "From Jerusalem the Great to Alexandria the Small," pp. 129–40.

61. See Josephus, *Jewish War* 1.1.1, 31–33; 9.4.190; 7.10.2–3, 420–36; *Antiquities* 13.3.1–3, 62–73; 14.8.1, 127–32; 20.10.3, 235–37; and *Against Apion* 2.5.51–55.

62. See the evidence collected by Gideon Bohak, "'Joseph and Aseneth' and the Jewish Temple in Heliopolis" (Ph.D. diss., Princeton University, 1994), pp. 67–72 and 94–99.

63. According to Tcherikover and Fuks, *Corpus Papyrorum Judaicarum*, pp. 244–46, the tone of the letter suggests that Onias "was a member of the court, known personally to the king." See also Parente, "Onias III' Death and the Founding of the Temple of Leontopolis," pp. 83–86.

64. For discussion of opposition to the priesthood in early rabbinic literature, see, for example, Louis Finkelstein, *Mevo le-Masekhtot Avot ve-Avot de-Rabbi Natan* (New York: Jewish Theological Seminary, 1961), pp. 10–13; and M. D. Herr, "Ha-Rezef she-be-Shalshelet Mesiratah shel ha-Torah le-Beirur ha-Historiografiah ha-Mikra'it ba-Hagutam shel Ḥazal," *Ẓion* 44 (1979) (*Sefer Zikaron le-Yiẓḥak Baer*), pp. 43–56 and the literature cited there. See also the discussion below.

65. Leviticus Rabbah, ed. Margaliot, p. 493.

66. With the exception of the parallel to this story in the Yerushalmi (see above). See also the discussion of a parallel in Josephus, below.

67. This point is not affected by the fact that priests are often referred to as "brothers" in rabbinic literature. The usage in this context is still ironic.

68. Rabbinic literature frequently, although not consistently, privileges acquired status over inherited status. See, for example, m. Eduyot 5:7 and 8:3, m. Avot 1:12 and 2:12, and m. Horayot 3:8; t. Yoma 5:6, t. Baba Meẓi'a 3:23, t. Horayot 2:8–10, and t. Menaḥot 13:21; Sifrei Numbers, ed. Ḥ. S. Horowitz (1917; reprint, Jerusalem: Wahrmann Books, 1966), p. 144; Sifrei Deuteronomy, ed. Finkelstein, pp. 112 and 402; Midrash Tannaim, ed. Hoffman, p. 104; Avot de-R. Natan, ed. Solomon Schechter (1887; corrected reprint, with an introduction by Menaḥem Kister, New York: Jewish Theological Seminary, 1997), versions A and B, pp. 14–15; y. Yoma 3:9 (41a) and y. Horayot 3:5 (48a); b. Pesaḥim 57a, b. Yoma 38a–b and 71b; b. Baba Kamma 38a, b. Sanhedrin 96a, and b. Horayot 13a; and Song of Songs Rabbah 3:5. See also Gedalya Alon, "The Sons of the Sages," in *Jews, Judaism, and the Classical World*, trans. Israel Abrahams (Jerusalem: Magnes Press, 1977), pp. 436–56, especially the sources cited at pp. 436–37; Ephraim E. Urbach, *The Sages: Their Concepts and Beliefs*, trans. Israel Abrahams (Jerusalem: Magnes Press, 1979), pp. 512–13 and 529; and Kalmin, *The Sage in Jewish Society*, pp. 1–24.

69. See Yiẓḥak Magen, "Har Gerizim-Ir Mikdash," *Kadmoni'ot* 23, nos. 3–4 (1990), pp. 87 and 90; Seth Schwartz, "John Hyrcanus I's Destruction of the Gerizim Temple and Judaean-Samaritan Relations," *Jewish History* 7, no. 1 (1993), p. 19, n. 3; and Bohak, "'Joseph and Aseneth' and the Jewish Temple in Heliopolis," pp. 110–12. Regarding the possible existence of other Jewish temples outside of Jerusalem, see Morton Smith, *Palestinian Parties and Politics That Shaped the Old Testament* (New York: Columbia University Press, 1971), pp. 92–93.

70. Josephus, *Antiquities* 11.8.2–7.

71. T. Sanhedrin 9:5 and y. Sanhedrin 6:3 (23b). These versions lack the phrase "When the sages heard about the matter." As noted, this term is primarily, although not exclusively, found in Baraitot recorded in the Bavli, a point to which I will return, below.

72. Scholars disagree as to when the Jews lost the power to execute people. There is general agreement, however, that at the latest the Romans took this power from them when the Temple was destroyed in 70 CE. See Büchler, *Ha-Sanhedrin*, pp. 420–31; Hugo Mantel, *Studies in the History of the Sanhedrin* (Cambridge, Mass.: Harvard University Press, 1961), pp. 291–94 and 316; and Urbach, *Ha-Halakhah*, pp. 53–55 and 253–54. For a preliminary survey of the types of cases adjudicated by Tannaim after the destruction of the Temple, see Cohen, "The Place of the Rabbi in

Jewish Society of the Second Century," pp. 157–73. In the corpus studied by Cohen, no capital cases were recorded.

73. The Tosefta, incidentally, uses the terminology "When the sages *learned* about the matter," and the Yerushalmi uses the phrase "When the sages *knew* about the matter." The distinction seems to me to be without significance.

74. As noted, the narrative is also partially paralleled in Song of Songs Rabbah.

75. The suggestion of Tchernowitz, "Ha-Zugot u-Veit Ḥonio," pp. 242–43, that the Alexandrian craftsmen referred to are priests of the Leontopolis temple (see above) is ingenious but purely speculative.

76. See note 73.

77. See the appendix to this chapter for discussion of usages of the phrase in b. Gittin 35a, b. Bekhorot 51b, b. Eruvin 21b, and possibly b. Baba Kamma 50a.

78. See above for discussion of t. Sukkah 4:28 and y. Sukkah 5:8 (55d) versus b. Sukkah 56b; y. Yoma 6:3 versus b. Menaḥot 109b–110a; y. Shevuot 6:5 (37a–b) versus b. Gittin 35a; and the Oxford manuscript of Megillat Ta'anit versus b. Rosh Hashanah 18b. See also the discussion of t. Bekhorot 6:14 and b. Bekhorot 51b in the appendix to this chapter.

79. With one dubious exception. See the discussion of b. Gittin 35a in the appendix to this chapter.

80. Only b. Eruvin 21b, b. Bekhorot 51a, and possibly b. Shabbat 121a involve sages.

81. B. Yoma 38a, b. Sukkah 56b, b. Rosh Hashanah 18b (the Hasmoneans were priests, and the narrative explicitly mentions Yoḥanan the high priest), b. Menaḥot 109b–110a, b. Bekhorot 51b, and the one uncertain case, b. Baba Kamma 50a.

82. B. Eruvin 21b. See the appendix to this chapter.

83. See the discussion of b. Shabbat 121a and b. Yoma 38a, above, and of b. Gittin 35a in the appendix to this chapter.

84. See, however, the reference to the work of Alyssa Gray in the introduction.

85. T. Bekhorot 6:14.

86. See also Hyman, *Toldot Tannaim ve-Amoraim*, pp. 524–29.

87. *Halakhot Gedolot*, ed. Ezriel Hildesheimer (Jerusalem: Mekiẓei Nirdamim, 1980), vol. 2, p. 323.

88. See *Dikdukei Soferim*, ed. Rabbinovicz, n. *khaf.*

89. See *Dikdukei Soferim: Gittin*, ed. Meir Feldblum (New York: Horeb, 1966), nn. on ll. 3 and 4; and *Dikdukei Soferim ha-Shalem: Gittin*, vol. 2, ed. Hillel Porush (Jerusalem: Makhon ha-Talmud ha-Yisre'eli ha-Shalem, 2001), nn. on l. 3, and n. 3, for variants of the names.

90. Literally, and euphemistically, "May poison benefit one of that woman's children." The printed text employs a circumlocution to avoid the woman's true phraseology, and presumably also the horrible effects that phraseology might have on the reader, speaker, and/or audience of the text.

91. See Louis Finkelstein, "The Men of the Great Synagogue (*circa* 400–170 B.C.E.)," in *The Cambridge History of Judaism*, ed. W. D. Davies and Louis Finkelstein (Cambridge: Cambridge University Press, 1989), vol. 2, p. 240. In contrast to Finkelstein, my claim is not that Rav's traditions tend to be accurate but simply that they tend to be early and Palestinian.

92. See, for example, Hyman, *Toldot Tannaim ve-Amoraim*, pp. 17–18.

93. Catherine Hezser, *Form, Function, and Historical Significance of the Rabbinic Story in Yerushalmi Neziqin* (Tübingen: Mohr/Siebeck, 1993), p. 230; and Stemberger, "Narrative Baraitot in the Yerushalmi," p. 64.

94. Y. Shevu'ot 6:5 (37a–b).

95. See David Halivni, *Mekorot u-Mesorot: Nashim* (Tel Aviv: Devir, 1968), pp. 536–38.

CHAPTER 4

1. For an excellent earlier discussion of the role of anxiety in rabbinic literature, see Christine E. Hayes, "Displaced Self-Perceptions: The Deployment of *Minim* and Romans in *B. Sanhedrin* 90b–91a," in *Religious and Ethnic Communities in Roman Palestine*, ed. Hayim Lapin (Bethesda, Md.: University Press of Maryland, 1998), pp. 283–85.

2. I noted in the introduction that I will indicate explicitly when the conclusions of a particular chapter are based on examination of compilations or tractates within compilations other than those specified in the preface. The conclusions of this chapter are based on an examination of the Tosefta (Berakhot-Sotah); Sifrei Deuteronomy; Genesis Rabba; Leviticus Rabbah; Lamentations Rabbah; Kohelet Rabbah; Pesikta de-Rav Kahana; y. Berakhot, y. Pe'ah, y. Demai, y. Kila'im, y. Shevi'it, y. Terumot, y. Ma'aserot, y. Ma'aser Sheni, y. Ḥallah, y. Orlah, y. Bikkurim, y. Shabbat, y. Eruvin, y. Pesaḥim, y. Sukkah, y. Rosh Hashanah, y. Moed Katan, y. Ḥagigah, y. Yevamot, y. Ketubot, y. Sotah, y. Kiddushin, y. Baba Kamma, y. Baba Meẓi'a, y. Baba Batra, y. Sanhedrin, y. Makkot, y. Avodah Zarah, and y. Niddah; b. Berakhot, b. Shabbat, b. Ḥagigah, b. Ketubot, b. Baba Meẓi'a, b. Sanhedrin, b. Avodah Zarah, b. Zevaḥim, b. Ḥullin, and b. Niddah.

3. See also Rubenstein, *Culture*, pp. 67–79.

4. Or, more accurately, those cases that we could be relatively certain depict rabbinic interactions with nonrabbis. See Catherine Hezser, *The Social Structure of the Rabbinic Movement in Roman Palestine* (Tübingen: Mohr/Siebeck, 1997), pp. 53–154; and Kalmin, *The Sage in Jewish Society*, pp. 23–24.

5. In addition to the traditions examined in detail below, see also y. Pe'ah 1:1 (15d) (Rabenu Hakadosh [i.e., R. Yehudah Hanasi] and Artaban [regarding Artaban, see Hyman, *Toldot Tannaim ve-Amoraim*, p. 243]); y. Shevi'it 9:1 (38d) (see also the parallels in y. Berakhot 1:1 [3a]; Genesis Rabba, ed. J. Theodor and Ḥ. Albeck [1903–39; corrected reprint, Jerusalem: Wahrmann Books, 1965], p. 945; and Pesikta de-Rav Kahana, ed. Bernard Mandelbaum [New York: Jewish Theological Seminary, 1962], pp. 193–94. See also Michael Chernick, "'Turn It and Turn It Again': Culture and Talmud Interpretation," *Exemplaria* 12, no. 1 [2000], pp. 67–68); y. Shabbat 12:3 (13c) (and parallel) (the family of councilmen, the family of commoners, and R. Yoḥanan); y. Yoma 1:5 (39a) (a Boethusian and his father); y. Ta'anit 4:6 (68d–69a) (Bar Koziba, Hadrian, and R. Elazar Hamoda'i); y. Baba Kamma 4:3 (4b) (Rabban Gamliel and two Roman soldiers); and y. Sanhedrin 1:6 (19d) (Antigonus and R. Yoḥanan ben Zakkai); t. Niddah 5:1 and the parallel in b. Niddah 33b (R. Yosi and a Sadducean woman); b. Shabbat 52a (R. Yehoshua ben Korḥa and a eunuch); Kohelet Rabbah 1:1:8:4 (R. Yonatan and heretics); Kohelet Rabbah 4:1:17 (R. Yoḥanan ben Zakkai and Shimon Sikhna, a digger of wells, cisterns, and caves); and the literature cited below. Palestinian rabbis also manifest their preoccupation with nonrabbinic opinion by telling stories whose point is to dramatize the rewards that will befall those who honor rabbis. See, for example, y. Horayot 3:6 (48a) (and parallel) (R. Eliezer, R. Yehoshua, R. Akiba, and Abba Yehudah [the story praises not only Abba Yehudah's generosity but also the honor he paid the rabbis]); and Kalmin, *The Sage in Jewish Society*, pp. 29–33. See also the traditions that express Pharisaic concern for the reaction of Sadducees, Boethusians, and occasionally *minim* to Pharisaic practices, often performed publicly in

deliberate violation of non-Pharisaic opinions to demonstrate the error of their opponents' ways: m. Sukkah 4:9; m. Ḥagigah 2:4; m. Menaḥot 10:3; m. Parah 3:3 and 3:7; t. Yoma 1:5; t. Sukkah 3:1; t. Ḥagigah 3:35; t. Sanhedrin 6:6; and other sources cited by Sussmann, "Ḥeker Toldot ha-Halakhah u-Megillot Midbar Yehudah," pp. 67–68, n. 220. See also chapter 7. It bears noting, furthermore, that the overwhelming majority of dialogues between rabbis and heretics (*minim*) are preserved in the Bavli, but involve Palestinian rabbis. See Richard Kalmin, "Christians and Heretics in Rabbinic Literature of Late Antiquity," *Harvard Theological Review* 87, no. 2 (1994), pp. 160–69, especially pp. 163–64, and see the discussion below. As noted in the introduction, this material is methodologically problematic, and its impact on my findings is very difficult to gauge.

6. Pesikta de-Rav Kahana, ed. Mandelbaum, pp. 297–98.

7. See b. Sanhedrin 100a and, with minor variations, b. Baba Batra 75a.

8. See Sokoloff, *Dictionary of Jewish Babylonian Aramaic*, p. 960; and Jastrow, *Dictionary*, p. 1270.

9. It is not even certain that he must be viewed as a member of a group.

10. I base this translation on that of Lee I. Levine, "R. Simeon b. Yohai and the Purification of Tiberias: History and Tradition," *Hebrew Union College Annual* 49 (1978), pp. 150–53; and Herbert W. Basser, "Uncovering the Plots: The Image of Rabbi Shimon bar Yohai," in *The 2001 Mathers Lecture, The 2001 Rosen Lecture, and Other Queen's University Essays in the Study of Judaism*, ed. Jacob Neusner (Binghamton, N.Y.: Global Publication, Binghamton University, 2001), pp. 47–49. For further discussion of either this particular story or the portrayal of R. Shimon ben Yoḥai in rabbinic literature, see Levine, "R. Simeon b. Yohai," pp. 143–85; Ophra Meir, "Sippur R. Shimon ben Yoḥai ba-Me'arah," *Alei Si'aḥ* 26 (1989), pp. 145–60; Rubenstein, *Talmudic Stories*, pp. 105–38; Ben-Zion Rosenfeld, "R. Simeon b. Yohai: Wonder Worker and Magician; Scholar, *Saddiq* and *Hasid*," *Revue des études juives* 158, nos. 3–4 (1999), pp. 351–86; Chernick, " 'Turn It and Turn It Again,' " pp. 63–103; and Yafa Binyamini, "Ha-Mythos shel Rabbi Shimon bar Yoḥai: Iyun be-Aggadat Ḥazal," *Meḥkerei Ḥag* 12 (2001), pp. 87–102.

11. See Chernick, " 'Turn It and Turn It Again,' " p. 66, n. 6.

12. Levine, "R. Simeon b. Yohai," p. 147, n. 17, suggests that the Aramaic *safra* may also mean "schoolteacher." See also Sokoloff, *Dictionary of Jewish Babylonian Aramaic*, p. 828.

13. For this translation of the Yerushalmi, see Basser, "Uncovering the Plots," p. 49; and Chernick, " 'Turn It and Turn It Again,' " p. 67. See also Michael Sokoloff, *A Dictionary of Jewish Palestinian Aramaic of the Byzantine Period* (Ramat-Gan, Israel: Bar Ilan University Press, 1992), p. 162.

14. It is not out of the question, however, that the Yerushalmi and Kohelet Rabbah versions of the story here are corruptions of one of the references to a vote in either Genesis Rabba or Pesikta de-Rav Kahana (see below), since the language is very similar. See Basser, "Uncovering the Plots," p. 49. Kohelet Rabbah, incidentally, has as R. Shimon's second antagonist Nikai'a the scribe, who is mentioned in y. Ma'aser Sheni 5:2 (56a) as a pious figure from the first century CE, during the time of the second Temple. The two references are difficult to reconcile chronologically, since R. Shimon bar Yoḥai lived well after the destruction of the Temple.

15. Pesikta de-Rav Kahana, ed. Mandelbaum, pp. 191–94.

16. Genesis Rabba, ed. Theodor and Albeck, pp. 943–45. The translation is based on that of Levine, "R. Simeon b. Yohai," pp. 146–47.

17. The *am ha-areẓ* says, "Did you not say that ben Yoḥai has purified Tiberias?"

18. See Sokoloff, *Dictionary of Jewish Palestinian Aramaic*, p. 436.
19. Ibid., p. 327.
20. Ibid., p. 36.
21. Literally, "this man," a euphemism.
22. Literally, "that man's."
23. See Sokoloff, *Dictionary of Jewish Palestinian Aramaic*, p. 36.
24. Ibid., p. 72.
25. "That man."
26. For further discussion of ancient rabbinic dream interpretation, including evidence that some rabbis accepted money for interpreting dreams, see Kalmin, *Sages, Stories, Authors, and Editors*, pp. 61–85. See there also regarding attitudes toward dream interpretation throughout the ancient world.
27. See also y. Ta'anit 4:6 (68d–69a) (a Samaritan, Hadrian, and R. Elazar Hamoda'i); y. Moed Katan 3:7 (83b) (and parallel) (R. Shimon ben Lakish and a Samaritan); y. Avodah Zarah 3:1 (42c) (R. Abahu, unnamed Samaritans, and unnamed Jews); y. Sanhedrin 2:5 (20d) (R. Ḥizkiyah and a Samaritan); and y. Avodah Zarah 5:3 (44d) (R. Yishmael bei R. Yosi and unnamed Samaritans).
28. Sokoloff, *Dictionary of Jewish Palestinian Aramaic*, p. 415.
29. Literally, but euphemistically, "By that man's life."
30. "That man."
31. Sokoloff, *Dictionary of Jewish Palestinian Aramaic*, p. 426.
32. See also b. Sanhedrin 100a (R. Yirmiyah, R. Zeira, and a "certain elder" who cites R. Yoḥanan).
33. See Jastrow, *Dictionary*, pp. 830 and 1396.
34. R. Meir's name can be translated "he gives light."
35. Jastrow, *Dictionary*, p. 229.
36. Possibly we are to understand R. Meir as having left the Romans, according to which his fellow sages react to his statements, but there is no hint of this in the text. It is by no means out of the ordinary for a midrash to attribute to non-Jews the ability to quote scripture.
37. B. Shabbat 30b. Much, but not all, of the story is in Hebrew, but it is not introduced by a technical term indicative of Tannaitic provenance.
38. I have translated the verse according to the midrashic meaning assigned to it by R. Gamliel. The translation of the Jewish Publication Society numbers this verse Jer. 31:8 and translates it: "Those with child and those in labor."
39. See Jastrow, *Dictionary*, p. 870.
40. This is not to suggest, of course, that relations between rabbis in the Babylonian study house are not sometimes depicted as strained, to say the least. See, for example, Kalmin, *Sages, Stories, Authors, and Editors*, pp. 21–42; and Rubenstein, *Talmudic Stories*, pp. 34–63. It is striking that the student's disrespect does not end in his death. This story, however, is part of a lengthy narrative chain whose major theme is the importance of patience on the part of a rabbi when dealing with other people, including the famous story of Hillel and the non-Jew, whom Hillel agrees to convert while standing on one foot. For further evidence of the self-consciousness of Babylonian rabbis to the issue of radical rabbinic exegesis, and of their depiction of this issue as one confronted by rabbis in the privacy of the rabbinic study house, see the famous story of Moses' posthumous visit to the study of R. Akiva in Menaḥot 29b. This story is transmitted by Rav Yehudah in the name of Rav, both of whom were early Babylonian Amoraim. The story exhibits self-consciousness about the gap between the unadorned written Torah, i.e., the Torah as it exists without interpretation, and the

Torah of midrashic exegesis, i.e., the Torah as interpreted by the rabbis. See also Hayes, "Displaced Self-Perceptions," pp. 283–85.

41. In addition to the sources cited here, see Hayes, "Displaced Self-Perceptions," pp. 260–89. See in particular her discussion of the ancient rabbis' differentiation between contextual and noncontextual interpretation, which she argues convincingly is not totally unlike modern methods of distinguishing between the two. See also Rafael Loewe, "The 'Plain' Meaning of the Scriptures in Early Jewish Exegesis," *Papers of the Institute of Jewish Studies*, ed. J. G. Weiss (Jerusalem: Magnes Press, 1964), pp. 140–85; Sarah Kamin, "Rashi's Exegetical Categorization with Respect to the Distinction between Peshat and Derash: According to His Commentary to the Book of Genesis and Selected Passages from His Commentaries to Other Books of the Bible," *Immanuel* 11 (1980), pp. 16–32; and *Rashi: Peshuto shel Mikra u-Midrasho shel Mikra* (Jerusalem: Magnes Press, 1986); Yaakov Elman, "'It Is No Empty Thing': Nahmanides and the Search for Omnisignificance," *Torah u-Madda Journal* 5 (1993), pp. 1–83; David Halivni, *Peshat and Derash: Plain and Applied Meaning in Rabbinic Exegesis* (New York: Oxford University Press, 1991), pp. v–x and 3–88; and Jay Harris, *How Do We Know This?* (Albany: State University of New York Press, 1995), pp. 1–72.

42. See Jastrow, *Dictionary*, p. 13.

43. *Derishah* and *ḥakirah*, technical terms for questions that the judges must pose to the witnesses.

44. Ed. Mandelbaum, p. 74. The following translation, with modifications, is based on that of Jacob Milgrom, *The JPS Torah Commentary: Numbers* (Philadelphia: Jewish Publication Society, 1990), p. 438.

45. See also Hayes, "Displaced Self-Perceptions," p. 279, and n. 66 on pp. 279–80, regarding b. Berakhot 10a and b. Yevamot 4a.

46. We find the following nine cases: y. Berakhot 9:1 (12d–13a) (five cases, to which we find a partial parallel in Genesis Rabba, ed. Theodor and Albeck, pp. 62–63); y. Shabbat 3:4 (6a) and parallel (Bar Kappara and a philosopher, and/or Avlat and Levi bar Sisi; see Hyman, *Toldot Tannaim ve-Amoraim*, p. 98). See also the dialogues between R. Yoḥanan ben Zakkai and Agnatos the general in y. Sanhedrin 1:6 (19c) and (19d); Leviticus Rabbah, ed. Margaliot, pp. 92–93; and Pesikta de-Rav Kahana, ed. Mandelbaum, p. 74. Hayes, "Displaced Self-Perceptions," pp. 170–71, n. 49, with reference to the cases involving R. Simlai in y. Berakhot 9:1 (12d–13a), overstates matters when she argues that all of Simlai's replies to his students are clearly more radical and less in conformity with the context than are his replies to the heretics. We are dealing with different tendencies, differing shades of gray, rather than with unambiguous distinctions between black and white. In addition, I am not fully convinced by Hayes's contention that these narratives reveal rabbinic "anxiety" about their interpretive methods. If she is correct, however, then these dialogues support my thesis all the more effectively. As noted above, according to one of two versions, a dialogue recorded in y. Shabbat 3:4 (6a) involves Avlat and Levi bar Sisi. Avlat is depicted elsewhere only in the Bavli in the presence of Shmuel, and Levi bar Sisi is a Palestinian rabbi who moved to Babylonia (see Hyman, *Toldot Tannaim ve-Amoraim*, pp. 859–60). According to this version, therefore, the scene of this dialogue would appear to be Babylonia (according to the version with Bar Kappara and the philosopher the scene is Palestine). There are no cases in the Bavli of this narrative form involving Babylonian rabbis. It is likely, therefore, that this story reflects a Palestinian context, despite the possibility that it is set in Babylonia.

47. Kalmin, *The Sage in Jewish Society*, p. 6.

48. See above for discussion of Kohelet Rabbah 1:1:9 (R. Meir and the Romans); and y. Sanhedrin 1:4 (R. Yoḥanan ben Zakkai and Agnatos the general). Many stories examined above pit the Palestinian rabbis against ordinary nonrabbis, which we do not find to be the case in stories involving Babylonian rabbis. See also Sifrei Deuteronomy, ed. Finkelstein, p. 401; y. Baba Kamma 4:3 (4b); and b. Baba Kamma 38a (Rabban Gamliel and two officials of the Roman government).

49. That is, in accordance with the original meaning of this expression (and the only meaning that makes sense), the exception that "tests" the rule. See also b. Sanhedrin 99b–100a, which bears careful scrutiny in light of the findings of this chapter. It needs to be borne in mind that the concern of the Amoraim in the latter discussion is interpretive; this chapter, in contrast, is based exclusively on the analysis of stories. We should be aware of the likelihood that the statements in b. Sanhedrin 99b–100a reveal little or nothing about the rabbis' extratextual preoccupations and attitudes, e.g., their attitudes toward real people in their midst (for more on this issue, see Hayes, *Between the Babylonian and Palestinian Talmuds*, pp. 3–11). The brief stories accompanying the interpretive comments (by Rava and Rav Papa, both of whom were mid-fourth-century Amoraim) are perhaps to be understood as fictions deriving from their exegetical remarks. Narratives in b. Shabbat 88a–b, b. Ta'anit 24b, and b. Niddah 20b depict interactions between Rava and nonrabbis (specifically, the Persian queen, Ifra Hurmiz, and her son, Shapur) that are not germane to my inquiry. The issue in these stories is not the rabbi's credibility qua rabbi, but as a representative of the Jewish people. In b. Niddah 20b, for example, the queen mother says to her son, "Come and see how wise the Jews are." Similar expressions are used in the other narratives as well.

50. The printed text reads "Sadducee," which is obviously incorrect. See *Dikdukei Soferim*, ed. Rabbinovicz, nn. *kuf* and *taf*; and Yonah Fraenkel, "Bible Verses Quoted in Tales of the Sages," *Scripta Hierosolymitana* 22 (1971), pp. 94–95, especially nn. 40 and 42. Fraenkel claims (n. 42) that the reading *mina bar bei rav* is found in all manuscripts, but the Florence manuscript in fact refers to him simply as a "heretic" (*mina*). In any event, it is likely that the reading *mina bar bei rav* is correct, first because it is the reading of most manuscripts, and second because it is easy to understand why a scribe shortened and "corrected" this version to the more customary "heretic" (*mina*), but not at all clear why a scribe would change *mina* to the peculiar and otherwise unprecedented locution *mina bar bei rav*.

51. Regarding the terms *bei rav* and *bar bei rav*, see Goodblatt, *Rabbinic Instruction in Sasanian Babylonia*, pp. 105–54, especially pp. 114–15.

52. The ensuing analysis owes much to that of Fraenkel, "Bible Verses," pp. 94–98. I do not specify my agreement and disagreement with him each step of the way.

53. For more on the Talmud's treatment of the blind Rav Sheshet, see b. Zevaḥim 96b and Kalmin, *Sages, Stories, Authors, and Editors*, pp. 7–8. Some traditions speak of Rav Yosef being blind, but whereas rabbinic sources treat blindness as Rav Sheshet's major defining feature, they treat it as a minor motif, as only one of many characteristics, where Rav Yosef is concerned.

54. See Fraenkel, "Bible Verses," p. 94, and p. 96, n. 44.

55. See *Dikdukei Soferim*, ed. Rabbinovicz, n. *reish*, for versions reading "They said to him," and "he said to them"; see also Fraenkel, "Bible Verses," pp. 95–98. According to this reading, however, the opening dialogue, the only part of the story that describes Rav Sheshet's humiliation is between Rav Sheshet and the heretic–rabbinic disciple alone.

56. According to an alternative reading, "Rav Sheshet spoke a word and there came forth sparks and singed his eyes." See *Dikdukei Soferim*, ed. Rabbinovicz, n. *taf*; and Fraenkel, "Bible Verses," pp. 95 and 98, n. 53.

57. See Fraenkel, "Bible Verses," p. 97, n. 49, and the parallels from Greek literature cited there.

58. It is conceivable, although not necessary, that the two versions of the story's endings are later additions to the narrative, by commentators uncomfortable with the heretic getting the final word and not being explicitly punished.

59. Interestingly, the only other case involves Rava (see b. Shabbat 88a–b). As noted, later Babylonian Amoraim (such as Rava) are frequently depicted as behaving in accordance with Palestinian models. It also bears noting that the name "Rava" is frequently confused with the name "R. Abba." There were apparently several Amoraim named R. Abba, and all of their statements, as far as we can determine, derive from Palestine. It is possible, therefore, that even this narrative depicts a dialogue between a heretic and a rabbi in Palestine. See also b. Ketubot 112a. Yaakov Elman, " 'He in His Cloak and She in Her Cloak': Conflicting Images of Sexuality in Sasanian Mesopotamia," in *Discussing Cultural Influences: Text, Context, and Non-Text in Rabbinic Judaism: Proceedings of a Conference on Rabbinic Judaism at Bucknell University*, ed. Rivka Kern-Ulmer (forthcoming) argues that a dialogue between Rav Kahana and a *mina* in b. Sanhedrin 37a is set in Babylonia. (I thank Professor Elman for providing me with a copy of his article in advance of its publication.) There were numerous rabbis named Rav Kahana, however, according to which this case as well might involve a later Babylonian Amora. See above, and see the conclusion. It is also possible that this story as well presupposes a Palestinian setting, despite Elman's cogent arguments in favor of a Babylonian setting. See Albeck, *Mavo la-Talmudim*, p. 175. Curiously, we find two standard halakhic debates between Babylonian Amoraim and Yaakov Mina'ah (b. Megillah 23a and b. Ḥullin 84a). There is no hint from the content of either dialogue that Yaakov Mina'ah (Yaakov the heretic [?]) is anything other than a conventional sage. (As noted several times, the absence of the title "Rabbi" introducing his name is not a clear indication of nonrabbinic status.) The only clear indication we get that Yaakov Mina'ah is a heretic is in b. Avodah Zarah 28a, in a story that places him in Israel, interacting with Palestinian rabbis. While it is extremely risky to do biography based on Talmudic sources, particularly when it involves reconciling sources that appear to conflict, it is possible that Yaakov is referred to as "the heretic" in Megillah and Ḥullin because of his apostasy later in life, while the account in Avodah Zarah depicts him after he apostasized. Even if this understanding is incorrect, Yaakov's two halakhic dialogues are certainly not characteristic of disputes between rabbis and heretics. The kind of disputes that concern me in this chapter—cases in which rabbis exhibit or express anxiety, self-consciousness, and the like—are certainly not evident in these dialogues.

60. Kalmin, "Christians and Heretics," pp. 163–65, especially p. 163 and p. 164, nn. 31 and 35, respectively.

61. Apparently according to one of two versions. See, however, *Dikdukei Soferim*, ed. Rabbinovicz, n. *taf*; and *Arukh ha-Shalem*, ed. Kohut, vol. 2, p. 40.

CHAPTER 5

1. See, for example, Mary Boyce, "Toleranz und Intoleranz im Zoroastrismus," *Saeculum* 21 (1970), pp. 325–43; and "Iconoclasm among the Zoroastrians," in *Christianity, Judaism and Other Greco-Roman Cults: Studies for Morton Smith at Sixty*, pt.

4, ed. Jacob Neusner (Leiden: Brill, 1975), pp. 93–111, especially p. 104; Mary Boyce and Frantz Grenet, *A History of Zoroastrianism*, vol. 3, *Zoroastrianism under Macedonian and Roman Rule* (Leiden: Brill, 1991) p. 66, especially n. 71, for a response to criticism by Gherardo Gnoli, *Zoroaster's Time and Homeland: A Study on the Origins of Mazdeism and Related Problems* (Naples: Instituto Universitario Orientale, 1980), pp. 220–22; Philippe Gignoux, "Religions and Religious Movements, pt. 1: Zoroastrianism," in *History of Civilizations of Central Asia*, vol. 3, *The Crossroads of Civilizations: A.D. 250 to 750*, ed. B. A. Litvinsky et al. (Paris: UNESCO, 1996), pp. 409–10; Morony, *Iraq after the Muslim Conquest*, pp. 283 (and the sources cited in n. 34), 291–92 (and the references cited in n. 74), and especially pp. 384–85 and 409–10. See also Russell, *Zoroastrianism in Armenia*, pp. 11, 154, 246, 481, and 494; Albert de Jong, *Traditions of the Magi: Zoroastrianism in Greek and Latin Literature* (Leiden: Brill, 1997), p. 350. See also N. N. Chegini and A. V. Nikitin, "Sasanian Iran: Economy, Society, Arts and Crafts," in *History of Civilizations of Central Asia*, ed. Litvinsky et al., vol. 3, pp. 44 and 63–65. Regarding rabbinic pronouncements on this subject, see Seth Schwartz, "Gamaliel in Aphrodite's Bath: Palestinian Judaism and Urban Culture in the Third and Fourth Centuries," in *The Talmud Yerushalmi and Graeco-Roman Culture*, vol. 1, ed. Schäfer, pp. 213–17; and Lee I. Levine, *The Ancient Synagogue: The First Thousand Years* (New Haven: Yale University Press, 2000), pp. 206–13 and 451–58.

2. The conclusions of this chapter are based on examination of the following tractates of the Bavli: Berakhot; Shabbat; Eruvin; Pesaḥim; Yoma; Rosh Hashanah; Sukkah; Beiẓah; Ta'anit; Megillah; Moed Katan; Ḥagigah; Ketubot; Sotah; Gittin; Baba Meẓi'a; Baba Batra; Sanhedrin; Makkot; Avodah Zarah; Zevaḥim; Ḥullin; Bekhorot; and Niddah. For purposes of comparison I also examined the following Palestinian compilations: Mekhilta de-R. Yishmael; Sifrei Deuteronomy; Leviticus Rabbah; and the following tractates of the Yerushalmi: Berakhot; Sanhedrin; and Avodah Zarah.

3. Kalmin, "Christians and Heretics," pp. 155–69.

4. See, for example, Gerald Blidstein, "R. Yohanan, Idolatry, and Public Privilege," *Journal for the Study of Judaism* 5, no. 2 (1974), p. 154; Schwartz, "Gamaliel in Aphrodite's Bath," p. 206; and *Imperialism and Jewish Society, 200 B.C.E. to 640 C.E.* (Princeton: Princeton University Press, 2001), pp. 129–76; Yaron Eliav, "Viewing the Scriptural Environment: Shaping the Second Commandment," in *The Talmud Yerushalmi and Graeco-Roman Culture*, vol. 3, ed. Peter Schäfer (Tübingen: Mohr/Siebeck, 2002), pp. 413–15; and "Al Avodah Zarah be-Veit ha-Merḥaẓ ha-Romi: Shtei He'arot," *Katedra* 110 (2004), pp. 173–80. For literary evidence, see, for example, Mekhilta de-R. Yishmael, ed. Horowitz and Rabin, pp. 223–26; y. Berakhot 2:1 (4b); y. Avodah Zarah 3:8 (43b); and y. Avodah Zarah 3:13 (43b); and see the discussion below. Zeev Weiss, however, in a paper entitled "Sculptures and Sculptural Images in the Urban Galilean Context," delivered at the conference "The Sculptural Environment of the Roman Near East: Reflections on Culture, Ideology, and Power," University of Michigan, Ann Arbor, November 7–10, 2004, observed that in Sepphoris and Tiberias, the two major rabbinic centers in late antique Palestine, archaeologists have found less evidence of statuary and images than in cities in Palestine that had less of a rabbinic presence. I thank Professor Weiss for showing me his paper in advance of its publication.

5. Compare the parallels to this tradition in y. Avodah Zarah 3:1 (42c) and Kohelet Rabbah 9:10.

6. In addition to the sources cited below, see also b. Avodah Zarah 48b–49a (Resh Lakish and R. Yoḥanan), which depicts water worshipped as an idol, thereby constituting a public nuisance. Compare the parallel in y. Shevi'it 8:11 (38b–c), and see Saul Lieberman, *Hellenism in Jewish Palestine* (New York: Jewish Theological Seminary,

1950), pp. 130–38, especially pp. 132–33; and Blidstein, "R. Yohanan, Idolatry, and Public Privilege," pp. 154–61; Schwartz, "Gamaliel in Aphrodite's Bath," pp. 216–17, n. 33; Levine, *The Ancient Synagogue*, pp. 451–58; and the primary and secondary sources cited by Eliav, "Viewing the Scriptural Environment," pp. 415–17.

7. The printed edition reads R. Menaḥem son of R. Yosi. See, however, *Dikdukei Soferim*, ed. Rabbinovicz, n. *pei*. See also Joseph M. Baumgarten, "Art in the Synagogue: Some Talmudic Views," *Judaism* 19, no. 2 (1970), p. 199; Yoel Florsheim, "R. Menaḥem (=Naḥum) ben Simai," *Tarbiẓ* 45 (1976), pp. 151–53; Schwartz, *Imperialism*, pp. 145–47; and chapter 3.

8. See Sokoloff, *Dictionary of Jewish Babylonian Aramaic*, p. 1168. Compare Jastrow, *Dictionary*, p. 762.

9. The word "statues" translates the word *andartaya*. For a discussion of this word, see Yosef Geiger, "Pulḥan ha-Shalitim be-Ereẓ-Yisrael ha-Romit," *Katedra* 111 (2004), p. 11, and n. 35, there. See also the discussion below.

10. See Sokoloff, *Dictionary of Jewish Babylonian Aramaic*, p. 1139.

11. See b. Avodah Zarah 50a, the discussion below, and the literature cited in note 7.

12. The literature on this story is extensive. See Schwartz, "Gamaliel in Aphrodite's Bath, pp. 203–17; and *Imperialism*, pp. 167–71; and, most recently, Azzan Yadin, "Rabban Gamaliel, Aphrodite's Bath, and the Question of Pagan Monotheism," *Jewish Quarterly Review* (forthcoming).

13. Regarding this name, see Dov Zlotnick, "Proklos ben PLSLWS," in *Sefer Zikaron le-R. Shaul Lieberman*, ed. Shamma Friedman (New York: Jewish Theological Seminary, 1993), pp. 49–52.

14. The continuation of this mishnah is clearly not part of the dialogue between Proclus and Gamaliel. See Yadin, "Rabban Gamaliel, Aphrodite's Bath, and the Question of Pagan Monotheism."

15. See, for example, Eliav, "Al Avodah Zarah be-Veit ha-Merḥaẓ ha-Romi," pp. 175–78.

16. See ibid., pp. 173–78, and the literature cited there.

17. The discussion continues: "And why was he called 'the son of the holy ones'? Because he would not even look at the image on a coin." This part of the discussion is not relevant to us, since coins were not the objects of cultic worship. Babylonian rabbis no less than Palestinian rabbis had to deal with coins that bore images of gods or kings, but we do not hear of any Babylonian rabbis who found such coins objectionable.

18. B. Avodah Zarah 43a.

19. B. Sanhedrin 64a. Regarding Bei Torta, see Oppenheimer, *Babylonia Judaica in the Talmudic Period*, pp. 359 and 367, n. 84. Regarding Rav Menasheh, see Albeck, *Mavo la-Talmudim*, p. 297. Both the locality and the Amora mark this as a story set in Babylonia.

20. Regarding the term *avodah zarah* as designating an idol or the object of idolatrous worship, see Noam Zohar, "Avodah Zarah u-Vitulah," *Sidra* 19 (2001–2), pp. 63–77. Zohar is referring to Tannaitic traditions, and it is an open question whether the term is used consistently as such in post-Tannaitic sources as well. I rely on context to determine the term's meaning. Here, an idol is clearly referred to.

21. See Yad Ramah, s.v. *Ve-ha-Po'er Aẓmo le-Pe'or zo hi Avodato*. The version of the story before us is problematic, since Rav Menasheh evidently bases his response on the distinction between a "stone" and a "clod." When he asks in the study house, however, the rabbis simply quote the mishnah (of which he is certainly aware) without

responding to his proposed distinction. This issue, while interesting from the point of view of the development of the text, is not germane to the discussion here.

22. See also b. Avodah Zarah 11b (Rav, quoted by Rav Ḥanan bar Rav), and Martin Jacobs, "Pagane Tempel in Palästina: Rabbinische Aussagen im Vergleich mit archäologischen Funden," in *The Talmud Yerushalmi and Graeco-Roman Culture*, vol. 2, ed. Peter Schäfer and Catherine Hezser (Tübingen: Mohr/Siebeck, 2000), pp. 147–51.

23. See below for discussion of manuscript variants, which do not affect my present discussion.

24. See b. Avodah Zarah 43b and the parallel in b. Rosh Hashanah 24b.

25. Regarding this synagogue, see Isaiah Gafni, "Batei-Keneset Ba'alei Zikah Historit be-Bavel ha-Talmudit," in *Batei-Keneset Atikim: Kovez̧ Meḥkarim*, ed. Aharon Oppenheimer et al. (Jerusalem: Yad Yiz̧ḥak Ben-Z̧vi, 1988), pp. 147–50, especially p. 148.

26. The printed edition of b. Rosh Hashanah 24b reads the names "Rav and Shmuel" before those of Abuha de-Shmuel and Levi. This is chronologically anomalous, and these names are missing in all manuscripts of b. Rosh Hashanah and are also not found in any versions of the parallel in b. Avodah Zarah.

27. Geiger, "Pulḥan ha-Shalitim," p. 11, and n. 35, observes that the story's term for statue, the Greek word *andarta*, usually (although not always) implies a statue of a person rather than of a god, which perhaps implies that the story does not deal with an object of worship.

28. See the references cited in note 1.

29. A third text, in b. Avodah Zarah 54b, is a purported dialogue between a philosopher and Rabban Gamaliel, in which the philosopher informs Rabban Gamaliel of a case in which there was a fire in his city, and the entire city was consumed by fire, with the exception of an idolatrous temple. This text, in other words, describes an idolatrous temple in a purportedly Palestinian context. My claim, of course, is not that traditions that purport to take place in Palestine never depict idols inside temples, but rather that some traditions in the Bavli depict idols in Palestine confronting rabbis as an everyday part of their lives, as opposed to idols in Babylonia, which rabbis have to go out of their way to confront, or which they hear of indirectly.

30. See Sokoloff, *Dictionary of Jewish Babylonian Aramaic*, p. 966.

31. See Hyman, *Toldot Tannaim ve-Amoraim*, p. 1079; and Albeck, *Mavo la-Talmudim*, p. 305. See also b. Avodah Zarah 48b, in the context of m. Avodah Zarah 3:8, which discusses an *Asherah*, a tree worshipped as an idol. A brief narrative there relates: "Rav Sheshet said to his attendant, 'When you arrive there, hurry me past.'" This narrative, however, provides no hint of where he is when he encounters the Asherah, unlike the Palestinian stories surveyed above, which establish clearly that the encounter takes place in an urban context. In addition, we are discussing statuary, and this narrative is therefore not, strictly speaking, germane to my inquiry. The Yerushalmi's discussion of the same mishnah (y. Avodah 3:8 [43b]), furthermore, contains several accounts of Palestinian rabbis encountering idols in public places, asking how to proceed, and being informed by their teachers that they should "Pass by it and blind its eye," which apparently means that they should not honor the idol by departing from their usual routine (see Blidstein, "R. Yohanan, Idolatry, and Public Privilege," p. 158). Might the idiom "blind its eye" have led to the story being told about Rav Sheshet, the proverbial blind rabbi, in its Babylonian retelling? See also the discussion of b. Berakhot 58a in chapter 4.

32. See the conclusion for a discussion of traditions that express this attitude. My claim, it bears emphasizing, is not that we never find the expression of such attitudes in the Bavli, but that alongside them we also find expressions of anxiety.

33. Urbach, *The Sages*, p. 22. See also Urbach, "The Rabbinical Laws of Idolatry in the Second and Third Centuries in the Light of Archaeological and Historical Facts," *Israel Exploration Journal* 9, nos. 3–4 (1959), pp. 154–55; and Ẓiona Grossmark, "Halakhot Avodah Zarah be-Takhshitim ke-Bavu'ah le-Yaḥasei Yehudim ve-Nokhrim be-Ereẓ-Yisrael bi-Yemei ha-Mishnah ve-ha-Talmud," in *Yehudim ve-Nokhrim be-Ereẓ-Yisrael bi-Yemei ha-Bayit ha-Sheni, ha-Mishnah ve-ha-Talmud*, ed. Aharon Oppenheimer et al. (Jerusalem: Yad Yiẓḥak Ben-Ẓvi, 2003), pp. 1–8. See also the secondary literature cited by Schwartz, *Imperialism*, p. 134, nn. 14–16.

34. Moshe Halbertal and Avishai Margalit, *Idolatry*, trans. Naomi Goldblum (Cambridge, Mass.: Harvard University Press, 1992), p. 2, are even more extreme: "The fight against idolatry, which was a central theme in biblical religion, disappeared during the period of the second Temple. . . . The temples of Baal and Astarte ceased to be real enemies; they no longer threatened the hegemony of God in the Jewish community, and the problem of the temptation of idolatry was removed from the spiritual agenda of the period."

35. Lieberman, *Hellenism in Jewish Palestine*, pp. 120–21.

36. Ibid., p. 116. Lieberman (n. 8) mentions "the polemics in Rome between the Rabbis and the philosophers (Mishnah *'Abodah Zarah* IV. 7; *Tosefta* ibid. VI. 7 . . .) as well as the disputations of the philosopher and Rabban Gamaliel (*TB* ibid. 54b and parallel . . .)," but he notes that they "lack the specific features of *Leitzanuta de-'Abodah Zarah*, the derision of idol worship, or the refutation of its principles." See also George Foot Moore, *Judaism in the First Centuries of the Christian Era*, vol. 1 (Cambridge, Mass.: Harvard University Press, 1932), p. 363, who writes: "The teachers of Palestine, addressing themselves to men of their own religion, did not feel it necessary to polemicize against polytheism and idolatry as the Hellenistic literature does." Luitpold Wallach, "A Palestinian Polemic against Idolatry: A Study in Rabbinic Literary Forms," *Hebrew Union College Annual* 29 (1945–46), p. 389, finds such polemics in Palestinian literature, but he makes no attempt to find them in Babylonian literature. See pp. 398–99 and 401 for an attempt to explain the purpose of the polemic. Wallach clearly finds it inadmissible that some Jews (let alone rabbis!) were attracted to idol worship after the destruction of the second Temple, and that the rabbis found it necessary to "demonstrate" its inefficacy. See there for his explanation of these polemics in rabbinic literature.

37. Lieberman, *Hellenism in Jewish Palestine*, pp. 116–18.

38. Urbach, "The Rabbinic Laws of Idolatry," p. 164. See pp. 158–60 and 229–38, however, where Urbach claims that rabbis disagreed about the threat posed by idol worship to Judaism, with some sages ruling leniently because they viewed the threat as minimal and others ruling more strictly because they took the threat more seriously. See also Lieberman, *Hellenism in Jewish Palestine*, p. 126.

39. See Urbach, "The Rabbinic Laws of Idolatry," p. 236; and Baumgarten, "Art in the Synagogue," pp. 201 and 206. Compare Mireille Hadas-Lebel, "Le paganisme à travers les sources rabbiniques des IIe et IIIe siècles: Contribution à l'étude du syncrétisme dans l'empire romain," in *Aufstieg und Niedergang der römischen Welt* 2:19/2 (1979), p. 398, who argues that the rabbis worried about the susceptibility of the Jewish community to the attractiveness of idolatry. See also Levine, *The Ancient Synagogue*, p. 210, n. 48. For evidence of the attractiveness of idolatry for Jews in late antique Palestine, see Immanuel Friedheim, "Yehudim Ovdei Avodah-Zarah be-Ereẓ-Yisrael bi-Tekufat ha-Mishnah ve-ha-Talmud," *Divrei ha-Kongress ha-Olami ha-Shneim-Asar le-Mada'ei ha-Yahadut*, div. 2, *Toldot Am Yisrael* (Jerusalem: Ha-Igud ha-Olami le-Mada'ei ha-Yahadut, 2000), pp. 21–44. Friedheim also distinguishes between rabbis, who

fiercely condemned idolatry, and nonrabbinic Jews, some of whom were attracted to idol worship. See, however, pp. 27–38, where Friedheim discusses traditions, also discussed in this chapter (see below), which suggest that even some rabbis were impressed by the power of idols. For evidence that some Palestinian Jews worshipped idols, see pp. 42–43.

40. See also Schwartz, *Imperialism*, pp. 132–76; and Martin Goodman, "The Jewish Image of God in Late Antiquity," in *Jewish Culture and Society under the Christian Roman Empire*, ed. Richard Kalmin and Seth Schwartz (Leuven: Peeters, 2003), pp. 133–45.

41. As noted in the preface, according to a growing consensus of scholars, the final redaction of the Bavli took place in the sixth or seventh centuries CE. The Yerushalmi appears to have been edited in the late fourth or early fifth centuries CE. With regard to the continuing vitality of paganism in the Roman Empire, see Ramsey Macmullen, *Paganism in the Roman Empire* (New Haven: Yale University Press, 1981), pp. 62–94; R. Lane Fox, *Pagans and Christians* (London: Penguin, 1986); John North, "The Development of Religious Pluralism," in *The Jews among Pagans and Christians in the Roman Empire*, ed. J. Lieu et al. (London: Routledge, 1992), pp. 174–93; Mary Beard, John North, and Simon Price, eds., *Religions of Rome*, vol. 1, *A History* (Cambridge: Cambridge University Press, 1998), pp. 387–88; Schwartz, *Imperialism*, pp. 129–76; and Friedheim, "Yehudim Ovdei Avodah-Zarah," pp. 21–27. See also Levine, *The Ancient Synagogue*, p. 210, and p. 456, n. 69.

42. B. Moed Katan 25b.

43. See, for example, b. Megillah 13a (R. Yoḥanan and R. Shimon ben Pazi).

44. See, for example, b. Shabbat 56b regarding King Solomon.

45. For vivid Christian and Muslim accounts of pagan worship in Iran both before and after the Muslim conquests, see Morony, *Iraq after the Muslim Conquest*, pp. 386–87, 394, 397–400, and 414–15. As with rabbinic traditions, it is unclear whether or not or to what extent these accounts are fictional. For a discussion of some of the diverse ways in which an idol can be perceived to possess power, see Halbertal and Margalit, *Idolatry*, pp. 37–54, and see the literature cited at p. 259, n. 8.

46. See also the collections of stories in Mekhilta de-R. Yishmael, ed. Horowitz and Rabin, pp. 223–26; and Mekhilta de-R. Shimon bar Yoḥai, ed. Y. N. Epstein and E. Z. Melamed (1955; reprint, Jerusalem: Yeshivat Sha'arei Raḥamim, 1990), pp. 146–48, both of which hammer away in exhaustive detail at the point that there is no efficacy to idol worship.

47. The Hebrew word translated here as "idols" is singular, but here and throughout I have rendered the word in the plural in an attempt to convey the best English sense of the passage.

48. Literally, "it." See note 47.

49. Compare the version of this exchange in Mekhilta de'R. Yishmael, ed. Horowitz and Rabin, p. 220; and see the analysis of Yadin, "Rabban Gamliel, Aphrodite's Bath, and the Question of Pagan Monotheism."

50. See the previous story. I have altered the translation of this verse slightly to reflect the midrashic understanding.

51. For further discussion of this story, see Friedheim, "Yehudim Ovdei Avodah-Zarah," pp. 36–38, and the literature cited there.

52. For variant readings of this text, see ms. New York JTS 44830, ed. Abramson, p. 51a. Haggadot ha-Talmud, Ein Yaakov, and Yalkut Shimoni all lack the sentence "It appears to them in a dream and says to them, 'Slaughter a man for me and I will bring rain.'" Urbach, *The Sages*, p. 698, n. 27, prefers this reading, which probably arose for

apologetic reasons, out of discomfort with the implication that the rabbis attribute reality to the idol. I think the contested phrase is an integral part of the tradition, however, and it is found in the Munich manuscript and attested by R. Ḥananel and the Ri. See the discussion below.

53. I have translated according to the midrashic meaning of the passage. The translation of the Jewish Publication Society renders "He scorns the scorners."

54. Obviously there is no contradiction between this claim and the fact that the traditions are also arranged in chronological order.

55. Pagans in fact did challenge Christianity and Judaism on scriptural grounds. See, for example, Julian, *Against the Galileans* 155C–159E, who raises an objection similar to that raised in the rabbinic text, namely: How can God be called a jealous God? For Julian this was proof of the contradictory nature of the Bible. If God were jealous, He would destroy the competition. Since He does not, either He cannot (in which case He is not all-powerful) or He does not wish to, in which case pagan worship of a multitude of gods is in keeping with the will of the god of the Bible. See also the literature cited by Yadin, "Rabban Gamliel, Aphrodite's Bath, and the Question of Pagan Monotheism."

56. Zunin's assertion that "there is no reality to idols" need not imply that he is a Jew (or a Christian), since some pagans rejected idol worship. See the literature cited by Yadin, "Rabban Gamaliel, Aphrodite's Bath, and the Question of Pagan Monotheism."

57. Compare Friedheim, "Yehudim Ovdei Avodah Zarah," pp. 36–37. Further study is necessary to determine whether rabbis ever use parables when responding to non-rabbinic Jewish interlocutors, other than (1) those explicitly identified as heretics; and (2) those who, according to the rabbis, through their actions or words weaken or deny their connection to the Jewish people.

58. For further discussion of this phrase, see chapter 4.

59. Two Palestinian Amoraic statements in y. Avodah Zarah 4:7 (44a), based on the mishnah that served as the starting point of the collection analyzed above, reflect similar but not identical attitudes. It will be helpful to briefly compare them to the Babylonian material surveyed above, although a systematic study of statements in Palestinian rabbinic compilations of late antiquity remains a desideratum.

> (1) R. Naḥman in the name of R. Mena, "In the future, idols will spit in the faces of their worshippers and disappear from the world. What is the [scriptural] proof? 'All those who worship idols will be ashamed'" (Ps. 97:7).
>
> (2) R. Naḥman in the name of R. Mena, "In the future, idols will come and bow before the Holy One, blessed be He, and disappear from the world. What is the [scriptural] proof? 'All of the gods will bow to Him'" (Ps. 97:7).

These statements express an intense desire for the humiliation of idols and idol-worshippers, and for demonstration of their submission to God. They present a brief eschatological vision with what appears to be confidence, but the very need to make such statements and to transmit them to posterity betrays dissatisfaction with present reality, and expresses the desire for vengeance upon and humiliation of pagans and the objects of their worship. These statements reveal the depth of the anger of at least one rabbi in the face of the status quo in Roman Palestine. This rabbi vents his frustration at the perseverance, indeed the flourishing, of idols and idol-worshippers in the Jewish homeland, although his statements are too brief to permit determination of whether or not he views them as attractive to Jews and even rabbis and therefore as cause for anxiety. The text reads "Rav Naḥman," incidentally, which would appear to establish his identity as a Babylonian. There was a Palestinian rabbi named Naḥman, however, who is most likely referred to here, since it fits chronologically for him to quote R. Mena. Perhaps the scribe copied "Rav Naḥman" (instead of "R. Naḥman") because of his familiarity with the much better-known Babylonian Amora by that name.

60. See also the parallel in Sifrei Numbers, ed. Horowitz, p. 171; and y. Sanhedrin 10:2 (28d). See also Friedheim, "Yehudim Ovdei Avodah-Zarah," pp. 41–42, for a comparison of the Bavli's version of the story with Palestinian versions.

61. See note 60.

62. The form of worship described in this story is certainly a rabbinic invention. The rabbis knew about the cult of Ba'al Pe'or only through biblical accounts. Their description of it is a play on the word "Pe'or," deriving it from the Hebrew word "po'er," "to expose."

63. Regarding the Sasanian kings' conception of themselves as gods, see V. B. Lukonin, "Political, Social and Administrative Institutions, Taxes and Trade," in *The Cambridge History of Iran*, ed. Yarshater, vol. 3, pt. 2, pp. 694–95; and Wiesehöfer, *Ancient Persia*, pp. 165–66. Along similar lines, we find a much more cordial dialogue, ostensibly between R. Yehoshua ben Korḥa, a Tanna, and an unnamed Roman emperor, in b. Ḥullin 59b–60a. This dialogue depicts the emperor wanting to see and to feed the Jewish God, and the rabbi convincing him that it is impossible to do so. While it should not surprise us that a Palestinian tradition dramatizes such a dialogue, we cannot discount the possibility that it reflects a Babylonian Amoraic milieu. It lacks a parallel in any Palestinian compilation, it is in Aramaic, and it lacks a technical term indicative of Tannaitic provenance. Both its Tannaitic and its Palestinian character are therefore subject to doubt.

64. This story is paralleled in a Palestinian compilation, Lamentations Rabbah 1:16. For my purposes, the differences between the Babylonian and Palestinian versions are inconsequential, since both are angry polemics against idolatry. Compare the version in Lamentations Rabbah, ed. Buber, p. 84. Compare also Pesikta Rabbati 43. The rabbinic versions also reflect anxiety, although the anxiety is not about the attractiveness of idol worship to Jews in the rabbinic present, which I showed in the collection analyzed above, but rather anxiety over the fate of Jewish heroes who are forced to give their lives rather than worship idols, anxiety over the possibility that Jewish powerlessness and pagan power demonstrate God's rejection of the Jewish people.

65. For earlier scholarly discussion comparing the various versions, see, for example, Gerson D. Cohen, "Ma'asei Ḥannah ve-Shivat Banehah be-Sifrut ha-Ivrit," in *Sefer ha-Yovel li-Kevod Mordechai Menaḥem Kaplan*, ed. Moshe Davis (New York: Jewish Theological Seminary, 1953), pp. 109–23 (Hebrew section); Aharon Agus, *The Binding of Isaac and Messiah: Law, Martyrdom and Deliverance in Early Rabbinic Religiosity* (Albany: State University of New York Press, 1988), pp. 11–32; and Galit Hasan-Rokem, *Web of Life: Folklore and Midrash in Rabbinic Literature* (Stanford: Stanford University Press, 2000), especially pp. 114–25. See also Robin Darling Young, "The 'Woman with the Soul of Abraham': Traditions about the Mother of the Maccabean Martyrs," in *"Women Like This": New Perspectives on Jewish Women in the Greco-Roman World*, ed. Amy-Jill Levine (Atlanta: Scholars Press, 1991), pp. 67–81; and the bibliography listed in n. 1, there.

66. Idol worship was not a matter of vital concern in Fairfield, Connecticut, where I went to Hebrew school in the early 1960s, yet students there learned this story,

and it made a big impression. The story resonated with us because it was said to be proof of the Jewish invention of monotheism and thus a crucial proof of the Jewish contribution to western civilization and a response to Christian claims of superiority, and/or Jewish feelings of inferiority. I doubt that the story served the same purpose in the Palestinian and Babylonian rabbinic centers of late antiquity.

67. See, however, Oppenheimer, *Babylonia Judaica in the Talmudic Period*, pp. 179–235, who notes that Maḥoza, a prominent rabbinic settlement in the mid-fourth century, was a suburb of the capital city, Ctesiphon-Seleucia-Bei Ardashir, which already in the first century CE was a large city with a mixed population, including many Jews.

68. See note 1.

69. Boyce, "Iconoclasm among the Zoroastrians," p. 107; Russell, *Zoroastrianism in Armenia*, p. 483; and Morony, *Iraq after the Muslim Conquest*, p. 287.

70. Russell, *Zoroastrianism in Armenia*, p. vi. See also pp. 114–15, 193, 196, 199–200, and 247–48. Russell, like Mary Boyce, characterizes these reforms as "iconoclastic," using an ambiguous term that I prefer to avoid.

71. See the references cited in note 18 of the introduction.

72. See D. M. Lang, "Iran, Armenia, and Georgia," in *The Cambridge History of Iran*, ed. Yarshater, vol. 3, pt. 1, p. 505; and Geoffrey Herman, "The Story of Rav Kahana (BT Baba Qamma 117a–b) in Light of Armeno-Persian Sources," in *Irano-Judaica 6: Studies Relating to Jewish Contacts with Persian Culture throughout the Ages*, ed. Shaul Shaked and Amnon Netzer (Jerusalem: Ben-Zvi Institute, forthcoming), and the sources cited in n. 43, there. I thank Mr. Herman for sharing a manuscript version of his article prior to its publication.

73. See Russell, *Zoroastrianism in Armenia*, p. 515. See also note 16 in the introduction.

74. See Russell, *Zoroastrianism in Armenia*, p. 528. It was only in 428 CE that the Sasanians succeeded in stamping out the Armenian Arsacid challenge to their legitimacy, but by that time Armenia had been a Christian country for close to a century.

75. See the traditions collected by Friedheim, "Yehudim Ovdei Avodah-Zarah," pp. 27–40.

76. Lieberman, *Hellenism in Jewish Palestine*, p. 121.

77. See Morony, *Iraq after the Muslim Conquest*, p. 292, n. 74, who observes that "Christians rarely distinguished between Magians and pagans, called both heathens . . . and assumed that Magians worshiped idols."

CHAPTER 6

1. See the introduction.

2. See also Robert Brody, "Judaism in the Sasanian Empire: A Case Study in Religious Coexistence," in *Irano-Judaica: Studies Relating to Jewish Contacts with Persian Culture throughout the Ages*, vol. 2, ed. Shaul Shaked and Amnon Netzer (Jerusalem: Ben-Zvi Institute, 1990), pp. 52–62, who argues that the Persians, for the most part, did not intend to persecute Babylonian Jews. They interfered with Jewish practices when those practices offended Zoroastrian religious principles. This chapter, however, concentrates on the third century, and is not intended as a characterization of Sasanian policy toward the Jews throughout the entire period of their rule. See the discussion below.

3. See, for example, Wiesehöfer, *Ancient Persia*, pp. 210–15.

4. See also 1 Chron. 1:5.

5. Tiras is the last brother mentioned in the verse, indicating his status as the youngest. Rav Yosef's tradition identifying Tiras as Persia implies that Persia is the youngest, demonstrating why it makes sense to identify Persia as "the young of the flock."

6. Aphrahat, a Christian from Persia who wrote in the first half of the fourth century CE in the vicinity of rabbinic Babylonia (see the introduction), interprets the second beast in Daniel 7 as a reference to the kingdom of Media and Persia, and the fourth beast as a reference to the kingdom of the sons of Esau, i.e., to the Greeks and Romans. Yet the ram, now symbolizing Shapur, fights the fourth beast, which is the Roman Empire. According to Aphrahat, the Roman Empire, which is Christian, will not be defeated until the coming of Christ. The parallels to Rav's view are obvious. See Brock, "From Antagonism to Assimilation," p. 17.

7. According to the printed edition, Rav responds with a statement that is a mixture of Aramaic and Hebrew: "[Aramaic:] Yes; [Hebrew:] it is a decree of the King." See, however, *Dikdukei Soferim*, ed. Rabbinovicz, n. *daled*, who observes that the one Aramaic word "Yes" is missing in all manuscripts, as well as in the first edition of Ein Yaakov and a manuscript of Yalkut Shimoni.

8. The printed edition reads "to him," an obvious error. See *Dikdukei Soferim*, ed. Rabbinovicz, n. *hei*. See also Moshe Beer, "Gezerotav shel Kartir al Yehudei Bavel," *Tarbiẓ* 55, no. 4 (1986), p. 531, n. 30.

9. See *Dikdukei Soferim*, ed. Rabbinovicz, n. *vav*, who points out that the Aramaic phrase "First, because they destroy synagogues" is obviously a later addition to the text (since "Aramaic is not the language of a Baraita") and is missing in many versions. See also Rabbinovicz's comments regarding the phrase "and also."

10. See *Dikdukei Soferim*, ed. Rabbinovicz, n. *lamed*, for versions with a Hebrew preposition (*vav*). Most versions, however, have an Aramaic preposition (*daled*).

11. Gafni, *Yehudei Bavel*, pp. 39–40, and 116. See also Krauss, *Paras ve-Romi ba-Talmud u-va-Midrashim*, pp. 30–31; Geo Widengren, "The Status of the Jews in the Sasanian Empire," *Iranica Antiqua* 1 (1961), pp. 128–30; Jacob Neusner, *A History of the Jews in Babylonia* (Leiden: Brill, 1966), vol. 2, pp. 36–37; E. S. Rosenthal, "Le-Milon ha-Talmudi," in *Irano-Judaica: Studies Relating to Jewish Contacts with Persian Culture Throughout the Ages*, vol. 1, ed. Shaul Shaked and Amnon Netzer (Jerusalem: Ben-Zvi Institute, 1982), pp. 63–64 and the literature cited at p. 131, n. 49; and Moshe Beer, "Ha-Reka ha-Medini u-Fe'iluto shel Rav be-Bavel," *Ẓion: Sefer Yovel* 50 (1985), p. 160; and "Gezerotav shel Kartir," pp. 530–32.

12. See, for example, Rosenthal, "Le-Milon ha-Talmudi," pp. 54–58; Daniel Sperber, "On the Unfortunate Adventures of Rav Kahana: A Passage of Saboraic Polemic from Sasanian Persia," in Shaked and Netzer, *Irano-Judaica*, vol. 1, pp. 83–100; Gafni, *Yehudei Bavel*, pp. 194–97; and "Ha-Yeshivah ha-Bavlit la-Or Sugyat B.K. 117a," *Tarbiẓ* 49, nos. 1–2 (1980), pp. 292–301; Adiel Schremer, "'Akshei lei ve-Okmei': Iyun Eḥad be-Sugyat ha-Bavli, Baba Kamma 117a," *Tarbiẓ* 66, no. 3 (1997), pp. 403–15; Shamma Friedman, "The Further Adventures of Rav Kahana: Between Babylonia and Palestine," in *The Talmud Yerushalmi and Graeco-Roman Culture*, vol. 3, ed. Peter Schäfer (Tübingen: Mohr/Siebeck, 2002), pp. 247–71; and "Sippur Rav Kahana ve-R. Yoḥanan (BK 117a–b) ve-Anaf Nusaḥ Geniza-Hamburg," in *Sefer Zikaron li-Kevod Meyer Feldblum* (forthcoming); and Herman, "The Story of Rav Kahana."

13. Or whoever attributed the statement to Rav. See also b. Gittin 59b, where the same expression, "the package is undone," is attributed to Abaye in a different context.

14. This consideration, of course, is important evidence in favor of the first version, but it is less than fully probative, since it is possible that Rav's second statement (part K) represents the view of those who accept the first version of Rav's response (part G). See the discussion below.

15. What is convincing and what is not, however, is in the mind of the beholder.

16. Perhaps it will be objected that it is unlikely that Rav would prefer his own opinion to that of the Tanna, R. Yehudah b'R. Ilai (part D). Several considerations, however, neutralize this argument. First, Rav is a very early Amora, who on occasion disagrees with Tannaim. Second, R. Yehudah b'R. Ilai's statement is quoted by Amoraim (R. Yoḥanan, quoted in turn by Rabbah bar bar Ḥanah), and such statements are often not treated in the Talmud as "pure" Tannaitic statements. Third, Rav has the backing of a Tannaitic tradition of his own (part J), and fourth, it is not unusual for Amoraim to overrule Tannaim when midrash aggadah (nonlegal exegesis of scripture) is involved.

17. It is important to respond to a potential argument one might be tempted to make in *favor* of the second version as the original. This argument bases itself on the language of parts E–I. Both the objection of Rav Kahana and Rav Asi (part F) and the second version of Rav's response (part I) are in Aramaic, while the first version of Rav's response (part G) together with Rav's original statement (part E) are in Hebrew. With regard to the different languages used in this discussion, see Rosenthal, "Le-Milon ha-Talmudi," p. 63. As noted repeatedly throughout this book, often a change of language within a discussion or statement is indicative of a change of speaker or an editorial interpolation, according to which the first version of Rav's response (part G) would appear to derive from a different source from the objection of Rav's interlocutors (part F) and the second version of Rav's response (part I). I am convinced this is not the case here, however, for it is easy to account for the fact that some parts of the discussion are in Hebrew and others are in Aramaic. Rav's opening statement is in Hebrew because his statement is declarative. Rav is asserting what he considers to be a fact about the future course of events, and such statements, particularly those attributed to Amoraim as early as Rav, tend to be in Hebrew. The rest of the discussion, however, is argumentational, i.e., it consists of an objection and a response, and Talmudic argumentation is typically formulated in Aramaic. See Kraemer, "On the Reliability of Attributions in the Babylonian Talmud," pp. 182–86. The argument from language is not useful in the present instance as a tool by which to divide the discussion into diverse sources, i.e., to conclude that the first version of Rav's response is a later addition. For this first version (part G) is in Hebrew because the Hebrew phrase "It is a decree of the King" is found explicitly in a Baraita quoted later on in the discussion as support for Rav's statement. Rav (or whoever attributed the statement to Rav) is in all likelihood employing the language of the Baraita. See also the discussion of b. Moed Katan 25b–26a, below.

18. See Rosenthal, "Le-Milon ha-Talmudi," p. 131, n. 47.

19. It also bears mentioning that the argument of the second version of Rav's response depends on equating the Persians' destruction of synagogues (or a synagogue) with the Romans' destruction of the Temple. With regard to this equation, see Gafni, "Batei-Keneset Ba'alei Zikah Historit," pp. 161–62; and *Yehudei Bavel*, pp. 116–17.

20. For example, when passages from documents are quoted, for example, in m. Ketubot 4:7–8 and 10–12.

21. There is reason to believe, furthermore, that the Aramaic phrase in the Baraita is a post-Talmudic addition. According to Judith Hauptman, Baraitot introduced by the

phrase "It is also taught thus [in a Baraita]" have been subjected to late editorial tampering, and if Hauptman is correct, then even the later editors responsible for the phrase "It is also taught thus [in a Baraita]" and for the Baraita as currently formulated minus the Aramaic phrase were unaware of the second version of Rav's statement. See Judith Hauptman, *Development of the Talmudic Sugya: Relationship between Tannaitic and Amoraic Sources* (Lanham, Md.: University Press of America, 1988), pp. 1–13. Compare Simcha Goldsmith, "The Role of the *Tanya Nami Hakhi Baraita*," *Hebrew Union College Annual* 73 (2002), pp. 133–56.

22. The manuscript is Yemenite and dates from 1608. As several scholars have noted, Yemenite textual traditions are to be taken very seriously, albeit with appropriate caution, as possible evidence of authentic early readings, even when they depart significantly from the "received," more mainstream versions and traditions. See, for example, Saul Lieberman, *Midreshei Teiman*, 2nd ed. (Jerusalem: Wahrmann Books, 1970), pp. 3–42; Gafni, "Ha-Yeshivah ha-Bavlit la-Or Sugyat B. K. 117a," p. 301, n. 39; and Sperber, "On the Unfortunate Adventures of Rav Kahana," p. 100.

23. Complicating matters even further is the fact that the section of ms. JTS Rab. 218 cited immediately above is currently bracketed with quotation marks, and a reading copied by a different scribe, virtually identical to that of the printed edition, has been added in the margin. See the discussion below.

24. More precisely, the reading in the body of ms. JTS Rab. 218.

25. Rosenthal, "Le-Milon ha-Talmudi," p. 64, is therefore not fully accurate when he ridicules earlier scholars who commented on this discussion and claims that the phrase "They also destroy synagogues" is not missing in any manuscript.

26. Daniel Boyarin, *Intertextuality and the Reading of Midrash* (Bloomington: Indiana University Press, 1990), pp. 1–21; and Hayes, *Between the Babylonian and Palestinian Talmuds*, pp. 3–20.

27. Or whoever attributed these statements to Rav.

28. Compare Beer, "Ha-Reka ha-Medini," p. 160.

29. See Rosenthal, "Le-Milon ha-Talmudi," pp. 63 and 131, n. 47; and Beer, "Ha-Reka ha-Medini," p. 160.

30. Some of these names cannot be identified with certainty, but there is scholarly unanimity that they all refer to religious minorities in the Persian Empire.

31. See MacKenzie, "Kerdir's Inscription," pp. 42 (synoptic text in translation), 54 (transcription), 58 (translation), and 64 (commentary). Wiesehöfer, *Ancient Persia*, p. 199, translates: "And the Jews, Buddhists, Hindus, Nazarenes, Christians, Baptists and Manichaeans were smashed in the empire, their idols destroyed, and the habitations of the idols annihilated and turned into abodes and seats of the gods." See also the translation and commentary of Martin Sprengling, "Kartir, Founder of Sasanian Zoroastrianism," *American Journal of Semitic Languages and Literatures* 57 (1940), pp. 220–23; and *Third Century Iran: Sapor and Kartir* (Chicago: Oriental Institute, 1953); Widengren, "The Status of the Jews," p. 130; and Rosenthal, "Le-Milon ha-Talmudi," pp. 88–89, nn. 133–36. Neusner, *A History of the Jews in Babylonia*, vol. 2, p. 18, and n. 1, claims to be quoting Sprengling's translation, but his rendering of the translation is incomprehensible in several places, and he gives the wrong page reference to Sprengling's article.

32. Compare Frye, *The Heritage of Persia*, p. 210.

33. Friedman, "Al Derekh Ḥeker ha-Sugya," p. 30.

34. Beer, "Ha-Reka ha-Medini," for example, pp. 155–57, 163, and 168–69; and "Gezerotav shel Kartir," pp. 529–30, n. 27 (compare Beer's discussion on pp. 530–32, where he minimizes the problems that the Zoroastrian priests caused the Jews during

Rav's lifetime). See also Amnon Netzer, "Ha-Sasanim ba-Talmud ha-Bavli," *Shevet ve-Am* 7, n.s. no. 2 (1973), p. 252.

35. Beer, "Ha-Reka ha-Medini," pp. 158–63. See also pp. 170–72.

36. *Igeret Rav Sherira Gaon*, ed. Benjamin Lewin (Haifa, 1920), p. 97.

37. According to this reconstruction, instead of *alef, taf, samekh, reish, vav,* the scribe or oral performer rendered *alef, samekh, taf, reish, vav,* reversing the order of *samekh* and *taf.* My description of precisely how this variant came about is deliberately vague. I thank Robert Brody of the Hebrew University for helping me formulate matters in this fashion.

38. *Seder Tannaim ve-Amoraim*, ed. Kalman Kahan (Frankfort am Main: Ḥermon, 1935), p. 6. See also Nahum Brüll, "Die Entstehungsgeschichte der babylonischen Talmuds als Schriftwerk," *Jahrbücher für jüdische Geschichte und Literatur* 2 (1876), p. 12, n. 8, who proposed long ago that Rav Sherira and *Seder Tannaim ve-Amoraim* were describing the same event. Brüll in fact suggests that metathesis has taken place between the forms *istatru* ("were destroyed") and *itasru* ("were closed"), although *Seder Tannaim ve-Amoraim* uses the Hebrew form *harsu* ("they destroyed"). See Kalman Kahan, introduction to *Seder Tannaim ve-Amoraim*, ed. Kahan, p. 27, who casts doubt on Brüll's claim.

39. More precisely, the most original version we are capable of reconstructing.

40. For a discussion of accounts in early medieval Persian sources, which make no mention of the destruction of synagogues, see Widengren, "The Status of the Jews," p. 143. See also the discussion below.

41. See Jacob Neusner, *A History of the Jews in Babylonia* (Leiden: Brill, 1970), vol. 5, pp. 60–72, and the literature cited there.

42. The printed edition mistakenly reads "Rabbah" instead of "the rabbis." See Rosenthal, "Le-Milon ha-Talmudi," pp. 38 and 71, n. 15; *Dikdukei Soferim: Gittin*, ed. Feldblum, nn. on l. 42; and *Dikdukei Soferim ha-Shalem: Gittin*, vol. 1, ed. Hillel Porush (Jerusalem: Makhon ha-Talmud ha-Yisre'eli ha-Shalem, 1999), p. 163, nn. on ll. 24 and n. 42.

43. Regarding the term *ḥabara* (pl. *ḥabarei*), see *Geschichte der Perser und Araber zur Zeit des Sasaniden*, ed. Nöldeke, p. 68, n.1; the literature cited in Beer, "Ha-Reka ha-Medini, p. 156, n. 6; and "Al Shalosh Gezerot she-Nigzeru al Yehudei Bavel be-Me'ah ha-Shelishit," in Shaked and Netzer, *Irano-Judaica*, vol. 1, pp. 27–28, n. 11; Rosenthal, "Le-Milon ha-Talmudi," pp. 71–74, nn. 23–25; and Sokoloff, *Dictionary of Jewish Babylonian Aramaic*, p. 429.

44. Rosenthal, "Le-Milon ha-Talmudi," pp. 38–42.

45. For further discussion of this tendency of the anonymous editors, see Kalmin, "The Formation and Character of the Babylonian Talmud," in *The Cambridge History of Judaism*, ed. Katz, vol. 4, p. 846.

46. B. Berakhot 24b and b. Shabbat 41a. See also b. Ketubot 111a, where we find: "Said Rav Yehudah, 'Whoever dwells in Babylonia, it is as if he dwells in the land of Israel.'" See also Kalmin, *The Sage in Jewish Society*, pp. 51–57 and 59–60, for discussion of the frequent depiction of Rav Yehudah as chief spokesman for the idea that Babylonian rabbinic genealogy was superior to that of rabbis in Palestine.

47. At least in comparison to what rabbinic authors claim Israel endured at the hands of the Romans. See chapter 1. See also Neusner, *A History of the Jews in Babylonia*, vol. 3, p. 18, who writes: "It seems incongruous that so slight an inconvenience—the removal of a lamp... should have elicited such anguished despair." See also appendix 1 to this chapter.

48. Compare, for example, Neusner, *A History of the Jews in Babylonia*, vol. 2, pp. 35–36; Beer, "Al Shalosh Gezerot," pp. 25–37; and Rosenthal, "Le-Milon ha-Talmudi," pp. 42 and 58–59.

49. Sokoloff, *Dictionary of Jewish Babylonian Aramaic*, p. 1108.

50. Meiri, *Beit ha-Beḥirah: Yevamot*, ed. Shmuel Dikman (Jerusalem: Makhon ha-Talmud ha-Yisre'eli ha-Shalem, 1962), p. 233, s.v. *kevar*, writes: "Because they would rejoice and do business with them on the days of their festivals." It is likely that the phrase "and do business with them" is Meiri's interpretation rather than his version of the text. Meiri's interpretation was probably motivated by the fact that the rabbis nowhere mention the issue of "rejoicing on the days of their festivals," but the issue of "doing business with them on the days of their festivals" exercises them a great deal. See the discussion below.

51. The phrase "as it is said" connects the quotation of 1 Sam. 12:15 immediately following to the discussion of the three decrees immediately preceding. The phrase, however, is most likely a later addition to the text. See *Dikdukei Soferim ha-Shalem: Yevamot*, ed. Liss, p. 423, nn. on l. 31. The significance of this fact will be discussed below.

52. See Beer, "Al Shalosh Gezerot," pp. 26–27 and 37. Compare the discussion below.

53. Beer, "Al Shalosh Gezerot," p. 29.

54. Ibid., pp. 26–37; and Brody, "Judaism in the Sasanian Empire," p. 58. Compare Meiri, s.v. *kevar*.

55. It is not entirely clear whether this tradition claims that the Persians do this themselves, or force the Jews to do it.

56. As noted, however, the reading "as it is said" is most likely a later addition, according to which Rabbah bar Shmuel's statement is a separate tradition, and is not quoted by the authors of the "three decrees" tradition as proof for their claim that the dead are disinterred on account of the sin of rejoicing on the festivals of the Persians.

57. The relative chronology of parts D and E will be discussed below.

58. Beer, "Al Shalosh Gezerot," pp. 25–37; and Brody, "Judaism in the Sasanian Empire," p. 58. See also Meiri, s.v. *kevar*; R. Avraham min he-Har, s.v. *gazru al shalosh*; and Rivan, s.v. *gazru gezerot*.

59. See chapter 1, and the story of R. Ḥanina ben Teradion and R. Elazar ben Perata, also on b. Avodah Zarah 17b.

60. Geoffrey Herman, written communication, March 10, 2004. For more detailed discussion, see Herman, "Ha-Kohanim be-Bavel," pp. 147–52. Compare Shaul Shaked, "Zoroastrian Polemics against Jews in the Sasanian and Early Islamic Period," in Shaked and Netzer, *Irano-Judaica*, vol. 2, p. 93; Brody, "Judaism in the Sasanian Empire," p. 58; and Gafni, *Yehudei Bavel*, pp. 41–42. See also Beer, "Al Shalosh Gezerot," pp. 30–36.

61. See, for example, Beer, "Al Shalosh Gezerot," pp. 27 and 37; Brody, "Judaism in the Sasanian Empire," p. 58. Beer, pp. 29–37, would like to interpret part D as both a list of three pairs of (1) divine punishment/Babylonian Jewish transgression, and (2) Persian punishment/Babylonian Jewish offense against the Persians. Only by doing great violence to the text is Beer able to interpret the tradition as a historical chronicle converted into a sermon.

62. Friedman, "Al Derekh Ḥeker ha-Sugya," pp. 25–26.

63. It is also peculiar that with all of the extensive discussion of interactions between Jews and idolaters in tractate Avodah Zarah, nowhere else is there the slightest concern for Jews "rejoicing on their festivals." See the discussion below.

64. See the phraseology of Beer, "Al Shalosh Gezerot," p. 35: "The Talmud includes the matter [of disinterring the dead] in a literary/typological framework and lists it as one of the three decrees." Might Beer be sensitive to the likelihood that the issue of "disinterring the dead" derives from a different source than the rest of the tradition?

65. As noted several times throughout this book, the term "originally" refers to the most original form of the tradition that we can reconstruct.

66. See the first chapter of Bavli Avodah Zarah. The closest we come to discussion of the sin of rejoicing on the holidays of idolaters is found in b. Avodah Zarah 8a. There, however, the reference is to Jews celebrating with an idolater who throws a wedding party for his son. A wedding party is clearly not the same as a "festival" (*eid*). See also b. Avodah Zarah 16a and 64b–65a.

67. See Meiri, s.v. *kevar*; and the references cited in Beer, "Al Shalosh Gezerot," p. 36.

68. Shamma Friedman, "Mivneh Sifruti be-Sugyot ha-Bavli," in *Divrei ha-Kongress ha-Olami ha-Shishi le-Mada'ei ha-Yahadut* (Jerusalem: Ha-Igud ha-Olami le-Mada'ei ha-Yahadut, 1977), div. C, vol. 3, pp. 391–96. See also Jeffrey L. Rubenstein, "Some Structural Patterns of Yerushalmi *Sugyot*," in *The Talmud Yerushalmi and Graeco-Roman Culture*, ed. Schäfer, vol. 3, pp. 303–13.

69. Friedman, "Mivneh Sifruti," pp. 391–96; and Halivni, *Mekorot u-Mesorot: Nashim*, pp. 271–72.

70. *Dikdukei Soferim ha-Shalem: Yevamot*, ed. Liss, nn. on ll. 29–30 and pp. 422–23, nn. 113–18. See also Friedman, "Al Derekh Heker ha-Sugya," p. 30. It is possible, although less likely, that part D was passed down in fragmentary condition, with one of the three punishments lost in transmission. Such incomplete transmission is a common phenomenon in the ancient world, and it would not be at all shocking to encounter it here. It will be recalled that part D opens with the phrase "They decreed three [punishments] on account of three [crimes]," and the third punishment was perhaps added by later editors whose text of the tradition listed only two. In other words, it is possible that the later editors inherited a tradition that specified three crimes but only two punishments; they needed a third punishment to "complete" the tradition.

71. Compare Beer, "Al Shalosh Gezerot," p. 27.

72. See, for example, Kalmin, *Sages, Stories, Authors, and Editors*, pp. 193–212, and the references cited there.

73. Their subordinate status is shown by the fact that they are unnamed. See also Beer, "Al Shalosh Gezerot," p. 27.

74. One could argue with difficulty that part D is intended as the words of an omniscient narrator, and is not intended as the continuation of either party to the conversation in part C. This leaves unresolved, however, the problem of the change of language, and also makes for a very abrupt transition between part C and part D, a transition so abrupt that it very likely led to the reading of Rashi and several other medieval commentators, which is a very problematic attempt to smooth the transition between the two parts. In all likelihood Rashi's reading (s.v. *amru lei* and *amar lahem*) is an emendation by commentators struggling to read part D as the continuation of the dialogue in part C. See *Dikdukei Soferim ha-Shalem: Yevamot*, ed. Liss, p. 422, n. 112.

75. It is quite possible that the editors who placed part D after part C intended to present the former as the continuation of the latter. My point, however, is that this (hypothesized) editorial interpretation is most likely not an accurate reflection of the traditions' actual relationship. See Magid Mishneh on Rambam, Mishneh Torah, Laws

of Fasts 2:3, whose reading of the text apparently differs greatly from all other witnesses.

76. Beer, "Al Shalosh Gezerot," pp. 27–28. See also Beer, "Ha-Reka ha-Medini," pp. 155–63, especially p. 160; and Beer, "Kartir," pp. 529–32. Beer claims unconvincingly that even if part D is understood to be independent of part C, it can be assigned reliably to the beginning of Sasanian rule in the first half of the third century. See also Julius Fürst, "Geschichte der jüdischen Literatur in Babylonien," *Literaturblatt des Orients* 14 (1847), p. 212; Zechariah Frankel, *Mevo ha-Yerushalmi* (Breslau, 1870), p. 97b; Neusner, *A History of the Jews in Babylonia*, vol. 2, pp. 35–36; and the literature cited in Rosenthal, "Le-Milon ha-Talmudi," pp. 128–29, n. 6.

77. Rosenthal, "Le-Milon ha-Talmudi," pp. 41–42; 58–59; and 128–29. See also Widengren, "The Status of the Jews," pp. 124–31; and Gafni, *Yehudei Bavel*, p. 40, n. 96. Compare Eli Aḥdut, "Ha-Polmos ha-Yehudi-Zoroastri ba-Talmud ha-Bavli," in *Irano-Judaica*, vol. 4, *Studies Relating to Jewish Contacts with Persian Culture Throughout the Ages*, ed. Shaul Shaked and Amnon Netzer (Jerusalem: Ben-Zvi Institute, 1999), p. 25, who dates the three decrees to the "third century."

78. See, for example, Friedman, "Al Derekh Ḥeker ha-Sugya," p. 20; Goodblatt, "The Babylonian Talmud," pp. 154–56, and the literature cited there; and Halivni, *Mekorot u-Mesorot: Shabbat*, pp. 5–18.

79. See note 51 and see the discussion immediately following.

80. *Dikdukei Soferim ha-Shalem: Yevamot*, ed. Liss, p. 423, nn. on l. 31.

81. See also Joshua Schwartz, "Tension between Palestinian Scholars and Babylonian Olim in Amoraic Palestine," *Journal for the Study of Judaism* 11 (1980), pp. 78–94; Isaiah Gafni, "Expressions and Types of 'Local Patriotism' among the Jews of Babylonia," in Shaked and Netzer, *Irano-Judaica*, vol. 2, p. 69; and Rubenstein, *Culture*, p. 97.

82. See Ferdinand Justi, *Geschichte des alten Persiens* (Berlin: G. Grote, 1879), p. 200.

83. *Ausgewählte Akten persischer Märtyrer*, trans. Oskar Braun (Kempten, Germany: Jos. Kösel, 1915), pp. 1 and 116; Geo Widengren, *Die Religionen Irans* (Stuttgart: W. Kohlhammer, 1965), p. 279; Beer, "Al Shalosh Gezerot," p. 33.

84. Otakar Klima, *Manis Zeit und Leben* (Prague: Czechoslovakian Academy of Sciences, 1962), pp. 218; 278, n. 5; and 520; *Ginza, der Schatz, oder, Das grosse Buch der Mandäer*, trans. Mark Lidzbarski (Göttingen: Vandenhoeck and Ruprecht, 1925), pp. x, 16, and 35; and Beer, "Al Shalosh Gezerot," p. 33, n. 29.

85. Mary Boyce, *Zoroastrians: Their Religious Beliefs and Practices* (London: Routledge, 1979), p. 121. See also Boyce and Grenet, *A History of Zoroastrianism*, vol. 3, p. 130.

86. *Ausgewählte Akten persischer Märtyrer*, trans. Braun, p. 163; *Auszüge aus syrischen Akten persischer Märtyrer*, trans. Georg Hoffmann (1880; reprint, Nendeln, Liechtenstein: Kraus, 1966), p. 39.

87. Beer, "Al Shalosh Gezerot," pp. 35–36.

88. The Persian decree against "meat" likewise cannot be pinned to down a particular time period or event in Persian history. See the literature cited in note 60.

89. See *Dikdukei Soferim*, ed. Rabbinovicz, n. *shin*; and Epstein, *Mavo le-Nusaḥ ha-Mishnah*, p. 968.

90. Based on the parallel to this Baraita in y. Moed Katan 3:7 (83b), the derivation from scripture would appear to be the continuation of the Baraita. The question "What is the [scriptural] source?" is in Aramaic in the Bavli (*minalan*) but is Hebrew in the Yerushalmi (*minayin*). In the Bavli, the Baraita is interrupted by

Amoraic and anonymous commentary, a perfectly common phenomenon, but in the Yerushalmi, the Baraita is not interrupted. See also *Massekhet Semaḥot* 9:19, ed. Michael Higger (1931; reprint, Jerusalem: Makor, 1970), pp. 175–76.

91. In the Bavli, this phrase is likewise in Aramaic (*di-khetiv*). In the Yerushalmi, the quotation from scripture is not introduced by a technical term.

92. Mss. Munich 140, and Opp. Add. Fol. 23 (366) Oxford read "Rav Yehudah" instead of "Shmuel." The reading "Shmuel," which is the reading of most manuscripts and medieval testimonia, is preferable, since Shmuel is depicted as conversing or interacting with Shapur several times in the Bavli (b. Berakhot 56a; b. Sukkah 53a; b. Sanhedrin 98a). See also part F, where all versions read "Shmuel." So close was the identification between Shmuel and Shapur in the minds of the rabbis that Shmuel was referred to several times as "Shapur the king" (see b. Baba Kamma 96b; b. Baba Meẓi'a 119a; b. Baba Batra 115a), but Rav Yehudah never is. See also the discussion below. The reading "Rav Yehudah" may have arisen because of the proximity of the word *Yehuda'ei* ("Jews"). Mss. Munich 140 and Opp. Add. Fol. 23 (366) Oxford are so closely related, furthermore, that the two together only comprise a single textual witness. Compare Gafni, *Yehudei Bavel*, p. 263, n. 102.

93. See Saul Lieberman, "Palestine in the Third and Fourth Centuries," *Jewish Quarterly Review* 37 (1946), p. 36, n. 331.

94. See appendix 2 to this chapter, where I elaborate on this point.

95. Compare Gafni, *Yehudei Bavel*, pp. 262–63.

96. It is possible, of course, that the two traditions were emended once they became juxtaposed to one another in this discussion, in which case their striking similarities are no indication that they derive from a single source. When speculating about emendations by later editors or transmitters, of course, anything is possible, and we have little choice but to rely on the texts as they exist before us, unless compelling evidence leads us to suspect editorial tampering.

97. See chapters 1, 2, and 3.

98. See the discussion below.

99. It is also possible, although unlikely, that part G is the continuation of Shapur's statement to Shmuel (part F).

100. Perhaps for this reason, Sokoloff, *Dictionary of Jewish Babylonian Aramaic*, p. 548, says that the meaning of the phrase *kal yetrei* (translated here as "the noise of the [Persian] bows") is uncertain.

101. See Lieberman, "Palestine in the Third and Fourth Centuries," p. 35 and n. 323; and "Ha-Perush," in *Yerushalmi Nezikin*, ed. E. S. Rosenthal (Jerusalem: Ha-Akademi'ah ha-Le'umit ha-Yisre'elit le-Mada'im, 1983), p. 182.

102. See *Geschichte der Perser und Araber zur Zeit des Sasaniden*, ed. Nöldeke, p. 32; and Lieberman, "Palestine in the Third and Fourth Centuries," p. 35, n. 323.

103. In my reconstruction, the response to the objection is introduced by the phrase "[Shmuel] said to them" and reads as follows: [Shmuel said to them], "They only said [that one rends ones garments upon hearing bad news] in the case of the majority of the community in conformity with what happened" [to Saul, Jonathan, the soldiers of the Lord, and the House of Israel]. I base this reading on ms. Opp. Add. Fol. 23 (366) Oxford, which reads *alef-lamed*, an abbreviation indicating direct dialogue, although it is not clear according to this reading whether the speaker or the addressee is singular or plural. I base myself further on Ein Yaakov and ms. Munich 140, both of which read *amar lei* ("he said to him") as well as on ms. Vatican 108, which reads these words in the margin. Rabbinovicz, *Dikdukei Soferim*, n. *yud*, maintains: "We can explain this reading with difficulty," indicating clearly that he prefers the reading of the

printed edition, according to which part D is not Amoraic dialogue, but rather a response by the anonymous editors. The difficulty noted by Rabbinovicz, however, disappears if we understand the reading "he said to him" as a mistaken attempt to decipher the abbreviation *alef-lamed*, which later scribes incorrectly expanded to *amar lei*. The correct reading is preserved in ms. Oxford (*alef-lamed*), and the abbreviation *alef-lamed* is actually short for "he said to them," *amar lehu*, and refers to Shmuel responding to those who informed him of the action of Shapur the king ("They said to Shmuel, 'Shapur the [Persian] king killed 12,000 Jews in Caesarea Mazaca,' and he did not rend [his garments]"). It bears mentioning, furthermore, that while mss. Vatican 134 and Harl. 5508 (400) British Museum do not read part D as Shmuel's response to his informants, these manuscripts do read it as the continuation of part C rather than as deriving from the anonymous editors. These manuscripts connect parts C and D by the conjunction *vav* ("and"), according to which they form a unified source.

104. In all likelihood, Shmuel's statement is in Hebrew, despite the fact that the rest of the discussion is in Aramaic because his response fits perfectly as an interpretation of the Baraita. Were it to be detached from its argumentational setting, it would work perfectly as such an interpretation, and would require neither the addition nor the subtraction of any words to make sense directly based on the Baraita. In addition, Shmuel is making a declarative statement rather than responding to an objection, so his statement does not constitute argumentation and therefore, according to the rules of Talmudic discourse, need not be phrased in Aramaic. Such interpretations, particularly those attributed to early Amoraim such as Shmuel, are generally formulated in Hebrew. It bears mentioning that in b. Yoma 10a, analyzed above in detail, Rav responds in Hebrew to the Aramaic objection of Rav Asi and Rav Kahana (part G: "It is a decree of the King").

105. See Lieberman, "Palestine in the Third and Fourth Centuries," p. 36, n. 331, who says explicitly: "Although *TB [Moed Katan 26a]* decided that the law of the tearing of the garments applied only in the case where the slaughtered masses consisted of the majority of the nation, *it was only a justification for the behavior of Samuel*; the Palestinian Talmud does not mention the limitation" (emphasis added).

106. See, for example, David Zvi Hoffmann, *Mar Samuel, Rector der jüdischen Akademie zu Nehardea in Babylonien* (Leipzig; O. Leiner, 1873), pp. 37–48; J. Obermyer, *Die Landschaft Babylonien im Zeitalter des Talmuds und des Gaonats* (Frankfurt am Main: I. Kauffman, 1929), p. 264; Neusner, *A History of the Jews in Babylonia*, vol. 2, pp. 44–46 and 64–72; and Gafni, *Yehudei Bavel*, p. 42.

107. See the introduction, and chapters 4 and 5.

108. See, however, Moshe Beer, *Rashut ha-Golah bi-Yemei ha-Mishnah ve-ha-Talmud* (Tel Aviv: Devir, 1976), pp. 179–84, who observes that the Bavli attributes to Babylonian rabbis no direct criticisms of the exilarch, but only of the exilarch's "household," or "slaves."

109. See, for example, Halivni, *Midrash, Mishnah, and Gemara*, pp. 76–77 and 87–92. In b. Sanhedrin 17a, for example, Babylonian Amoraim claim that one cannot become a prominent judge if one is unable to devise 150 arguments supporting the proposition that a reptile is ritually pure, despite the fact that the Torah explicitly labels it impure. See also b. Eruvin 13b and b. Sanhedrin 17b. It is conceivable, although, for reasons noted above, less likely, that the editors in this instance had political as well as exegetical motives. For according to the discussion as currently structured, King Shapur was a righteous king who never killed Jews, with the exception of the Jews of Caesarea Mazaca, who had it coming to them. According to this understanding, the

anonymous editorial machinations are at least in part designed to teach a lesson about the need for political quietism, to demonstrate logically the folly of armed rebellion against Persian authority.

110. It should also be noted that some versions of the question before Rav make no mention of Hanukah, according to which the situation is the same as in the story of Rabbah bar bar Ḥanah in b. Gittin 16b–17a (see above). See Rosenthal, "Le-Milon ha-Talmudi," pp. 58–64.

111. See Rosenthal, "Le-Milon ha-Talmudi," pp. 60–61 and 129–30.

112. See note 6 in chapter 1.

113. See, however, note 110.

114. Frequently, the anonymous editors attempt to respond to an objection multiple times. They suggest inadequate responses at first, explain why they are inadequate, and save the best one, the one that will not be refuted, for last. In such a situation, the editors' motive once again appears to be *lehagdil Torah u-leha'adirah* ("to increase Torah learning and make it glorious"), and in the process to explain why the final answer is superior to the rejected responses. It would have been possible to quote the final answer first, eliminating the need to cite the rejected answers, but this would have resulted in the diminution of Torah learning: we would not appreciate fully the superiority of the final answer, and would not know why other answers did not work as well. This common technique of the anonymous editors is not applicable in this instance, however, since we are dealing not with two (or more) answers to a single objection, only one of which is valid, but with single answers to two different objections, both of which stand in the end and neither of which is rejected as inadequate. One gains a false impression from the discussion as currently formulated, namely, that the second response works only to resolve the second objection.

CHAPTER 7

1. See Dor, *Torat Ereẓ-Yisrael be-Bavel*, for example, pp. 11–84.

2. See the conclusion.

3. The term "Josephus-like traditions" is intended to leave open the possibility that in several instances the Bavli and Josephus drew narratives from an earlier compilation no longer extant. See appendix 1 to this chapter.

4. As is well known, the printed texts of the Talmud often read "Sadducees," but examination of the manuscripts and medieval *testimonia* reveals that the correct reading is *minim*, "heretics." I have relied on Sussmann, "Ḥeker Toldot ha-Halakhah,'" pp. 44–45, n. 147; 46; 48–49, n. 166; 50, n. 168; 51–52, n. 171; and 53–55, n. 176; and Günter Stemberger, *Jewish Contemporaries of Jesus: Pharisees, Sadducees, Essenes* (Minneapolis: Fortress Press, 1995), pp. 38–66, for identification of the cases in which the correct reading is "Sadducees."

5. See also Sussmann, "Ḥeker Toldot ha-Halakhah," pp. 50–51, n. 168. Compare Anthony Saldarini, *Pharisees and Sadducees in Palestinian Society* (Edinburgh: T and T Clark, 1989), pp. 231–35. See also pp. 298–308, especially the bibliography cited at p. 298, n. 1.

6. Jean Le Moyne, *Les sadducéens* (Paris: Librairie Lecoffre, 1972), pp. 357–79; and Sussmann, "Ḥeker Toldot ha-Halakhah," p. 57, n. 185.

7. It bears emphasizing that my claim is not that the Sadducees actually were literalists, accepting only teachings they found "explicitly" in the Bible, but rather that the Sadducees are sometimes portrayed in this fashion in Josephus and in the Bavli. See the discussion below.

8. Regarding the connection between Josephus and several traditions in the Bavli, see Cohen, "Parallel Historical Traditions in Josephus and Rabbinic Literature," pp. 7–14; Stemberger, *Jewish Contemporaries of Jesus*, pp. 106–9; and chapters 2 and 3 here.

9. See the introduction.

10. In addition to the passages surveyed below, compare b. Eruvin 68b and m. Eruvin 6:2. According to m. Eruvin 6:2 (a Palestinian tradition), Sadducees are legally differentiated from non-Jews with regard to the laws of carrying within a courtyard on the Sabbath. According to the tradition in the Bavli, in contrast, the majority view of the Tannaim on this subject is that Sadducees have the status of non-Jews. See also Le Moyne, *Les sadducéens*, pp. 117–18. Compare also b. Sukkah 48b–49a and the parallels in y. Sukkah 4:8 (54d) and y. Yoma 1:5 (39a). See also t. Sukkah 3:16; Raymond Harari, "Rabbinic Perceptions of the Boethusians" (Ph.D. diss., New York University, 1995), pp. 145–64; and appendix 2 to this chapter for discussion of variation in rabbinic sources between Sadducees and Boethusians. Finally, see b. Baba Batra 115b and Rashbam, s.v. *Amar Rav Huna amar Rav, "Kol..."*

11. To my knowledge, this expression is without parallel elsewhere in rabbinic literature.

12. Or an individual.

13. See *Dikdukei Soferim*, ed. Rabbinovicz, n. *zayin*, who records one manuscript that lacks the phrase "to exclude the Sadducees" in the body of the text, and has it only in the margin. As noted throughout this book, manuscript variation is often indicative of a later editorial or a post-Talmudic addition to a text. In addition, several manuscripts have the Aramaic phrase responding to the question, also in Aramaic, "What is this?" If the interpolation were post-Talmudic, then it would fall outside the purview of this study.

14. M. Yoma 1:5.

15. The version in b. Menaḥot 65a–b features a controversy between Rabban Yoḥanan ben Zakkai and a Boethusian, and contains many of the same motifs. Due to the derivative character of the version in b. Baba Batra 115b–116a (see appendix 3 to this chapter), it is unlikely that Rav and Rav Huna, depicted as quoting the Baraita, were acquainted with the version before us. Compare Noam, *Megillat Ta'anit*, pp. 367–68. Stemberger, *Jewish Contemporaries of Jesus*, p. 63, also claims that the story in Baba Batra borrowed motifs from Menaḥot, but he does not justify his claim. The story in Baba Batra is paralleled in the Florence manuscript of Megillat Ta'anit (see Noam, *Megillat Ta'anit*, pp. 86–87 and 223–25). As noted in chapters 1 and 3, Noam argues that the earliest versions of the scholion to Megillat Ta'anit are of Palestinian origin. This is most likely not the case here, since the reading shared in common by Baba Batra and Megillat Ta'anit is a later reworking of the story in b. Menaḥot. In addition, in the case before us only the Florence manuscript of the scholion records the parallel, and as noted in chapter 3, Noam characterizes this manuscript as "more Babylonian" than the Oxford manuscript. In this case, it is likely that the "Babylonian" character of the Florence manuscript is the result of scribal contamination of the manuscript based on the Bavli. Shamma Friedman, "Shenei Inyanei Ḥanukah be-Skolion shel Megilat Ta'anit" (unpublished manuscript), argues plausibly that sometimes the version of a tradition in the Bavli is based on that of the scholion of Megillat Ta'anit, and sometimes the reverse is true. I thank Professor Friedman for showing me his manuscript in advance of its publication.

16. The following translation, with modifications, is based on that of Israel W. Slotki, *Baba Bathra* (London: Soncino, 1935), pp. 475–76.

17. Jastrow, *Dictionary*, p. 1156. Compare Levy, *Wörterbuch*, vol. 4, p. 28.

18. The term translated here as "old man" often has the meaning "elder" in rabbinic literature. In that sense the term is an expression of respect. In this context, the translation "old man" makes better sense.

19. See y. Baba Batra 8:1 (16a). See also t. Yadayim 2:20 (Boethusians vs. Pharisees), and the discussion below.

20. The following quotation is part of a lengthy discussion in b. Berakhot 28b–29a. The material quoted here probably originated independently of the larger discussion and was placed in its present context by later editors. For my present purposes, the larger context is irrelevant and is therefore omitted.

21. The term *tenan* generally introduces the quotation of a mishnah. The first half of the statement ("Do not trust yourself until the day of your death") is, in fact, found verbatim in m. Avot 2:4, while the second half is found in Pesikta de-Rav Kahana (see below), a post-Tannaitic midrashic compilation. The Bavli, apparently, intends to designate both halves as Tannaitic in origin.

22. Pesikta de-Rav Kahana, ed. Mandelbaum, p. 176.

23. See also Kalmin, *The Sage in Jewish Society*, pp. 61–67.

24. See also chapter 2 for further discussion of this story.

25. I omit the account of the origin of the Sadducees and Boethusians in Avot de-R. Natan, version B chap. 10 and version A chap. 5, ed. Schechter, p. 26, since Avot de-R. Natan was probably redacted later than the period surveyed in this study. While it probably contains some (much?) earlier material, it is difficult to determine whether or not any particular statement is early. The relevance of this tradition to the present study is therefore highly questionable. For the same reason, I also omit from the discussion traditions in the scholion of Megillat Ta'anit that lack parallels in ancient texts. See chapters 1 and 3.

26. Sifrei Numbers, ed. Horowitz, p. 121.

27. See also Shaye J. D. Cohen, "The Significance of Yavneh: Pharisees, Rabbis, and the End of Jewish Sectarianism," *Hebrew Union College Annual* 55 (1984), p. 39, n. 30.

28. See also Pesikta de-Rav Kahana, ed. Mandelbaum, p. 176, discussed above in connection with b. Berakhot 29a. T. Ḥagigah 3:35 may also be relevant: "A table that became impure, it is immersed at the appropriate time [*bi-zemano*], even on the Sabbath. It happened that they immersed the menorah [used in the Temple] on a holiday [*yom tov*] and the Sadducees said, 'Come and see the Pharisees who immerse the moon [*me'or ha-levanah*].'" Perhaps this story is critical of the Sadducees for ridiculing the Pharisees, but if so the criticism is quite muted. The Sadducees are not punished for their behavior, nor is it even explicit in the story that they are halakhically incorrect. See m. Ḥagigah 3:8; Saul Lieberman, *Tosefta ki-Feshutah*, vol. 5 (New York: Jewish Theological Seminary, 1962), p. 1336; and Stemberger, *Jewish Contemporaries*, p. 51. See also Sussmann, "Ḥeker Toldot ha-Halakhah," pp. 65–68, according to whom the Sadducees are not ridiculing the Pharisees. According to several portrayals in Palestinian and Babylonian sources, the Sadducees restrict their opposition to the theoretical realm, confining themselves to halakhic opinions contrary to those of the sages. With the exception of the occasional zealot, these stories claim, Sadducees are harmless, although the exceptional Sadducee who defies the sages in practice is in several instances a high priest, and is thus in a position to inflict significant damage to the community, since he plays a key role in the sacrificial cult. These occasional zealots, however, are swiftly punished with death at the hands of heaven, and the danger they pose is therefore localized and contained. See t. Parah 3:8; t. Niddah 5:3; b. Yoma 19b;

and b. Niddah 33b. See also t. Yoma 1:8 and y. Yoma 1:5 (39a–b) (par. y. Sukkah 4:8 [54d]) (involving Boethusians). We find the same motif in Josephus, *Antiquities* 18.15 and 18.17. Compare Stemberger, *Jewish Contemporaries of Jesus*, p. 63. One of these stories, t. Parah 3:8, is truncated, and parts of it are difficult to understand. It appears to contain the motif, familiar to us from other stories, of the father of the high priest accepting his son's death as punishment for his acting in accordance with Sadducean opinion. This story lacks, however, a clear statement of the obedience of Sadducees in general to the halakhic opinions of the sages.

29. Babylonian traditions: 8 out of a total of 21 (b. Berakhot 29a [twice]; b. Yoma 4a and b. Yoma 19b; b. Sukkah 48b–49a; b. Kiddushin 66a [twice]; and b. Baba Batra 115b–116a). Palestinian traditions: 1–3 out of a total of 18–19 (Pesikta de-Rav Kahana, ed. Mandelbaum, p. 11, and possibly Sifrei Numbers, ed. Horowitz, p. 121; and y. Eruvin 1:1 [18c]). Phrased in statistical terms, 38 percent of the Babylonian traditions about Sadducees are critical, as opposed to only 5–17 percent of the Palestinian traditions (although this sample is too small to be statistically significant). See also Stemberger, *Jewish Contemporaries of Jesus*, pp. 46–66; and Joseph M. Baumgarten, "The Pharisaic-Sadducean Controversies about Purity and the Qumran Texts," *Journal of Jewish Studies* 31, no. 2 (1980), pp. 165–69.

30. As noted, we find 18–19 traditions in Palestinian compilations and 21 in the Bavli. The 18–19 Palestinian traditions are found in m. Eruvin 6:2; m. Makkot 1:6; m. Parah 3:7; m. Niddah 4:2; m. Yadayim 4:6; m. Yadayim 4:7 (twice); t. Ḥagigah 3:35; t. Parah 3:7–8; t. Niddah 5:2–3; Sifra Aḥarei Mot Perek 3:11; Sifrei Numbers, ed. Horowitz, p. 121; Sifrei Deuteronomy, ed. Finkelstein, p. 231; Midrash Tannaim, ed. Hoffman, p. 117 (the text of this tradition, however, has probably been influenced by that of the parallel in the Bavli); y. Eruvin 1:1 (18c); y. Yoma 1:5 (39a–b); y. Sukkah 4:8 (54d) (and parallel); y. Baba Batra 8:1 (16a); Pesikta de-Rav Kahana, ed. Mandelbaum, p. 176; and possibly y. Sukkah 4:8 (58d) (and parallel). See also y. Sanhedrin 6:2 (23b). The 21 traditions in the Bavli are found in b. Berakhot 29a; b. Yoma 4a, 19b (twice), and 53a; b. Sukkah 48b–49a; b. Ḥagigah 16b (and parallel); b. Kiddushin 66a (twice); b. Baba Batra 115b–116a (twice); b. Sanhedrin 33b, 52b, and 90b; b. Horayot 4a and 4b; b. Menaḥot 65a; and b. Niddah 33b–34a (three times). B. Kiddushin 66a presents a particular problem, since the term "Sadducee" is not explicitly used but the comment by Rav Naḥman bar Yiẓḥak, and the editorial addition by the anonymous editors (see below) clearly assumes the story to be about Sadducees. The comment by Abaye in b. Berakhot 29a (see above) also has in mind this tradition, or one closely resembling it. I have therefore included it in my list of Bavli examples. In compiling the above figures, we count exact parallel traditions within a single compilation as one. I count as one cases in which the Sadducees are mentioned more than once in a single discussion, unless they are mentioned by more than one tradition within the discussion. For example, I count as two cases in which Sadducees are mentioned once in a single Baraita and then again in an Amoraic statement based on the Baraita. I also count as two cases in which the Sadducees are mentioned in two Amoraic statements. I count as one cases in which Sadducees are mentioned more than once in the Mishnah or Tosefta but the two usages occur within a single tradition; if they occur within separate traditions, I count them as two. To determine whether or not more than one tradition is involved, I do not rely on the traditional numbering system, since these divisions are later impositions onto the text and are often not consistent from one manuscript to the next. Instead, I attempt to determine whether or not a particular tradition or set of opinions would be quoted in the Talmud as a single tradition or as multiple traditions. It is certainly possible that I have incorrectly

categorized and counted some traditions, but this fact does not have a significant impact on my findings, since the errors will tend to cancel one another out. That is, if according to my criteria, I mistakenly inflate the number of cases in which Sadducees are mentioned in the Bavli, I will very likely do the same for the Yerushalmi, since I employ the same criteria for both compilations.

31. The exception is b. Baba Batra 115b–116a. See also b. Kiddushin 66a.

32. Cohen, "The Significance of Yavneh," pp. 39–40, points out that "the amoraim of Babylonia, begin to see themselves more clearly as the descendants of the Pharisees." See also Jaffee, *Torah in the Mouth*, pp. 52–60. Might this explain in part why the Bavli dislikes Sadducees, the traditional enemies of the Pharisees, whom Babylonian Amoraim came to view as their progenitors? This explanation, however, simply defers the problem, since the answer to one question ("Why is the Bavli anti-Sadducee?") raises another, equally difficult question ("Why do Babylonian rabbis identify with Pharisees?"). Perhaps it would be preferable to argue that the Bavli's dislike of the Sadducees and its greater sympathy for Pharisees, the Sadducees' opponents, are attributable to a single cause. Our task is to determine what that cause might have been.

33. I say "similar" because Palestinian traditions about Sadducees tend to be neutral, but not positive.

34. Kalmin, *The Sage in Jewish Society*, pp. 61–67 and 135–38.

35. Or what they considered to be Sadducean traits. See the discussion below. See also Martin Goodman, "A Note on Josephus, the Pharisees and Ancestral Traditions," *Journal for Jewish Studies* 50, no. 1 (1999), pp. 17–18; and Albert I. Baumgarten, "The Pharisaic Paradosis," *Harvard Theological Review* 80, no. 1 (1987), pp. 64–65 and 70.

36. Regarding Josephus's description of the Sadducees, see *Antiquities* 13.297 and 408; and 17.41. See also the discussion below.

37. Ben Zion Wacholder, *The Dawn of Qumran: The Sectarian Torah and the Teacher of Righteousness* (Cincinnati, Ohio: Hebrew Union College Press, 1983), pp. 141–69 and 264–70; and Yaakov Elman, "The World of the 'Sabboraim': Cultural Aspects of Post-Redactional Additions to the Bavli," paper delivered at the conference "Creation and Composition: The Contribution of the Bavli Redactors (Stammaim) to the Aggada," New York University, February 9–10, 2003, argue for the existence of proto-Karaite groups in Babylonia during these centuries. See also Elman, "Acculturation to Elite Persian Norms," pp. 38–43, who collects texts that describe Rava, a mid-fourth-century Babylonian rabbi, clashing with nonrabbis over the issue of rabbinic authority vis-à-vis the Bible. This question merits systematic study. For further discussion of possible connections (or the lack thereof) between Karaites and earlier Jewish groups, see, for example, Naphtali Wieder, *The Judean Scrolls and Karaism* (London: East and West Library, 1962), pp. 253–57; Yoram Erder, "Eimatai Heḥel ha-Mifgash shel ha-Kara'ut im Sifrut Apokrifit ha-Kerovah le-Sifrut ha-Megilot ha-Genuzot?" and "Divrei Teshuvah"; and Ḥaggai Ben-Shammai, "He'arot Metodi'ot le-Ḥeker ha-Yaḥas bein Kara'im le-Vein Kitot Yehudi'ot Kedumot (be-Heksher ha-Islami ve-ha-Ereẓ-Yisre'eli)," *Katedra* 42 (1987), pp. 54–68 and 85–86; and 69–84, respectively; Sussmann, "Ḥeker Toldot ha-Halakhah," pp. 45, n. 147 and 59, n. 187; and Robert Brody, *The Geonim of Babylonia and the Shaping of Medieval Culture* (New Haven: Yale University Press, 1998), pp. 85–95. Regarding the possibility of the continued existence in Palestine of Sadducees after the destruction of the Temple, perhaps for centuries, see Martin Goodman, "Sadducees and Essenes after 70 CE," in *Crossing the Boundaries; Essays in Biblical Interpretation in Honour of Michael D. Gouldner*, ed. Stanley E. Porter et al. (Leiden: Brill, 1994), pp. 347–56.

38. See Erder, "Eimatai," pp. 54–68; and Brody, *The Geonim of Babylonia*, pp. 85 and 88–89.

39. Erder, "Eimatai," p. 57.

40. Brody, *The Geonim of Babylonia*, p. 88.

41. B. Kiddushin 70a–b.

42. As noted in the previous chapter, one exception appears to have been the exilarch, whom Babylonian rabbis seem to have criticized only indirectly, via criticisms of the exilarch's servants, or his "household." The exilarch, however, was a politically powerful individual who had police power and would have been capable of inflicting great harm on the rabbis. Presumably proto-Karaites (if they existed) would not have been.

43. We read there:

> (A) Mishnah: [In the case of] monetary matters, they bring back [the accused] both for [possible] exoneration [following conviction] and for [possible] conviction [following exoneration]. [In the case of] a capital crime, they bring back [the accused] for [possible] exoneration [following conviction] but not for [possible] conviction [following exoneration].
>
> (B) Talmud: Said R. Ḥiyya bar Abba said R. Yoḥanan, "Provided that [the court] erred regarding a matter with which the Sadducees disagree."
>
> (C) But regarding a matter with which the Sadducees agree,
>
> (C1) it is a matter of "Go and read in [the children's] schoolhouse [*zil karei bei rav*]."

This brief discussion, like the discussion in b. Horayot 4a (see above), asserts that Sadducees accept scripture but reject rabbinic tradition. And like Horayot 4a and for the same reasons, the concluding sections, (C) and (C1), probably derive from the anonymous editors rather than from the early Amoraim (B). See the discussion below. Incidentally, part C is in Hebrew, but it does not stand by itself, without the Aramaic part (C1). If (C1) is a later addition to the statement, therefore, as I believe it is, then part C is also a later addition.

44. See Goodblatt, *Rabbinic Instruction in Sasanian Babylonia*, pp. 108–9.

45. See Catherine Hezser, *Jewish Literacy in Roman Palestine* (Tübingen: Mohr/Siebeck, 2001), pp. 68–72 and 75–84. As David Halivni pointed out in a paper delivered at the conference "Creation and Composition: The Contribution of the Bavli Redactors (Stammaim) to the Aggada," New York University, February 9–10, 2003, there are several references in the Bavli to "books of aggadah," but they are never said to have been studied by children.

46. Friedman, "Al Derekh Ḥeker ha-Sugya," pp. 25–26.

47. As also noted throughout this book, the term "originally" refers to the most "original" form of the statement that we are at present capable of reconstructing. It is possible, of course, that the statement looked different in earlier stages of development, but these are at present inaccessible to us.

48. Perhaps the expression "Go and read in [the children's] schoolhouse" is a proverb, and it is common to find popular proverbs rendered in Aramaic in rabbinic sources. This consideration may partly explain the change in language from Hebrew to Aramaic. This consideration, however, leaves unexplained a statement by Rav Sheshet in b. Horayot 4b, to be examined in detail below.

49. See note 47.

50. See Goodman, "A Note on Josephus," pp. 17–20.

51. See the preface and the introduction.

52. R. Ḥananel quotes the reading of the printed edition, but reports an alternative reading: "[If the court] rules concerning a matter in the Torah, [the members of the court] are exempt." According to this reading, this statement is not relevant to my inquiry since it does not mention the Sadducees.

53. Albeck, *Mavo la-Talmudim*, pp. 39–43.

54. Actually, the two statements. See note 43.

55. As well as that on b. Sanhedrin 33b.

56. See also chapter 2.

57. I am not convinced by the arguments of Ephraim E. Urbach, "Ha-Derashah ki-Yesod ha-Halakhah u-Va'ayat ha-Soferim," *Tarbiẓ* 27, nos. 2–3 (1958), p. 181; and *Ha-Halakhah*, p. 181, n. 52, in favor of the reading "written and lying," i.e., written and officially published in an archive. Urbach's claim depends upon emendation of the text (removal of the words "in a corner") and upon acceptance of a reading of the story attested only in some versions of a sixteenth-century anthology, Aggadot ha-Talmud.

58. Josephus, *Antiquities* 13.288–300.

59. I refer to Josephus's observation in the lengthy passage quoted above: "The Pharisees had passed on to the people certain regulations handed down by former generations and not recorded in the laws of Moses, for which reason they are rejected by the Sadducean group, who hold that only those regulations should be considered valid which were written down, and those which had been handed down by former generations need not be observed." See the discussion below.

60. See also Josephus, *Antiquities* 13.372–76.

61. See note 43.

62. And b. Sanhedrin 33b. See the discussion above.

63. With regard to the question of the date of the advent of this conception, see Peter Schäfer, "Das 'Dogma' von der mündlichen Torah im rabbinischen Judentum," in *Studien zur Geschichte und Theologie des Rabbinischen Judentums* (Leiden: Brill, 1978), pp. 153–97; and Stemberger, *Jewish Contemporaries of Jesus*, p. 94, n. 108. See also Jaffee, *Torah in the Mouth*, p. 10, who argues that for centuries there existed a distinction in practice between texts transmitted orally and in writing, without the crystallization of the concept of the oral Torah versus the written Torah. It is not out of the question that the same conceptual difference distinguishes the statement of Rav Naḥman bar Yiẓḥak and the later addition by the anonymous editors.

64. Mason, *Flavius Josephus on the Pharisees*, p. 217.

65. Ibid., p. 243. See also pp. 230–45. For further discussion of this passage, see Neusner, *Rabbinic Traditions about the Pharisees before 70*, pt. 3, pp. 163–65; Ellis Rivkin, *A Hidden Revolution* (Nashville, Tenn.: Abington, 1978), pp. 41–42; Baumgarten, "The Pharisaic Paradosis," pp. 64–65, 69, and 72, n. 33; Jaffee, *Torah in the Mouth*, pp. 50–52; Stemberger, *Jewish Contemporaries of Jesus*, pp. 93–95; Goodman, "A Note on Josephus," pp. 17–20, and the literature cited on p. 18, n. 3, there; and Daniel Boyarin, "The Diadoche of the Rabbis; Or, Judah the Patriarch at Yavneh," in *Jewish Culture and Society*, ed. Kalmin and Schwartz, p. 297, n. 318. Compare Urbach, "Ha-Derashah ki-Yesod ha-Halakhah," p. 181; Joseph M. Baumgarten, "The Unwritten Law in the Pre-Rabbinic Period," *Journal of Jewish Studies* 3 (1972), pp. 7–29; and Saldarini, *Pharisees and Sadducees*, p. 308 (but see p. 117, there).

66. See appendix 1 to this chapter.

67. See the discussion of b. Kiddushin 66a, above.

68. Josephus also depicts the Sadducees negatively in *Jewish War* 2.166 and *Antiquities* 20.199.

69. See, for example, Cohen, "Parallel Historical Traditions," pp. 13–14; and chapter 2 here.

70. Scholars disagree about the significance and derivation of the name "Boethusians." According to one view adopted by several scholars, the correct reading of the name in rabbinic texts is "Beit Sin." See, for example, Lieberman, *Tosefta ki-Feshutah*, vol. 4, pp. 870–71. I use the conventional spelling "Boethusians," however, to avoid unnecessary confusion. The issue of the original spelling and pronunciation of the name has no bearing on my findings.

71. For earlier discussions of the Boethusians, see, for example, M. D. Herr, "Mi Hayu ha-Baytosin?" in *Divrei ha-Kongress ha-Olami ha-Shevi'i le-Mada'ei ha-Yahadut* (Jerusalem: Ha-Igud ha-Olami le-Mada'ei ha-Yahadut, 1981), vol. 3, pp. 1–20, and the literature cited there.

72. See especially y. Yoma 1:5 (39a), where an opinion is attributed first to the Boethusians and subsequently to the Sadducees. Scholars have noted that the Tosefta prefers the term "Boethusians" to "Sadducees," using the term "Sadducee" in only one case, and referring to Boethusians even when parallel traditions use the term "Sadducee." This phenomenon has yet to receive a satisfactory explanation. See also Le Moyne, *Les sadducéens*, pp. 101–2; and Sussmann, "Ḥeker Toldot ha-Halakhah," pp. 51–52, n. 171, and pp. 52–53.

73. See also Sussmann, "Ḥeker Toldot ha-Halakhah," pp. 48–49 and nn. 166–67, who observes that the portrayal of Sadducees in rabbinic texts differs from the portrayal of Boethusians, in that the former, in contrast to the latter, are never mentioned in connection with calendrical matters or the dates of holidays.

74. See Josephus, *Antiquities* 13.298, who describes the Pharisees as having "the masses as their ally." See also *Antiquities* 13.401 and 18.17.

75. See note 28.

76. For further discussion of these texts, see Harari, "Rabbinic Perceptions of the Boethusians," pp. 235–53.

77. The reading of the printed text, *gadrum*, "fenced," should be emended to *garerum*, "dragged." See Jastrow, *Dictionary*, p. 272.

78. See, for example, m. Yadayim 4:6–7 compared to t. Yadayim 2:20. In the former case, Sadducees "cry out" against the Pharisees; in the latter, Boethusians "cry out" against them.

79. See also y. Sukkah 4:8 (51d) (and parallel), where this story is alluded to and quoted in part. The Yerushalmi does not inform us whether its version of the story reads "Boethusian" or "Sadducean."

80. It bears mentioning that according to Josephus, *Antiquities* 13.372, the villain of the story is Alexander Jannaeus, a Hasmonean king.

81. The conventional transliteration of this term is *kal ve-ḥomer*. See, however, Strack and Stemberger, *Introduction to the Talmud and Midrash*, p. 21.

82. See the references cited in note 19.

83. See the Tannaitic parallel in t. Yadayim 2:20.

84. According to the rabbis, human beings have the power to determine when the new month is proclaimed, which affects the date on which holidays are celebrated. If the rabbinical court decides to fix the new moon on Wednesday, a holiday celebrated on the fifteenth of that month will fall on a different date than if the new moon is fixed on Thursday, i.e., one day later. This is not at all the same, however, as

acknowledging the court's right to decide if the holiday is to be celebrated on the fifteenth of a given month, for example, or on the twentieth of that month.

CONCLUSION

1. See chapter 7. The term "literature," obviously, does not imply writing when the reference is to ancient rabbis. For another example of a story attested in Josephus and in the later stratum of the Babylonian Talmud, but not in Palestinian rabbinic literature, see *Antiquities* 14.168–76 and b. Sanhedrin 19a–b. Most of the differences between Josephus's and the Bavli's versions of the story can easily be attributed to Babylonian editors, who in all likelihood introduced Babylonian motifs and preoccupations into the story. For example, Herod is the villain of the Josephan tale, but the Bavli's villain is Yannai, in conformity with the Bavli's tendency to depict Yannai as the prototypical wicked king (see chapters 2 and 7). In addition, the king's opponent in the Bavli's story is Shimon ben Shetach rather than Samaias in Josephus, in line with the Bavli's tendency to portray Shimon ben Shetach as Yannai's major antagonist (see b. Berakhot 48a, b. Kiddushin 66a, and b. Sanhedrin 107b). Finally, it is likely that the conclusion of the story in the Bavli is the product of later editors who brought it in line with the mishnah (m. Sanhedrin 2:2), as I have repeatedly noted was the motive for the Bavli's editorial changes in chapters 2 and 3. The story is introduced into the Talmud by the anonymous editors based on a statement by Rav Yosef, an Amora of the early fourth century. For further discussion of this story, see Cohen, *Josephus in Galilee and Rome*, p. 253, n. 29; and "Parallel Historical Traditions in Josephus and Rabbinic Literature," pp. 9–10 (Cohen concludes, p. 10, that the narrative under discussion is one of the cases in which "the rabbinic and the Josephan accounts differ in numerous details . . . but the identity of the stories is clear nevertheless"); Efron, *Ḥikrei ha-Tekufah ha-Ḥashmona'it*, pp. 158–62; Goodblatt, *The Monarchic Principle*, pp. 112–13; and Kalmin, *The Sage in Jewish Society*, pp. 65–67.

2. See the discussion of the story involving Abuha de-Shmuel and Levi in b. Avodah Zarah 43b (paralleled in b. Rosh Hashanah 24b), in chapter 5.

3. See chapter 4.

4. See chapters 2 and 3.

5. See the literature cited in note 20 of the introduction.

6. See Dor, *Torat Ereẓ Yisrael be-Bavel*; and "Teshuvah le-Ma'amaro shel A. Goldberg," *Tarbiẓ* 34, no. 1 (1964), p. 98; Epstein, *Mevo'ot le-Sifrut ha-Amoraim*, pp. 79 and 297; Urbach, *Ha-Halakhah*, pp. 207, 214–16, and 318, n. 55; Gafni, *Yehudei Bavel*, pp. 107–8; Eliezer Segal, *Case Citation in the Babylonian Talmud: The Evidence of the Tractate Neziqin* (Atlanta: Scholars Press, 1990), pp. 35–59; Strack and Stemberger, *Introduction to the Talmud and Midrash*, pp. 218–19; Kalmin, *Sages, Stories, Authors, and Editors*, pp. 87–94; Pinhas Hayman, "Alteration and Change in the Teachings of R. Yohanan ben Nafha through Transfer from Israel to Babylonia" (Ph.D. diss., Yeshiva University, 1989); "Disputation Terminology and Editorial Activity in the Academy of Rava bar Yosef bar Hama," *Hebrew Union College Annual* 72 (2001), pp. 61–83, especially p. 62; and "From Tiberias to Mehoza: Redactorial and Editorial Processes in Amoraic Babylonia," *Jewish Quarterly Review* 93, nos. 1–2 (2002), pp. 117–48. See also the discussion and the literature cited below.

7. Dor emphasized the special connection between Rava "and his school" to the opinions of R. Yoḥanan, but he also emphasized the special affinity of later Babylonian

rabbis for Palestinian learning in general (pp. 15–16, n. 7; p. 16, n. 1; p. 24; p. 36, especially n. 12; pp. 66–73; 77; 79–115; and 127–40).

8. See note 6. See, however, Avraham Goldberg, "Ḥadirat ha-Halakhah shel Ereẓ Yisrael le-Tokh Masoret Bavel ke-Fi she-Hi Mishtakefet mi-Tokh Perek Arvei Pesaḥim," *Tarbiẓ* 33, no. 4 (1964), pp. 337–48; and Ephraim B. Halivni, *Kelalei Pesak ha-Halakhah ba-Talmud* (Lud, Israel: Makhon Haberman le-Meḥkerei Sifrut, 1999), pp. 102–4. Halivni's arguments are primarily directed against a detail of Dor's claim that Rava favored the authority of R. Yoḥanan. I am interested in showing the special affinity of mid-fourth-century (and later) Babylonian rabbis for traditions and modes of behavior deriving from Palestine and beyond, and Halivni's arguments do not challenge that thesis.

9. Christine E. Hayes, *Gentile Impurities and Jewish Identities: Intermarriage and Conversion from the Bible to the Talmud* (Oxford: Oxford University Press, 2002), pp. 190–91.

10. B. Baba Batra 21a. See Gafni, *Yehudei Bavel*, pp. 107–8. See also b. Megillah 26a vis-à-vis y. Megillah 3:2 (74a); Josephus *Jewish War* 2.569; and *Antiquities* 4.287, cited by Gafni on p. 108, n. 82. See also pp. 109–12, where Gafni documents the transformation of the Babylonian synagogue from a place of prayer alone to a place of learning as well. In this respect, the Babylonian synagogue comes to resemble the Palestinian synagogue, and the two traditions that portray a "Palestinianized" Babylonian synagogue involve rabbis of the mid–fourth century and later. See also pp. 138–48, for Gafni's discussion of Babylonian rabbinic attitudes toward conversion.

11. Kalmin, *Sages, Stories, Authors, and Editors*, pp. 87–88. See also pp. 89–91.

12. Or *Ba'a*.

13. B. Baba Meẓia 57a (Rava-Ḥasa-R. Ami [see *Dikdukei Soferim*, ed. Rabbinovicz, nn. *bet* and *gimel*]); and b. Ḥullin 53b (Rav Papi-Rav Bibi bar Abaye).

14. For an additional respect in which later Babylonian rabbinic literature conforms to Palestinian rabbinic models, see b. Sanhedrin 8a (the anonymous editors based on a statement by Rav Naḥman bar Yiẓḥak) and Kalmin, *The Sage in Jewish Society*, pp. 94–100. In addition, as noted in chapter 4, Rava appears to be the only Babylonian Amora to be depicted as coming in contact with *minim* ("heretics"), while portrayals of contact between *minim* and Palestinian rabbis are relatively frequent. See also Kalmin, *The Sage in Jewish Society*, pp. 38–39, where I describe the Palestinian rabbinic practice of addressing nonrabbis affectionately as "my son," or "my daughter," and p. 128, n. 52, where I discuss a possible instance of the same phenomenon involving a later Babylonian Amora.

15. Kalmin, *Sages, Stories, Authors, and Editors*, pp. 46–47, 58–59, and 89–94.

16. Dor, *Torat Ereẓ Yisrael be-Bavel*, p. 13; and Kalmin, *Sages, Stories, Authors, and Editors*, pp. 46–47.

17. Kalmin, *Sages, Stories, Authors, and Editors*, pp. 58–59. See also Dor, *Torat Ereẓ-Yisrael be-Bavel*, pp. 11–84 and 94–113.

18. See Carey A. Moore, "Judith, Book of," in *The Anchor Bible Dictionary*, ed. David Noel Freedman (New York: Doubleday, 1992), vol. 3, p. 1123.

19. The translation is that of Carey A. Moore, *The Anchor Bible: Judith* (Garden City, N.Y.: Doubleday, 1985), p. 14.

20. This is not to suggest that all or even most Palestinian rabbis believed that the urge to worship idols disappeared among Jews during the second Temple period (see Friedheim, "Yehudim Ovdei Avodah-Zarah," pp. 27–40). Rather, my claim is that

the idea is attested in rabbinic Palestine, and that it is not attested in Babylonia until the mid–fourth century.

21. See Albeck, *Mavo la-Talmudim*, pp. 155–56. The fact that R. Ḥanina's opinion is juxtaposed to that of Rav makes it likely that R. Ḥanina bar Ḥama, a Palestinian rabbi, is referred to.

22. On the other hand, later editors (how late, we cannot say) may have reformulated Rav's statement to fit the context (i.e., as an alternative to R. Ḥanina's view), according to which they, rather than Rav, are acquainted with R. Ḥanina's opinion.

23. It is true that the names Rav Ashi and R. Asi often interchange, so we cannot exclude the possibility that the story involves the third-generation Palestinian R. Asi. However, the story's use of the term *pirka*, which almost without exception is used in stories and traditions involving Babylonian rabbis (see, for example, Goodbatt, *Rabbinic Instruction*, pp. 171–96), renders this possibility quite remote.

24. See Friedheim, "Yehudim Ovdei Avodah-Zarah," p. 29, n. 46. See also b. Sanhedrin 63b–64a, where we find a tradition that describes the partial neutralization of the urge to worship idols. See also the parallel in b. Yoma 69b. Originally, however, the tradition referred to the sexual impulse, and it was the anonymous editors of b. Sanhedrin 63b–64a who interpreted it as referring to idol worship. According to the Saul Lieberman database, "This is it" is the reading of the following manuscripts of b. Sanhedrin 64a: (1) Yad ha-Rav Herẓog; (2) Florence 7–9 I II; (3) Munich 95 (the words "urge of idolatry" are written in the margin). "This is it" is also the reading of ms. JTS 270 218 EMC of b. Yoma 69b. Mss. Vatican 134 and Munich 6 of Yoma; and Kahlsruhe Reuchlin 2 of Sanhedrin 64a read "The prophet said to Israel, 'This is the one of whom it is said, "This is Wickedness"'" (Zekh. 5:8). Ms. JTS 271 1623 EMC of Yoma reads: "The prophet said to Israel, 'Grab it.'" The printed edition and ms. Munich 95 of Yoma 69b read "The prophet said to Israel, 'This is the urge to worship idols.'" See *Dikdukei Soferim*, ed. Rabbinovicz, n. *vav*, on Yoma 69b, according to which the Oxford manuscript reads "the evil urge to worship idols." The manuscripts that mention "the [evil] urge to idolatry" have almost certainly been "corrected" by scribes wishing to conform the tradition to its context in Sanhedrin 63b–64a, which demands that it deal with idolatry. This is most likely the interpretation of the later anonymous editors, however, rather than an integral part of the tradition, which refers to sexual temptation. The logic of the interpretation of the anonymous editors is the similarity between the urge to worship idols and the urge to engage in forbidden sex asserted by several Talmudic traditions.

25. B. Berakhot 10b (Abaye or Rava); b. Taanit 21b–22a (Abaye and Abba the bloodletter); b. Baba Meẓia 22a (Amemar, Mar Zutra, Rav Ashi, and Mari bar Isak); and b. Ḥullin 133a (the anonymous editors, Rav Safra, Rava, Rav Yosef, and a priest). See below for a discussion of strikingly similar traditions in Palestinian compilations. See also the references cited in the notes immediately following, and the discussion below of similar motifs, in traditions in Palestinian compilations.

26. B. Shabbat 23b (Rava); and b. Ketubot 52b–53a (Rav Papa, Yehudah bar Maremar, and Abba Sura'ah).

27. B. Sanhedrin 27a–b (Rav Papi and Bar Ḥama).

28. B. Shabbat 23b (Rava); b. Nedarim 81a (Rav Sheshet b. d'Rav Idi, Mar Zutra, and Rav Ashi); b. Yevamot 45b (Rava and Rav Mari bar Rachel); and b. Baba Batra 149a (Rava and Rav Mari, the son of Isur the convert). See also the discussion below.

29. B. Rosh Hashanah 6a (Rava); b. Ketubot 67b (Rava); b. Baba Batra 9a (Rav Papa and Rav Sama b. de-Rav Yeyva); and b. Baba Batra 10a (Rav Papa and Ḥiyya bar Rav Midifti).

30. B. Kiddushin 71a (Rav Naḥman bar Yiẓḥak); b. Kiddushin 71a (Abaye); and b. Kiddushin 72b (Rav Zevid Minehardea and Amemar).

31. See the literature cited in the introduction.

32. I have translated the verse in accordance with its midrashic meaning (see below). The translation of the Jewish Publication Society renders "You give them their food when it is due."

33. See Sokoloff, *Dictionary of Jewish Babylonian Aramaic*, p. 434.

34. See also b. Rosh Hashanah 6a (Rava). A story in b. Baba Batra 9a, also involving later Babylonian rabbis (Rav Papa and Rav Sama b. de-Rav Yeyva), makes the same point. See also b. Ketubot 67b, where Rava and Rav Papa are the only rabbis who comment on several Tannaitic sources that emphasize the importance of giving charity directly to the poor.

35. It is unlikely that R. Yoḥanan and R. Shimon ben Lakish quoted a statement by R. Elazar. There has evidently been some editorial tampering with the story.

36. See also Kalmin, *The Sage in Jewish Society*, p. 43, and the traditions cited in p. 130, n. 67, there.

37. See Sokoloff, *Dictionary of Jewish Babylonian Aramaic*, p. 1110.

38. It is unclear whether "Doron" is the name of a person or a place.

39. We find the identical motif in Lamentations Rabbah 3:17 (R. Abahu and Yosi Reisha); and y. Terumot 2:3 (41c) (R. Ḥama bar Ḥaninah and his father at the springs of Geder) (see also the parallel in y. Shabbat 3:1 [5d]).

40. Literally, "let his eye be dimmed."

41. See Sokoloff, *Dictionary of Jewish Babylonian Aramaic*, pp. 442, 594, and 978.

42. Ibid., pp. 193 and 1051.

43. The syntax suggests that the rabbi is speaking to the defendant, Bar Ḥama, although it is surprising that Bar Ḥama would be addressed in this fashion.

44. See Sokoloff, *Dictionary of Jewish Babylonian Aramaic*, p. 599.

45. For another example preserved in a Palestinian compilation and involving a Palestinian rabbi, see y. Sotah 1:4 (16d) (R. Meir).

46. Literally, "distanced it."

47. Literally, "to distance and to bring near."

48. Kalmin, *The Sage in Jewish Society*, pp. 51–60.

49. A nazir vows to abstain from drinking wine and cutting the hair.

50. For this interpretation of the mishnah, see, for example, b. Kiddushin 69b (R. Elazar).

51. Regarding this place name, see Oppenheimer, *Babylonia Judaica in the Talmudic Period*, p. 189, n. 40. Compare Ben-Ẓion Eshel, *Yishuvei ha-Yehudim be-Bavel bi-Tekufat ha-Talmud* (Jerusalem: Magnes Press, 1979), pp. 144–45.

52. See, for example, b. Kiddushin 70a–b. See also Urbach, *Ha-Halakhah*, pp. 214 and 318, n. 53.

53. Literally, "Rav Mari, [Isur's] son, was born in [a state of] holiness but was not conceived in a state of holiness."

54. See Sokoloff, *Dictionary of Jewish Babylonian Aramaic*, p. 892.

55. See Albeck, *Mavo la-Talmudim*, p. 369. Compare Hyman, *Toldot Tannaim ve-Amoraim*, pp. 903–5, and Gafni, *Yehudei Bavel*, p. 139, n. 85.

56. See Kalmin, *The Sage in Jewish Society*, pp. 46–47, and the references cited there. I have not yet found the motif, however, in Palestinian compilations, but only in the Bavli.

57. See Kalmin, *The Sage in Jewish Society*, pp. 31–32. Thus far, however, I have found only one such tradition in a Palestinian compilation. See t. Avodah Zarah

3:9–10; b. Ketubot 62b–63a (R. Akiba, Ben Kalba Savu'ah, and R. Akiba's wife); b. Nedarim 51a (Rabbi and Ben Elasha); b. Sanhedrin 99a (R. Yoḥanan).

58. Regarding the expression *Ẓurba mei-Rabbanan,* see Sokoloff, *Dictionary of Jewish Babylonian Aramaic,* pp. 956–57. I am not as confident as Sokoloff that the precise nuance of the term is "a member of an intermediate scholarly class between the common people and the scholars." First, the term *ẓurba* is often missing in manuscripts and medieval testimonia (it is, in fact, suspect here; see *Dikdukei Soferim,* ed. Rabbinovicz, n. *yud*), and second, the expression's meaning is not consistent. A systematic study of the expression is a desideratum.

59. Kalmin, *The Sage in Jewish Society,* p. 32. See also b. Ketubot 52b–53a (Rav Papa, Yehudah bar Maremar, and Abba Sura'ah).

60. See also b. Nedarim 81a (Rav Sheshet b. de-Rav Idi, Mar Zutra, and Rav Ashi); and Kalmin, *The Sage in Jewish Society,* pp. 42–43. It is possible, although unlikely, that Rava is referring only to men of rabbinic ancestry who aspire to become rabbis themselves, but not to men of nonrabbinic ancestry.

61. See Sifrei Deuteronomy, ed. Finkelstein, pp. 415–16; Genesis Rabba, ed. Theodor and Albeck, pp. 841, 843, 1220–21, and 1262–63; Leviticus Rabbah, ed. Margaliot, pp. 110–14, 570–71, and 669–71; and y. Sotah 7:4 (21d) and Ephraim E. Urbach, "Magamot Dati'ot ve-Ḥevrati'ot be-Torat ha-Ẓedakah shel Ḥazal," *Ẓion* 16 (1951), p. 25, n. 176. See also Kalmin, *The Sage in Jewish Society,* pp. 29–32, and the references cited at pp. 125–26 and nn. 14 and 21.

62. A *Ẓurba mei-Rabbanan.* See note 58.

63. See Kalmin, *The Sage in Jewish Society,* pp. 75–79 and 140–42, and the references cited there. For other later Babylonian traditions that make the same point, see b. Ta'anit 24a (and *Massekhet Ta'anit,* ed. Henry Malter [New York: American Academy for Jewish Research, 1930], p. 106, nn. on l. 8); and b. Sanhedrin 102b (the anonymous editors) and the discussion of this tradition in Kalmin, *The Sage in Jewish Society,* pp. 49–50. Another Babylonian tradition makes the same point (b. Ta'anit 22a [Rav Beroka Ḥoza'ah; see Oppenheimer, *Babylonia Judaica,* pp. 86–90]), but we cannot date the protagonist of the story.

64. Peter Brown, "Eastern and Western Christendom in Late Antiquity: A Parting of the Ways," in *Society and the Holy in Late Antiquity* (Berkeley: University of California Press, 1982), pp. 184–85.

65. See *Dikdukei Soferim,* ed. Rabbinovicz, n. *zayin,* for variants of the name.

66. See also b. Ḥullin 133a (Rava, Rav Safra, Rav Yosef [the teacher of both rabbis], and the anonymous editors); and the discussion in Kalmin, *The Sage in Jewish Society,* pp. 30–31.

67. Or Rava. See note 65.

68. See also, for example, b. Pesaḥim 10a; b. Ketubot 27a; b. Baba Batra 138a; and b. Ḥullin 89a; and Dor, *Torat Ereẓ Yisrael be-Bavel,* p. 12. In general, we find such transmissional confusion between rabbis who are contemporaries, and who are either both from Babylonia or both from Palestine.

69. As noted in the preface, the Yerushalmi appears to have been edited late in the fourth or early in the fifth century. The latest rabbis mentioned in it by name lived in the latter part of the fourth century, and it has a layer of anonymous editorial discourse much thinner than that of the Bavli. See Bokser, "An Annotated Bibliographical Guide to the Study of the Palestinian Talmud," p. 55; and Strack and Stemberger, *Introduction to the Talmud and Midrash,* pp. 188–89. Compare Sussmann, "Ve-Shuv le-Yerushalmi Nezikin," pp. 101–5.

70. See, for example, Friedman, *Talmud Arukh*, vol. 1, pp. 31–37, especially n. 90 on p. 33; and "La-Aggadah ha-Historit ba-Talmud ha-Bavli"; Rubenstein, *Talmudic Stories*, pp. 24–26, and the copious literature cited in nn. 96–97 at pp. 310–11. A systematic study of this issue is a desideratum, which unfortunately cannot be undertaken here.

71. Gray, *A Talmud in Exile*, pp. 1–39; Rubenstein, *Culture*, pp. 1–11 and 16–142; Boyarin, *Border Lines*, pp. 151–225.

72. Millar, *The Roman Near East*, p. 510. See also pp. 516–17.

73. Chapters 2 and 3 were also concerned with literature rather than behavior.

Bibliography

SECONDARY SOURCES

Aderet, Avraham. *Mei-Ḥurban li-Tekumah: Derekh Yavneh be-Shikum ha-Umah.* Jerusalem: Magnes Press, 1990.

Agus, Aharon. *The Binding of Isaac and Messiah: Law, Martyrdom and Deliverance in Early Rabbinic Religiosity.* Albany: State University of New York Press, 1988.

Aḥdut, Eli. "Ha-Polmos ha-Yehudi-Zoroastri ba-Talmud ha-Bavli." In Shaked and Netzer, *Irano-Judaica,* vol. 4, pp. 17–40.

Albeck, Ḥanokh. *Mavo la-Talmudim.* Tel Aviv: Devir, 1969.

Alon, Gedalya. *Toldot ha-Yehudim be-Ereẓ Yisrael bi-Tekufat ha-Mishnah ve-ha-Talmud.* 2 vols. Tel Aviv: Ha-Kibuẓ ha-Me'uḥad, 1952–55.

———. "Paritin: Le-Toldot ha-Kehunah ha-Gedolah be-Sof Yemei Bayit Sheni." In *Meḥkarim be-Toldot Yisrael bi-Yemei Bayit Sheni u-bi-Tekufat ha-Mishnah ve-ha-Talmud,* vol. 1, pp. 48–76. Tel Aviv: Ha-Kibuẓ ha-Me'uḥad, 1957.

———. "Nesi'uto shel Rabban Yoḥanan ben Zakkai." In *Meḥkarim be-Toldot Yisrael bi-Yemei Bayit Sheni u-bi-Tekufat ha-Mishnah ve-ha-Talmud,* vol. 1, pp. 253–74. Tel Aviv: Ha-Kibuẓ ha-Me'uḥad, 1957.

———. "The Sons of the Sages." In *Jews, Judaism and the Classical World,* trans. Israel Abrahams, pp. 436–57. Jerusalem: Magnes Press, 1977.

Asmussen, Jes P. "Christians in Iran." In Yarshater, *The Cambridge History of Iran,* vol. 3, pt. 2, pp. 924–48.

Baer, Yiẓḥak. "Yerushalayim bi-Yemei ha-Mered ha-Gadol." *Ẓion* 36, nos. 3–4 (1971), pp. 127–90.

Bammel, Ernst. "Der achtundzwanzigster Adar." *Hebrew Union College Annual* 28 (1957), pp. 109–13.

Barnes, T. D. "Constantine and the Christians of Persia." *Journal of Roman Studies* 75 (1985), pp. 126–36.

Basser, Herbert W. "Uncovering the Plots: The Image of Rabbi Shimon bar Yohai." In *The 2001 Mathers Lecture, the 2001 Rosen Lecture, and Other*

Queen's University Essays in the Study of Judaism, ed. Jacob Neusner, pp. 37–62. Binghamton, N.Y.: Global Publication, Binghamton University, 2001.

Baumgarten, Albert I. "Rabbi Judah I and His Opponents." *Journal for the Study of Judaism* 12, no. 2 (1981), pp. 135–72.

———. "The Pharisaic Paradosis." *Harvard Theological Review* 80, no. 1 (1987), pp. 63–77.

———. "Rabbinic Literature as a Source for the History of Jewish Sectarianism in the Second Temple Period." *Dead Sea Discoveries* 2, no. 1 (1995), pp. 14–57.

Baumgarten, Joseph. "Art in the Synagogue: Some Talmudic Views." *Judaism* 19, no. 2 (1970), pp. 196–207.

———. "The Unwritten Law in the Pre-Rabbinic Period." *Journal for the Study of Judaism* 3 (1972), pp. 7–29.

———. "The Pharisaic-Sadducean Controversies about Purity and the Qumran Texts." *Journal of Jewish Studies* 31, no. 2 (1980), pp. 57–70.

Beard, Mary, John North, and Simon Price, eds. *Religions of Rome*. Vol. 1. *A History*. Cambridge: Cambridge University Press, 1998.

Becker, Adam. "Devotional Study: The School of Nisibis and the Development of 'Scholastic' Culture in Late Antique Mesopotamia." Ph.D. diss., Princeton University, 2004.

Beer, Moshe. *Rashut ha-Golah bi-Yemei ha-Mishnah ve-ha-Talmud*. Tel Aviv: Devir, 1976.

———. "Al Shalosh Gezerot she-Nigzeru al Yehudei Bavel be-Me'ah ha-Shelishit." In Shaked and Netzer, *Irano-Judaica*, vol. 1, pp. 25–37 (Hebrew section).

———. "Ha-Reka ha-Medini u-Feiluto shel Rav be-Bavel." *Ẓion: Sefer Yovel* 50 (1985), pp. 155–72.

———. "Gezerotav shel Kartir al Yehudei Bavel." *Tarbiẓ* 55, no. 4 (1986), pp. 525–39.

Ben-Ḥayyim-Trifon, Daliah. "Ha-Reka ha-Politi ha-Penimi shel Mered Bar-Kokhba." In Oppenheimer and Rapaport, *Mered Bar-Kokhba: Meḥkarim Ḥadashim*, pp. 13–26.

———. "Ha-Kohanim mei-Ḥurban Bayit Sheni ve-ad Aliyat ha-Noẓrut." Ph.D. diss., University of Tel Aviv, 1985.

Ben-Shamai, Ḥaggai. "He'arot Metodi'ot le-Ḥeker ha-Yaḥas bein Kara'im le-Vein Kitot Yehudi'ot Kedumot (be-Heksher ha-Islami ve-ha-Ereẓ-Yisre'eli)." *Katedra* 42 (1987), pp. 69–84.

Binyamini, Yafa. "Ha-Mythos shel Rabbi Shimon bar Yoḥai: Iyun be-Aggadat Ḥazal." *Meḥkerei Ḥag* 12 (2001), pp. 87–102.

Blidstein, Gerald. "R. Yohanan, Idolatry, and Public Privilege." *Journal for the Study of Judaism* 5, no. 2 (1974), pp. 154–61.

Bohak, Gideon. "'Joseph and Aseneth' and the Jewish Temple in Heliopolis." Ph.D. diss., Princeton University, 1994.

———. "CPJ III, 520: The Egyptian Reaction to Onias' Temple." *Journal for the Study of Judaism* 26, no. 1 (1995), pp. 32–41.

———. *Joseph and Aseneth and the Jewish Temple in Heliopolis*. Atlanta: Scholars Press, 1996.

Bokser, Baruch M. *Post Mishnaic Judaism in Transition: Samuel on Berakhot and the Beginnings of Gemara*. Chico, Calif.: Scholars Press, 1980.

———. "An Annotated Bibliographical Guide to the Study of the Palestinian Talmud." In *Aufstieg und Niedergang der römischen Welt* 2:19/2 (1979). Reprinted in *The Study of Ancient Judaism*. Vol. 2, *The Palestinian and Babylonian Talmuds*, ed. Jacob Neusner, pp. 1–119. New York: Ktav, 1981.

———. "Wonder-Working and the Rabbinic Tradition: The Case of Hanina ben Dosa." *Journal for the Study of Judaism* 16, no. 1 (1985), pp. 42–92.
Bowersock, Glen W. "A Roman Perspective on the Bar Kokhba Revolt." In *Approaches to Ancient Judaism*, vol. 2, ed. William Scott Green, pp. 131–41. Chico, Calif.: Scholars Press, 1980.
Boyarin, Daniel. *Intertextuality and the Reading of Midrash*. Bloomington: Indiana University Press, 1990.
———. *Carnal Israel: Reading Sex in Talmudic Culture*. Berkeley: University of California Press, 1993.
———. *Dying for God: Martyrdom and the Making of Christianity and Judaism*. Stanford: Stanford University Press, 1999.
———. "The Diadoche of the Rabbis; Or, Judah the Patriarch at Yavneh." In Kalmin and Schwartz, *Jewish Culture and Society under the Christian Roman Empire*, pp. 285–318.
———. *Border Lines: The Partition of Judaeo-Christianity*. Philadelphia: University of Pennsylvania Press, 2004.
Boyce, Mary. "Toleranz und Intoleranz im Zoroastrismus." *Saeculum* 21 (1970), pp. 325–43.
———. "Iconoclasm among the Zoroastrians." In *Christianity, Judaism and Other Greco-Roman Cults: Studies for Morton Smith at Sixty*, pt. 4, ed. Jacob Neusner, pp. 93–111. Leiden: Brill, 1975.
———. *Zoroastrians: Their Religious Beliefs and Practices*. London: Routledge, 1979.
Boyce, Mary, and Frantz Grenet. *A History of Zoroastrianism*. Vol. 3. *Zoroastrianism under Macedonian and Roman Rule*. Leiden: Brill, 1991.
Brakke, David. *Athanasius and the Politics of Asceticism*. Oxford: Clarendon Press, 1995.
Breuer, Yoḥanan. "Gadol mei-Rav Rabbi, Gadol mei-Rabbi Rabban, Gadol mei-Rabban Shemo." *Tarbiẓ* 66, no. 1 (1997), pp. 41–59.
Brock, Sebastian. "Christians in the Sasanian Empire: A Case of Divided Loyalties." In *Religion and National Identity: Studies in Church History*, ed. Stuart Mews, pp. 1–19. Oxford: Blackwell, 1982.
———. "From Antagonism to Assimilation: Syriac Attitudes to Greek Learning." In Garsoïan et al., *East of Byzantium*, pp. 17–34.
———. "Eusebius and Syriac Christianity." In *Eusebius, Christianity, and Judaism*, ed. Harold W. Attridge and Gohei Hata, pp. 212–34. Detroit, Mich.: Wayne State University Press, 1992.
Brody, Robert. "Judaism in the Sasanian Empire: A Case Study in Religious Coexistence." In Shaked and Netzer, *Irano-Judaica*, vol. 2, pp. 52–62.
———. *The Geonim of Babylonia and the Shaping of Medieval Culture*. New Haven: Yale University Press, 1998.
———. "Stam ha-Talmud ve-Divrei ha-Amoraim. Paper delivered at the World Congress of Jewish Studies, Jerusalem, July 31–August 4, 2005.
Brown, Peter. "The Diffusion of Manichaeism in the Roman Empire." *Journal of Roman Studies* 59 (1969), pp. 92–103.
———. "Eastern and Western Christendom in Late Antiquity: A Parting of the Ways." In *Society and the Holy in Late Antiquity*, pp. 166–95. Berkeley: University of California Press, 1982.
———. "The Rise and Function of the Holy Man in Late Antiquity." *Journal of Roman Studies* 61 (1971), pp. 80–101. Reprinted, with additions, in *Society and*

the Holy in Late Antiquity, pp. 103–52. Berkeley: University of California Press, 1982.

Brüll, Nahum. "Die Entstehungsgeschichte der babylonischen Talmuds als Schriftwerk." *Jahrbücher für jüdische Geschichte und Literatur* 2 (1876), pp. 1–123.

Bubis, Mauricio. "Am Yisrael bein Paras le-Romi: Ha-Imut bein Malkhut Paras ve-ha-Keisarut ha-Romit, ve-Hashpa'atah al Ḥayyei ha-Yehudim bi-Tekufat ha-Talmud." Ph.D. diss., Hebrew University, 1990.

Büchler, Adolf. *Ha-Sanhedrin bi-Yerushalayim u-Veit ha-Din ha-Gadol she-be-Lishkat ha-Gazit*. Jerusalem: Mosad ha-Rav Kuk, 1974 (*Das Synedrin in Jerusalem und das Grosse Beth-din in der Quaderkammer des jerusalemischen Tempels*).

Bundy, David. "Christianity in Syria." In Freedman, *The Anchor Bible Dictionary*, vol. 1, pp. 970–79.

Cameron, Alan. *The Mediterranean World in Late Antiquity* AD *395–600*. London: Routledge, 1993.

Chegini, N. N., and A. V. Nikitin. "Sasanian Iran: Economy, Society, Arts and Crafts." In Litvinsky et al., *History of Civilizations of Central Asia*, vol. 3, pp. 35–77.

Chernick, Michael. " 'Turn It and Turn It Again': Culture and Talmud Interpretation." *Exemplaria* 12, no. 1 (2000) (*"Turn It Again": Jewish Medieval Studies and Literary Theory*), pp. 63–103.

Cohen, Gerson D. "Ma'asei Ḥannah ve-Shivat Banehah be-Sifrut ha-Ivrit." In *Sefer ha-Yovel li-Kevod Mordechai Menaḥem Kaplan*, ed. Moshe Davis, pp. 109–23 (Hebrew section). New York: Jewish Theological Seminary, 1953.

Cohen, Shaye J. D. *Josephus in Galilee and Rome: His Vita and Development as a Historian*. Leiden: Brill, 1979.

———. "The Significance of Yavneh: Pharisees, Rabbis, and the End of Jewish Sectarianism." *Hebrew Union College Annual* 55 (1984), pp. 27–53.

———. "Parallel Traditions in Josephus and Rabbinic Literature." In *Proceedings of the Ninth World Congress of Jewish Studies*, div. 2, vol. 1, pp. 7–14. Jerusalem: World Union of Jewish Studies, 1986.

———. *From the Maccabees to the Mishnah*. Philadelphia: Westminster Press, 1987.

———. "The Place of the Rabbi in Jewish Society of the Second Century." In *The Galilee in Late Antiquity*, ed. Lee I. Levine, pp. 157–73. New York: Jewish Theological Seminary, 1992.

———, ed. *The Synoptic Problem in Rabbinic Literature*. Providence, R.I.: Brown Judaic Studies, 2000.

De Jong, Albert. *Traditions of the Magi: Zoroastrianism in Greek and Latin Literature*. Leiden: Brill, 1997.

Delcor, M. "Le temple d'Onias en Égypte: Réexamen d'un vieux problème." *Revue Biblique* 75, no. 2 (1968), pp. 188–203.

Derenbourg, Joseph. *Essai sur l'histoire et la géographie de la Palestine*. Paris, 1867.

Dodgeon, Michael H., and Samuel N. C. Lieu, eds. *The Roman Eastern Frontier and the Persian Wars (*AD *226–363): A Documentary History*. London: Routledge, 1991.

Dor, Ẓvi. "Teshuvah le-Ma'amaro shel A. Goldberg." *Tarbiẓ* 34, no. 1 (1964), p. 98.

———. *Torat Ereẓ Yisrael be-Bavel*. Tel Aviv: Devir, 1971.

Downey, Glanville. *A History of Antioch in Syria: From Seleucus to the Arab Conquest*. Princeton: Princeton University Press, 1961.

Drijvers, Hans. "The Persistence of Pagan Cults and Practices in Christian Syria." In Garsoïan et al., *East of Byzantium*, pp. 35–43.

Efron, Yehoshua. *Ḥikrei ha-Tekufah ha-Ḥashmona'it*. Tel Aviv: Ha-Kibuẓ ha-Me'uḥad, 1980.

———. "Milḥemet Bar-Kokhba le-Or ha-Masoret ha-Talmudit ha-Ereẓ-Yisre'elit ke-Neged ha-Bavlit." In Oppenheimer and Rapaport, *Mered Bar-Kokhba: Meḥkarim Ḥadashim*, pp. 47–105.

Eliav, Yaron. "Viewing the Scriptural Environment: Shaping the Second Commandment." In Schäfer, *The Talmud Yerushalmi and Graeco-Roman Culture*, vol. 3, pp. 413–15.

———. "Al Avodah Zarah be-Veit ha-Merḥaẓ ha-Romi: Shtei He'arot." *Katedra* 110 (2004), pp. 173–80.

Elman, Yaakov. "The Suffering of the Righteous in Palestinian and Babylonian Sources." *Jewish Quarterly Review* 80, nos. 3–4 (1990), pp. 315–39.

———. "Righteousness as Its Own Reward: An Inquiry into the Theologies of the Stam." *Proceedings of the American Academy of Jewish Research* 57 (1991), pp. 35–67.

———. " 'It Is No Empty Thing': Nahmanides and the Search for Omnisignificance." *Torah u-Madda Journal* 5 (1993), pp. 1–83.

———. *Authority and Tradition: Toseftan Baraitot in Talmudic Babylonia*. Hoboken, N.J.: Ktav, 1994.

———. "How Should a Talmudic Intellectual History Be Written? A Response to David Kraemer's *Responses*." *Jewish Quarterly Review* 89, nos. 3–4 (1999), pp. 361–86.

———. "Marriage and Marital Property in Rabbinic and Sasanian Law." In *Rabbinic Law in Its Roman and Near Eastern Context*, ed. Catherine Hezser, pp. 227–76. Tübingen: Mohr/Siebeck, 2003.

———. "The World of the 'Sabboraim': Cultural Aspects of Post-Redactional Additions to the Bavli." Paper presented at the conference "Creation and Composition: The Contribution of the Bavli Redactors (Stammaim) to the Aggada," New York University, February 9–10, 2003.

———. "Acculturation to Elite Persian Norms and Modes of Thought in the Babylonian Jewish Community of Late Antiquity." In *Netiot LeDavid: Jubilee Volume for David Weiss Halivni*, ed. Ephraim Halivni et al., pp. 31–56. Jerusalem: Orhot Press, 2004.

———. " 'He in His Cloak and She in Her Cloak': Conflicting Images of Sexuality in Sasanian Mesopotamia." In *Discussing Cultural Influences: Text, Context, and Non-Text in Rabbinic Judaism: Proceedings of a Conference on Rabbinic Judaism at Bucknell University*, ed. Rivka Kern-Ulmer. Forthcoming.

———. "Middle Persian Culture and Babylonian Sages: Accommodation and Resistance in the Shaping of Rabbinic Legal Traditions." In *Cambridge Companion to Rabbinic Literature*, ed. Charlotte E. Fonrobert and Martin S. Jaffee. Cambridge: Cambridge University Press. Forthcoming.

Epstein, J. N. *Mevo'ot le-Sifrut ha-Amoraim*. Jerusalem: Magnes Press, 1962.

———. *Mavo le-Nusaḥ ha-Mishnah*. 2nd ed. Jerusalem: Magnes Press, 1964.

Erder, Yoram. "Divrei Teshuvah." *Katedra* 42 (1987), pp. 85–86.

———. "Eimatai Heḥel ha-Mifgash shel ha-Kara'ut im Sifrut Apokrifit ha-Kerovah le-Sifrut ha-Megilot ha-Genuzot?" *Katedra* 42 (1987), pp. 54–68.

Eshel, Ben-Ẓion. *Yishuvei ha-Yehudim be-Bavel bi-Tekufat ha-Talmud*. Jerusalem: Magnes Press, 1979.

Fiey, J.-M. "Aones, Awun et Awgin (Eugène). Aux origins du monachisme mésopotamien." *Analecta Bollandiana* 80 (1962), pp. 52–81.

———. "Topographie chrétienne de Mahoze." *L'Orient Syrien* 12 (1967), pp. 397–420.

Finkelstein, Louis. *Mevo le-Masekhtot Avot ve-Avot de-Rabbi Natan*. New York: Jewish Theological Seminary, 1961.

———. "The Men of the Great Synagogue (*circa* 400–170 B.C.E.)." In *The Cambridge History of Judaism*, vol. 2, ed. W. D. Davies and Louis Finkelstein, pp. 229–44. Cambridge: Cambridge University Press, 1989.
Fitzmayer, Joseph A., and Daniel J. Harrington. *A Manual of Palestinian Aramaic Texts*. Rome: Biblical Institute Press, 1978.
Florsheim, Yoel. "R. Menaḥem (=Naḥum) ben Simai." *Tarbiẓ* 45, nos. 1–2 (1975–76), pp. 151–53.
Flusser, David. "Ha-Hishkiḥah Am Yisrael et ha-Ḥashmona'im bi-Yemei ha-Beina'im?" *Katedra* 75 (1995), pp. 36–54.
Fowden, Garth. "The Pagan Holy Man in Late Antique Society." *Journal of Hellenic Studies* 102 (1982), pp. 33–59.
———. *Empire to Commonwealth: Consequences of Monotheism in Late Antiquity*. Princeton: Princeton University Press, 1993.
Fox, R. Lane. *Pagans and Christians*. London: Penguin, 1986.
Fraenkel, Yonah. "Bible Verses Quoted in Tales of the Sages." *Scripta Hierosolymitana* 22 (1971), pp. 80–99.
———. *Darkhei ha-Aggadah ve-ha-Midrash*. 2 vols. Givatayim, Israel: Yad la-Talmud, 1991.
Frankel, Zechariah. *Mevo ha-Yerushalmi*. Breslau, 1870.
Freedman, David Noel, ed. *The Anchor Bible Dictionary*. 6 vols. New York: Doubleday, 1992.
Friedheim, Immanuel. "Yehudim Ovdei Avodah-Zarah be-Ereẓ-Yisrael bi-Tekufat ha-Mishnah ve-ha-Talmud." In *Divrei ha-Kongress ha-Olami ha-Shneim-Asar le-Mada'ei ha-Yahadut*, div. 2, *Toldot Am Yisrael*, pp. 21–44. Jerusalem: Ha-Igud ha-Olami le-Mada'ei ha-Yahadut, 2000.
Friedman, Shamma. "Mivneh Sifruti be-Sugyot ha-Bavli." In *Divrei ha-Kongress ha-Olami ha-Shishi le-Mada'ei ha-Yahadut*, div. 3, vol. 3, pp. 391–96. Jerusalem: Ha-Igud ha-Olami le-Mada'ei ha-Yahadut, 1977.
———. "Al Derekh Ḥeker ha-Sugya." In *Perek ha-Ishah Rabbah ba-Bavli*, pp. 7–45. Jerusalem: Jewish Theological Seminary, 1978.
———. "Al ha-Aggadah ha-Historit ba-Talmud ha-Bavli." In *Sefer Zikaron le-R. Shaul Lieberman*, ed. Shamma Friedman, pp. 119–64. Jerusalem: Saul Lieberman Institute for Talmudic Research, 1993.
———. *Talmud Arukh*. Vol. 1, *Ha-Perushim*. Jerusalem: Jewish Theological Seminary, 1990.
———. *Talmud Arukh*. Vol. 2, *Ha-Nusaḥim*. Jerusalem: Jewish Theological Seminary, 1996.
———. "Ha-Baraitot ba-Talmud ha-Bavli ve-Yaḥasam le-Makbiloteihen she-ba-Tosefta." In *Atarah le-Ḥayim: Meḥkarim be-Sifrut ha-Talmudit ve-ha-Rabbanit li-Kevod Professor Ḥayim Zalman Dimitrovsky*, ed. Daniel Boyarin et al., pp. 163–201. Jerusalem: Magnes Press, 2000.
———. "The Further Adventures of Rav Kahana: Between Babylonia and Palestine." In Schäfer, *The Talmud Yerushalmi and Graeco-Roman Culture*, vol. 3, pp. 247–71.
———. "Shenei Inyanei Ḥanukah be-Skolion shel Megilat Ta'anit." Unpublished paper, 2004.
———. "Sippur Rav Kahana ve-R. Yoḥanan (BK 117a–b) ve-Anaf Nusaḥ Geniza-Hamburg." In *Sefer Zikaron li-Kevod Meyer Feldblum*. Forthcoming.
Frye, Richard N. *The Heritage of Persia*. Cleveland: World, 1963.
———. *The Golden Age of Persia: The Arabs in the East*. New York: Harper & Row, 1975.
———. *The History of Ancient Iran*. Munich: Beck, 1984.

Fürst, Julius. "Geschichte der jüdischen Literatur in Babylonien." *Literaturblatt des Orients* 14 (1847), pp. 210–15.
Gafni, Isaiah. "Ha-Yeshivah ha-Bavlit la-Or Sugyat B. K. 117a." *Tarbiẓ* 49, nos. 1–2 (1979–80), pp. 292–301.
———. "Ḥiburim Nestorianim ki-Makor le-Toldot Yeshivot Bavel." *Tarbiẓ* 51, no. 4 (1982), pp. 567–76.
———. "Expressions and Types of 'Local Patriotism' among the Jews of Babylonia." In Shaked and Netzer, *Irano-Judaica*, vol. 2, pp. 63–71.
———. "Batei-Keneset Ba'alei Zikah Historit be-Bavel ha-Talmudit." In Oppenheimer et al., *Batei-Keneset Atikim*, pp. 147–54.
———. *Yehudei Bavel bi-Tekufat ha-Talmud*. Jerusalem: Merkaz Zalman Shazar le-Toldot Yisrael, 1990.
———, ed. *Merkaz u-Tefuẓah: Ereẓ Yisrael ve-ha-Tefuẓot bi-Yemei Bayit Sheni, ha-Mishnah ve-ha-Talmud*. Jerusalem: Merkaz Zalman Shazar le-Toldot Yisrael, 2004.
Garsoïan, Nina G. "Byzantium and the Sasanians." In Yarshater, *Cambridge History of Iran*, vol. 3, pt. 1, pp. 568–92.
———. "Armenia in the Fourth Century: An Attempt to Redefine the Concepts 'Armenia' and 'Loyalty.'" *Revue des études arméniennes* 8 (1971), pp. 341–52. Reprinted in *Armenia between Byzantium and the Sasanians*. London: Varorium Reprints, 1985.
———. "Prolegomena to a Study of the Iranian Aspects of Arsacid Armenia." *Zeitschrift für armenische Philologie* 90 (1976), pp. 177–234. Reprinted in *Armenia between Byzantium and the Sasanians*, pp. 1–46. London: Variorum Reprints, 1985.
Garsoïan, Nina G., et al., eds. *East of Byzantium: Syria and Armenia in the Formative Period*. Washington, D.C.: Dumbarton Oaks, 1982.
Geiger, Yosef. "Ha-Gezerah al ha-Milah u-Mered Bar-Kokhba." *Ẓion* 41, nos. 3–4 (1976), pp. 139–47.
———. "Pulḥan ha-Shalitim be-Ereẓ-Yisrael ha-Romit." *Katedra* 111 (2004), p. 11.
Geller, Markham J. "Alexander Jannaeus and the Pharisee Rift." *Journal of Jewish Studies* 30, no. 3 (1979), pp. 202–11.
Gero, Stephen. "The See of Peter in Babylon: Western Influences on the Ecclesiology of Early Persian Christianity." In Garsoïan et al., *East of Byzantium*, pp. 45–51.
Gignoux, Philippe. "Religions and Religious Movements, Part One: Zoroastrianism." In Litvinsky et al., *History of Civilizations of Central Asia*, vol. 3, pp. 403–12.
Gillman, Ian, and Hans-Joachim Klimkeit. *Christians in Asia before 1500*. Richmond, England: Curzon Press, 1999.
Ginzberg, Louis. "He'arot le-Arukh ha-Shalem." In *Additamenta ad Librum Aruch Completum*, ed. Samuel Krauss, pp. 417–37. Vienna: Alexander Kohut Foundation, 1937.
Gnoli, Gherardo. *Zoroaster's Time and Homeland: A Study on the Origins of Mazdeism and Related Problems*. Naples: Instituto Universitario Orientale, 1980.
Goehring, James E. "The Origins of Monasticism." In *Eusebius, Christianity, and Judaism*, ed. Harold W. Attridge and Gohei Hata, pp. 235–55. Detroit, Mich.: Wayne State University Press, 1992.
———. "Withdrawing into the Desert: Pachomius and the Development of Village Monasticism in Upper Egypt." *Harvard Theological Review* 89 (1996), pp. 267–85.

Goldberg, Avraham. "Ḥadirat he-Halakhah shel Ereẓ Yisrael le-Tokh Masoret Bavel ke-Fi she-Hi Mishtakefet mi-Tokh Perek Arvei Pesaḥim." *Tarbiẓ* 33, no. 4 (1964), pp. 337–48.

———. "The Babylonian Talmud." In *The Literature of the Sages*. Pt. 1, *Oral Torah, Halakha, Mishna, Tosefta, Talmud, External Tractates*. Compendia Rerum Iudaicarum ad Novum Testamentum, sec. 2. Vol. 3, The Literature of the Jewish People in the Period of the Second Temple and the Talmud, ed. Shmuel Safrai, pp. 323–45. Assen: Van Gorcum, 1987.

Goldenberg, Robert. *The Nations That Know Thee Not: Ancient Jewish Attitudes toward Other Religions*. New York: New York University Press, 1998.

Goldsmith, Simcha. "The Role of the *Tanya Nami Hakhi Baraita*." *Hebrew Union College Annual* 73 (2002), pp. 133–56.

Goodblatt, David. *Rabbinic Instruction in Sasanian Babylonia*. Leiden: Brill, 1975.

———. "Towards the Rehabilitation of Talmudic History." In *History of Judaism: The Next Ten Years*, ed. Baruch M. Bokser, pp. 31–44. Chico, Calif.: Scholars Press, 1980.

———. "The Babylonian Talmud." In *Aufstieg und Niedergang der römischen Welt* 2:19/2 (1979). Reprinted in *The Study of Ancient Judaism*. Vol. 2, *The Palestinian and Babylonian Talmuds*, ed. Jacob Neusner, pp. 120–99. New York: Ktav, 1981.

———. "Ha-To'ar 'Nasi' ve-ha-Reka ha-Dati-Ideologi shel ha-Mered ha-Sheni." In Oppenheimer and Rapaport, *Mered Bar-Kokhba: Meḥkarim Ḥadashim*, pp. 113–32.

———. *The Monarchic Principle: Studies in Jewish Self-Government in Antiquity*. Tübingen: Mohr/Siebeck, 1994.

Goodman, Martin. "Sadducees and Essenes after 70 CE." In *Crossing the Boundaries: Essays in Biblical Interpretation in Honour of Michael D. Gouldner*, ed. Stanley E. Porter et al., pp. 347–56. Leiden: Brill, 1994.

———. "A Note on Josephus, the Pharisees and Ancestral Traditions." *Journal of Jewish Studies* 50, no. 1 (1999), pp. 17–20.

———. "The Jewish Image of God in Late Antiquity." In Kalmin and Schwartz, *Jewish Culture and Society under the Christian Roman Empire*, pp. 133–45.

Gray, Alyssa. *A Talmud in Exile: The Influence of Yerushalmi Avodah Zarah on the Formation of Bavli Avodah Zarah*. Providence, R.I.: Brown Judaic Studies, 2005.

Green, William Scott. "What's in a Name? The Problematic of Rabbinic 'Biography.'" In *Approaches to Ancient Judaism: Theory and Practice*, ed. William Scott Green, pp. 77–96. Missoula, Mont.: Scholars Press, 1978.

———. "Palestinian Holy Men: Charismatic Leadership and Rabbinic Tradition." In *Aufstieg und Niedergang der römischen Welt* 2:19/2 (1979), pp. 619–47.

Grossmark, Ẓiona. "Halakhot Avodah Zarah be-Takhshitim ke-Bavu'ah le-Yaḥasei Yehudim ve-Nokhrim be-Ereẓ-Yisrael bi-Yemei ha-Mishnah ve-ha-Talmud." In *Yehudim ve-Nokhrim be-Ereẓ-Yisrael bi-Yemei ha-Bayit ha-Sheni, ha-Mishnah ve-ha-Talmud*, ed. Aharon Oppenheimer et al., pp. 1–8. Jerusalem: Yad Yiẓḥak Ben-Ẓvi, 2003.

Gruen, Erich S. "The Origins and Objectives of Onias' Temple." In *Studies in Memory of Abraham Wasserstein*, vol. 2, ed. H. M. Cotton et al., pp. 47–70 (*Scripta Classica Israelica* 16 [1997]).

Hadas-Lebel, Mireille. "Le paganisme à travers les sources rabbiniques des IIe et IIIe siècles: Contribution à l'étude du syncrétisme dans l'empire romain." In *Aufstieg und Niedergang der römischen Welt* 2:19/2 (1979), pp. 397–489.

Halbertal, Moshe, and Avishai Margalit. *Idolatry*, trans. Naomi Goldblum. Cambridge, Mass.: Harvard University Press, 1992.

Halevi, A. A. *Sha'arei ha-Aggadah.* Tel Aviv: A. Armony, 1963.
———. *Ha-Aggadah ha-Historit-Biografit le-Or Mekorot Yevani'im ve-Latini'im.* Tel Aviv: A. Armony, 1975.
Halevy, Yiẓḥak. *Dorot ha-Rishonim.* 4 vols. 1897–1939. Reprint, Jerusalem, 1967.
Halivni, David. *Mekorot u-Mesorot: Nashim.* Tel Aviv: Devir, 1968.
———. *Mekorot u-Mesorot: Yoma-Ḥagigah.* Jerusalem: Jewish Theological Seminary, 1975.
———. *Mekorot u-Mesorot: Shabbat.* Jerusalem: Jewish Theological Seminary, 1982.
———. *Midrash, Mishnah, and Gemara: The Jewish Predilection for Justified Law.* Cambridge, Mass.: Harvard University Press, 1986.
———. *Peshat and Derash: Plain and Applied Meaning in Rabbinic Exegesis.* New York: Oxford University Press, 1991.
Halivni, Ephraim Beẓalel. *Kelalei Pesak ha-Halakhah ba-Talmud.* Lud, Israel: Makhon Haberman le-Meḥkerei Sifrut, 1999.
Hampel, Ido. "Megillat Ta'anit." Ph.D. diss., Tel Aviv University, 1976.
Harari, Raymond. "Rabbinic Perceptions of the Boethusians." Ph.D. diss., New York University, 1995.
Harris, Jay. *How Do We Know This?* Albany: State University of New York Press, 1995.
Harris, William V. "On the Applicability of the Concept of Class in Roman History." In *Forms of Control and Subordination in Antiquity,* ed. Toru Yuge and Masaoki Doi, pp. 598–610. Leiden: Brill, 1988.
Hasan-Rokem, Galit. *Web of Life: Folklore and Midrash in Rabbinic Literature.* Stanford: Stanford University Press, 2000.
Hauptman, Judith. *Development of the Talmudic Sugya: Relationship between Tannaitic and Amoraic Sources.* Lanham, Md.: University Press of America, 1988.
———. *Rereading the Mishnah: A New Approach to Ancient Jewish Texts.* Tübingen: Mohr/Siebeck, 2005.
Hayes, Christine E. *Between the Babylonian and Palestinian Talmuds: Accounting for Halakhic Difference in Selected Sugyot from Tractate Avodah Zarah.* Oxford: Oxford University Press, 1997.
———. "Displaced Self-Perceptions: The Deployment of *Minim* and Romans in *B. Sanhedrin 90b–91a.*" In *Religious and Ethnic Communities in Roman Palestine,* ed. Hayim Lapin, pp. 249–89. Bethesda; University Press of Maryland, 1998.
———. *Gentile Impurities and Jewish Identities: Intermarriage and Conversion from the Bible to the Talmud.* Oxford: Oxford University Press, 2002.
Hayman, Pinhas. "Alteration and Change in the Teachings of R. Yohanan ben Nafha through Transfer from Israel to Babylonia." Ph.D. diss., Yeshiva University, 1989.
———. "Disputation Terminology and Editorial Activity in the Academy of Rava bar Yosef bar Hama." *Hebrew Union College Annual* 72 (2001), pp. 61–83.
———. "From Tiberias to Mehoza: Redactorial and Editorial Processes in Amoraic Babylonia." *Jewish Quarterly Review* 93, nos. 1–2 (2002), pp. 117–48.
Hayward, Robert. "The Jewish Temple of Leontopolis: A Reconsideration." *Journal of Jewish Studies* 33, nos. 1–2 (1982) (*Essays in Honour of Yigal Yadin*), pp. 429–43.
Heinemann, Yiẓḥak. *Darkhei ha-Aggadah.* Jerusalem: Magnes Press, 1970.
Hengel, Martin. *Judentum und Hellenismus: Studien zu ihrer Begegnung unter besonderer Berücksichtigung Palästinas bis zur Mitte des 2. Jhs. V. Chr.* Tübingen: Mohr, 1969.
———. *Judaism and Hellenism.* 2 vols. Philadelphia: Fortress Press, 1974.
Henning, W. B. "The Great Inscription of Sapur I." *Bulletin of the School of Oriental Studies* 9 (1939), pp. 823–49.

Herman, Geoffrey. "Ha-Kohanim be-Bavel bi-Tekufat ha-Talmud." Master's thesis, Hebrew University, 1998.

———. "The Story of Rav Kahana (BT Baba Qamma 117a–b) in Light of Armeno-Persian Sources." In Shaked and Netzer, *Irano-Judaica*, vol. 6. Forthcoming.

Hermann, Georgina. "Naqsh-i Rustam 6: The Roman Victory of Shapur I and The Bust And Inscription of Kerdir," in *Iranische Denkmäler*, fasc. 13, "The Sasanian Rock Reliefs at Naqsh-i Rustam," pp. 13–33. Berlin: Dietrich Reimer, 1989.

Herr, M. D. "Persecutions and Martyrdom in Hadrian's Days." *Scripta Hierosolymitana* 23 (1972), pp. 85–125.

———. "The Participation of Galilee in the 'War of Qitus' or in the 'Bar Kosba Revolt.'" *Katedra* 4 (1977), pp. 67–73.

———. "Ha-Reẓef she-be-Shalshelet Mesiratah shel ha-Torah le-Beirur ha-Historiografiah ha-Mikra'it ba-Hagutam shel Ḥazal." *Ẓion* 44 (1979) (*Sefer Zikaron le-Yiẓḥak Baer*), pp. 43–56.

———. "Mi Hayu ha-Baytosin?" In *Divrei ha-Kongress ha-Olami ha-Shevi'i le-Mada'ei ha-Yahadut*, vol. 3, pp. 1–20. Jerusalem: Ha-Igud ha-Olami le-Mada'ei ha-Yahadut, 1981.

Hezser, Catherine. *Form, Function, and Historical Significance of the Rabbinic Story in Yerushalmi Neziqin*. Tübingen: Mohr/Siebeck, 1993.

———. *The Social Structure of the Rabbinic Movement in Roman Palestine*. Tübingen: Mohr/Siebeck, 1997.

———. *Jewish Literacy in Roman Palestine*. Tübingen: Mohr/Siebeck, 2001.

Hirsch, S. A. "The Temple of Onias." In *Jews' College Jubilee Volume*, pp. 39–80. London: Luzac, 1906.

Hoffman, David Zvi. *Mar Samuel: Rector der jüdischen Akademie zu Nehardea in Babylonien*. Leipzig: O. Leiner, 1873.

Hyman, Aharon. *Toldot Tannaim ve-Amoraim*. 1910. Reprint, Jerusalem: Makhon Peri ha-Arez, 1987.

Irshai, Oded. "'Ateret Rosho ke-Hod ha-Melukhah Ẓanuf Ẓefirat Shesh le-Kavod u-le-Tiferet': Li-Mekomah shel ha-Kehunah be-Ḥevrat ha-Yehudit shel Shilhei ha-Et ha-Atikah." In *Reẓef u-Temurah: Yehudim ve-Yahadut be-Ereẓ Yisrael ha-Bizantit-Noẓrit*, ed. Lee I. Levine, pp. 67–106. Jerusalem: Merkaz Dinur le-Ḥeker Toldot Yisrael, 2004.

Isaac, Benjamin, and Aharon Oppenheimer. "The Revolt of Bar Kokhba: Ideology and Modern Scholarship." In Benjamin Isaac, *The Near East under Roman Rule: Selected Papers*, pp. 220–56. Leiden: Brill, 1998.

Jacobs, Martin. "Pagane Tempel in Palästina: Rabbinische Aussagen im Vergleich mit archäologischen Funden." In *The Talmud Yerushalmi and Graeco-Roman Culture*, vol. 2, ed. Peter Schäfer and Catherine Hezser, pp. 139–59. Tübingen: Mohr/Siebeck, 2000.

Jaffee, Martin S. *Torah in the Mouth: Writing and Oral Tradition in Palestinian Judaism, 200 BCE–400 CE*. Oxford: Oxford University Press, 2001.

Jastrow, Marcus. *A Dictionary of the Targumim, Talmud Babli, Yerushalmi, and Midrashic Literature*. 1886–1903. Reprint, New York: Judaica Press, 1971.

Jeremias, Joachim. *Jerusalem in the Time of Jesus*. Trans. F. H. and C. H. Cave. Philadelphia: Fortress Press, 1969.

Jones, A. H. M. "The Social Background of the Struggle between Paganism and Christianity." In *The Conflict between Paganism and Christianity in the Fourth Century*, ed. Arnaldo Momigliano, pp. 17–37. Oxford: Clarendon, 1963.

Justi, Ferdinand. *Geschichte des alten Persiens*. Berlin: G. Grote, 1879.

Kalmin, Richard. "Christians and Heretics in Rabbinic Literature of Late Antiquity." *Harvard Theological Review* 87, no. 2 (1994), pp. 155–69.

———. "The Modern Study of Ancient Rabbinic Literature: Yonah Fraenkel's *Darkhei ha'aggadah veha-midrash.*" *Prooftexts* 14 (1994), pp. 189–204.

———. *Sages, Stories, Authors, and Editors in Rabbinic Babylonia.* Atlanta: Scholars Press, 1994.

———. *The Sage in Jewish Society of Late Antiquity.* London: Routledge, 1999.

———. "Rabbinic Portrayals of Biblical and Post-Biblical Heroes." In Cohen, *The Synoptic Problem in Rabbinic Literature,* pp. 119–41.

———. "Rabbinic Traditions about Roman Persecutions of the Jews: A Reconsideration." *Journal of Jewish Studies* 54, no. 1 (2003), pp. 21–50.

———. "The Formation and Character of the Babylonian Talmud." In *The Cambridge History of Judaism,* vol. 4, *The Late Roman-Rabbinic Period,* ed. Steven Katz, pp. 840–76. Cambridge: Cambridge University Press, 2006.

Kalmin, Richard, and Seth Schwartz, eds. *Jewish Culture and Society under the Christian Roman Empire.* Leuven: Peeters, 2003.

Kamin, Sarah. "Rashi's Exegetical Categorization with Respect to the Distinction between Peshat and Derash: According to His Commentary to the Book of Genesis and Selected Passages from His Commentaries to Other Books of the Bible." *Immanuel* 11 (1980), pp. 16–32.

———. *Rashi: Peshuto shel Mikra u-Midrasho shel Mikra.* Jerusalem: Magnes Press, 1986.

Kasher, Arye. *The Jews in Hellenistic and Roman Egypt.* Tübingen: Mohr/Siebeck, 1985.

Kettenhofen, Erich. *Die römisch-persischen Kriege des 3. Jahrhunderts n. Chr.* Wiesbaden: Ludwig Reichert, 1982.

Kieval, Philip. "The Talmudic View of the Hasmonean and Early Herodian Periods in Jewish History." Ph.D. diss., Brandeis University, 1970.

Kimelman, Reuven. "Ha-Oligarkiah ha-Kohanit ve-Talmidei ha-Ḥakhamim bi-Tekufat ha-Talmud." *Ẓion* 48, no. 2 (1983), pp. 135–47.

Klein, Shmuel. "Die Baraita des Vierundzwanzig Priestabteilhungen." Ph.D. diss., University of Heidelberg, 1909.

———. "Review of Paul Kahle: *Masoreten des Westens.*" *Monatschrift für die Geschichte und Wissenschaft des Judentums* 73, nos. 1–2 (1929), pp. 69–73.

Klima, Otakar. *Manis Zeit und Leben.* Prague: Czechoslovakian Academy of Sciences, 1962.

Kohut, Alexander, ed. *Arukh ha-Shalem.* 8 vols. 1878–92. Reprint, Vienna: Menorah, 1926.

Kraemer, David C. "On the Reliability of Attributions in the Babylonian Talmud." *Hebrew Union College Annual* 60 (1989), pp. 175–90.

Krauss, Samuel. *Griechische und lateinische Lehnwörter im Talmud, Midrasch und Targum.* Vol. 2. 1899. Reprint, Hildesheim: G. Olms, 1964.

———. *Paras ve-Romi ba-Talmud u-va-Midrashim.* Jerusalem: Mosad ha-Rav Kuk, 1948.

Lang, D. M. "Iran, Armenia, and Georgia." In Yarshater, *The Cambridge History of Iran,* vol. 3, pt. 1, pp. 505–36.

Lapin, Hayim. Review of *The Sage in Jewish Society of Late Antiquity,* by Richard Kalmin. Paper presented at the AAR/SBL conference in Nashville, Tennessee, November 19, 2000.

Le Moyne, Jean. *Les sadducéens.* Paris: Librairie Lecoffre, 1972.

Levine, Lee I. "R. Simeon b. Yohai and the Purification of Tiberias: History and Tradition." *Hebrew Union College Annual* 49 (1978), pp. 143–85.

———. "Ha-Ma'avak ha-Politi bein ha-Perushim li-Ẓedukim bi-Tekufat ha-Ḥashmona'it." In *Perakim be-Toldot Yerushalayim bi-Yemei Bayit Sheni: Sefer Zikaron le-Avraham Shalit*, ed. Aharon Oppenheimer et al., pp. 61–83. Jerusalem: Yad Yiẓḥak Ben-Ẓvi, 1980.

———. *The Ancient Synagogue: The First Thousand Years*. New Haven: Yale University Press, 2000.

Levy, Jacob. *Neuhebräisches und chaldäisches Wörterbuch über die Talmudim und Midraschim*. 2nd rev. ed. Lazarus Goldschmidt. 4 vols. Berlin: Benjamin Harz, 1924.

Lieberman, Saul. "The Martyrs of Caesarea." *Annuaire de l'Institut de philologie et d'histoire orientales et slaves* 7 (1939–44), pp. 395–446.

———. "Palestine in the Third and Fourth Centuries." *Jewish Quarterly Review* 37, no. 1 (1946), pp. 31–54.

———. *Hellenism in Jewish Palestine*. New York: Jewish Theological Seminary, 1950.

———. *Tosefta ki-Feshutah*. 10 vols. Jerusalem: Jewish Theological Seminary, 1955–88.

———. *Midreshei Teiman*. 2nd ed. Jerusalem: Wahrmann Books, 1970.

———. "Redifat Dat Yisrael." In *Sefer Yovel li-Kevod Shalom Baron*, vol. 3, ed. Saul Lieberman and Arthur Hyman, pp. 213–45. Jerusalem: American Academy for Jewish Research, 1975.

———. "Ha-Perush." In *Yerushalmi Nezikin*, ed. E. S. Rosenthal, pp. 113–223. Jerusalem: Ha-Akademi'ah ha-Le'umit ha-Yisre'elit le-Mada'im, 1983.

Litvinsky, B. A., et al., eds. *History of Civilizations of Central Asia*. Vol. 3, *The Crossroads of Civilizations, A.D. 250 to 750*. Paris: UNESCO, 1996.

Loewe, Raphael. "The 'Plain' Meaning of the Scriptures in Early Jewish Exegesis." In *Papers of the Institute of Jewish Studies*, ed. J. G. Weiss, pp. 140–85. Jerusalem: Magnes Press, 1964.

Lukonin, V. B. "Political, Social and Administrative Institutions, Taxes and Trade." In Yarshater, *The Cambridge History of Iran*, vol. 3, pt. 2, pp. 681–746.

Luria, B. Z. "Hordos ha-Melekh." In *Sefer Shmuel Yeivin: Meḥkarim ba-Mikra, Arkiologiah, Lashon, ve-Toldot Yisrael*, ed. Shmuel Abramski et al., pp. 501–38. Jerusalem: Kiryat Sefer, 1970.

Mackenzie, D. N. "Kerdir's Inscription." In *Iranische Denkmäler*, fasc. 13, "The Sasanian Rock Reliefs at Naqsh-i Rustam," pp. 35–72. Berlin: Dietrich Reimer, 1989.

Macmullen, Ramsey. "Social Mobility and the Theodosian Code." *Journal of Roman Studies* 54 (1964), pp. 49–53.

———. *Roman Social Relations, 50 B.C. to A.D. 284*. New Haven: Yale University Press, 1974.

———. *Paganism in the Roman Empire*. New Haven: Yale University Press, 1981.

Magen, Yiẓḥak. "Har Gerizim-Ir Mikdash." *Kadmoni'ot* 23, nos. 3–4 (1990), pp. 70–96.

Mandel, Pinḥas. "Aggadot ha-Ḥurban: Bein Bavel le-Ereẓ Yisrael." In Gafni, *Merkaz u-Tefuẓah*, pp. 141–58.

Mango, Marlia M. "The Continuity of the Classical Tradition in the Art and Architecture of Northern Mesopotamia." In Garsoïan et al., *East of Byzantium*, pp. 115–34.

Mantel, Hugo. *Studies in the History of the Sanhedrin*. Cambridge, Mass.: Harvard University Press, 1961.

Mason, Steve. *Flavius Josephus on the Pharisees: A Composition-Critical Study*. 1991. Reprint, Boston: Brill Academic, 2001.
Meeks, Wayne A. *Jews and Christians in Antioch in the First Four Centuries*. Missoula, Mont.: Scholars Press, 1978.
Meir, Ophra. "Sippur R. Shimon ben Yoḥai ba-Me'arah." *Alei Siaḥ* 26 (1989), pp. 145–60.
Milgrom, Jacob. *The JPS Torah Commentary: Numbers*. Philadelphia: Jewish Publication Society, 1990.
Millar, Fergus. *The Roman Near East, 31 BC–AD 337*. Cambridge, Mass.: Harvard University Press, 1993.
Milns, R. D. "Alexander the Great." In Freedman, *The Anchor Bible Dictionary*, vol. I, pp. 146–50.
Modrzejewski, Joseph Meleze. *The Jews of Egypt: From Rameses II to Emperor Hadrian*. Trans. Robert Coraman. Philadelphia: Jewish Publication Society, 1995.
Moore, Carey A. *The Anchor Bible: Judith*. Garden City, N.Y.: Doubleday, 1985.
———. "Judith, Book of." In Freedman, *The Anchor Bible Dictionary*, vol. 3, pp. 1117–25.
Moore, George Foot. *Judaism in the First Centuries of the Christian Era*. Vol. 1. Cambridge, Mass.: Harvard University Press, 1932.
Morony, Michael G. *Iraq after the Muslim Conquest*. Princeton: Princeton University Press, 1984.
Moscovitz, Leib. "Bein Amoraim le-Orkhim: Hirhurim Metologi'im." Paper delivered at the World Congress of Jewish Studies, Jerusalem, July 31–August 4, 2005.
Murray, Robert. "The Characteristics of the Earliest Syriac Christianity," in Garsoïan et al., *East of Byzantium*, pp. 3–16.
Netzer, Amnon. "Ha-Sasanim ba-Talmud ha-Bavli." *Shevet ve-Am* 7, n.s. no. 2 (1973), pp. 251–62.
Neusner, Jacob. *A History of the Jews in Babylonia*. 5 vols. Leiden: Brill, 1965–70.
———. *Rabbinic Traditions about the Pharisees before 70*. 3 vols. 1971. Reprint, Atlanta: Scholars Press, 1999.
———. "How Much Iranian in Jewish Babylonia?" In *Talmudic Judaism in Sasanian Babylonia: Essays and Studies*, pp. 139–47. Leiden: Brill, 1976.
———. *Judaism, The Classical Statement: The Evidence of the Bavli*. Chicago: University of Chicago Press, 1986.
———. *Making the Classics in Judaism*. Atlanta: Scholars Press, 1989.
Noam, Vered. "Le-Nusaḥav shel ha-'Skolion' le-Megillat Ta'anit." *Tarbiẓ* 62, no. 1 (1993), pp. 55–99.
———. "Shetei Eduyot al Netiv ha-Mesirah shel Megillat Ta'anit ve-al Moẓa'o shel Nusaḥ ha-Kilayim le-Be'urah." *Tarbiẓ* 65, no. 3 (1996), pp. 389–416.
———. *Megillat Ta'anit: Ha-Nusaḥim, Pesharam, Toldoteihem, be-Ẓeruf Mahadurah Bikortit*. Jerusalem: Yad Yizḥak Ben-Ẓvi, 2003.
North, John. "The Development of Religious Pluralism." In *The Jews among Pagans and Christians in the Roman Empire*, ed. J. Lieu et al., pp. 174–93. London: Routledge, 1992.
Obermyer, J. *Die Landschaft Babylonien im Zeitalter des Talmuds und des Gaonats*. Frankfurt am Main: I. Kaufman, 1929.
Oppenheimer, Aharon. *Babylonia Judaica in the Talmudic Period*. Wiesbaden: Ludwig Reichert, 1983.
———. "Bar-Kokhba ve-Kiyum ha-Miẓvot." In Oppenheimer and Rapaport, *Mered Bar-Kokhba: Meḥkarim Ḥadashim*, pp. 140–46.

———. "Taharat ha-Yiḥus be-Bavel ha-Talmudit." In *Eros, Erusin ve-Isurim*, ed. Israel Bartal and Isaiah Gafni, pp. 71–82. Jerusalem: Merkaz Zalman Shazar le-Toldot Yisrael, 1998.

Oppenheimer, Aharon, and Uriel Rapaport, eds. *Mered Bar-Kokhba: Meḥkarim Ḥadashim*. Jerusalem: Yad Yiẓḥak Ben-Ẓvi, 1984.

Oppenheimer, Aharon, et al., eds. *Batei-Keneset Atikim: Kovez̤ Ma'amarim*. Jerusalem: Yad Yiẓḥak Ben-Ẓvi, 1988.

Parente, Fausto. "Onias III' Death and the Founding of the Temple of Leontopolis." In *Josephus and the History of the Greco-Roman Period: Essays in Memory of Morton Smith*, ed. F. Parente and J. Sievers, pp. 69–98. Leiden: Brill, 1994.

Perikhanian, Anait. "Iranian Society and Law." In Yarshater, *The Cambridge History of Iran*, vol. 3, pt. 2, pp. 627–80.

Pines, Shlomo. "He'arot al Tikbolet ha-Kayemet bein Munaḥim Suri'im u-vein Munaḥim shel Lashon Ḥazal." In *Sefer Zikaron le-Yaakov Friedman*, ed. Shlomo Pines, pp. 205–13. Jerusalem: Ha-Makhon le-Mada'ei Yahadut, 1974.

Porton, Bezalel. *Archives from Elephantine: The Life of an Ancient Jewish Military Colony*. Berkeley: University of California Press, 1968.

Rabello, Alfredo Mordechai. "Gezerat ha-Milah ke-Eḥad ha-Gormim le-Mered Bar-Kokhba." In Oppenheimer and Rapaport, *Mered Bar-Kokhba: Meḥkarim Ḥadashim*, pp. 27–46.

———. "The Ban on Circumcision as a Cause for Bar Kokhba's Rebellion." *Israel Law Review* 29, nos. 1–2 (1995), pp. 176–214.

Rabinowitz, Z. W. *Sha'arei Torat Bavel*. Jerusalem: Jewish Theological Seminary, 1961.

Rajak, Tessa. "Hasmonean Dynasty." In Freedman, *The Anchor Bible Dictionary*, vol. 3, pp. 67–76.

Reiness, H. Z. *Be-Ohalei Shem*. Jerusalem: M. Newman, 1983.

Rivkin, Ellis. *A Hidden Revolution*. Nashville, Tenn.: Abington, 1978.

Rokeaḥ, David. "Zekhariah ben Avkulas: Anvetanut O Kana'ut?" *Ẓion* 53, no. 1 (1988), pp. 53–56.

———. "Be-Khol Zot Misḥak Milim: Teguvah." *Ẓion* 53, no. 3 (1988), pp. 317–22.

Rosenfeld, Ben-Zion. "R. Simeon b. Yohai: Wonder Worker and Magician; Scholar, *Saddiq* and *Hasid*." *Revue des études juives* 158, nos. 3–4 (1999), pp. 351–86.

Rosenthal, David. "Arikhot Kedumot ba-Talmud ha-Bavli." In *Meḥkerei Talmud*, ed. David Rosenthal and Yaakov Sussmann, vol. 1, pp. 155–204. Jerusalem: Magnes Press, 1990.

Rosenthal, E. S. "Le-Milon ha-Talmudi." In Shaked and Netzer, *Irano-Judaica*, vol. 1, pp. 63–131.

———. "Mashehu al Toldot ha-Nusaḥ shel Masekhet Pesaḥim (Bavli)." In *Talmud Bavli, Masekhet Pesaḥim; Ketav-Yad Sason-Lunzer u-Mekomo be-Masoret ha-Nusaḥ*, pp. 5–59. London: Valmadona Library, 1985.

Rostovtzeff, Michael I. "*Res Gestae Divi Saporis* and Dura." *Berytus* 8, fasc. I (1943), pp. 17–60.

Rousseau, Philip. *Ascetics, Authority and the Church in the Age of Jerome and Cassian*. Oxford: Oxford University Press, 1978.

———. "Ascetics as Mediators and as Teachers." In *The Cult of Saints in Late Antiquity and the Early Middle Ages*, ed. James Howard-Johnston and Paul A. Hayward, pp. 45–59. Oxford: Oxford University Press, 1999.

Rubenstein, Jeffrey L. *Talmudic Stories: Narrative Art, Composition, and Culture*. Baltimore, Md.: Johns Hopkins University Press, 1999.

———. "Some Structural Patterns of Yerushalmi Sugyot." In Schäfer, *The Talmud Yerushalmi and Graeco-Roman Culture*, vol. 3, pp. 303–13.
———. "The Thematization of Dialectics in Bavli Aggada." *Journal of Jewish Studies* 53, no. 2 (2002), pp. 1–14.
———. *The Culture of the Babylonian Talmud*. Baltimore, Md.: John Hopkins University Press, 2004.
Rubin, Zeev. "The Roman Empire in the *Res Gestae Divi Saporis*: The Mediterranean World in Sasanian Propaganda." In *Ancient Iran in the Mediterranean World: Proceedings of an International Conference in Honour of Professor Józef Wolski held at the Jagiellonian University, Cracow, in September, 1996*, ed. Edward Dąbrowa, pp. 176–85. Cracow: Jagiellonian University Press, 1998 (*Electrum: Studies in Ancient History*).
Russell, James R. *Zoroastrianism in Armenia*. Cambridge, Mass.: Harvard University, Department of Near Eastern Languages and Civilizations, 1987.
———. "Christianity in Pre-Islamic Persia: Literary Sources." In *Encyclopaedia Iranica*, vol. 5, ed. Ehsan Yarshater, pp. 523–28. Costa Mesa, Calif.: Mazda, 1992.
Safrai, Shmuel. *Ha-Aliyah le-Regel bi-Yemei Bayit Sheni*. Tel Aviv: Am ha-Sefer, 1965.
Saldarini, Anthony. *Pharisees and Sadducees in Palestinian Society*. Edinburgh: T and T Clark, 1989.
Sartre, Maurice. *The Middle East under Rome*. Trans. Catherine Porter and Elizabeth Rawlings. Cambridge, Mass.: Harvard University Press, 2005.
Savvidis, Kyriakos. "Armenia." In *Der neue Pauly: Enzyklopädie der Antike*, vol. 2, ed. Hubert Cancik and Helmuth Schneider, pp. 10–11. Stuttgart: Metzler, 1997.
Schäfer, Peter. "R. Aqiva und Bar Kokhba." In *Studien zur Geschichte und Theologie des rabbinischen Judentums*, pp. 65–121. Leiden: Brill, 1978.
———. "Das 'Dogma' von der mündlichen Torah in rabbinischen Judentum." In *Studien zur Geschichte und Theologie des rabbinischen Judentums*, pp. 153–97. Leiden: Brill, 1978.
———. *Der Bar Kokhba-Aufstand: Studien zum zweiten jüdische Krieg gegen Rom*. Tübingen: Mohr/Siebeck, 1981.
———. "Hadrian's Policy in Judaea and the Bar Kokhba Revolt: A Reassessment." In *A Tribute to Geza Vermes: Essays on Jewish and Christian Literature*, ed. Phillip R. Davies and Richard T. White, pp. 281–303. Sheffield, England: Sheffield Academic Press, 1990. (*Journal for the Study of the Old Testament* series 100)
———, ed. *The Talmud Yerushalmi and Graeco-Roman Culture*. 3 vols. Tübingen: Mohr/Siebeck, 1998–2002.
———. "'From Jerusalem the Great to Alexandria the Small': The Relationship between Palestine and Egypt in the Graeco-Roman Period." In Schäfer, *The Talmud Yerushalmi and Graeco-Roman Culture*, vol. 1, pp. 129–40.
———, ed. *The Bar Kokhba War Reconsidered: New Perspectives on the Second Jewish Revolt against Rome*. Tübingen: Mohr/Siebeck, 2003.
Schremer, Adiel. "'Akshei lei ve-Okmei': Iyun Eḥad be-Sugyat ha-Bavli, Baba Kamma 117a." *Tarbiẓ* 66, no. 3 (1997), pp. 403–15.
———. Review of *The Sage in Jewish Society of Late Antiquity*, by Richard Kalmin. *Ẓion* 60, no. 2 (2000), pp. 229–35.
———. "Li-Mesorot Nusaḥ ha-Tosefta: Iyun Rishoni be-Ikvot Shaul Lieberman." *Jewish Studies: An Internet Journal* 1 (2002), pp. 11–43. Available at www.biu.ac.il/JS/JSIJ/jsij1.html.
Schwartz, Daniel. "Hordos ba-Mekorot ha-Yehudim." In *Ha-Melekh Hordos u-Tekufato*, ed. Mordechai Naor, pp. 38–42. Jerusalem: Yad Yiẓḥak Ben-Ẓvi, 1984.

———. "Od li-She'elat 'Zekhariah ben Avkulas: Anvetanut O Kana'ut?'" *Ẓion* 53, no. 3 (1988), pp. 313–16.
———. *Studies in the Jewish Background of Christianity.* Tübingen: Mohr/Siebeck, 1992.
———. "Yehudei Miẓra'im bein Mikdash Ḥonio le-Mikdash Yerushalayim u-le-Shamayim." *Ẓion* 62, no. 1 (1997), pp. 7–22. A revised version appears in Gafni, *Merkaz u-Tefuẓah*, pp. 37–55.
———. *Sefer Makabim Bet: Mavo, Targum, Perush.* Jerusalem: Yad Yiẓḥak Ben-Ẓvi, 2004.
Schwartz, Joshua. "Tension between Palestinian Scholars and Babylonian Olim in Amoraic Palestine." *Journal for the Study of Judaism* 11 (1980), pp. 78–94.
Schwartz, Seth. *Josephus and Judaean Politics.* London: Brill, 1990.
———. "John Hyrcanus I's Destruction of the Gerizim Temple and Judaean-Samaritan Relations." *Jewish History* 7, no. 1 (1993), pp. 9–25.
———. "Gamaliel in Aphrodite's Bath: Palestinian Judaism and Urban Culture in the Third and Fourth Centuries." In Schäfer, *The Talmud Yerushalmi and Graeco-Roman Culture*, vol. 1, pp. 203–17.
———. *Imperialism and Jewish Society, 200 B.C.E. to 640 C.E.* Princeton: Princeton University Press, 2001.
Segal, Eliezer. *Case Citation in the Babylonian Talmud: The Evidence of the Tractate Neziqin.* Atlanta: Scholars Press, 1990.
———. *The Babylonian Esther Midrash.* 3 vols. Atlanta: Scholars Press, 1994.
Segal, M. H. *A Grammar of Mishnaic Hebrew.* 1927. Corrected reprint, Oxford: Clarendon, 1970.
Shaked, Shaul, and Amnon Netzer, eds. *Irano-Judaica: Studies Relating to Jewish Contacts with Persian Culture throughout the Ages.* 6 vols. Jerusalem: Ben-Zvi Institute, 1982–.
———. "Zoroastrian Polemics against Jews in the Sasanian and Early Islamic Period." In Shaked and Netzer, *Irano-Judaica*, vol. 2, pp. 85–104.
Slotki, Israel W., trans. *Baba Bathra.* London: Soncino, 1935.
Smallwood, E. Mary. *The Jews under Roman Rule: From Pompey to Diocletian.* Leiden: Brill, 1976.
Smith, Morton. *Palestinian Parties and Politics That Shaped the Old Testament.* New York: Columbia University Press, 1971.
Sokoloff, Michael. *A Dictionary of Jewish Palestinian Aramaic of the Byzantine Period.* Ramat-Gan, Israel: Bar Ilan University Press, 1992.
———. *A Dictionary of Jewish Babylonian Aramaic of the Talmudic and Geonic Periods.* Ramat-Gan, Israel: Bar Ilan University Press, 2002.
Southern, Pat. *The Roman Empire from Severus to Constantine.* London: Routledge, 2001.
Sperber, Daniel. "On the Unfortunate Adventures of Rav Kahana: A Passage of Saboraic Polemic from Sasanian Persia." In Shaked and Netzer, *Irano-Judaica*, vol. 1, pp. 83–100.
Sprengling, Martin. "Kartir, Founder of Sasanian Zoroastrianism." *American Journal of Semitic Languages and Literatures* 57, no. 2 (1940), pp. 197–228.
———. *Third Century Iran: Sapor and Kartir.* Chicago: Oriental Institute, 1953.
Stemberger, Günter. "The Maccabees in Rabbinic Tradition." In *The Scriptures and the Scrolls: Studies in Honour of A. S. Van der Woude on the Occasion of His Sixty-fifth Birthday*, ed. F. Garcia Martinez et al., pp. 193–203. Leiden: Brill, 1992.

———. *Jewish Contemporaries of Jesus: Pharisees, Sadducees, Essenes.* Minneapolis: Fortress Press, 1995.

———. *Introduction to the Talmud and Midrash.* Trans. Markus Bockmühl. 2nd ed. Edinburgh: T and T Clark, 1996.

———. "Narrative Baraitot in the Yerushalmi." In Schäfer, *The Talmud Yerushalmi and Graeco-Roman Culture,* vol. 1, pp. 63–81.

———. Review of *The Synoptic Problem in Rabbinic Literature,* edited by Shaye J. D. Cohen. *Journal for the Study of Judaism* 33, no. 3 (2002), pp. 324–25.

Stern, Menahem. *Greek and Latin Authors on Jews and Judaism.* 3 vols. Jerusalem: Israel Academy of Arts and Sciences, 1974–80.

———. "Aspects of Jewish Society: The Priesthood and Other Classes." In *The Jewish People in the First Century: Historical Geography, Political History, Social, Cultural and Religious Life and Institutions.* Compendia Rerum Iudaicarum ad Novum Testamentum, sec. 1, vol. 2, ed. Shmuel Safrai and Menahem Stern, pp. 561–630. Assen: Van Gorcum, 1976.

Stern, Sacha. "Attribution and Authorship in the Babylonian Talmud." *Journal of Jewish Studies* 45, no. 1 (1994), pp. 28–51.

Strack, Herman, and Günter Stemberger. *Introduction to the Talmud and Midrash.* Trans. Markus Bockmühl. 1991; reprint, Minneapolis: Fortress Press, 1992.

Sussmann, Yaakov. "Sugyot Bavli'ot li-Sedarim Zera'im ve-Tohorot." Ph.D. diss., Hebrew University, 1969.

———. "Ḥeker Toldot ha-Halakhah u-Megillot Midbar Yehudah: Hirhurim Talmudi'im Rishonim la-Or Megillat 'Mikẓat Ma'asei ha-Torah.'" *Tarbiẓ* 59, no. 1 (1989–90), pp. 11–76.

———. "Shuv al Yerushalmi Nezikin." In *Meḥkerei Talmud,* vol. 1, ed. David Rosenthal and Yaakov Sussmann, pp. 55–133. Jerusalem: Magnes Press, 1990.

———. "'Ha-Yerushalmi Ketav-Yad Ashkenazi,' ve-'Sefer Yerushalmi.'" *Tarbiẓ* 65, no. 1 (1996), pp. 37–63.

Tcherikover, Victor A. *Hellenistic Civilization and the Jews.* Philadelphia: Jewish Publication Society, 1966.

Tchernowitz, H. "Ha-Zugot u-Veit Ḥonio." In *Sefer ha-Yovel li-Khevod Levi Ginzberg,* pp. 232–47. New York: American Academy for Jewish Research, 1946.

Thomson, Robert W. "The Formation of the Armenian Literary Tradition," in Garsoïan et al., *East of Byzantium,* pp. 135–50.

Urbach, Ephraim E. "Magamot Dati'ot ve-Ḥevrati'ot be-Torat ha-Ẓedakah shel Ḥazal." *Ẓion* 16, nos. 3–4 (1951), pp. 1–27.

———. "Ha-Derashah ki-Yesod ha-Halakhah u-Va'ayat ha-Soferim." *Tarbiẓ* 27, nos. 2–3 (1958), pp. 166–82.

———. "The Rabbinical Laws of Idolatry in the Second and Third Centuries in the Light of Archaeological and Historical Facts." *Israel Exploration Journal* 9, nos. 3–4 (1959), pp. 149–65 and 229–45.

———. *Ḥazal: Pirkei Emunot de-De'ot.* 2nd ed. Jerusalem: Magnes Press, 1971.

———. *The Sages: Their Concepts and Beliefs.* Trans. Israel Abrahams. Jerusalem: Magnes Press, 1979.

———. *Ha-Halakhah: Mekoroteha ve-Hitpatḥutah.* Givatayim, Israel: Yad la-Talmud, 1984.

VanderKam, James G. "Simon the Just: Simon I or Simon II." In *Pomegranates and Golden Bells: Studies in Biblical, Jewish, and Near-Eastern Ritual, Law, and Literature in Honor of Jacob Milgrom,* ed. David P. Wright et al., pp. 303–18. Winona Lake, Ind.: Eisenbrauns, 1995.

Van Rompay, Lucas. "The Christian Syriac Tradition of Interpretation." In *Hebrew Bible/Old Testament: The History of Its Interpretation*, vol. 1, pt. 1, ed. Magne Saebo, pp. 612–41. Göttingen: Vandenhoeck and Ruprecht, 1996.

Visotzky, Burton L. *Fathers of the World: Essays in Rabbinic and Patristic Literatures.* Tübingen: Mohr/Siebeck, 1995.

Vööbus, Arthur. *The Statutes of the School of Nisibis.* Stockholm: Estonian Theological Society in Exile, 1962.

Wacholder, Ben Zion. *The Dawn of Qumran: The Sectarian Torah and the Teacher of Righteousness.* Cincinnati, Ohio: Hebrew Union College Press, 1983.

Wallach, Luitpold. "A Palestinian Polemic against Idolatry: A Study in Rabbinic Literary Forms." *Hebrew Union College Annual* 29 (1945–46), pp. 389–401.

Ward-Perkins, J. B. "The Roman West and the Parthian East." *Proceedings of the British Academy* 51 (1985), pp. 174–99.

Weisehöfer, Josef. *Ancient Persia from 550 BC to 650 AD.* Trans. Azizah Azodi. London: I. B. Taurus, 1996.

Weiss, Zeev. "Sculptures and Sculptural Images in the Urban Galilean Context." Paper presented at the conference "The Sculptural Environment of the Roman Near East: Reflections on Culture, Ideology, and Power," University of Michigan, Ann Arbor, November 7–10, 2004.

Widengren, Geo. "The Status of the Jews in the Sasanian Empire." *Iranica Antiqua* 1 (1961), pp. 117–62.

———. *Die Religionen Irans.* Stuttgart: W. Kohlhammer, 1965.

Wieder, Naphtali. *The Judean Scrolls and Karaism.* London: East and West Library, 1962.

Yadin, Azzan. "Rabban Gamaliel, Aphrodite's Bath, and the Question of Pagan Monotheism." *Jewish Quarterly Review* (forthcoming).

Yahalom, Yosef. *Az be-Ein Kol: Seder ha-Avodah ha-Ereẓ Yisre'elit ha-Kadum le-Yom ha-Kippurim.* Jerusalem: Magnes Press, 1996.

Yankelevitch, Rafael. "Neḥunion Aḥia: Li-She'elat Zehuto be-Ma'aseh Ḥananyah ben Aḥiv shel Rabbi Yehoshua." In *Milet: Meḥkerei ha-Univeritah ha-Petuḥah be-Toldot Yisrael ve-Tarbuto*, vol. 2, ed. Shmuel Ettinger et al., pp. 137–41. Tel Aviv: Ha-Universitah ha-Petuḥah, 1984.

———. "Mikdash Ḥonio: Meẓi'ut ve-Halakhah." In *Yehudim ve-Yahadut bi-Yemei Bayit Sheni, Ha-Mishnah ve-ha-Talmud*, ed. Aharon Oppenheimer et al., pp. 107–15. Jerusalem: Yad Yiẓḥak Ben-Ẓvi, 1993.

Yarshater, Ehsan, ed. *The Cambridge History of Iran.* Vol. 3, pts. 1–2, *The Seleucid, Parthian and Sasanian Periods.* Cambridge: Cambridge University Press, 1983.

———. "Iranian National History." In Yarshater, *The Cambridge History of Iran*, vol. 3, pt. 1, pp. 359–477.

Yisraeli-Taran, Anat. *Aggadot ha-Ḥurban.* Tel Aviv: Ha-Kibuẓ ha-Me'uḥad, 1997.

Young, Robin Darling. "The 'Woman with the Soul of Abraham': Traditions about the Mother of the Maccabean Martyrs." In *"Women Like This": New Perspectives on Jewish Women in the Greco-Roman World*, ed. Amy-Jill Levine, pp. 67–81. Atlanta: Scholars Press, 1991.

Zeitlin, Solomon. "Megillat Ta'anit as a Source for Jewish Chronology and History in the Hellenistic and Roman Periods." Pts. 1–3. *Jewish Quarterly Review*, n.s. 9 (1918–19), pp. 71–102, and 10 (1919–20), pp. 49–80 and 237–90.

Zlotnick, Dov. "Proklos ben PLSLWS." In *Sefer Zikaron le-R. Shaul Lieberman*, ed. Shamma Friedman, pp. 49–52. New York: Jewish Theological Seminary, 1993.

Zohar, Noam. "Avodah Zarah u-Vitulah." *Sidra* 19 (2001–2), pp. 63–77.

PRIMARY TEXTS, CRITICAL EDITIONS, MANUSCRIPTS, AND COLLATIONS OF VARIANT READINGS

Aggadot ha-Talmud. Unknown Spanish author. 1511. Reprint, Jerusalem: Bamberger and Vahrman, 1961.
Albeck, Hanokh, ed. *Shishah Sidrei Mishnah*. 6 vols. Tel Aviv: Devir, 1957–59.
Avraham min he-Har (Abraham of Montpelier). *Commentary on Nedarim and Nazir*. Ed. M. Y. Blau. New York, 1962.
Braun, Oskar, trans. *Ausgewühlte Akten persischer Märtyer*. Kempten, Germany: Jos. Kösel, 1915.
Buber, Solomon, ed. *Lamentations Rabbah*. 1899. Reprint, Hildesheim: G. Olms 1967.
Dewing, Henry Bronson, trans. Procopius, *Works*. 7 vols. Cambridge, Mass.: Harvard University Press, 1914–40.
Dikman, Shmuel, ed. Meiri, *Beit ha-Beḥirah*. Jerusalem: Makhon ha-Talmud ha-Yisre'eli ha-Shalem, 1962.
Enelow, H. G., ed. R. Israel ibn Al-Nakawa, *Menorat ha-Ma'or*. New York: Bloch, 1931.
Epstein, J. N., and E. Z. Melamed, eds. *Mekhilta de-R. Shimon bar Yoḥai*. 1955. Reprint, Jerusalem: Yeshivat Sha'arei Raḥamim, 1990.
Feldblum, Meyer, ed. *Dikdukei Soferim: Gittin*. New York: Horeb, 1966.
Finkelstein, Louis, ed. *Sifrei Deuteronomy*. 1939. Reprint, New York: Jewish Theological Seminary, 1969.
Foerster, Richard, ed. Libanius, *Opera*. 12 vols. Leipzig: B. G. Tübner, 1903–27.
Higger, Michael, ed. *Massekhet Semaḥot*. 1931. Reprint, Jerusalem: Makor, 1970.
Hildesheimer, Ezriel, ed. *Halakhot Gedolot*. 3 vols. Jerusalem: Mekiẓei Nirdamim, 1980.
Hoffman, David Zvi, ed. *Midrash Tannaim*. 1908–9. Reprint, Jerusalem: Books Export Enterprises, 1984.
Hoffmann, Georg, trans. *Auszüge aus syrischen Akten persischer Märtyer*. 1880; reprint, Nendeln, Liechtenstein: Kraus, 1966.
Ḥorev, Yehudah, and Moshe Katsenelenbogen, eds. R. Israel ibn Al-Nakawa, *Menorat ha-Ma'or*. Jerusalem: Mosad ha-Rav Kuk, 1961.
Horowitz, Ḥ. S., ed. *Sifrei Numbers*. 1917. Reprint, Jerusalem: Wahrmann Books, 1966.
Horowitz, Ḥ. S., and I. A. Rabin, eds. *Mekhilta de-R. Yishmael*. 1931. Reprint, Jerusalem: Wahrmann Books, 1966.
Jeffreys, Elizabeth, et al., trans. *The Chronicle of John Malalas*. Melbourne: Australian Association for Byzantine Studies, 1986.
Josephus. *Against Apion, Antiquities, Jewish War, Life*. Ed. Henry St. James Thackeray, Ralph Marcus, A. W. K. Green, and Louis H. Feldman. 9 vols. Cambridge, Mass.: Harvard University Press, 1926–65.
Kahan, Kalman, ed. *Seder Tannaim ve-Amoraim*. Frankfurt am Main: Ḥermon, 1935.
Lewin, Benjamin, ed. *Igeret Rav Sherira Gaon*. Haifa, 1920.
Lidzbarski, Mark, trans. *Ginza, der Schatz, oder, Das grosse Buch der Mandäer*. Göttingen: Vandenhoeck and Ruprecht, 1925.
Lieberman, Saul, ed. *Deuteronomy Rabbah*. 2nd ed. Jerusalem: Shalem, 1992.
Liss, Avraham, ed. *Dikdukei Soferim ha-Shalem: Yevamot*. Jerusalem: Ha-Makhon ha-Yisre'eli ha-Shalem, 1988.
Maharam Shif. In back of standard editions of the Babylonian Talmud.
Maharsha. In back of standard editions of the Babylonian Talmud.
Malter, Henry, ed. *Massekhet Ta'anit*. New York: American Academy for Jewish Research, 1930.

Mandelbaum, Bernard, ed. *Pesikta de-Rav Kahana*. New York: Jewish Theological Seminary, 1962.

Margaliot, Mordechai, ed. *Leviticus Rabbah*. 1956–58. Reprint, New York: Jewish Theological Seminary, 1993.

Nöldeke, Theodor, ed. *Geschichte der Perser und Araber zur Zeit des Sasaniden: Aus der arabischen Chronik des Tabari*. 1897. Reprint, Leiden: Brill, 1973.

Porush, Hillel, ed. *Dikdukei Soferim ha-Shalem: Gittin*. Jerusalem: Makhon ha-Talmud ha-Yisre'eli ha-Shalem, 1999.

Rabbinovicz, Rafael, ed. *Dikdukei Soferim*. 12 vols. 1866–97. Reprint, Jerusalem: Ma'ayan ha-Ḥokhmah, 1960.

Rabinovitz, Ẓvi Moshe, ed. *Ginzei Midrash*. Tel Aviv: University of Tel Aviv, 1977.

Rashbam (Shlomo ben Meir). In standard editions of tractate Baba Batra of the Babylonian Talmud.

Rashi (Shlomo ben Yiẓḥak). In standard editions of the Babylonian Talmud.

Ratshaby, Yehudah, ed. Zekhariah al-Dahri, *Sefer ha-Musar*. Jerusalem: Makhon Ben-Ẓvi, 1965.

Ri (R. Yiẓḥak ben Yosef mi-Corbeil; one of the Ba'alei ha-Tosafot). In standard editions of the Babylonian Talmud.

Rivan (Yehudah ben Binyamin Harofe Anav).

R. Ḥananel (Rabbenu Ḥananel of Qayrawan). On the side of the page in standard editions of the Babylonian Talmud.

Schechter, Solomon, ed. *Avot de-R. Natan*. 1887. Corrected reprint, with an introduction by Menahem Kister, New York: Jewish Theological Seminary, 1997.

Sofer, Avraham, ed. Meiri (Menaḥem ben Shlomo), *Bet ha-Beḥirah al Massekhet Avodah Zarah*. Jerusalem: ha-Teḥiyah, 1964.

Tashbaẓ (Teshuvot R. Shimshon ben Ẓadok). Jerusalem: Kolel Taharat Yom Tov, 1973.

Tanakh: The Holy Scriptures: The New Jewish Publication Society Translation According to the Traditional Hebrew Text. Philadelphia: Jewish Publication Society, 1988.

Tcherikover, Victor A., and Alexander Fuks, eds. *Corpus Papyrorum Iudaicarum*. Cambridge, Mass.: Harvard University Press, 1957.

Theodor, J., and Ḥ. Albeck, eds. *Genesis Rabba*. 1903–39. Corrected reprint, Jerusalem: Wahrmann Books, 1965.

Valdman, Ḥayim Yosef, ed. Yaakov ben Shlomo ibn Ḥabib, *Sefer Ein Ya'akov*. Jerusalem: Mifal Ein Ya'akov, 1994.

Whitby, Michael, and Mary Whitby, eds. and trans. *The History of Theophylact Simocatta: An English Translation with Introduction and Notes*. Oxford: Clarendon, 1986.

Wright, Wilmer Cave, trans. *The Works of the Emperor Julian*. 3 vols. London: William Heinemann, 1913–23.

Yad Ramah (Meir Todros Halevi Abulafia). Commentary to tractate Sanhedrin. Warsaw, 1895.

Yalkut Hamakhiri (Makhir ben Abba Mari). Berlin, 1894.

Yonge, Charles D., trans. Ammianus Marcellinus, *The Roman History during the Reigns of the Emperors Canstantius, Julian, Jovianus, Valentinian, and Valens*. 8 vols. London: Henry G. Bohn, 1862.

General Index

Abaye, 152–53, 159–60, 162–67, 176, 182, 185
Abuha de-Shmuel, 108
Aggadah, viii, 38, 59
Agnatos the general, 96
Agrippas the general, 111
Aḥa, R., 93–94
Aḥa bar Huna, Rav, 67, 70–71
Akiba, R., 27–29, 32–33, 82, 85, 108, 112–14
Albeck, Ḥanokh, 158
Alexandria, 75–76, 79
Ami, R., 139, 142, 144
Amoraim, Babylonian
  attitudes toward genealogical purity, 3, 12, 175, 182–84
  attitudes toward idols and cultic worship, 8, 103–4, 108–20, 177–78
  and their avoidance of contact with nonrabbis, 3–4, 103–4, 119, 173
  and the breakdown of social barriers to contact with nonrabbis starting in the mid-fourth century, 178–82
  and the depiction of later generations as behaving according to earlier Palestinian norms, 10, 98, 100 and n. 59
  and their desire for interaction with their social superiors, 9–10, 98
  and their greater willingness to emend earlier traditions, 37–39, 59, 61, 82
  internal focus of, 3–4, 8–9, 15, 19, 35, 37, 47, 59, 98, 101, 120–21, 144, 149, 173–74
  and their lack of sensitivity to nonrabbinic criticism, 87–88, 90, 92–96, 98–101, 174
  and their limited contact with idols, 103–8, 116, 119–20, 173
  and their magnification of the importance of the rabbis during the Second Temple period, 37–85
  and their minimization of the role of kings, 40–41, 43, 58–59
  and their perception of the transition from Parthian to Sasanian rule, 122–46
  and their preference for scriptural exegesis over logical arguments, 125–27
  and their receptivity to nonrabbinic literature. *See* Nonrabbinic traditions in rabbinic compilations

Index of Rabbinic and Other Ancient Sources

This index contains references to sources discussed in the text and also in significant references in the notes. Most sources are not indexed because the large number of these would have produced an overburdened index. Sources from the Mishnah, Tosefta, Yerushalmi, and Bavli are all cited according to the editions listed on pp. xiii–xiv.

Mekhilta de-R. Yishmael is cited according to the Horowitz and Rabin edition; Sifrei Numbers according to the Horowitz edition; Sifrei Deuteronomy according to the Finkelstein edition; Genesis Rabbah according to the Theodor and Albeck edition; Pesikta de-Rav Kahana according to the Mandelbaum edition; and Megillat Ta'anit according to the edition of Vered Noam.

All other rabbinic compilations are cited according to the standard printed editions. Josephus and Julian are cited according to the Loeb Classical Library edition.

RABBINIC SOURCES